DEMOCRACY
A MAN-SEARCH

DEMOCRACY
A MAN-SEARCH

By
LOUIS H. SULLIVAN

INTRODUCTION BY ELAINE HEDGES

GREENWOOD PRESS, PUBLISHERS
WESTPORT, CONNECTICUT

The Library of Congress has catalogued this publication as follows:

Library of Congress Cataloging in Publication Data

Sullivan, Louis Henri, 1856-1924.
  Democracy.

  1. Philosophical anthropology. 2. Democracy.
I. Title.
[BD450.S85 1973]   128'.3   72-10700
ISBN 0-8371-6617-9

Grateful acknowledgment is made to The Art Institute of Chicago for permission to publish the Louis H. Sullivan manuscript in the Burnham Library of Architecture and to the Ford Foundation for financial assistance in publishing this volume.

Copyright © 1961 All rights reserved
Wayne State University Press

Originally published in 1961
by Wayne State University Press, Detroit

Reprinted with the permission
of Wayne State University Press

First Greenwood Reprinting 1973

Library of Congress Catalogue Card Number 72-10700

ISBN 0-8371-6617-9

Printed in the United States of America

ACKNOWLEDGMENTS

I would like to thank Mrs Dorothy Norman for allowing access to her copy of *Democracy* as well as her correspondence with L. J. Salter and George Elmslie, and to thank Mr Salter for permission to quote from his correspondence. I am indebted to Miss Ruth E. Schoneman of the Burnham Library, The Art Institute of Chicago, for her help in supplying information about various manuscript problems. Thanks are due also to Dr Edgar P. Richardson, Director of The Detroit Institute of Arts, for his part in bringing this book into being. Any student of Sullivan is indebted to Professor Hugh Morrison's study, *Louis Sullivan;* particular thanks are due him for supplying me with additional information on Sullivan not contained in his book.

E.H.

INTRODUCTION

By
Elaine Hedges

Like many another American artist Louis Sullivan has had to wait for recognition. During his lifetime he did enjoy a brief period of fame, from 1880 to 1895, the years of his partnership with Dankmar Adler. Then, Sullivan was designing such famous structures as the Wainwright Building in St. Louis, the Chicago Auditorium (now Roosevelt University) and the Walker Warehouse; experimenting in the use of skeleton construction and contributing to the design of the skyscraper; and producing, as quickly as his pencil could travel across the page, sheet upon sheet of that ornamentation which Frank Lloyd Wright considered his greatest achievement. But this period of quick and even whirlwind success, when Sullivan was helping make the Chicago Loop what Sigfried Giedion later called it, the center of architectural development for the world, was followed by some thirty years of growing poverty and neglect.

INTRODUCTION

The unhappy severance of his partnership with Adler, through whose contacts most of the commissions had come, was partly responsible for Sullivan's professional decline; contributing, too, was Sullivan's quick temper, which often led him, in the years when he was in business for himself, to quarrel with clients and lose commissions. But also important was the impact of the Chicago Exposition of 1893. Under the auspices of Eastern architects like Charles McKim and Richard Hunt, called in to direct the Fair by a city still unwilling to assert its independence of Eastern standards, the Exposition, with its weak-rooted cuttings from Eastern hothouses, as Sullivan called the buildings, spawned that revival of interest in Classical and Renaissance styles which was effectually to curtail the demand for his work. In the years that followed there were some commissions: most notably the Schlesinger Mayer (later Carson Pirie Scott & Co.) Building, on which Sullivan worked intermittently between 1899 and 1904; otherwise, only an occasional bank in a small midwestern town, or a cemetery monument.

Sullivan's biography, in the years after 1907, makes unhappy reading. In 1908 he lost his country home which was located in Ocean Springs, Mississippi. In 1909 he had to auction off his household effects—books, paintings, furniture, rugs—and dismiss his faithful assistant (and later literary executor) George Grant Elmslie. 1910 saw the termination of his membership in the Chicago Club. By 1918 he was forced to vacate his suite of offices, held since the building was first constructed, in the Auditorium Tower. And by then he had been living for about ten years in a succession of small, cheap Chicago hotels. Friends helped support Sullivan in the last years of his life: fellow members of the Cliff Dwellers Club, who subsidized the writing and publication of his last book, *The Autobiography of an Idea* (1924).[1]

It was his writings—some essays and articles, a long prose poem, but particularly the three books, *Kindergarten Chats*, *Democracy*, and *The Autobiography*—that spiritually sustained Sullivan during this long final period of his life. His writings became more and more the major outlet for his seemingly inexhaustible energies, more and more his sole available form of commitment. He would coop himself up, at the Chicago or Cliff Dwellers Club, or in his office or hotel room, and, smoking heavily and drinking quantities of strong black coffee, write on into the small hours of the morning. (Again and again, as one reads the manuscript of *Democracy*, one finds such notations at the ends of chapters as "completed 2:15 a. m.," or

---

[1] For the fullest account of Sullivan's life see Willard Connely, *Louis Sullivan As He Lived* (New York, 1960). Cf. also John McAndrew, "Who Was Louis Sullivan?" *Arts*, v. 31, no. 2 (November, 1956), 22–27, for speculation on the importance to Sullivan of his association with Adler and a brief discussion of his unhappy later years.

INTRODUCTION

"3:00," or "4:30.") Frank Lloyd Wright describes Sullivan on his deathbed, impatiently waiting for the first published copy of *The Autobiography:* "The book meant life to him now." [2]

Two of the books Sullivan composed during these years are recognized today as an essential part of his contribution to modern architecture. As critics like Sigfried Giedion and Lewis Mumford have attested, the impact on contemporary architecture—American and European—of the theory of organic or functional art contained in *Kindergarten Chats* and *The Autobiography* has been widespread and profound. Indeed, Sullivan's closest critic, Hugh Morrison, believes that his influence on contemporary architecture is to be traced more to his writings than to his buildings.[3] The books of Sullivan's most illustrious pupil, Frank Lloyd Wright, whether actually influenced by Sullivan's writings or not, show striking similarities of thought and style. For the layman, too, Sullivan's writings have been richly suggestive. For example John Szarkowski, in the foreword to his excellent volume of photographs of Sullivan's buildings, attributes the origin of his own interest in Sullivan to the "intoxicating, inspiring writings." [4]

Given such recognition, it is surprising that so little attention has been paid to the third book Sullivan wrote: that its very existence, in fact, has gone almost unnoticed. Between 1906 and 1908 Sullivan drafted, revised and completed the manuscript which he entitled *Democracy: A Man-Search*. His longest work and his most ambitious, it was never published in his lifetime. In 1940-41 about twenty pages of the text were published in the magazine *Twice a Year*,[5] and since 1949 the entire text has been available in a microcard edition published by the Free Public Library of Louisville, Kentucky. Otherwise, little notice has been taken of a work whose availability means, as Morrison has said, that "the source materials are finally at hand for a new and more complete appraisal of Sullivan's many-sided genius." [6] *Democracy* does contribute richly to our understanding of the thought of one of America's major architects. In addition, in its

---

[2] *Genius and the Mobocracy* (New York, 1949), p. 74.

[3] Sigfried Giedion, *Space, Time and Architecture* (Cambridge, Mass., 1949), pp. 283-284, 310-317, and passim; Lewis Mumford, *Roots of Contemporary American Architecture* (New York, 1952), pp. 74-81; Hugh Morrison, *Louis Sullivan* (New York, 1952), p. 268.

[4] *The Idea of Louis Sullivan* (Minneapolis, 1956), foreword.

[5] Nos. 5-6 (Fall-Winter, 1940, Spring-Summer, 1941), pp. 17-28: an edited version which draws chiefly on the opening section of the work.

[6] Introduction to the microcard edition.

own right, it is a frequently moving statement of a great artist's faith in the democratic ideal.

* * * *

Fully to appreciate *Democracy* one should approach it through Sullivan's earlier work, *Kindergarten Chats,* and through a general awareness of his aims as a writer. Readers of *Kindergarten Chats* or *The Autobiography* know that Sullivan's was a commitment—a dedication, in fact—that went far beyond architecture. Describing his activity in Chicago in the eighteen-eighties and nineties, he once said that he had pursued "aggressive research in creative architecture, and, simultaneously, . . . studies in the reality of man." From technical questions of architecture to metaphysical explorations of man's reality might "seem a far cry," he admitted.[7] But Sullivan had been profoundly impressed by his reading in Walt Whitman, and also in Taine; and he had early acquired a deep sense of the interrelatedness of all aspects of life in society, of the organic nature of life and therefore of culture.[8] And underlying this sense (which was of course one source of his organic or functional theory of art) was an unswerving faith—also richly sustained by Whitman—in individual man, man who had created both society and art. Genuine creativity in any art, Sullivan therefore believed, must be rooted in an understanding of man; and specifically of democratic man. It was in *Democracy* that Sullivan's exploration of the reality of democratic man received its fullest expression.

Democracy developed many of the ideas previously presented in *Kindergarten Chats.* The latter was ostensibly an introduction to the first principles of architecture (it was published in installments in a Cleveland magazine, *Interstate Architect and Builder,* from February, 1901 to February, 1902). But it might almost be described as a Transcendental [9]

[7] *Autobiography* (New York, 1924), p. 299.

[8] Sullivan's indebtedness to Whitman has been discussed by such critics as F. O. Matthiessen, *American Renaissance* (New York, 1941), pp. xv–xvi, 144, 592; Donald Egbert, "The Idea of Organic Expression and American Architecture," Stowe Persons, ed., *Evolutionary Thought in America* (New Haven, 1950), pp. 336–396; and Richard P. Adams, "Architecture and the Romantic Tradition: Coleridge to Wright," *American Quarterly,* v. ix, no. 1 (Spring, 1957), 55–58. Taine, whom Sullivan read in Paris in 1874, gave him what he calls in *The Autobiography* a "new and shining" idea—that "the art of a people is a reflex or direct expression of the life of that people," p. 233.

[9] As used in this Introduction to indicate the organicism of such American writers as Emerson and Thoreau, "Transcendentalism" is not to be confused with Sullivan's use of the word, in the lower case, in *Democracy* (see Group II, chapter 1, for example), to indicate the Kantian theory of a dualism between "pure reason" and the "thing-in-itself," to which he was opposed.

tract. Sullivan began by examining buildings, but he quickly moved behind their façades. He "read" a building, as Emerson might read a book: "its external aspect--considered . . . as a revelation of character";[10] and he had soon demonstrated that the characters, both of the architect and of the society he expressed and served through his work, were corrupt, in need of reform. Banks masquerading as Roman temples, libraries surmounted by Gothic turrets, office buildings sporting caducei—the whole eclectic display of post-Exposition architecture was symbol and symptom of a deep-rooted falseness in American life and in the individual. *Kindergarten Chats* was devoted to reforming the individual—the student whom Sullivan conducted through the dialogues that comprise the work. "I subject him to certain experiences and allow the impressions they make on him to infiltrate."[11]

The experiences were primarily of and in nature. Absorption in nature made the student's imagination receptive, led him to penetrate through its forms to the reality beneath. *Kindergarten Chats* was structured in terms of the seasons, and the climax of each stage of the student's growth was prompted by some dramatic natural experience. In guiding the student through the awakening of summer, the "lucidity and calm" of autumn, the "depths and darkness" of winter, and the "optimism" of spring, Sullivan was, as he later explained, analogizing the process of man's natural growth (from childhood to adolescence and maturity) and of his spiritual growth.[12] He was also utilizing a technique common to writers like Thoreau and Whitman, in order to communicate a vision like theirs. By the end of the book he had richly displayed this vision: of an organic nature, that functioned through balanced and recurring seasonal rhythms, ceaselessly unfolding, growing and dying, expressing its ends, or functions, through patterns, or forms, that drew their beauty from the honesty and economy, that is to say the naturalness, of their expression. It was a "fluent conception of . . . *continuity*"[13] which Sullivan wished the student to grasp.

[10] Claude Bragdon, ed. (Lawrence, Kansas, 1934), p. 18. All quotations are taken from this edition. The more recent edition, Isabella Athey, ed. (New York, 1947), contains revisions Sullivan made in the text in 1918, that is, after completing *Democracy*. Since we are interested in tracing the development of his thought, Bragdon's is the preferable edition.

[11] *Ibid.*, p. ix. Cf. Whitman, "The reader is to do something for himself, . . . must . . . construct indeed the poem, argument, history, metaphysical essay—the text furnishing the hint, the clue, the start or framework," *Democratic Vistas*, in *Complete Prose Works* (New York, 1914), p. 249.

[12] *Kindergarten Chats*, pp. x, 245.

[13] *Ibid.*, p. 58.

INTRODUCTION

While this vision of nature was the basis for Sullivan's esthetic of form and function, it was also, and more importantly in his man-centered philosophy, the basis for individual re-creation. By his own slow absorption in nature the student himself became "organic." He re-established within himself a natural harmony of thought and feeling, reason and emotion; a harmony denied, Sullivan felt, by current academic training, with its emphasis on the drily intellectual application of dead styles, and denied by other aspects of civilization as well. Sullivan's was a strenuous protest against what he saw as the overemphasis on intellect and the denial of the creative role of the emotions—a protest continued by his pupil, Frank Lloyd Wright. His counter-vision, of the organic or whole man, who has overcome false dualisms of head and heart, intellect and emotion, is the focal point of his thought. For until individual man discovers not only the organic quality of nature but the applicability of nature's lessons to himself, neither the architecture nor the society he creates can be genuine.

When, in *Democracy,* Sullivan turned his attention to American society as a whole, the new context led him to develop further certain ideas that *Kindergarten Chats* had merely touched upon. By studying man in relation to history and society, rather than in relation to nature, Sullivan began to move beyond romantic or Transcendental formulations, to emerge with conceptions that suggestively parallel some of the fundamental ideas of later thinkers like William James and John Dewey.

Kindergarten Chats itself, for all its resemblance to the work of Emerson, Thoreau or Whitman (its reliance on nature for both pedagogical device and structural principle; its use of indirection and of a romantic vocabulary of Head and Heart, Reason and Understanding; above all, its basic faith in the goodness and power of the "natural" man), nevertheless showed some of the effects of Sullivan's exposure to post-Civil War thought —for example, in its evolutionary, genetic and psychological emphases. By the eighteen-eighties and nineties, when Sullivan was working in Chicago, the romantic synthesis had of course for several decades been challenged by new speculation: evolutionary theory, scientific developments, religious skepticism. That Sullivan read widely in such areas is evident both from his *Autobiography* and from the books found in his library when it was sold in 1909. His *Autobiography* offers a generous sampling of his intellectual adventures: his introduction to psychology, philosophy and the music of Wagner through his friend and fellow-architect, John Edelmann; his excited responses to Taine, and to Spencer and Darwin. The library list is further informative. Represented there among others are Max Nordau, Renan, Alexander Bain, Ibsen, Veblen, Schopenhauer, and William James

INTRODUCTION

and Nietzsche. There were also many volumes of American and European history, including some by Fiske, Draper, Eggleston, Higginson, Bryce and Rawlinson, and five volumes of that favorite nineteenth-century popularization of science, *Appleton's Scientific Library*.[14]

Sullivan draws on such readings in *Democracy,* freely, often rashly, but often, too, with provocative results. His book is enormously ambitious: a study of "the physical, the mental, the emotional and spiritual facts of our civilization" (p. 41). Its point of departure is what Sullivan saw as the contemporary crisis in the United States, a crisis he called, invoking terms Whitman had used in *Democratic Vistas,* the point of choice between "Feudalism" and "Democracy."[15] The book is rooted in dismay, at what Sullivan, in the early 1900's, believed to be the widespread betrayal of the promise of America. The growing cleavage between rich and poor, political corruption, industrial exploitation, the spiritual, moral and educative failure of church and university—all are instanced as examples of the extent to which American society has fallen short of its promise.

Sullivan proposes to show how to regain this promise, and demonstration takes him back before the beginning of recorded time and forward again into the twentieth century. The book is organized into six groups of chapters. The first two groups, "Parting of the Ways" and "Face to Face," are an impassioned statement of the contemporary crisis. The third and fourth, "The Man of the Past" and "Dreams," offer an historical survey of man's search for reality. The fifth, "The Man of Today," presents crucial aspects of and significant character types in contemporary America. The last group, "The New Way," restates the solution to the crisis as Sullivan sees it. History, politics, religion, sociology, and science are all grist for his mill; and legend, fable, vision, poetry, dramatic monologue and dialogue combine with straight exposition to compose a book which is, in Morrison's words, "one copious outpouring of thought, feeling and image."[16]

The germ of *Democracy* was contained in a statement Sullivan made toward the end of *Kindergarten Chats.* "Current ideas concerning democracy are so vague," he wrote, "and current notions concerning man's powers so shapeless, that the man who shall clarify and define, who shall

[14] *Autobiography,* pp. 206-209, 233, 254-255; *Catalogue at Auction at our Salesrooms no. 185 Wabash Ave., Monday, Nov. 29 (1909) 10:30 a. m. Household Effects, Library, Oriental Rugs, Paintings, etc. of Mr. Louis Sullivan.* Williams, Barker and Severn Co. Auctioneers (Burnham Library, Chicago).

[15] Sullivan's original terms, as the holograph shows, were "Absolutism" and "Justice." Midway through his second group of chapters he changed, and the earlier chapters were later revised to conform to the new choice of terms.

[16] Introduction to the microcard edition.

xiii

interpret, create and proclaim in the image of Democracy's fair self, will be the destined man of the hour. . . . The world is waiting for such man [sic] as for a Messiah." [17] In himself becoming such a Messiah, Sullivan seems to have drawn heavily on another source besides Whitman. While his role in the book as national voice, man of largest sensibility, obviously owes much to Whitman, his conception of the role, as well as much of the book's tone and style, seem clearly indebted to his reading in Nietzsche. A "well-worn" copy of *Thus Spake Zarathustra* found in Sullivan's library seems to have formed there a companion-piece to *Leaves of Grass*.[18] The similarities between *Democracy* and *Zarathustra* are worth noting. Both books originate in the same awareness of man's power; and both pursue the same inquiry, a redefinition of the self, "to create," in Nietzsche's words, "freedom for new creating." [19] And redefinition of the self involves for both what Sullivan once described as "a complete reversal and inversion of the commonly accepted intellectual and theological concept of the Nature of man." [20] Like Nietzsche, Sullivan would locate God, or spiritual power, within man himself: recognize in man the source of all values. But where he differed, and most radically, from Nietzsche was in his refusal to limit the notion of the superman to the aristocratic few. Sullivan was eager participant in the fin-de-siècle cult of the superman. In *The Autobiography* he describes himself as living in a "maze of hero-worship," records his admiration for Wagner's Siegfried, and for Michelangelo, "the man of super-power, the glorified man," and insists finally that the idea of power is "the IDEA permeating and dominating this narrative of a life-experience." [21] And he enacted the idea in his own life. Both Wright, in his book on Sullivan, *Genius and the Mobocracy,* and George Elmslie, in his correspondence, refer to Sullivan as "The Master." And one of Sullivan's still unpublished works, a prose poem entitled "The Master," incorporates, according to Elmslie, "famous phases of a master's life."

But Sullivan remained Whitman's disciple. He conceived his mission in *Democracy* to be that of engendering in every man a belief in his own power and potential. While he might employ what one could call Zarathustrian methods to achieve this end—not only is his book a composite of poetry and philosophy, ethics and satire, it is full of terse, "prophetic"

---

[17] *Kindergarten Chats,* p. 137.
[18] *Louis Sullivan,* p. 225. The auction catalogue lists a copy of *Thus Spake Zarathustra,* trans. Alexander Tille (New York, 1896).
[19] *Zarathustra* (New York, 1896), p. 27.
[20] *Autobiography,* p. 248.
[21] *Ibid.,* pp. 176, 234, 330.

INTRODUCTION

utterances, large portions of it are written in an apocalyptic style, and the whole work is colored by the presence of the speaker or narrator as Poet who has brooded long in solitude, come down now into the market place to utter his prophecy and challenge—such methods are always put at the disposal of Sullivan's democratic ideas.

* * * *

To trace these ideas means to reorder, somewhat, materials scattered throughout the book, to impose a prose logic on a work that, threatening always to burst the bonds of any containing form, introduces its ideas only to drop them, circle back, reiterate and extend them later.

The book contains, particularly in the third and fourth groups of chapters, but also partly in the first, a survey of man's mental and moral development that recapitulates a survey sketchily presented in *Kindergarten Chats* and now made the basis for fuller readings. Sullivan reads man's past, particularly the religious and scientific systems he has invented, as a series of efforts in self-understanding. Throughout his history man has been seeking to know himself, to fathom his own nature and being. So far he has failed. Fear, ignorance, suspicion, the urge to self-preservation have led him to create social inequalities, to perpetrate wars, to invent false gods and to construct intellectual systems that have tended to distort the truth of his own powers. Sullivan tries to recapture the feelings of primitive man: his ignorant wonder at the cycle of day and night, his fear of a nature he could not comprehend, which led him "painfully . . . to erect structures of his emotions and thoughts that might stand as symbols, mediators, transitions between the unknown world without and the unknown world within" (p. 24). Succeeding religious systems—Egyptian, Oriental, and especially Catholic—are similarly so many "gorgeous fabrics" which man has hung as "veils between himself and the vast unknown" (p. 25). They are myths, constructed by man to assuage his fears, to explain the origin of powers that can be found actually to reside within man himself. They are largely the products of self-distrust, the attribution to a "God" of man's own essential capacities. Sullivan includes in Group IV a long study of the Catholic Church. The substitution of a feudal God for the democratic Christ, the growth of the Church under Constantine into a worldly institution, the evolution of priest into feudal overlord, and the defeat of an aspirant Democracy at the hands of the Inquisition—all are offered as proofs of the denial, throughout history, of man's essential powers.[22]

---

[22] The anti-Catholicism evident in *Democracy* was even more pronounced in the original version. The holograph contains lengthy diatribes against "cunning priests"

Science is similarly interpreted, as a new language through which man has tried to explore himself and nature; and a similar conclusion is reached, that once again man attributed to abstractions an independent existence. "Force" and "matter" were hypostatized as "God" had been; and so the separation of man from nature, and from himself, continued: the new language of science threatened thus to betray its creator. It is significant that in *Democracy* Sullivan singles out aspects of Darwinian and Spencerian theories for special criticism. He attacks the "law of natural selection" and the "survival of the fittest," *"laissez faire"* and the Spencerian theory of a "progression from simple to complex, from homogeneous to heterogeneous" (pp. 54, 58). As his *Autobiography* records, Sullivan originally thought the theory of evolution "stupendous"; [23] and insofar as the theory ministered to his belief in progress he of course retained it. But while he had also originally shared the widespread post-Civil War faith in Spencer's system, by the time of *Democracy* he had rejected Spencer, as William James had done, and for much the same reason. The Spencerian system was dualistic, "external," reducing the universe to matter and force, passive and active. Sullivan recognized in it a continuation of the dualisms of soul and body, mind and nature, "pure reason" and the "thing-in-itself" which had plagued man's thinking throughout history. He sees in later scientific developments, such as the discovery of radium, indications of man's readiness to abandon such false separations, and to recognize a universe that is basically composed of energy, and therefore, in Sullivan's favorite term, of potentiality for "power."

The rapidity and simplification of this historical survey through which Sullivan whirls the reader make it seem brash indeed. His Beaux Arts history professor, according to *The Autobiography,* described Sullivan's historical imagination as "vivid, amazing and rash"; and Sullivan said of his approach to history during his student days in Paris that "history became . . . a moving drama, and he sole spectator." [24] Of course, the survey he

who made "suckers" of the people. Group III, chapter 2, "Feudalism," is in the holograph more largely concerned with the Catholic Church, the "supreme monument of feudalism." Nevertheless it is worth noting that Sullivan also remarked in the holograph that, "Were I a Churchman to no other Church would I go." If one must have Feudalism, he continued, the Catholic Church is its most "beautiful and persuasive expression." Although too much of the language of the final version of *Democracy* is still bitter and crude, in revising the book Sullivan did tone down even stronger language and eliminated many passages of invective: passages referring not merely to the Catholic Church but to business, labor, diplomacy, education, etc.

[23] *Autobiography,* p. 255.

[24] *Ibid.,* pp. 232, 237.

gives in *Democracy* is melodramatically oversimplified; and undoubtedly the simplification comes partly from the example of such books as John Draper's *History of the Intellectual Development of Europe,* which Sullivan read, he recorded, with "absorbing interest." [25] Draper's book, devoted to illustrating the "orderly progress of civilization" [26] by describing the triumph of science in its conflict with the Catholic Church, was a popular post-Civil War reinterpretation of history in the light of new scientific and evolutionary theory. As his library reveals, Sullivan acquired much of his knowledge of contemporary intellectual developments from such popularizations.

But it is important to appreciate what Sullivan intended. "Almost everything," Whitman had asserted in *Democratic Vistas,*

> that has been written, sung, or stated, of old, with reference to humanity under the feudal or oriental institutes, religions, and for other lands, needs to be re-written, re-sung, re-stated, in terms consistent with the institutions of these States, and to come in range and obedient uniformity with them.[27]

Sullivan undoubtedly saw himself as doing just this: as rewriting history in the light of what he believed to be the most valid contemporary ideals, the most urgent contemporary aspirations. For the purpose of his historical survey is of course to afford further support for the organic views already advanced in *Kindergarten Chats.* A reading of man's history (and Sullivan's reading, as we shall see, was not so different from the one John Dewey would give twenty years later in *The Quest for Certainty*) reinforces the thesis, which *Kindergarten Chats* had first developed, that man is divided —split. He has set himself against himself, and so against his neighbors, society and nature. And if in *Kindergarten Chats* Sullivan's intention was to inspire man to re-create himself, his strategy in *Democracy* is to demonstrate the logical identity of such individual re-creation with that of society as a whole. For, once he has established, historically and psychologically, that dualisms are erroneous, that "there is, in essence neither a within nor a without, neither subjective nor objective" (p. 46), no essential separation between man and nature, between the "I" and the "not-I," Sullivan proceeds to derive the socio-ethical corollary: of man's responsibility, not only to himself but to his fellow man. Sullivan's vision of democracy is rooted in this belief in interrelatedness and mutual responsibility.

[25] *Ibid.,* p. 253.
[26] (New York, 1876), v. 1, p. iv.
[27] *Democratic Vistas,* p. 249.

But he does not rest with asserting the ethical principle. He develops in *Democracy* an epistemological approach, one that aligns him even more explicitly with James and Dewey. From recognizing the union of man and nature Sullivan moves to recognizing the union of thinker and thing, of thinker and thought. In *Kindergarten Chats,* in a chapter on "Thought," "that extraordinary agent," he had made the crucial statement that "your test will always be--results; for real thinking brings real results." [28] In *Democracy,* especially in its penultimate chapter, he reiterates and enlarges upon the idea: "by no possibility can we separate thought from the things we call physical. There is no dividing line--no threshold. There are merely phases of consciousness . . ." (p. 382). Thought has two aspects: attention, or becoming aware; and reflection, or becoming purposeful. Thought alters situations, and herein lies man's creativity. Sullivan discovers the origin of thought in primitive man's first impulse to fashion something for immediate use, in his first impulse to seek repose from the confusion of what he did not understand. Thought, whether it originates in the "flow and pressure of tradition," or as "a reaction from specific environment," is essentially power: to change, to produce, to create new situations (p. 29). "There is no phase of human activity that is not a situation"; and "The completed value of thinking consists in its use in planning--that is, in the creation of new situations." In fact, "the power of thought must create the situation in advance" (p. 383).

A "true democracy" is the situation to be created. And Sullivan has by now provided for its creation historically, psychologically, and philosophically. His reading of history, plus vivid descriptions, included in the book, of the contemporary American scene, establish the urgent need; his reading of man and nature the ready possibility. More, he insists upon the readiness of the possibility to the point where his concepts begin to remind one strikingly of statements in William James's essay, "The Will to Believe." For, once the process of thinking is seen as a "doing," a further assertion follows: that the democratic situation *can be* created if sufficiently believed in. Sullivan argues, not only that "the thought of a people is to be read in the acts of a people; . . . the acts of a people are its thought," but that *"refraining* from action is a definite act, expressing positive thought" (p. 28). Living thus becomes a "dramatic . . . ever-present moment" (p. 17), with every thought and every action a choice: between Feudalism and Democracy, isolation and responsibility, selfishness and altruism. And since the choice between Feudalism and Democracy is, quite fundamentally, a moral and even a religious choice—"architecture," Sullivan

[28] *Kindergarten Chats,* p. 51.

once stated, "is not an art but a religion, and that religion but part of a greater religion of Democracy," [29]—it qualifies thus as one of the options which, for James in "The Will to Believe," were "forced, living and momentous," and which were to be decided, therefore, by our "passional nature" (the exercise of which, described as "heart" or "emotion" Sullivan had argued for so strenuously in *Kindergarten Chats*). For what is involved, if we seem not to decide, is, in James's words, "the same risk of losing the truth." [30] Americans can choose to create the democratic situation; faith in the fact will help create the fact.

The formulation of this ideal is the logical final step, the culmination of Sullivan's organicism. A comparison with John Dewey may suggest its full relevance. In *The Quest for Certainty* (1929) Dewey spelled out a similar interpretation of history, beginning with primitive man, his search for security by propitiating the powers that environed him, his self-distrust and fear leading him to create a realm of unchangeable absolutes and of self-transcendent knowledge. And Dewey's further discussion, of the invidious distinction between thinking and action fostered by Greek philosophers, their separation of a "higher realm of fixed reality" from an "inferior world of changing things" represents, of course, his attack on the same dualism against which Sullivan was protesting. Sullivan is further at one with Dewey in recognizing the central importance of scientific developments in reversing the traditional relation of knowledge to action. As an architect, a worker with tools and materials, Sullivan had grasped the true involvement of thinking with doing; and so he was freed from that "depreciation of action, of doing and making . . . cultivated by philosophers" which Dewey spent so much of his philosophical career crusading against.[31] As Morrison has said, "To Sullivan in his later years there could be no real creation in architecture without the stimulus of a definite and actual problem that had to be solved, a need that had to be filled." [32]

Sullivan, furthermore, clearly comprehended the implications of this idea, not only for the individual artist, but for society as a whole. To recognize that thinking is an act, and that acts have consequences, is to recognize the social nature of thought. This was Dewey's starting point; and while Dewey of course went far beyond Sullivan in specific exploration

[29] Claude Bragdon, "Letters from Louis Sullivan," *Architecture* (July, 1931), p. 10.
[30] *The Will to Believe* (New York, 1912), p. 11.
[31] *Intelligence in the Modern World: John Dewey's Philosophy*, ed. Joseph Ratner (New York, 1939), pp. 275–279, 288, 237.
[32] *Louis Sullivan*, p. 46.

of American social and political realties, the general principles on which he proceeded are those which Sullivan held. That "democracy is a name for a life of free enriching communion," its "keynote . . . the necessity for the participation of every mature human being in formation of the values that regulate the living of men together"; that its foundation is "faith in the capacities of human nature," and that it "had its seer in Walt Whitman"—these statements by Dewey represent also Sullivan's basic beliefs.[33]

One naturally wonders whether Sullivan was specifically influenced by either James or Dewey. The evidence is inconclusive. We do know, from the library list, that Sullivan owned the 1905 edition of James's *Principles of Psychology,* and that he also owned two works, *The Intellect and the Senses* and *The Emotions and the Will,* by Alexander Bain, the English philosopher whom both James and Charles Sanders Peirce referred to as having influenced the course of American pragmatic thought.[34] On the other hand, Hugh Morrison does not recall, from his talks and correspondence about Sullivan with George Elmslie, any reference to James or Dewey.[35] Of course, most of James's and a good bit of Dewey's writings were in print by the time *Democracy* was begun. *The Will to Believe,* first delivered as an address in 1896, was published in 1897; and other of James's essays and articles might have come Sullivan's way through such periodicals as *Scribner's, The Nation* and *The Atlantic Monthly.* In the 1890's Dewey was teaching at the University of Chicago and publishing his early studies on ethics and education. One wonders whether Sullivan was aware of the existence, at this time, of what James in 1904 called "The Chicago School" of philosophers.[36] There is no evidence to indicate that he was, but the similarity of his ideas and concerns to those of Dewey remains impressive. Nor should the parallelism between *The School and Society* (1899) and *Kindergarten Chats* go unnoticed. Dewey's fight against equating education with exclusively intellectual interests, his insistence that "if we identify ourselves with the real instincts and needs of childhood, and ask only after its fullest assertion and growth, the discipline and information and culture of adult life shall all come in their due season," and his assertion that "the primary root of all educative activity is in the instinctive,

---

[33] *Intelligence in the Modern World,* p. 400.
[34] Cf. Philip Wiener, *Evolution and the Founders of Pragmatism* (Cambridge, Mass., 1949), p. 19.
[35] Letter to Elaine Hedges from Hugh Morrison, March 22, 1954.
[36] *Collected Essays and Reviews,* ed. Ralph Barton Perry (New York, 1920), p. 445.

INTRODUCTION

impulsive attitudes and activities of the child," [37] immediately remind us of Sullivan's basic assumptions in his first book.

Kindergarten Chats was completed about a year or so after *The School and Society* was published, but many of its ideas had been expressed earlier, in articles and addresses which Sullivan composed and delivered during the 1890's. One concludes, on the basis of available evidence, that Sullivan found his own way to pragmatic-instrumentalist formulations. He obviously grasped quickly and acutely the relevance to his own thinking of various ideas and theories encountered in his reading. For the rest he seems logically and for the most part independently to have extended and developed his thought from its nineteenth-century romantic base to some of the conclusions reached more or less simultaneously by philosophers like James and Dewey.

*   *   *   *

But to appreciate the similarities of Sullivan's thinking in *Democracy* to that of James and Dewey is not to argue that his book should be read as a philosophical treatise. One emphasizes his ideas for the sake of appreciating his deep affinity with an American tradition of thought; of recognizing the validity he found, as a consciously democratic artist, in forms of both romantic-Transcendental and pragmatic-instrumentalist philosophies. (One feels sure that Sullivan would have endorsed Dewey's major work on esthetics, *Art as Experience* [1934].) Meanwhile, however, *Democracy* is far from being essentially a logical, reasoned demonstration of ideas. It is a manifesto: a call, like *Democratic Vistas,* for an increased consciousness, a new moral order "in these States." As such it contains not only historical interpretation and philosophical speculation, but vision and celebration, criticism and exhortation. Sullivan's disciple Claude Bragdon's description of *Kindergarten Chats* might almost equally well be applied to *Democracy:* "Large, loose, discursive, a blend of the sublime and the ridiculous, as though Ariel had collaborated with Caliban, . . . one of the most provocative, amazing, amusing, astounding, inspiring things that I have ever read." [38]

Democracy has, in other words, the virtues but also the defects—and, unhappily, these in abundance—of manifestoes. There is an impassioned

---

[37] *The School and Society* (Chicago, 1899), p. 71; "Froebel's Educational Principles," *The Elementary School Record* (a series of monographs, edited by Dewey, published by the University of Chicago, February 1900–December 1900), p. 143.

[38] *Autobiography,* Foreword, p. 8.

sense of conviction, of dedication, which the rhetoric sometimes finely communicates; but there is also a terrible simplification of issues, a melodramatic banality and a crudeness of language, the result of Sullivan's determination to "Shock and Jar," to provide "object lessons . . . for the millions" (p. 260).

The object lessons only sporadically succeed. In Group V of the book Sullivan presents and presumably explores particular types of modern American man—the business man, the politician, the monopolist, the worker. But the portraits are crude oversimplifications, their language blatant and coarse. Sullivan's invective, against graft and hypocrisy, against food poisoning, rot-gut whisky, patent medicines and special railroad privileges for freight, is so shrill as to become embarrassing. He is somewhat more successful in other chapters in the same group, in which (possibly profiting from his reading in Veblen, whose works were also found in his library), he attacks cant and pretension in American life. The idea at least, if not always the accomplishment, is noteworthy as he exposes the true "functions" which hide themselves behind the false "forms" of words like "success," "common sense," "practicality," and "business." (And one of the most interesting chapters in the book, Group I, chapter 5, is an exposé, before the age of the semanticists, of words as masks or labels.)

But if Sullivan's sense of crisis all too often hurries him into a prose more frenzied than formed, sometimes this same sense of crisis manages to create its own conviction. Thus with his outraged vision of life in a typical American city (Group II, chapter 6), the description succeeds, by dint of its very exaggeration, in capturing the hectic pace and the disorder of urban life—the chaotically crowded buildings, the hurrying people, the frantic trade. His inventory, in this word picture, of mills, factories, hotels, boarding houses, mansions and sweat shops, puts to new use Whitman's famous cataloguing device. Sullivan is not celebrating the plenitude of America, but emphasizing the discrepancy between promise and achievement, exposing the contradictions aand absurdities into which man has fallen.

So too he composes verse, suggesting Whitman as modified by Nietzsche, which is intended to challenge man's self-imposed isolation. It is a verse that goads more often than it glorifies the common man. Whitman's "I" is re-examined. If Sullivan as the speaker is the soul or spirit, the voice of Democracy or Life, the identification of speaker and ideal is nevertheless often ironic, and the sense of alienation creates a sometimes unmanageable dialectic:

INTRODUCTION

I am thy heart!!
Maniac! You have crept into my heart, to ransack it. . . .

Speak! Am I not thyself?!
No, No!!--Yes,--my weaker self. . . .

Even though thou knowest me not,
Yet am I Creator, Preserver;
I am Life, I am thy heart!
I am Disturber, Aspirer.
I am Truth.   (pp. 241, 240, 242).

As these fragments from a long verse dialogue show, Sullivan's messianic impulse led him to employ a rhetoric that not only surges but shrieks, not only chants but clamors. His prose is replete with dashes, underlinings, exclamation points and capitalizations (a punctuation that, according to those who knew him, captures his emphatic, taunting manner of speech). If frequently his language and rhythms are drawn from Whitman, Nietzsche and the Bible, they seem also drawn, at other times, from the political platform and the revivalist's bench. Too often Sullivan's style, as well as the almost brutally repetitious nature of the book, dissolves rather than clarifies a point. The topic drifts from him, wanders through a poem or a dialogue, and is finally swept away in incantation. Despite his shrewd awareness of the danger of abstract terms he is too prone to use them himself: e.g., "there is a sublimely great and simple worker for us all:--It is that Worker whose name is Life!" (p. 329). Thus too with the incessantly invoked contrast between Feudalism and Democracy. Feudalism too easily becomes a diabolical principle; and Sullivan's style, in consequence, might almost be described as an attempt at exorcism.

The book, in other words, is charged with anxiety: an anxiety that Sullivan quite rightly found "close under the surface" (p. 30) of American life, and an anxiety undoubtedly aggravated by his own precarious personal situation at the time. Whereas in *Kindergarten Chats* his role as teacher was on the whole amiably conceived—despite occasional sarcasm there was room enough for humor, and for geniality—in *Democracy* the patient teacher is replaced by the peremptory prophet. Sullivan insists more; his writing takes on more pronounced tones of struggle, of assertiveness, and of dismay. L. J. Salter, who prepared parts of *Democracy* for publication in *Twice a Year,* aptly described Sullivan's style as both "full of vigorous phrases—words that stick to the tongue," and as containing "patterns of speech . . . that bristle and irritate. My poor brain has grown a rash from it! . . . He frequently harps on a theme 'till it leaves a bruise on the mind." [39]

* * * *

Morrison, referring briefly to *Democracy* in his book on Sullivan, "hazards the opinion" that the work will some day be considered "one of the great literary achievements of modern times." [40] One can hardly agree with this opinion. For all its intermittent power and persuasiveness, its insights and its frequently forceful use of language, *Democracy* is much too seriously flawed by tedious redundancy, simplification, shrillness, and sometimes sheer silliness. It remains, nonetheless, impressive: a moving testimonial, forged by love and rage, to Louis Sullivan's faith in democratic man, and hence to his faith in the possibilities of a democratic art and way of life.

That Sullivan believed it important to formulate, in *Democracy*, his philosophy of man and society is quite consistent with his specific ideas on the nature and function of architecture. His conception of functional architecture included a theory of "expressive form," by which the moral or social function of a building was equally as important as the building's more narrowly utilitarian purpose. Thus Sullivan could and frequently did concentrate his attention on the façades of his buildings, on that ornamentation which Frank Lloyd Wright considered to be his greatest contribution, rather than on their interior construction. Lewis Mumford, in fact, has concluded that Sullivan contributed little that was new to the interior design of the skyscraper; his interest was in redesigning the exterior, making it a statement of the social, and therefore of the moral, meaning of the "tall building." Wright himself continued Sullivan's broad interpretation of functionalism. "Buildings," Wright once said, "are a synthesis of society and civilization in a system of philosophy and ethics, if they are organic architecture." [41] Looked at in this way, *Democracy* is Louis Sullivan's laudably ambitious if not always successful attempt to define American "society and civilization" within "a system of philosophy and ethics," and thus to provide that rich background of meaning that might, he hoped, inspire creative work not only in architecture and the other arts but—he would have insisted—in the art of living as well.

[39] Letters to Dorothy Norman, May 27, 1939; August 24, 1939.
[40] *Louis Sullivan*, p. 237.
[41] *Genius and the Mobocracy*, p. 64.

A NOTE ON THE TEXT

The history of the text of *Democracy* is somewhat complicated. In what follows reference will be made to the original pencilled manuscript, and to four typescripts: two carbons signed by Sullivan and two typed copies of one of the carbons.

Sullivan's literary executor, George Grant Elmslie, had in his possession two typed carbons of *Democracy,* signed by Sullivan, as well as the original pencilled manuscript. He gave the manuscript to the Avery Library, Columbia University in 1937, and one of the signed carbons to The Art Institute of Chicago in 1941. The microcard edition, published in 1949 by the Free Public Library of Louisville, Kentucky, is based on this carbon. The second signed Sullivan carbon was reproduced in two typed copies by Mr. Robert Olmsted of Oak Park, Illinois in 1940. Mr. Olmsted retained one copy and gave the other to Elmslie. Elmslie in turn gave the second signed carbon to Mrs. Dorothy Norman of New York City, who had published excerpts from *Democracy* in her magazine, *Twice a Year*. After Elmslie's death his typed copy was given to The Art Institute of Chicago by his heirs.

The two signed Sullivan carbons, representing his revisions of the holograph, are both dated in his hand as completed on April 18, 1908. However, there are slight differences between them, specifically in the phrasing of chapter headings and in the wording of chapter I, Group I. Investigation to determine which version should be considered definitive has unearthed no conclusive information. However, in 1953 Mr. Olmsted referred to his typescript as based on a "2nd revision" of *Democracy;* and Elmslie's correspondence with Mrs. Norman indicates that he preferred the second carbon. Comparison with the holograph, furthermore, strongly indicates that this second carbon represents a later revision by Sullivan. In this second version the phrasing of chapter I is tighter, and less ornate. Adjectives, adverbs and qualifying phrases found in the first signed carbon are omitted. The holograph shows that Sullivan's procedure in composing *Democracy* was first to write out his ideas fully, even loosely. Deletions of material, from sentences and paragraphs to blocks of pages, followed, as did stylistic tightening. Rhetoric was toned down, redundancies and flowery verbiage eliminated. It therefore seems clear that the version of *Democracy* herein reproduced was Sullivan's final revision.

A collation of the Elmslie typescript with the Norman carbon on which it is based verifies its accuracy.

The Elmslie text has been faithfully reproduced in the following pages including such matters as Sullivan's punctuation and variant spellings, e.g.

    Mahommed and Mahomet
    enquiry and inquiry
    gaged and gauged
    Budda and Buddha
    phantasy and fantasy

The manuscript presented certain difficulties, and in some cases it was not possible to discern the intent of the author. There is an early reference to *eight* million population; later the word is *eighty*. Rather than edit we have let both words stand. The word *strom* is used in connection with water. Since *strom* is a German word for *stream* we have left it. As an invariable rule everything has been exactly reproduced with the

A NOTE ON THE TEXT

exception of instances where we found obvious typographical and typists' errors on the following manuscript pages:

Page	line		Page	line	
4	12:	*hypcrite* for hypocrite	101	12:	*respons* for responds
11	11:	*percursor* for precursor	102	15:	*throughout the the length* (repetition)
11	26:	*ecstacy* for ecstasy	103	:	*devois* for devoid
17	24:	*annointed* for anointed	105	:	*repellant* for repellent
21	13:	*diaphonous* for diaphanous	108	6:	*innoculated* for inoculated
35	3:	*fills* for flies	108	26:	*innoculated* for inoculated
40	10:	*portentuous* for portentous	109	17:	*fedual* for feudal
40	25:	*tumultous* for tumultuous	113	9:	*anthithesis* for antithesis
41	8:	*prophesy* for prophecy	115	:	*orgie* for orgy
42	1:	*then then open* (repetition)	119	16:	" " "
			120	13:	*thet* for that
42	24:	*essense* for essence	122	6:	*thoights* for thoughts
55	20:	*drouse* for drowse	127	7:	*thoights* for thoughts
56	7:	*durtive* for furtive	142	3:	*hypcritical* for hypcritical
57	24:	*graons* for groans			
62	2:	*structur* for structure	145	21:	*bolume* for volume
63	11:	*phantams* for phantoms	147	21:	*Blase* for Blasé
63	23:	*was* for as	147	22:	*dyspectic* for dyspeptic
66	1:	*hetrogeneous* for heterogeneous	148	12:	*irrisistible* for irresistible
68	13:	*unheardof* for unheard-of	151	22:	*feat* for feast
			156	1:	*fream* for dream
68	17:	*boatsfully* for boastfully	156	20:	*irrisistible* for irresistible
70	16:	*anadynes* for anodynes	166	21:	*envelope* for envelop
76	7:	*himselfl* for himself	170	25:	*theit* for their
76	17:	*ma,* for man	176	8:	*Mediterannean* for Mediterranean
76	19:	*he* for He			
77	2:	*strong* for string	176	21:	*S little* for A little
88	24:	*al* for all	176	22:	*pariently* for patiently
89	17:	*lay* for law			
94	17:	*bobb* for bob	182	20:	*Listenting* for Listening
98	10:	*Jolly Rodger* for Roger	187	2:	*god* for dog

xxvii

A NOTE ON THE TEXT

Page 194	line 6: *baded* for based	Page 295	line 3: *ruppressing* for suppressing
199	24: *Ie* for It	297	20: *some* for come
202	22: *ter,* for term	302	5: *hi,self* for himself
208	6: *instittutions* for institutions	310	27: *whatsoere* for whatsoe'er
212	27: *paeon* for paean	311	1: *his* for this
214	27: *depracatory* for deprecatory	313	19: *vicilization* for civilization
215	23: *arrogent* for arrogant	316	13: *dominnered* for domineered
216	10: *gret* for great	318	1: *despided* for despised
216	24: *whatsoere* for whatsoe'er	319	9: *srumise* for surmise
220	16: *whatsoere* for whatsoe'er	319	24: *wil* for will
228	24: *seflsame* for selfsame	326	1: *anbormal* for abnormal
229	24: *Gos* for God	330	7: *ouw* for our
232	10: *whcih* for which	341	8: *Se money* for See money
233	15: *pracfical* for practical	341	8: *tha phantom* for the phantom
233	26: *unmistakeably* for unmistakably	347	11: *poverty-striken* for poverty-stricken
245	12: *sacntion* for sanction	349	18: *pachrymose* for lachrymose
247	16: *a nde pessimism* for and pessimism	353	12: *multutudinous* for multitudinous
250	8: *portentuous* for portentous	356	10: *them* for then
253	9: *gispels* for gospels	357	19: *Loathsomly* for Loathsomely
253	10: *Relio-dramatic* for Religio-dramatic	359	12: *Fedual* for Feudal
255	15: *lillies* for lilies	369	12: *al* for all
265	1: *spcial* for social	369	24: *darma* for drama
266	5: *masscres* for massacres	376	18: *And the,* for And then
269	12: *thet* for they	384	11: *magiv* for magic
277	14: *preogatives* for prerogatives	384	21: *guadily* for gaudily
277	20: *of of the world* (repetition)	385	1: *a a mob* for a mob
282	11: *saty* for stay	390	28: *supiration* for suspiration
286	3: *suoreme* for supreme	391	14: *emninent* for eminent
290	23: *portentuous* for portentous	392	17: *offenseive* for offensive
293	22: *sawy* for sway	394	11: *aa* for as

A NOTE ON THE TEXT

Page 399	line 7: *understand* for understands	Page 462	line 24: *appaling* for appalling
400	21: *I you canot* for If you cannot	464	20: *ida* for idea
401	17: *rodomantade* for rodomontade	465	26: *extremeity* for extremity
406	9: *ignminy* for ignominy	466	14: *fedual* for feudal
410	20: *portentuous* for portentous	475	5: *unawarem* for unaware
415	22: *ceils* for veils	492	8: *vpid* for void
418	14: *breed* for breeds	496	17: *meana* for means
426	19: *hom* for home	501	4: *diaphonous* for diaphanous
430	18: *bevause* for because	523	2: *estrangemen* for estrangement
440	20: *vpice* for voice	530	8: *GPAFT* for GRAFT
447	28: *hi,self* for himself	533	1: *all other other thoughts* (repetition)
451	8: *unforgetable* for unforgettable	533	16: *undreamed of* for undreamed-of
451	19: *assininity* for asininity	535	4: *suppresion* for suppression
455	19: *wont* for won't	541	5: *in so far* for insofar
456	26: *ia* for is	545	3: *distrubance* for disturbance
456	27: *wont* for won't	545	15: *and they why and how* for and the why and how
457	27: *brakesm* for brakes		
458	8: *sonambulist* for somnambulist		
459	28: *appaling* for appalling	559	14: *paring of your ways* for parting of your ways
460	2: *appaling* for appalling		

Obscurities in the text have been faithfully reproduced. They are designated by an asterisk (*). In some instances we have suggested a possible intent of the obscure passage in a footnote.

Apparent lacunae have been collated with the Norman copy. These are designated by [brackets].

The text has been reproduced faithfully with passages such as the one on pages 77–81 where the obvious rhyme scheme would suggest a different verse arrangement.

  To avoid needless duplications in this book, the manuscript's "Plan of Contents," and "Index" have been deleted. The "Index" duplicates with minor typographical differences the "Plan of Contents" and both of these are given in our Table of Contents.

A NOTE ON THE TEXT

One problem relating to the text remains unsolved. Although Sullivan dated his two signed copies of *Democracy* April 18, 1908 the holograph shows that a rough draft of the entire final section of the book (Group VI) was composed between May and July, 1908; and it is apparent, from a comparison with the signed carbons, that this rough draft predated the version of the chapters in Group VI which are found in the signed carbons. Perhaps some future scholar may be able to explain the discrepant dating, which, meanwhile, has no bearing on this publication of the text.

DEMOCRACY
A MAN-SEARCH

INTRODUCTION

That man creates in the image of his thought is our thesis.

* * * *

Since the beginning, all institutions have come out of the multitudes, as their dreams, taking shape. So shall they come hereafter. The dreams are to be new; for ours is a new day. Ours is a wonder-day of ocean cables, land-lines, railways, machine tools, daily papers, printing press,--in short a day in which communication, production, distribution are reaching vibrant meanings they had not in the past. Meanings which confront us, to make the way plain.

These new elements are of man's reality. They are modes of his free creative spirit. They are so new, they seem to have sprung full-born of his earth-grip. Yet they but herald a greater coming. The elemental dream of the ages shall achieve full voice in the advent of Democracy.

This vast articulating dream is not now particular to place, people, mere nationality; it is earth-round. Our world knits daily more compact, more cogent; the peoples grow simpler-minded, alerter, clearer-eyed, firmer willed. Their ancient polychromatic thought is turning white. Its power begins to change in facility, in range and focus. Object lessons are not now alone for the few, the old chosen of God; they are becoming visible and clear to the millions, the new chosen of Spirit. The primordial dream of man is shaping true.

* * * *

Feudalism has had its day. It is about to pass. The end is not yet. But the beginning of the end of man's self-eclipse is here--the time is here at last. The clocktick now records fateful history in the swift making. There is no recession. We shall see what we shall see. We of today are in the thick action of the world's sublimest drama.

* * * *

It may thus be well to make a reconnaissance; to go from place to place, surveying the field from different angles and levels, now far, now near, that we may form a reasonable notion of what it all portends, and how and why this crisis has come upon us--this cataclysm of birth. To make as it were a few brief field-notes. Such is the purpose of this book. To make a sketch of man in the setting of his natural powers. To picture forth his historic folly.

Thus speaking, a few tendencies, long obscured, are now becoming clear. One of these is fundamental, namely, that man naturally seeks man. But in this search, he has been thwarted, because of his weakness: How and why--we shall see.

So, too, man has sought a God; but in this search he likewise has been thwarted, out of his own weakness--and we shall see how and why.

Thus history condenses into this: The God-Search and the Man-Search are in effect but two interchangeable aspects of a single aspiration--the search, by man's spirit, for the integral Spirit of Universal Life.

* * * *

Man has stood, and stands, isolated, a wanderer, a stranger in his own history; far from a God, far from Man, far from Self,--even while

INTRODUCTION

seemingly so close, so vividly close to Earth, and Self, and Gods, and Man. It is important that we know how and why this was so, and still is so.

To sketch this how, and why, is of the dramatic urge of the book. It is its tragic component; its passage through the great Shadow.

* * * *

To search man, to penetrate that ubiquitous aspect of his fear which we call hypocrisy, and to find actually in him powers, of which he has not dared to dream, is of the new Dream of Democracy. It is the passage from the shadow into the light.

* * * *

Since the beginning, man has held himself evil; such is historic man's recorded estimate of himself; for he lived in a world of fear.

Strange!--man still lives in that same world. He has not faith in man. His intellect inhibits such a faith.

* * * *

When man was the natural animal, trusting to instinct, he may not have been unhappy; but with the birth of his conscious intellect his troubles began. They increased, thereafter, in manifold, until he has turned every use into abuse, every blessing into a curse, in a tangle of fatuity. His conscious intellect poisoned him;--it envenomed him with phantasms. It awakened cruelty--the abnormal ego.

* * * *

Yet always with a heavy heart he has hoped, he knew not why. And always the rosy dawn of his life became a sombre and stormy day, he knew not how. So he died, in weariness--others came after, an endless throng, melting into earth, seemingly without avail.

* * * *

Yet, as slow time moved, man caught glimpses, here and there. Here and there, men more clear-eyed than their fellows, saw certain things, spoke certain words,--and were crucified or not.

But, with it all, the conscious intellect in man frightened him-- Hence he thought only of self, and perpetually thus made enemies. For he, dreaming enemies, they came to make a weariness of his life. So he shrank selfish, hard, self-centered.

Out of the dreams of fear he made civilizations, which grew, decayed, and fell. Because, in his fear, he had found neither God, nor Man, nor himself nor the Earth. Elaborately searching, he had not found how and why he was unreal.

* * * *

It is important to note that some nineteen centuries ago, a new doctrine, a new view of God and Man came obscurely into being, on the verge of the Western world. A view which gave man a fleeting, partial glimpse of himself, of the neighbor and of a God of the spirit and of the heart.

The thoughtful mind must hold this birth momentous.

It must indeed have seemed to a man of the past, that a dawn of joy and of peace had come at last for the weary soul.

It was not to be.

The priest came anew into his own.

* * * *

Some have called this spiritual advent Christianity--a term now misleading, because insufficient.

Others see in that obscure birth the semi-conscious beginning of Democracy--a word growing steadily more luminous, because all-sufficing.

* * * *

Soon after the death of this symbol-man, he, so called, of Nazareth, the Sun-God was restored. On the ruin of one man's simple hope, the perversion and betrayal of his heart's desire, arose the Church. The real tragedy of the Galilean is found not on the Cross. Thus perished the beginnings of justice. It was but a gleaming in the night.

* * * *

The free spirit of Man cannot wholly be repressed, even by himself. Nor can the sense of justice wholly be driven from his heart, even by himself. He cannot forever forswear realities. He cannot forever forswear himself.

The free spirit of the Man of Nazareth--the reputed man of the people, the historic image of their pathetic dream--lived after him as indeed it had lived, in them, long before him. Lived on,--an outcast. The little source of light must bide its time.

* * * *

INTRODUCTION

Amid the darkness, there came, in time, another gleam. The enquiring intellect, despite all repression by the phantasmal intellect, slowly stood forth. There came another shock, another birth,--the birth of a material sun and a material earth which a man dreamed and found to be true. So died the Sun God. This stupendous announcement was to the conscious, material, logical intellect, what the announcements of the Nazarene were to the heart and the spirit.

It was another Inversion.

It awakens in the modern mind, the thought that all ideas that men have held sacred may likewise prove in fact ghostly inversions of the reality of man's own powers.

* * * *

Came the unfolding to man of the spread of the physical earth.

Came the westward crossing of the Atlantic. A new dreamer announced a new world.

Came emotional happenings.

Came Luther's rebellion.

* * * *

These intellectual, physical and emotional happenings marked the opening chapter of modern western history. Man's conscious intellect, changing not a whit in character, had grown in its grasp of the world. His heart remained negligible. The neighbor was still an enemy--with whom man combined against other enemies. Combined for plunder and against plunder.

* * * *

Science had arisen--a pale new light.

* * * *

Came revolt against Kings. Man's intellect, becoming aggressive, turned to man in a political way. Men began to reason together concerning what they fantastically called man's natural rights--not hefting the difference between man's rights and his natural powers. They nevertheless dreamed their dream. It came true in Revolutions. So in blood and fire came a new birth, and the beginning of a new chapter, but not a new book. It was always the same book. Men still looked at externals, and exalted abstractions. They still believed abstractions could serve in place of justice.

* * * *

Meanwhile science sought to banish certain fears; but it let the great intellectual superstitions alone:--it shared them.

* * * *

Over the vast area of America men now began to spread apace, carrying with them a notion of self-government. They naively said it was of the people, by the people, for the people. It was indeed. They wished to be free. They did not know how. They mistook isolation for freedom.

In their midst, slavery had sprung quickly from its ancient root;--why not? When the crisis came, and this people split and clashed, the crude Democracy won; and for a time it feasted upon the illusion of triumph.

But men began to crowd; and thus arose out of the fertility of the land and out of that rough and ready aspect of Feudalism, which they called Democracy, the great God, Cash--speedily to fill the sky. Men forsook all else. Their dream of individual selfish power and dominion, the full ferocity of what they called Liberty, was about to come true. Their new God said: "Betray all, worship me. I wish sons in my image," so the people dreamed that if they might but betray enough, there might again be earth-gods. The dream has come true.

* * * *

The object lesson was vast. Thus there came heretical dreamers:--the old, old voices of the wilderness. The conscious intellect had, in some, become more responsive, more inclusive, warmer; it had partly communed with the heart; and there arose, out of their dreams, another God which said:--Search the heart and find Justice there, for I am the God of the Neighbor!

So the men began searching for Justice where the new God said, where the voice of long ago had said it was:--hidden, in the heart of each man, waiting there, through the ages, to be found.

* * * *

The progress of this search they are proclaiming, each in his way. A new power is gathering; a new storm phalanxing; an overture murmuring.

The Gods are at war in the dusk of our dawn.

The ancient war of the Powers of the Dark and the Light.

* * * *

So rises our curtain on man and his world of dreams.

* * * *

GROUP I—PARTING OF THE WAYS

Chapter 1 "What is the Use?"
Chapter 2 The Point of the Ways
Chapter 3 Night and Day
Chapter 4 "Too Busy"
Chapter 5 Revolution (*A Turning Movement*)

CHAPTER 1 "WHAT IS THE USE?"

The cry of the old world. The tragic cry of the heart.
How often is it heard, how oftener is it unheard? It was the cry of yesterdays, it is the cry of today, of this hour. It has been uttered in every tone, every accent, every modulation, in badinage, in cynicism, in ferocity, in despair. It is a question answering and unanswered. From the depths it rises as bubbles.

Yet this cry will not down. It ever seeks an answer, expecting none, satisfied with none, denying all answers, while ever, through the ages, through the rise and fall of civilizations, it raises its persistent mournful query.

It compels attention. At the very outset it appears, raising a fateful, deprecating hand, as a guardian of the hinge of the door we would open.

To ignore this first demand is to ignore all--to end in folly. Is but to write a word upon the door and then depart in foolish hope, leaving it closed.

Shall we then, too, write our little word upon the door, and, satisfied, depart as cheerful madmen, or shall we, when we are at the wall wherein this door is set, the wall that rises up for every one who thinks alertly, look first at this pensive figure in the stillness and the twilight to see if indeed it be not a ghost, a phantom, and at least lay hold upon the handle of the door, and pull, to see, if it in truth be not unlocked, and then to swing it open, and see what?--*Reality?* and the sunshine?

How often has this specter said to me, said it persuasively, said in frozen tones:

"What is the use? Why are you here, alone, in this still hour? This is no door. The wall alone is real. It was raised by Fate and not by Man. For what is Man? I am the questioner. Hark!--there is no answer save the soft hush of my knuckle-bone upon the adamant. What is the use? Return whence you came. It is vain to look at me so steadfastly. For I am real; you are unreal.

"Courage? Others have had that. You are not the first to come. Others have come long before. Others have come, believing, also, that there was a door.

Millions upon shadowy millions have come. They did not even know a wall was here, they broke their hearts against it,--and are gone. Did not Job of old, come to this wall, sit here beside me in sackcloth, wailing? Did he not cry to his God: "O, for an umpire between Thee and me!" He saw me not.

Did not your Jesus come here, radiant, sweet, proclaiming joy, and a door that would open? Had he not courage? But his cross came here too. It was planted here beside what you call a door. To that cross he was nailed, the iron passed into his soul, with dying gasp he cried aloud: "My God, why hast thou forsaken me!"--with dimming eyes, he saw the wall that Fate had reared. He saw me not. It was I who stood at the foot of his cross. Alone I. Nor did I move, there was no need, the cross was planted here beside me. And many a cross, before that one, has been set up here, many since, many are to come. And many a noble heart's desire has been slain here, and many shall be--the hearts of those I could not and cannot dissuade, of those who believed me phantom and believed their own dreams real.

"WHAT IS THE USE?"

Do not tell me of Siegfried, his re-forging of the splintered sword, of Siegfried and the Dragon, of Siegfried and the circle of fire, holding sweet life within. Those are but fables, illusions of hope, dramas of the North. Do not tell me that spring-sun melts winter's ice. For that does not avail. Winter comes again remorselessly, to freeze the heart of Spring, to stillness. For Spring is man's destruction; it drives him mad even as it still the soul, to lock up all in ice, to cover all in snow, to blanket all with flees before oncoming death. The twinkle you call Life is futile in flight from dark to dark. Have not countless millions lived, have not these same swarms died like flies, utterly forgotten? What is the use? Ask not me, ask Death, great peaceful Death, what is the use? For Death answers with its one word--death!

"You talk of freedom? Vain!--You are free to die! Close but your eyes,--all things die. You would do good? Vain! Illusion that you are, what is this good, but a sure road to destruction! You do not believe! Try it--and die.

"Do you not know you are blockaded, and a vagrant on the high seas? Do you not know that man has ever said, evil is real--that in his heart this is the thing he surely knows?

"Did not your great King Solomon say: Vanity of Vanities--all is vanity and vexation of spirit. Are you then grown wiser!

"Does not your priest say that your hope is after death? For he must lie that he may live--just as all men have ever done, do now, and must ever do. There is no hope, here or there--for hope is man's illusion.

"You say that a God reigns over all? The God kills you as he kills all. He daily tears the heart and throws it on the earth. He daily breaks the back. Sorrow is your companion, not God. Sorrow is merciful. For did not your God kill the one man who asked to be his son, who asked of him to be as a merciful father here, and take away the bitter cup? Your God! Vain! This God is your Betrayer!

"You would earn the gratitude of men? Fool! You wish vipers at your heel, dogs at your throat? You would slap men in the face to earn their gratitude? You would call them by their real names, not Mr. This, not the Honorable That, but Thief, Liar, Scoundrel, Hypocrite, Coward, Murderer, Betrayer,--to earn their gratitude! What is the Use? Keep quiet; or you in turn will ask an unseen God to take away the bitter cup--the sign of gratitude. And you shall, as you should, be denied. And then you will come here again, this time with your cross, here, where I am forever and forever, and your breaking heart shall surely say, My God, My God, why hast Thou forsaken also me!--as I have heard it said, long, long, long. I will be here when you are gone. Here as ever; here by the door of illusion; the door of hope; the door of Justice, which the light of wit have writ upon, and safely gone their way. But the door at which the great heart breaks. Here will I wait for the Next; and I shall see the same passion, the same agony, the same ending, as I have seen from the beginning, as I shall see unto the last.

"Go. Return to the hearts of your people. Be vile and you shall live--for such keep away from the door.

"I am your friend. I would warn. For I am old.

"You would make a book into a door? You would turn it on the hinge of Life, believing that as it slowly opens there will spread a prospect of which men have dreamed and which is now become real--a promised land for which man was thought by his God, and by his God's handmaid, Nature, furnished as a home, and that his neighbor therein is his friend?

"You would show that this wall was built by men, and might be removed by men at a breath if but so they willed? Vain! Go write your words in the desert sands while a tempest sweeps. Go write them with your finger-tip in the quiet pool.--It were one. For Life is but a mocking mirror --and a storm--and dust. And man is but a useless finger, moved by a useless soul, writing therein.

"Go. Return to the follies in which you were born--your birthright --your inheritance which all respect. For your coming is but madness here.

"Return! Awake! Sit down--and write that all is for the best. That the Lord giveth--to some; and taketh away--from others. That thus it has been, that thus it shall be, that thus it should be. That a Providence regards the sparrow's fall. That He will consider man--hereafter, in due time. But do not write that man must seek man now. For that you will be rended as they turn. Thus would you write your knell, thus would you come to me for the last time.

"I am your friend. You have seen me. But you know not who or what I am. Nor shall any. So, go--before you persuade yourself that neither the wall is here nor I. For that is self-destruction. I am here, invisible alone to the blind--And here I shall remain.

"You would call as a voice in the wild? Go pluck at the stars--they are near. Speak softly--the mountains will come. Say 'peace' to the flood, say 'wait,' to the sun, pray and your God will answer--so will the Wilderness answer. For have you not heard: 'I asked them for bread, they gave me a stone'? Go: Ask the stars for meat and drink, but ask not man for Justice. The sun will give you his light without stint. So your own will give you hate.

"WHAT IS THE USE?"

What is the use? What is the Use?

Ask now your futile soul, your futile God:--What is the use? They will deceive you now as ever--for such is your heart's desire.

"But ask not me--For I am Truth.

"You will not go! You will stay here by me, and see Fate face to face! You will lay your hand upon the door! And throw it open wide! That all may see! You will not come again! You are here now! You will not bring a cross! You will blow down the wall with a breath! Spring shall-- once and for all, prevail! You know the meaning of the seasons! You questioned them before you questioned me! Beware!--Siegfried! There is a crow, a forest and a spear! And there are men--and passions cold as ice! And there are sheep which bleat and run away!

"You say you have hailed the sun? You say there is a greater sun that would rise and shine into the hearts of men! You say: Light, Light! More Light!

"Siegfried! Beware!

"What is the use! What is the use!

"The Great Sun rises but to set.

"Night! Night! Eternal night is Man's repose.

" 'Tis there, alone, the wicked cease from troubling, and the weary and the righteous are hushed.

"Siegfried, Siegfried! Shall I have warned you, alas, in vain? If so: Farewell until we meet.

"The Great Sun-Star now seeks to break apart the night!

"So: Go! This time in peace."

CHAPTER 2 THE POINT OF THE WAYS

With unfolding of intellect and increase in knowledge-capacity there has ever arisen within the minds of men a passion for isolation. It has grown with the growing certitude of possession and power. It has gained in intensity with its dream of power. It has thrown the man back upon himself, self-centering him, compressing him within a rigid mold of illusion.

With other men the reverse process has held. As the intellect of such man enlarges it looks passionately outward, seeking his fellows and a channel of communication.

These types are separate only in seeming. They are in reality two aspects of the essential nature of man. For initiative is the plastic germ of

THE POINT OF THE WAYS

action in all men. It signifies choice. Thus the two types set forth represent merely diverging directions of growth. For man is single. Notwithstanding all appearances to the contrary, men are in essence all alike; and in all of them, the individual choice of action is the primary social fact, the immediate factor of the will, determining the massive social growth.

Thus in his ever-flowing moment of initiative, the man is clearly at the parting of two ways--The one leading him away from his fellow men, and the other toward them. Upon the choice of the way has ever depended and now as surely depends the course of those two great factors in the social history of man, which we shall call Feudalism and Democracy. Even in so minute, so obscure a beginning have the forces of expansion and repression their origin and parting. And in this same small way the sense of possession begins to move into that perversion which leads to disaster.

Today, this hour, to every man comes this critical choice of a way. Throughout all the past it came hourly to each man. It was then, it is now the parting of the ways; and in his simple choice brood the vast consequences that are involved, in mass, in the terms wrong and right.

Not once in a lifetime has each man this choice to face, not once only does he choose; but all his life long--daily, hourly, ever and again insistently, persistently, inexorably does this choice confront him. In every thought he chooses, in every act, great or small, open or hidden, he records the choice.

He must choose and record as he proceeds; for, ever before him, at every instant is the parting of his ways; he must go either to the left or to the right, he must move either away from his people or toward them. Thus each man leaves his trail.

So dramatic is this ever-present moment, so persistent in the stillness its query "Which way?" So unescapable is an answer, so exactly to the center of each man's being does the sharp enquiring point of this ever-parting-of-the-ways present itself always, and not to be banished, not to be denied; not only demanding an answer but securing it, that each and every man, at every instant, whether he realizes it or not, whether he wish or no, puts himself definitely in the great balance of human affairs as one who gives his life-force either to Feudalism or to Democracy. That is, plain as daylight he chooses, and his acts so announce him--as one who lives either for the good of all the people, or for their hurt--and his own.

Thus, historically, have Feudalism and Democracy, in their minute initiatives in each man of the multitudes, rested side by side at the point of the Parting of the Ways.

Ideas concerning property or possessions have been too severely constricted. They must be freed, that they may grow and expand, as our democratic consciousness enlarges. For not only material objects, but thoughts, feelings, emotions, instinctive powers are likewise possessions or property. Thus property, in its broad human sense implies all that may be used, and communicated.

If we fail to take this larger view, we fail accordingly to grasp, the full past and present meaning of the two great passions in history, which have been for each race, for each civilization in its turn, and with all the intensity of life and death, the stupendous partings of the ways which have signified in fateful solemnity, in poignant pathos, those miseries of the peoples of the past, whose multitudes have made the long procession into the depths of pessimism, into that abyss which has swallowed people after people, and from whose depths still arises as a sigh of futility the ghostly call, "What is the use?"

To this wraith the heart of the watcher of today, pondering these places, long vacant, in the yearning past, gives answer, query for query, What was the abuse?

How supinely have the thoughtful even, taken things for granted. Here, spread out as a great moving picture lies the past. All is motion, all swarms, all spawns, all is pullulation, activity, yearning, ambition, sorrow and fantasy; as rich growths, spring up religions, philosophies, poetries, arts, crafts. And all that we seem to have seen therein has been the rise and fall of Kingdoms, the emergence, growth, splendor and decay of religions;-- because we have taken it for granted that there was naught else to see; because it was always the same story, the same play with varying settings. And, because it always has been, so, we have assumed it must forever so be:-- That such is man, such is his fate. That thus he was born, thus he must live, thus die. That nations were but as individuals, and must perforce suffer in birth, in blighted hopes, in disease, decay and death; that they must sink into the tombs of the nations--without avail. That the story is always of a splendor which is the mere and sure precursor of decay.

So have we busied ourselves writing about these things, describing them with careful minuteness of detail; descriptions futile, seemingly, as the things described, and but confirmatory of a pessimism seemingly ineradicable, seemingly planted and rooted in man by an all-powerful and malignant Fate which in hatred creates beauty but to blight it with a sinister smile.

Man has been a searcher. Inquisitive, industrious, tireless. He has probed and pried and untied and unraveled; he has looked close into himself; he has examined with minute care the very entrails of his thoughts. And he has looked far away from himself, at the mountains, the seas, the deserts, at the sun, the changing wondrous moon, the glory of the stars. And he has looked far, far away, at many times, to his many Gods. He has regarded them in adoration, in hope, in fear, in trembling; he has sought to join them in ecstasy and in holy calm; or he has looked at his Gods very near, very gently, affectionately, furtively. And with all this looking in, and all this looking out, this gazing afar and this searching nearby, he has looked over, under, around about and beside the one thing of all he should have seen, and known and rejoiced in:--The divinity in the heart of his fellow man. Thus the reality of his fellow did not dawn upon him through the translucent atmosphere of the fair earth. For he, firmly believing himself to be his own enemy, and that it must be so--for his Gods had revealed to him that he was fragile, looked upon all things and all men as opposed to him, and, so believing, he opposed them.

Thus it came that in searching all things, and even passionately seeking a one God, he did not seek Man:--even though he literally separated man into his anatomical parts; even though at times and places he plucked out and ate the very heart whose hate, love and valor he thought he knew, and even though as time went on he wrote and talked much about it:--even so close did man come to man, seeing him not--even though there was much said about the soul.

Man thus approached so near to man that the presence obscured the reality. He could not discern him. He was not yet come near enough. He did not go direct. He did not seek aright. He saw not man. He saw his own vision of man.

So the true man-search has been thus far but gleams of intuition, of genius; here and there flickering and sparkling through the past. In the main, nevertheless, this search has betokened a deep instinct; it was ever the cry of a small still voice; a life-urge, against which man the timorous, the powerful, the crafty, and therefore the unhappily self-centered, mendacious, and easily alarmed in his conscious, possessive and isolative intellect --has persistently, anxiously and blindly stifled in his heart.

Thus has the writing of history consisted in painstaking and elaborate sifting and statement of multitudinous facts, with the small central fact omitted;--the one vital, pivotal fact on which has turned the thought of man; the very hinge on which the historical door, immobile, with the fine writing and the pictures on it, must be swung--that we may see past the opaque screen of men and discern the *net man*--and after that to swing back

DEMOCRACY: *a man-search*

another door, this time, in the net man, that we may look into his inmost sanctuary, to see what goes on there, and what is the minute axis on which has turned and still turns his splendid and sumptuous misery.

So we must seek where man has not sought before--although he says he has; and although he has spun out of himself many ardent religions which proclaim that he has and does. For there is no tissue of man's weaving that is the thousandth part so fine, so resistant, so delicately obscuring as is his hypocrisy--nothing so close to him--close as a cocoon. Through this living screen we must insinuate, and push, and press home until we reach the real man; until we confront him, and greet him where he lives, as he believes safe, in his solitude of one--and then and there put and push home to him questions that have not before been asked peremptorily. Questions which, of their very nature permit of no denial, no evasion. For we shall go straight down to the point of the parting-of-the-ways. Standing there, we shall confront him, and to man--real man to real man. We shall press home first the question, of most profound import to us all:--"Which way? For thou art the man! Which way?" On this delicately stable point of the parting-of-the-ways we shall remain. It is the judgment-seat--and we shall enquire:--"What is the abuse?" And we shall never be dislodged; for on this minute point we shall be solid at the center of all things--at the center of man's choice:--There, where man has said and says his conscience has resided and resides. Whereas this conscience has been, ever, but the shift of his intellect. But Justice resides there, at the point of the parting-of-the-ways. This truth each man knows, even though he has denied it more than thrice. For man has evaded; has surreptitiously shifted the seat of Justice.

We shall thus surely lay our hand upon the latch of the Door in the wall of Illusion. No sepulchral presence shall appall or dissuade--surely no man.

The Great Parting-of-the-Ways is now become too clear in the dawn of our daybreak. Our Crisis is upon us:--and Our New Day. The Parting is too momentous. It is all in all. The beginning and the to-be-all! And we shall see that there is indeed a use! We shall find that it is not as we have supposed--as we have supinely taken for granted: The Phantom beside the Door is to clarify in the dawning and take spirit form and flesh as feudal man himself. For it is feudal man and none other who has said and now says: "What is the use?" It is feudal man who has been the Great Denier. His denial we shall dissolve. For we shall illuminate the heart, expand the range of the creative power of the mind, and certify the spiritual integrity of man. In the so doing, we shall but tell the true story of Democracy.

CHAPTER 3 NIGHT AND DAY

Since the beginning night has entranced the eyes of man, working through their transparency many wonders in his tremulous imagination. Far back in what we call the twilight of history--though it was full daylight then, sure enough, and men were practical then as now, and very close to the earth and their wants--far back there, on the rim of our horizon, men watched the stars and marvelled. Out in the open, where the full dome of the sky rested stable and supreme on the earth, through the soft deep gleamed countless gems, intimately near, serene, eternal; their light shone through men's eyes, and the man felt himself companion of the stars--so benign, so silent. In the stillness of his soul he felt their stillness. The night thus seemed magical to him, and beauteous, because of the shining stars. In the midst of the great assembly he saw some which moved slowly among the others, and these he called the wanderers. It seemed to him that they must have to do with his destiny--why, he did not know--but so they impressed his receptive mood--for he too deemed himself as one on a journey. The fair moon too, he saw. To her his heart went out in greeting. It seemed to him that the pure and winsome moon, also, must be bound up in some way with the course of his life.

But there were other places, other nights--nights of dismay, of heavy blackness, through forest, mountain and plain of wildly roaring wind, rain and dazzling crashes--all overwhelming. The man seemed small within such fury. Such nights sank into his heart--they too seemed bound up in the weaving of his strange stormy life--a life in which he felt lonely among giant happenings. So, many nights made many moods with him. These many moods and many nights seemed, all, to hold a mystery in common. With him mystery meant power; power meant something other, greater than himself--a something confronting which he felt fragile, his little life seeming but of feeble tenure. So night made in him a night; created in his soul a wonderland of darkling powers and sublimity. In the fascinations of this darkness his adolescent soul dwelt, wandering near and far. As in a vast domain he went here and there, alone with the stars, the storms, the other wanderers, in the company of the pale, placid moon. Here and there he sat hushed, alone with his forebodings, his perplexities, his mysteries, his ponderings; alone in a night growing deeper, unfathomable to his reach,--but very near, closing up to him, holding him, clasping his fantasy. In the night came to him sleep with dreaming. In visions of the night his soul seemed surely to go forth, far and near, finding vivid adventure. Night became for him more and more real, more and more portentous, as his mind awakened and awakened--in darkness. While the night grew ever more real, steadily it changed and doubled upon itself, becoming ever more unreal, moving apart from him, withdrawing, and gathering in, opposed to him, and yet appealing more deeply and more deeply.

Night seemed at last to him to have become fleeting and floating, yet, nevertheless, and oppressively, an eternal presence, a menace,--a disquieting, nay an appalling, absence. It seemed to him to have become a pit into which his life must sink; an abyss in which his soul must, in the end, be engulfed, lost, forever and forever. For in the dark he feared--he knew not what fell agency he feared. In the dark lurked a nameless dismay, for him, at times a terror--an agony of unrest within rest, a sombre imprisonment, endless and not to be escaped, to which, in the bitter ending of all, it must be his fate to yield. For he seemed helpless, alone, yet not alone.

NIGHT AND DAY

But the man also many a time saw darkness break from its secret covert and flee away as before a pursuer; many a pale gray-white dawn he saw; many a time he saw the east sky flush as with raging fire, the great sun rise in his might. An awakening with courage arose [also] * in the soul of the man, greeting his lord of day, as the sun-god, dazzling overwhelming mounted on high to the throne of the heavens, taking dominion over all the land, all men and things thereon, the power of powers, the glory of glories in the highest,--world without end, as it seemed to the soul of the man. And the man looked far over the brilliant land. In the heaven above he saw the doer of it all, and looked with joy and fear, and rapture and blessing and praise upon the radiant glory of the countenance of his redeemer. So rose and lived the Sun-God in the soul of the man,--and for him it was day-- and it was good:--and the mighty separation of darkness and light took on utterance within him, and this he poured forth over land and sea and sky-- and for him the God became the anointed of his soul.

And many a time he saw the sun decline,--he saw his god go to his rest far in the west--and again the night came creeping on, came the still hour, the hush of twilight, the silhouettes of dusk; the stars again came out of the deep, the obscurity thickened, for the great sun, the friend, had departed, and the dark power had returned. And the darkness deepened to its utmost pitch, and again waned, and again the sun arose, and the trial of strength went on, and on, night and day, day and night, throughout the man's life. Who should have him? Who should hold him at the last? In the darkness the sun seemed a dream and far away, and in the lightness the night seemed a dream and far away. But each returned and returned, and each strove for dominion over the heavens and over the man and his soul-- so it seemed to him. And in the man's perplexity each became a living thing, a power of powers, a mighty presence and a mighty absence,--and a spirit, ever near him, ever far; both, mightier than he. So arose in his soul a companion god,--a Prince of Darkness. And all things slowly coupled for him--for all about him seemed in opposition and conflict. Well he himself knew love and hate. He saw storms in the day and fires by night and by day. He saw tranquility and turbulence around and about him, and felt them within him. He knew the east and the west, north and south, right and left, up and down, in and out, forward and back; he knew one and many, health and sickness, strength and weakness, victory, defeat. And he knew abundance and famine; and he knew that some had more, others less. And, withal, these things seemed strangely intermingled, confused and confounded, even as they tended to separate more positively and clearly within

* From Norman copy.

his thoughts, his life experiences--his many joys and sorrows, the sweetness and the bitterness of his career, and the rise and downfall of his kind. And he knew of revenge, of lust, of hatred, of wrath, and he knew of smiles and tears--of punishment and reward. He knew of strength greater than his and of weakness even feebler than his. He knew a measure of freedom and a measure of hard bondage--and yet he knew also mercy, and pity, and tenderness, and he cherished deep affections. He knew loyalty and treachery. He knew enemies and friends, and he knew victory, pillage and plunder; catastrophe, destruction, flood and conflagration, rapine and ruin. And he knew murder by stealth, and torture, and sacrifice, and propitiation.

And against all this intricacy his mind struggled; for he wished to know. To him, the how, the why were strange enigmas, appalling riddles. For while some things seemed clearly for his good, others as clearly for his hurt, all seemed fickle, uncertain, shifting, unstable, passive, imperturbable. For the man wished to know; he wished peace, certitude; he wished explanations, that he might seek and find repose--that he might somehow, somewhere find a balance between himself,--the great world of mystery and power, which surrounded him, and the world, even of greater mystery, that seemed within him. So he sought to construct explanations and systems. Painfully he sought to erect structures of his emotions and thoughts that might stand as symbols, mediators, transitions between the unknown world without and the unknown world within. For he too, seemed to himself double--his soul seemed separate and apart. So he said, body and soul, of himself; and of all other things he said, substance and spirit; thus each thing seemed animated by a spirit, and so seemed all things. For he gave to them as a gift, abundantly of his spirit. And from their spirits, which he thus discerned, he added to the abundance of his spirit, for he held them in communion and esteem. Thus the man peopled himself without and within with souls, to which he ministered in spirit and which ministered to him in spirit. There were thus for him many spirits of the day and of the night; slowly they congregated into two great companies--for man had little by little thought, within himself, of that without himself which might do good or evil for him; and which, slowly, he pushed further away from himself, and exalted far, far above himself,--as mighty powers.

Thus the man of the past propelled his thoughts far forward, so that they live in our lives this day. But our thoughts go back to him perhaps more calmly, for our fears are not quite his fears--and in the abundance of our patient searching the man seems not dead but rather sleeping and dreaming, and with our rising light upon light he seems at times to waken and to live and breathe and walk upon the earth. His heart becomes our heart, His life our life. Patiently, tranquilly we look into his soul. For he was much to us. He lived for us. His soul put itself bravely against huge enigmas, heroically his mind sought to solve problems that are still our problems. So the man of the past is ourselves in the drift of our intellectual career. For men are all alike. He was like us; we are like him; and through the air of the ages our spirits commune with his spirit; and the eternal oneness of man comes to us more and more.

Thus the man of the past struggled for us that we might be free. Many were his tasks. Many his grand explorations. And of all dramas, the colossal blind struggle of his spirit to be free, is that drama which, in its pathos, its sublime tragedy, and ever up-springing hope, awakens and holds our deepest sympathy,--our profoundest sense of consonance in man.

The man of the Past made many systems, attempted many trial balances with Destiny; for thus it had to be. Of the countless threads of his life spun out of self and dyed of many hues--some he wove with and some he embroidered. Gorgeous fabrics of his thought thus he made. He hung them high, as great veils, before all eyes. He hung them as veils between himself and the vast unknown--veils that seemed to him ample, that seemed, to him, in his fascination, translucent, radiant, living, real--real to his diaphanous longings, real to his burning heart's desire, real to his last and lost earthly hopes--real to his agonies.

Others, as with stones he built upon the tenuous foundations of the solid deep. Sublime structures they. Seemingly, to him, indestructible, imperishable. Vast in scale they rose to his sonorous call from the depths of his soul, from the depths of all souls; reaching on high, they stood in air, dazzling, symmetrical, sumptuously rich and bejewelled with words. He gazed upon his works,--the man of the Past,--in awe for the dreams which seemed true. Dreams which seemed sufficient, enduring,--even to his own strangely indwelling soul, even as the sun, the stars seemed eternal--even as they so seemed ever in imposing contrast with his little life, and his great life, flickering together briefly between whence and whither, or wandering tragically as the blind in company of the blind.

So labored for us the man of the Past. Great pioneer, facing his many fates. In truth his works have endured, for we know them in part, and they are for us to measure, to weigh, to ponder. What they were--we are. How great was his faith and his sorrow!

* * * *

The man of the Past has left a crystalline statement of the impress on him and his forebears of night and day, which statement he elaborated, through ever-forming and phantasing conceptions of light and darkness, into simple stupendous, co-equal, world-heaven and hell-ruling powers of good and evil. The fabric of this dream, this veil, this explanation, was wrought by one Zoroaster, a thousand years or some such matter prior to our era. Its appearance is an aspect of high focal power, in the unfolding and presentation of man's thought.

The dazzling Persian imagery of the system of Zoroaster need not here especially concern us. Nor need his alleged career as poet, religious maniac, political intriguer and martyr. Suffice it that he, as religio-dramatic poet split man's life through the center as with a glittering axe, and That which is One, fell asunder. Its fundamental idea involves opposition, contrast, separation; that all things, all agencies, fall into opposing exactly equal couples. This system of coupled equal opposites he wove and embroidered in minute detail and in grandiose display, to the extremity of philosophic comprehensiveness and poetic phantasy. On high, ruled the coupled gods Good and Evil--in eternal, fruitless, equal might and warfare. From the one God hung, as a cloud-like train, a brilliant hierarchy and army of angels; from the other God, a sombre hierarchy and myriad of demons. Thus the powerful philosophy of Zoroaster, a philosophy which had of necessity to appear and take shape out of night and day, out of the very nature of man and his perplexities, a view of life gestated by the hopes and fears of generations upon generations so long ago, forms one of the many deep streams of thought, flowing through the centuries and now confluent within the drifting estuary of our modern thinking,--hence in a most subtle fashion in our acts of today. We shall see why and how man made his gods.

CONTENTS

Introduction by Elaine Hedges vii

A Note on the Text xxv

DEMOCRACY
A MAN-SEARCH

INTRODUCTION 3

GROUP I: PARTING OF THE WAYS
chapter 1. "What is the Use?" 11
chapter 2. The Point of the Ways 16
chapter 3. Night and Day 21
chapter 4. "Too Busy" 27
chapter 5. Revolution (A Turning-Movement) 34

GROUP II: FACE TO FACE
chapter 1. Viewpoint 45
chapter 2. The Hermit 49
chapter 3. Streams in the Environment 56
chapter 4. The Man on the Street 63
chapter 5. Dance of Death 68
chapter 6. The Great City 94
chapter 7. The Luxury of the Poor 111
chapter 8. A Word 122

CONTENTS

GROUP III: THE MAN OF THE PAST

chapter 1. Historic Sketch 131
chapter 2. Feudalism 142
chapter 3. Democracy 148
chapter 4. The Multitudes 153

GROUP IV: DREAMS

chapter 1. God-Search 161
chapter 2. Man-Search 170
chapter 3. The Nazarene 180
chapter 4. Story of the Church 189
chapter 5. The Dream of Power 209
chapter 6. The Span of Life 219

GROUP V: THE MAN OF TODAY

chapter 1. Awakening 231
chapter 2. Money Talks 236
chapter 3. Business is Business 238
chapter 4. Economy 248
chapter 5. Success 256
chapter 6. The Practical Man 261
chapter 7. The Eminent Man 270
chapter 8. The Self-Made Man 274
chapter 9. The Politician 287
chapter 10. The Parasite 297
chapter 11. The Monopolist 309
chapter 12. The Worker-- Life! 324
chapter 13. Spirit 338
chapter 14. Dusk of Gods: Dawn of Ego 343
chapter 15. Wellspring 356

CONTENTS

GROUP VI: THE NEW WAY

chapter 1. Abuse   367

chapter 2. Art   369

chapter 3. Science   373

chapter 4. The Poet   379

chapter 5. Thought   381

chapter 6. Ego   385

CHAPTER 4 "TOO BUSY"

We are busy, we moderns, singularly engrossed. We have "no time," so we say, for we are "getting things done." It may be well to inquire if we are busy dying. Well to ask what we are getting done.

Granted we are busy, it will be well to see how far we are occupied with loss, how far with gain; to search out what we, a people, mean by gain, and what we understand by loss. For loss and gain, in broad and narrow have much to do with us.

A people, like a man, is ever at the parting of the ways; the one way meaning gain, the other loss for Democracy.

It is assumed, sometimes, that we far-westerners, we of America, are urged by an ideal, a dream, which we, calling it Democracy, formulate in words, as a government of a people, by a people, for a people. It will be part of a fruitful inquiry, in due time to note what these words have to do with our acts.

In assaying the value of our deeds, we have material enough at our hand, we need but the refiner's fire and the scales of a sure balance. So shall we melt and weigh in the fire and in the balance of our thought.

If we, a people, have been too busy to search out, accept and act upon the plain, simple truths of Democracy, we have been "busy" with loss. If we have assumed that what we hail as our gain, our Prosperity, can have stable value, regardless of a spiritual foundation, we have been busy with loss indeed.

In order to arrive at a just estimate of the values of our results as a people, in order to trace backward, from these results to their origins in the thought of the people, we shall assume it axiomatic that the thought of a people is to be read in the acts of a people; and that, in fact, the acts of a people are its thought. In view of the varied origins and transmission of the thoughts of a people, it may be assumed that this is scarcely place to pause for a discussion of this asserted axiomatic truth; but, rather, we may await its unfolding and clarification, until such origins and process of transmission shall have been searched, and set forth. But it may be said, here, that, by the acts of a people, is meant all the acts of all the people; that all acts contribute to social results, hence to the social environment; that, by the thought of a people, is meant all the thoughts of all the people; that thoughts, flowing into acts initiate, maintain and change the social environment. And, further, we are to note this special qualification, namely, that *refraining* from action is a definite act, expressing positive thought.

It is also here posited as axiomatic, that there is no such thing as negative thinking;--that all thinking, however feeble, irresolute, heedless, narrow, is positive; and that, in the same sense, all acts are positive; that however intense or weak may be the desire that the act shall negative something, such act is, nevertheless, positive. There is no such thing as passivity. It is an appearance only,--a mirage of an immense positive power.

In other words all thoughts, all acts, are in essence and in fact positive for the sufficient reason that they cannot be otherwise, for such, as will be later set forth, is the nature of the Life-impulse. In the same sense, will-power is positive. Whether it be strong or weak or vacillating it is still positive. And the desire of the will to negative something or to refrain from something is just as surely positive as is the desire of the will to assert something, to create something.

And, just as positive and negative under analysis coalesce into integral notion of power, so do all acts and all thoughts resolve clearly into a single positive energy whose marked characteristic is a slowly or swiftly flowing change. Thus does the notion of gain and loss insinuate itself into the essence of thought and action, and imply directions of flow. If we are to seek a reasonably clear view of social realities, as well as the realities of the world of nature and of man's consciousness, we must discard the notion that thought is fixed, and accept the more rational notion that it is mobile; for thought is but a manifestation of the ever-flowing Life-energy.

Hence, in a study of Democracy as a philosophy of life, it is of prime importance to arrive at the real thought of a people. The trail to this thought, is defined by the acts of a people. Beyond the thoughts of a people lie the origins of these thoughts. These origins are of a twofold nature; the one phase arising as a reaction from specific environment, the other coming as a flow and pressure of tradition. For the study of environment we have the facts of daily life; and for the study of social tradition we pass from a survey of the present through the gateway of history, which opens to view the prior environments and the flow of men's thoughts, the flow of racial and national thoughts through them, with the many reacting modifications. Thus History, in its humanistic use gives a view of the rhythmic flow of man's thoughts into acts, and the reaction of his thoughts from his acts, in an imposing, an inspiring drift, from the dawn of recorded events to the present hour.

Daily the continuity and significance of this historic flow is becoming clearer; and daily the consciousness is increasing in clarity and power that this flow has been ever onward--never backward--and that the race is moving toward a new domain. With the aid of this historical consciousness we may look with clearer eye upon the happenings of our own day, and realize, to the full, what it means when a great people comes to a crucial parting of the ways. This interest is rendered the more acute, the more solicitous, because of the awakening consciousness of the peoples of the world. This modern phenomenon is a something new under the sun. The import of the slow but sure awakening of the world-people lies in the instinctive urge of its arousing latent power, and the uses to which that power will be put.

The deepest of our own internal stresses has arisen from the act and the fact, that we, of all peoples, have said, the most flippantly and fatalistically, "What is the use?" This query we have posited against the spiritual first-principle whereupon depends our wholesome life as a people.

There are many reasons why, with us, liberty has become license, and freedom a menace to that very individualism by which we lay such store. But the appalling aspect of our fatalism and instability is revealed in the thought, the act, the fact, that with us, betrayal has become a fine art,--the one art that we have assiduously cultivated. The consequences of such betrayal in thought, in act and in fact, must be included in the reckoning.

If our studies are to eventuate in substantial good, we must face our facts as facts. For we shall find, as we progress, that the broader, the simpler the fact, the more intense is the personal application of the principle within it. Our fixed purpose is clearly and broadly to present vital aspects, in our man-search. And in our search for man we must pass from the facts of his acts, to and through his thoughts, until we reach his core. Inasmuch as he can go nowhere that his acts do not reveal him, we shall surely find him. The study of a people can have but one fruitful end, and that: to find the individual--and reckon with him. If we had not a sound and sane balance in which to weigh our social values, such attempt to search out man through his larger expression in a people would be futile. But the nature and accuracy of our Balance will be set forth, as speedily as the ground plan of our work will permit; for this delicate and supreme balance that we shall put to use is naught else than the integrity of the Life-impulse.

Thus the unwelcome part of our task, the very hard part of it, is to look steadily at that which is worst in ourselves.

We are not a happy people. We say we are; but the saying is negatived by our manifest unrest, our obvious lack of equipoise, our progressive disintegration. To be sure there is a certain broad division in this regard between the city dwellers and the country dwellers; but the distinction is superficial--wherever you may go you are sure to find anxiety close under the surface. Now why should a flourishing people be anxious, and why should a free people be anxious, unless it be, perchance, that the prosperity and the freedom are unreal? Why does the stress of living become daily tenser in a land overflowing, in a land whose resources have not as yet been drawn upon in an intensive way? A land in which famine is unknown:--Or, should we stop here, and say, a land in which a widespread spiritual famine prevails, though seemingly unknown and unsuspected?

Righteous indignation we have with us, to be sure; but toward what end does that avail? Plain perception of the few, but simple, realities of life will count for more. To make these realities stand forth clear is the whole of our task.

Schools, colleges, universities we have; but what do these avail, in that they do not sow the seeds of simple, vital truths--truths as essential to a democratic life as are air, food and water to the physical life?

Of what avail are they if they do not inculcate the little truth that betrayal is fatal to the aspirations of Democracy? [If they do not teach the plain truth that integrity is the mainstay of Democracy.] * To be sure they declare they teach these things; but in thought, in act, in fact they do not. For there is all the difference in the world between the conventional repetition of a traditional ghostly precept, and the clear, powerful presentation of the reasonableness behind a living truth; however small, however negligible that truth may appear within the immense maze of our civilization.

For this failure in efficiency of teaching there is naturally, a reason. This reason, this reluctance, this evasion, it will be a part of our work to search out.

Whence has come the minute and diversified ramification of graft? Did it originate in the big? By no means. It has come from the sanction of innumerable individuals; it has grown out of innumerable small desires, and merely flourished and flowered conspicuously in the big. For it is not a primary fact that thoughts work downward from what we call the top. The reality is that the few at the top derive their power for good or evil and are supported and sustained in that power directly and solely by the desire and sanction of the many; that is, by the thoughts of the multitude.

At any given time there exists a prevailing thought of all the people considered as a unit; and upon the creative power, uplift and sanction of this thought rests the special power of those whom this thought chooses to exalt, because of definite accord with it. This accord of thought is the key to the flowering of any aspect of any civilization. But as this dominant thought of the people waxes, wanes and changes, so does the power of the sanctioned,--individuals or institutions--wax, wane and change accordingly and with marvellous precision. As long as the few remain sane they clearly understand this sanction and its nature. When the sense of delegated power drives them mad, as invariably it does when the passion of possession seizes them as a mania, they forget the sanction, and go down,--after a brutal but useless struggle to retain the power, which, in their illusion, they have believed to be their own. This mad dream of power invariably takes the form of a desire to enslave all the people--and evolves a most plausible, cunning and intricate system of treachery. When the people awake to the object lesson, the feudal fabric, vast though it be, falls to the ground. Thus individuals come and go, but the people move on. The vanity of the sanctioned few inexorably leads them to believe that they determine the orbit

* From Norman copy.

in which the many move. No superstition could be more fantastic. The orbit, the inertia, the momentum, the creative power lies in the imagination and will of the people. It has always been so; it is so now. Hence, special virtues are exalted when the multitudes so feel and will; and when the exaltation of vice is particularly in evidence, it is a sure sign that these are dominant within the thought of the people. Hence if graft prevails it is a plain sign that the average man is in thought a grafter, that he sanctions graft. The fact that he will variously disclaim this allegation signifies nothing further than an indication of the variety of mask he elects to wear upon his secret thought. For the physical, tangible fact of graft is here; you meet it everywhere, under every imaginable guise, disguise, and disclaimer; therefore the creative cause is here also: for it is irrational to suppose that any broad social manifestation may exist unnurtured by the sanction of these secret thoughts which determine the expression of the will of a people. It cannot feed upon itself. It rises and falls as sensitively as the stream of a fountain. For the stream of a fountain cannot exist of itself. It is but an expression of water, pressure, and an organized mechanism.

It is our business to search out man regardless of his phrases and his attitudinizing. And it is to be a part of our business, in such search, to utilize the knowledge that the great forces of nature are silent, and that what really counts in human affairs is the concurrence of minute individual agencies released by a simple silent power,--the power of Choice.

Thus the will of a people but expresses the gathered choice of its individuals. And the will or choice of the specific individual, has, ever, a minute origin. It is his choice, his initiative, his will, his imagination, at the small, sharp, ever-recurrent parting of his ways. It is his conscious, deliberate estimate of the values of gain and loss, in the large and the small way. It is his immediate answer to the query: What is the use? It is his individual response to the query: Which way?; the individual expression of his conception of liberty; the exact expression of his secret estimate of himself, of his neighbor, and of the world.

That is to say: Every man, in every thought, hence in every act, casts a real ballot--the kind that counts and is surely Life-counted--either for Feudalism or for Democracy.

And thus it comes, that such individual choosing--a continuous intimate process--taken in bulk and continuously, constitutes the real plebiscite, the real referendum--the real initiative, the real creative act--which sanctions or changes the social status. It is just here that we, a multitudinous people, are very busy now.

"TOO BUSY"

In our search we shall see how deep we are engrossed in a mania of destruction. How far with us the feudal madness has progressed, and we shall search, also, if there be a leaven of work within the surging power of our thought as a people; a ferment which may bring about a massive change.

* * * *

CHAPTER 5 REVOLUTION

(A Turning-Movement)

    Men, as a rule, are not in the habit of loosening up words--of untying the package, and shaking the contents out to air. Hence they so generally regard words merely as brands or labels. It is thus men speak vaguely, queerly, and vacantly of Democracy--For, to them it is a word, a brand, a label, merely.

    Many have heard of the fisherman of long ago, who unsealed a jar he found on the shore; and of how, instanter, one of the great genii or spirits emerged from the opened little jar, and, swiftly expanding, filled the air and the whole sky, and became terrible to look upon--even as it had been contained in so small a thing.

And many have heard of Aladdin's lamp; and of Sinbad the Sailor and the Old Man of the Sea, and, reading or hearing these stories, of long ago, may have thought them curious, passing stories. And so they were and are--charming stories, gossamer weavings of the finely creative oriental mind, spinnings from the heart, and the intellect's delight--hues, and shades, and iridescences of the dainty, capricious and deep-seeing soul. Stories they were and are, but perennial symbols. For the "once upon a time" always means--now. "Once upon a time" is but a poetic and diverting way of saying "Now"! And the "once upon a time there was a prince" or the "once upon a time there was a fisherman" is a poetic and diverting way of saying--you and I--here and now; and of hinting at our universal powers. For all men become alike in the fluid, living solvent of the spirit. And, once the heart is released it flies farther and brings back more than did the dove of Noah's Ark. And that was another story, another allegory, another symbol, another poem, and another "once upon a time"--another you and I,--another here and now.

Did you ever breathe the breath of your spirit into a little frothy, watery, soapy word, and watch it swell and grow as you breathed, and grow and sway, become gaudily iridescent, and detach, and float away-- and burst, and vanish like a hope? No? Then you have not read "And the Lord God formed man of the dust of the ground, and breathed into his nostrils the breath of life: and man became a living soul"? And is not this, too, but another story, another poem, another "once upon a time," another here and now? And is not man an iridescent bubble, a watery film, that bursts and vanishes as a hope of that Spirit which breathes the breath? Is it not thus that "in Adam all die"? and was and is not Adam you and I?-- That child, the father of us men-children. That symbol-man the myth-father of us symbol-children. That dream of an ancient story teller. That poetic, diverting image of spiritual quintessence and of eternal creative power. That sure sign that in Adam all live. That grand allegory which signifies that when man breathes into the dust the breath of his life, that dust becomes, for him, alive. That, when man breathes the breath of his spirit into the common things, those things become spiritual realities--living souls. That, when man gives the breath of his life to the neighbor, that neighbor becomes for him a living soul--thus you and I.

Have you thought how a word may be melted, cast, forged and sharpened into a sword?

Have you thought how a word may be made gelatinous, and spun out of the mind as a gossamer thread, and wound, and wound about an idea, until the real meaning of that idea becomes totally hid, and the cocoon, the word, alone remains visible and believable? No? Have you thought that prosperity might be such a word? Have you thought that Justice might be such a word--so spun, so used?

Have you thought how a word might be made ductile, and drawn out into a wire invisible, but stronger than steel, and how this wire, this word, might be used to bind so subtly yet so firmly, that the many human souls so bound would think it natural and of their own limitation that they could move only just so far? that they could only do just such and such things? Have you thought that Education might be such a word, that Religion might be such a word? Have you thought how two or three words could be twisted into a powerful strand, and used to rope you off and apart with? That law, and order, might be two such words, so stranded and so used? That a word could be turned into a hair and fashioned into a snare to snare you with? That the word God might be so fashioned and so used? Have you thought just why and how men use words as blinds to hide behind? That respectability, eminence, might be such screen-words? Have you thought how and why men have erected structures of words as barriers with which to keep themselves apart?

Have you ever thought how one word may be made to look like another word? Have you thought how the word Injustice may be dressed to resemble the word Justice? Have you thought how words have been and are used as scarecrows? Have you ever thought how a word may be placed in front of another word to hide it--how the word, Prosperity, may be placed in front of the word, Corruption, so as to hide it? Have you ever thought who does this--and why? Do you know words are used as decoys? and who so use them? and when, where, how and why? No? Then it were well you begin at once to enquire how you, yourself use words.

Have you ever looked words face to face? Have you ever really touched them, to see if this one or that one be dead or alive? Have you ever thought how words are used, by yourself or by others, as masks placed over things that it is desired shall not be seen in their murderous reality? Do you know just when, where, by whom and how, these mask-words are so used--and precisely why? Think again:--Precisely why?--either by yourself, or others, or all! Have you ever thought of the word, Illusion, and what it means? Have you ever suspected that it means you? or rather have you looked upon it as upon the back of a mirror?

Have you ever thought of the word, Reality? Have you ever steadfastly and fearlessly looked at it? or have you looked upon it as upon the face of a mirror, and, seeing reflected therein the mask you wear, believed yourself to be real--believing your thoughts, your acts, your sense of justice to be real? or have you seen the mask, known it as such, and kept it as such?--and have still remained in illusion?

Have you ever thought much concerning the word, Man? Have you ever sought the living substance of that word? Have you ever sought to exhaust the meaning of the word? Have you ever drawn from it as from a deep well? Have you ever reflected that this word, Man, embraces and includes all other words--that it excludes not a single word?

When you wish to know the meaning of a word do you go to a dictionary, and are you satisfied with that? Or, unsatisfied with that, feeling a huge vacancy of meaning, do you go to man and his ways, to nature and her ways,--to Life and its ways, to The Spirit and its ways? Behind the word, Man, have you ever actually searched for the reality, man? Behind the word, Nature, have you ever searched for the reality, nature? Behind the word, Life, have you ever searched out the reality, Life? Behind the word, Spirit, have you ever searched for the Spirit? Or have these great words remained with you little words, mere labels of powers regarding which you have felt no concern, because you were "too busy" with things which seemed to you much more real, practical, and of greater consequence?--because you had "no time"--for you were "busy" getting real things done? Have you ever thought of what you are really getting done while you are so busy?--while you have had no time for such trivialities as man, nature, Life, and the all-spirit?

And have you really thought at all, concerning the word, Democracy? and have you tried to discern its true nature? have you sought to remove the husks that surround it and get to the kernel? No? Well, I have caught a glimpse of its spiritual meaning; and that is my chief reason for arranging these marks on paper.

Have you ever thought, largely, concerning little words? Such words as Why, How, When, When,* Where? Have you ever seen a little word expand from seeming harmless nothingness into a terrific significance, size and power? Have you ever seen a word condense out of a vague expanse of futility and strike like a bolt? No? Have you deemed words inert, and their home, their home,† their prison, the dictionary? Have you merely liked or disliked their sound? Did you not know that words may be charged with power--if but that power be drawn from the Great Life--by anyone whose brain is a conductor of the great life-current? Have you ever stopped to think that we are all naturally such conductors, but that we have told ourselves it is not so--and that, curiously enough, the eminent and the

* Probably should be *What*,.
† The repetition is in the MS.

pious have told us that same thing too, and that in return we have acquiesced? Have you ever stopped to enquire precisely why, and how, we have so told ourselves, and how and why the exalted have so told us, and precisely why and how we have acquiesced? Have you ever thought, in self-preservation, to do this, have you ever deemed this an essential to racial preservation; to the preservation of the neighbor? Have you ever deemed it of the highest human import to enquire exactly what the many have said to the few and what the few have said to the many throughout all historic time; and what the many say to the few and what the few say to the many Today? Here! Now! and precisely why the few say certain things to the many, and refrain from saying certain other things? That the successful few have in fact said to the many, merely things that the many had already said to themselves, and implicitly believed; and that the unsuccessful few had said to the many either those things which the many had not yet said to themselves, and hence did not yet believe, or things which the many had ceased to say or believe?

Have you thought much concerning the word, History? Had you supposed it to mean a book? Have you unsealed this little word and beheld the genius of man emerge and slowly, sublimely, fill the air--the terrible and beautiful spirit of man--that spirit, darkling, gloomy, radiant, many colored--floating like a huge portentous cloud rumbling with passion, forking with the madness of desire, gleaming and melting and metamorphosing with every hue and shading of emotion--and partly still, with brilliant heights, diaphanous shadows--moving, ever moving, and ever threatening, ever retreating,--far far away in purple stillness, near and nearer in fog and storm--dazzling white and high against an infinite azure, hung in the infinite stillness of flowing time and space?! and have you seen the cloud transform before your eyes and assume mean repulsive crapulous shapes, and take on a turgid, dreary aspect of desolation?

Or have you seen the reality, History, spread out as a vast domain with mountains, forests, deserts, rivers and plains and great seas--with many peoples coming and going, and the sun rising and setting and rising and setting again?

Or have you seen it, anon, as a great moving picture, filled with tumultuous action, with men and women, with armies and fleets, with glory and the fierce glut of war, with nation at nation like wolf at wolf over the spoils? And have you seen it in many many other ways? Have you seen it as yourself, as your prior experiences in the man of the past, your shaping heredity, and heritage? Have you seen it as your own longings, your ambition, and your grief? And have you seen it as your neighbor,--

his needs, his wants, his hopes, his illusions, his fatalities? And have you listened to its voice telling the story of us all, and the story of those who went long, long before and are gone over the rim of time; and the story, the hint, the prophecy of those that are yet to come? Has history remained with you a catalogue of dates, of squabbles, of puppets--of stage mannerisms?--or is it with you the great story of the highest animal, the story of his coming up out of the dust, and of his struggles, his perplexities, his long long search for peace amid the tumult? His own story of what he thought concerning Man, Nature, Life and the all-spirit.

Have you ever felt the past as a living, vibrant, pulsating reality? Have you ever reached out, with that living power, the imagination, to grasp the hand of the Man of the Past--to look into his eyes, to hear his voice, to call him brother--to feel him brother to you and yours,--to you and me? That this vast "once-upon-a-time" we call History, is our once-upon-a-time; that it may be brought so near that it becomes now!--for us--and we become then!, in spirit, in sympathy, as the heart goes to the heart, the mind to the mind, the soul to the soul--spirit to spirit--as all blends into the great spirit of the present and the past, living and breathing from eternity to eternity--living and breathing here, now, for you and me? If not so, then open again that which you have thought but a book, and read, with a new eye; listen, with a new sense; feel, with a new heart and enter into possession with a resurgent soul! For then you will have glimpsed what you and I mean, what the neighbor means, what Feudalism and Democracy mean, what the past signified, what the present signifies, what the future may, can and must have in store for those who are to follow us--and be of us--as we--have followed the man of the past, and are of him.

Have you thought about the word Revolution? You have heard it often, no doubt, and used it often. But have you thought of what it really means? Perhaps not. In that case it were high time you think clearly and sanely of what it has meant and means--For we are in revolution now--world-wide, deepening in intensity here.

In its broad sense, to be sure, revolution is a normal and continuous process, a concomitant of evolution, as we say, of unfoldment, of development, of the all-life process and progress; and, in this its deepest aspect, it is a phase of Nature's silentious power of motion and growth.

As all great manifestations of Nature's power arise and shape from out the concurrence and rhythmic association of myriad, minute, indeed, infinitesimal powers, so, in social affairs, revolutions arise out of seeming nothingness, out of obscure and minute initiatives, which, in essence and in fact, are the reactions of men's thoughts against the entire environment--social and physical--confluent with an urge that is the invincible push of Life working out its program.

In this sense Democracy is ever a Revolution; superficially it is a reaction from Feudalism, but the deeper truth is that Democracy is an aspiration, a great instinctive reality pushing up through a heavy overlay of illusion, and seeking form for its superb and calm spirit.

Thus, while every revolution, small or great, and of whatsoever nature, is in one sense a reaction, in a more germinal a more genetic sense it is an explicit work of Life.

Again, broadly speaking, revolutions are of two kinds, that is, two manifestations of one underlying energy, namely, revolutions of peace and revolutions of war. The former are essentially creative in nature, the latter volcanic cataclysms of destructive passion, seeking a way out by force. The former are fostered by self-liberation of body and mind, the latter by self-suppression of body and mind. The former lead to beneficent change in the thought-output of a people, and hence to improvement in the social environment, the latter leads to the knife, the torch and a tornado of reconstruction. Therefore the former are legitimate offspring of the democratic Spirit--the latter, inexorable children of Feudalism. Therefore are the former revolutions of hope, the latter of essential despair. Thus is a revolution feudal or democratic.

How, then, will our present revolution now in its formative beginnings swerve, as it meets the point of the parting of the ways?

In view of the rapid growth from within us of a colossal money Feudalism, with slavery an obvious goal, it might seem, at first blush that a revolution of blood can be the only logical or possible reaction. For an entire people, once believing itself free, is not easily enslaved--a chord is touched at last; there is a new and modern dead line somewhere--no one knows just where--and our golden idols may easily turn to clay and dust.

Yet, on the other hand, means of communication, appliances for spreading news, for transmission and interchange of thought, are such as have not been hitherto used or known. Ours is conspicuously a new day, with new mechanisms and a new technique. We have a widespread system of public schools--millions of copies of daily papers, great issues of weekly periodicals and of monthly magazines--the ever ready telegraph, a conspicuously small standing army without an overtly allied church; and, above all, the ocean cables, girdling the world, keep us in sensitive daily touch with the entirety of mankind and make us responsive in varying degree to its manifold, powerfully changing thoughts and activities. Our percentage of illiterates is small--nearly all the people read, write, and cipher.

The battle ground, and the mechanisms, processes and methods are new; but the marshalling forces, the gathering hosts of a people dividing against itself, are propelled by the same world-old force of Feudalism. It is still a matter of dog eat dog. We have not yet gotten beyond that.

The optimist, in the faith of his hope and belief in the goodness of men, may predict a happy turning movement, and a renewed life, a new step toward the happiness of man, as the outcome.

The pessimist may find food and more food for his disbelief in men, in their sanity, their honesty; more nourishment for his fixed idea of their imbecility, their brutality, cowardice and lust. He will have his according view of the outcome. He will have no doubt.

The alarmist will progress in vacillation.

The apathetic will go on his fat-witted way until events fall upon him. So, also, will the complacent.

There are men who say they do not see a hand-writing on the wall-- there are men who say they do.

But it is no part of our business to be either optimistic or pessimistic. It is our business to be sensitive and just; to draw aside the veil. To look clearly, steadily and reasonably at the physical, the mental, the emotional and spiritual facts of our civilization. To set forth the flow and drift of its activities within the larger currents of events, the mightier tide of Life. To analyze these, unsparingly, in their origins. To call things by their real names. To place man clearly and definitely within his environment and his environment as accurately about him. To place him squarely face to face with himself. To place the neighbor squarely before him, and him squarely before all the people, and all the people as squarely before the individual. To place all, collectively and individually, squarely before Life, and as squarely before the modern shaping Spirit. And then, with a word or two of warning, a word or two of pleading, acknowledging his freedom of will, and his possession of brain and heart--we will leave him to desire as he sees fit, to think as he sees fit, to act as he sees fit, and to add the consequences--whatsoever they may be--to the sum total of his social environment and our gift to posterity. But this much may be added: When we shall have completed our task, the meaning of gain and loss will be clear in its human aspect. The nature of Feudalism and of Democracy will have been defined with so cutting a precision that it will mean you. The integrity of man and the immensity of his natural powers will be set forth indelibly--and this, also,--will mean you--For such is the Man-Search.

* * * *

GROUP II—FACE TO FACE

Chapter 1   Viewpoint
Chapter 2   The Hermit
Chapter 3   Streams in the Environment
Chapter 4   The Man on the Street
Chapter 5   Dance of Death
Chapter 6   The Great City
Chapter 7   The Luxury of the Poor
Chapter 8   A Word

CHAPTER 1   VIEWPOINT

It has been the fashion among philosophers to assume that mind is something apart from the Cosmos and that there is another something, apart in the Cosmos, called the objective reality. Hence there is assumed to be a "pure reason," and, a "thing in itself" concerning which the pure reason reasons. This is called transcendentalism. It is supposed to stand for the uttermost reach of intellect. In actuality, in comparison with that men daily *do,* it is crude. The wayside weeds shame it. The real moonlight makes of it a will-o-the-wisp. The vigor of health turns it to nonsense.

Now such view is definitely laid to one side in this work, as particularly lacking in the truly human sense of humor, kindliness and sympathy.

In place of it is set forth the conception that all is life--that the Cosmos is life--that the desire and the flesh of man is life--that what we call Nature is life--that what we call motion is life--that all things within us (as we say) and without us (as we say) are modes of life: and that there is, in essence neither a within nor a without, neither subjective nor objective; that our thoughts concerning phenomena--in sympathy, and therefore in reality--are modes of life interplaying with modes of life, and that the interplay of phenomena is likewise thus related to us. That the animus of Life is Spirit. That the simplest thing is intelligible only when with our life we cordially accept it as life, and with our spirit accept it as spirit.

It is assumed the day is passing, wherein men seriously believe in a rigid dualism--in the fetish of matter as a something acted upon by another something called energy or force; in the fetish of mind as an "active" something apart from another "passive" fetish called Nature; in the fetish of soul as apart from a fetish called body.

For such conceptions are but survivals of the day and the night, of the feudal notions of good and evil, of the phantasmal notions of sin and redemption:--Survivals of the notion of an external God--as though there could be anything external--external to what? Survivals of the notion that man is apart from nature, exterior to nature--where could man go to get away from nature? Survivals of the notion that nature is apart from man, external to man--where would nature go to get away from man?

Thus, is here set up the conception that in all things the individual man may see himself, because Life is integral, therefore nothing is really foreign to man--not even his neighbor--and man has been really foreign to nothing--not even to his God.

But man has assumed otherwise--and has paid the price. That singular perversion of his intellect, called vanity, and that equally singular intellectual repression of his heart, called hypocrisy, have obscured his sanity of vision. So, to fortify himself in his vanity and hypocrisy, to "prove" that his vision is clear, he has invented philosophies, doctrines, religions, dogmas galore--vain and hypocritical as himself.

Stubbornly has man refused to see himself in the neighbor:--"What! Brother to vermin like that?," he has said. Yet if he will look upon the meanest and most wretched of his kind, look close, he will see in the meanness and wretchedness of that other the meanness of his own vanity and the wretchedness of his own hypocrisy. He will see, in "vermin like that," the vermin that crawl within his intellect.

For man cannot escape the neighbor--where will he go to escape the neighbor? And the neighbor cannot escape him--where will the neighbor go to escape him?

And if a man resolutely sets out to search for man, will he not find him? Surely he will. For where can the man escape--there is nowhere to go. But the man does not believe this--he thinks he has anywhere and everywhere to go--that is part of his folly, that is the key to his illusion. For does not the man say:--I am, I possess, I do this and I do that! Do I not harness nature? Am I not above the brutes?--And thus does he nurse his round of illusions, thus does he cherish his monomania, thus does he foster his illusory segregation from the rest--and thus is his pride complete. But thus also, does he prepare himself for us as a specimen, and make himself ready for us that we may condense the totality of his environment upon him from all directions--because in his fatuity he believes he is not like other men.

And if we take one of the mean and wretched, one of the "vermin," show to him one of the exalted, and say to him:--Neighbor, would you like to see yourself?--Behold what you have created! He would surely say:--No, it cannot be possible. Yet it is not merely possible, it is actual. For the man, the "vermin" believes not so much that he is not like the exalted, as that the exalted are not like him. And this is the key to his illusions. He does not know himself when he sees himself in the mighty; for he is a dreamer; his vanity lies in the luxury of self-abasement, his hypocrisy in his secret disdain of his kind. He is as complicated in his pride and stubbornness as the artificial few whose furniture is philosophy, economics, theology, etc. His fetish like their own is Self. He is as much a snob as they. And yet he is a man, whose thinking and feeling are none the more or less inane, luxurious and futile than theirs. For his vision is neither more nor less obscure than theirs in essence and in practical application in the way of life. For him, as for them, the neighbor is a stranger --and man an unknown quantity. Because he, too, believes that there are two things--himself and something which is not himself. He too has his pure reason and his objective reality. He too is a transcendentalist. So his folly is neither greater nor less than theirs. His sense of humor and kindliness is as wanting as theirs; and the gift of fear is the common possession--it is that which unites all men in that mutual antagonism we call civilization, whose handmaiden we say is Reason.

But we have a sieve through which to sift, and we shall sift through man.

Meanwhile, allowing the pure reason and the thing-in-itself to repose on the shelf, we will proceed. For eyes and ears, a little sensibility, a little looking back, around and forward, a scent of the trail, a little awareness, are all the baggage we need. For have we not man in his environment always with us? What more do we need? What more should we need? Have we not the man-of-the-Past, as well as the man of today? And have we not as a sure guide the sound of his eternal cry: What is the use? In our thought do we not carry the man to come?

CHAPTER 2 THE HERMIT

It appears to be a hobby, universal in the individual, to believe himself inscrutable. He hugs the unction that he really can and does live within the retirement of his innate self; that, safe, within this sanctuary, he draws a veil impenetrable and inviolable.

And so perhaps he might do, were not all men--being of common origin--essentially alike; alike even as the leaves of a given tree. For is not each and every leaf of an oak tree oak, even as root, trunk and branch are oak--even as the flowering, the nut of the tree is oak? And are not men leaves of a common tree, as it were? Are they not as one in root, in branch, in flower, in seed of their thought?

So when the simulacrum man seeks thus to recede within the real man, as we advance, we may draw aside the veil he believes he has securely drawn; and, after that, drawing--it may be--aside a translucent gossamer he knows not of, we may reveal the very thing he calls his soul-- and find it greatly differing from what he has supposed and still believes.

And also, thus, if as a people we are very busy, we, as searchers, must know concerning what fictions and what facts we as a people are thus busy. We must know, particularly, concerning what the individual is concerning himself--especially when he is sure he is alone. We must note those things concerning which he does not appear to be concerning himself either when alone or abroad in the world of men and things. We will note the fictions he carries with him into the world of men, the fictions he finds there, the fictions he fails to find there, and we will note what realities, if any, he carries into the world of men and things, and what realities, if any, he finds there; what realities are there, whether he finds them or not; and what corresponding realities are in him whether he suspects them or not, whether he officially denies them or not. We will note what he knows of words, how he uses words, why he uses them and when--and where--what relationship exists between realities and words as he uses them--and the relationship between his words and fictions--fictions which he believes unsuspected because he has drawn a veil before them and is alone with them even as in a sanctuary. We must put the man face to face with fictions and realities, with lies and facts, face to face with words and things--face to face with words and men--face to face with his vanity, his hypocrisy--face to face with the lies he has told, the truths he has concealed, the truths he has suppressed--the truths he has killed the neighbor for uttering. We must put him face to face with the neighbor he has wrecked--that he may see that his soul is not what he thought it was--that words are not what he thought them--that they may, perchance, bite him in the face and tear more terribly than he has torn. For he must be shown what the word, thief, means, what the word, liar, means, he must be taught what the word, murder, means--what it means in fact, not fiction--what murder means in reality--in monstrous reality--face to face--not in the illusion and delusion we call the law--not legal murder--real murder, quick and slow, and sure. He must be put face to face with the words destruction, disintegration, decay, death--and must be confronted with the realities that lie behind these words and in front of them and massed around them. He must be confronted with the word responsibility--personal responsibility--*his* responsibility--and asked if he knows what that word means, and if not, what it shall mean--when the reality behind it comes forth and looks upon him, steadfastly, face to face. He must be asked if he knows what thought and act signify,--his thoughts--

his acts--not in fiction, but in fact!, not academically--but for sure. Not transcendentally, but here! now! net!

He must be put face to face with thoughts he has shunned, and asked if he now dare kill openly as he would kill in secret--as he would sacrifice in the sanctuary behind the drawn veil, to the God of Gold in his inmost dwelling--in his inviolable privacy, behind the veil where he believes he can hide from the world of men and things and thoughts and action.

He must be handed the knife that he has slipped into a thought, and shown the friend with the mortal wound in the back--the wound must be traced to the wounder, in his seclusion, in his sanctuary--yea in his private office.

He must be confronted with the word, treachery, behind the veil; and the word, philanthropy, before the veil. He must be shown--what he knows and denies--that these words are interchangeable in his code--that the one is hitched to the other as by a chain of links--that when he moves one the other goes.

He must be confronted with the neighbor, in the sanctuary, and asked:--Do you know this man? Surely you must know him, you have drawn his blood; and surely you must know this neighbor's thousands upon thousands of brothers, for you have likewise drawn their blood, and it tasted good, and the children's blood, also, tasted good.

And he must be confronted with graves. They must be brought into the sanctuary, behind the veil, into the sealed solitude of one--and to him must be said:--Here are more of your neighbors--you must have loved them well, for did not you many a time ask your God to bless them and prosper them even as he had blessed and prospered you--and has he not of a verity done so! Did not their blood taste also good? And did not your God smile-your golden and affectionate god--smile upon you, his incarnate son, upon you, face to face, paternally, behind the veil--in the solitude of the sanctuary of your secret thought?

And he must be confronted by the peevish faces of children from his factories. For is not their blood exceeding fine of savor, and very welcome to the dainty palate of the god--in the stillness of the sanctuary, in the silence of sacrifice and worship and consecration? The blood of little ones is so sweet that the god of gold must need drool and drowse with the glut of it. Indeed all blood is good and savory. The blood of women, too, is good and sweet, the women in his sweat shops and his stores. For men and children and women are all alike to the Golden God of the secret soul, and their blood is equally sweet--if but there be enough, only enough, and more and more and more. For such is the God incarnate in the man, behind the veil of words, words, words, spun and woven and embroidered words, the veil of words which he believes he has drawn, at the door of the temple which we may not profane, the enclosure even of which we may not enter--lest we find not a man but a phantom beside a door, and lest we find a cross with a child upon it, crying foolishly. That cross is the sign by which he conquers--he of the veiled secret thought.

And we must take to him in the sanctuary, the bruised, the battered, the abandoned wives, with the furtive children at their skirts, wives and children gathered here, there and everywhere, collecting in troupes upon troupes, thousands of them, (and there is room for them all in the little sanctuary), that he may know what the word whiskey means when not labeled "poison" and marked with skull and cross-bones when he "rectifies" it--That he may know what the word rectification means in fiction and fact--so that he may learn to spell the word, with the same letters that others use in spelling destruction.

And the torn and maimed men, women and children, all the separated legs, and arms and heads, and the funerals, the weeping ones, the disconsolate, the crutches and the bandages, the surgeons, hospitals, coffins, paraphernalia and cemeteries must be brought to him, brought in thousands upon thousands, wailing, moaning, stiff and stark, ghastly and freshly ripped open, all brought into the sanctuary, into the stillness, the quiet where the man is safe, inscrutable,--Alone with his secret soul, that he may see for sure that these human fragments, this human residue came from the grade crossings of his railroads; that he may know that he spells the word dividends with the identical letters that others use to spell the word murder --That his secret thought means these frightful things--That these realities must meet his fiction face to face--That the mangled dead, the bereaved, the orphaned, the broken hearted--must meet his soul face to face in the solitude, in the ever-growing stillness, with no sound save the heart-beat quieted forever. And the universities and libraries, and churches, he upreared, with their presidents, professors, preachers, students, worshippers all, of the Sunday God, must be brought in, too, and placed near the stilled hearts, and the human fragments, and hearses, and the beaten and abandoned women and children, all in the sanctuary--and there is room for all --it is such a little one. And the Sunday God must be brought in, too, and made acquainted with the smiling Golden God--that they may greet in a brotherly god-like way, within the soul of the man. And the Christ on the Cross must be brought in, too, with the crown of thorns and the stripes, and the spiked hands and feet and the pierced side, (he who would save men from themselves) bleeding and moaning (why hast thou abandoned me!)--He also must enter into the soul of the man to meet with the two gods and the fragments, and the dividends and the tears, that the blood from the wounded breast, that breast which yearned for the neighbor, may drip, drop by drop, into his soul; that the blood of the Son of Man may render red the pallid thought in the secret soul of the man who would murder, and poison, and betray, and rot and rob and mangle in the sanctified name of the God of Gold--while the Christ groans, and the Sunday God looks foolish, and the Golden God smiles and dozes, and the preachers say "Cast thy burden upon the Lord and He will sustain thee"-- "Believe and ye shall be saved"--while the human fragments are stark and silent--, and the tears flow silently, and the furtive children wonder and the professors and transcendentalists gape on--all in the soul of the man, in the solitude grown populous, and real, and vivid--face to face with the mockery of Christian civilization--and its cant, its pride, vanity, hypocrisy--with its worship of Judas, with its heel on the neighbor's throat, with its very soul like the soul of the man in the sanctuary--with its secret lust withdrawn behind the veil of the Cross and the Christ--with the gentle Christ and the lilies before the veil, and the lust of blood behind the veil. Before the veil, the hot passion of love; behind the veil the icy passion of greed, the insatiate cannibal hunger--the hunger and the teeth to crack the bones of tenderness--Before the veil: Brothers in Christ!--Behind the veil: Assassination!

And why should the man not feel safe, secure, alone, behind the veil? Why, otherwise, should words have been invented? Of what possible use, otherwise, could be the words love, friendship, fidelity, truth, honor, Justice, unless to be woven and embroidered into a radiant veil behind which the man might pass with his secret soul--and find a sanctuary for his love?

And why need the man be great? Will not an obscure man do? Will not any man answer the requirements? Must our search be far to choose? Will not one of the common run qualify also?--Has not the "vermin" also his veil? Has he not also his sanctuary? Does he not also leave a trail of deeds; as he withdraws into that wondrous sanctity of self? Shall there be cant for the rich and none for the poor? Is hypocrisy alone for the eminently great, and lust alone for the few, and the iron heel alone for the mighty? Are these things not free to all? Are not words plentiful-- and are not secret desires, secret desires anywhere and everywhere? And is a man bounded by his clothing, or by cleanliness, or filth? Or by learning, or ignorance, or by poverty or wealth, or by palace or hovel? Are not all men free, is not each man free to retire within himself and commune with his secret thoughts? Must one know Greek to do that, or mathematics, or philosophy, or theology? Do not all men self-commune in a universal language when they are alone and carefully dumb with their thoughts?

And are these thoughts not the same? Sifted and sifted, are they not the same in all men? Do they not weigh out the same when divested of formality, etiquette, manners and customs, pomp and parade, filth and starvation, and misery, wretchedness and sorrow? Are not all men alike when they are sifted through each other? Are their thoughts not alike, when stripped alike of rags and purple and fine linen? Is one man's soul so different from another man's soul that we can build a religion upon the difference, rather [than]* upon the sameness--That we can build an enduring civilization upon the differences rather than upon the unique similarity? Is the soul of the bum in the gutter really so different from the soul of the University president, or the Captain of Industry, or the Senator, or the Preacher, or the Pope, or the Emperor, or the eminent lawyer? It is the fashion to say in scorn and disdain that they differ--But that is falsehood! Stripped of all pedantry, all vanity, pride, hypocrisy, stubbornness, wealth, poverty--With the veil torn away--These souls stand bare, naked, and alike! and the secret thought is alike in all--And that thought is--Murder! It is the fundamental fact. It is life's deepest urge in man's thought. The ruling passion of man's mind is to destroy life, because man's deepest fear, his ancient fear, is the fear of life.

You do not believe this? This is ghastly, and the hell of pessimism? So it is. But, look about, anywhere, get close,--you will see. It is there.

To be sure it is not customary to speak thus baldly. It is not deemed considerate. We have euphemisms for all occasions, and the word, murder, we dilute, in a sea of phrases, and evaporate in perfumed breezes of sentiment. We attenuate it in speech, and make artistic distinctions, and we spin it into a delicate thread wherewith we weave a garment to hide its nakedness--and we paint it and powder it, and convert it and baptize it, and hide it in a religion, and have wise men to write beautiful books in which they spell it benevolence, political economy, and the laws of trade, and the survival of the fittest and *laissez faire*. And we infuse it into a body of laws--and we inject it into an army and a navy--and we erect it into a great system of business enterprise. And we have philosophers to sublimate it, and theologians to glorify it. And upon it we found a civilization, just as the man of the past founded civilizations upon it. But it is murder just the same, and the fear of life just the same, and the superstitious hatred of the neighbor just the same, and it is completely mutual, and completely uni-

* Supplied. See following sentence.

versal, and completely individual just the same. In short it is you and I, and the secret thought we hold in common--The thought we hold in common with the man of the Past. Shall it be the thought we transmit to the man to come? Or will he say of us: "Having ears why did ye not hear, and having eyes why did ye not see? Why did ye not look in the right place? Why did ye not listen in the stillness? Why did ye not seek and find man? Had man a heart and ye knew it not, heard it not, saw it not, felt it not! O, man in the dawning day, Why didst thou deny me? Why didst thou look at my approaching spirit and say to me, in freezing tones:-- What is the use--What is the use? I am real--you are unreal--The great heart comes here but to break--This is no door, it is a wall which Fate has reared, and here it shall remain forever and forever. And many shall come and many shall pass away--without avail! unto the last! and lost!

There we are, you and I, at the great parting of the ways, at the gain or loss of our being; and we are busy, very very busy--too busy to live. We are busy in our night: "getting things done." Face to face with minus. Unknowing plus. Lacking eyes, ears, sensibility. Lacking the scent of the trail. Filled with distrust and a fear of Life. Civilized cowards.

CHAPTER 3 STREAMS IN THE ENVIRONMENT

It is generally held in our thought that man is highly complex in his physical structure, processes, thoughts, emotions, longings, regrets, and the involved melodrama and tragedy of his life-history, past and present. It is impressed upon us by teachers, preachers, philosophers, friends and guides that man is fearfully and wonderfully made, and is battling against forces which seek his destruction. We are told that man is highly specialized in his functions and faculties, and is acted upon by highly diversified forces. These faculties, functions, and forces have been elaborately analyzed and specified, ever more minutely, and ever with an increasing aspect and complexity of estrangement. Our attention has thus, as it were, been surreptitiously directed to details, fixed upon details, riveted upon them; and our minds diverted and obscured by them. It is not strange that from the pressure of this host of details arises in us a vague sense of individual helplessness and insignificance; and that the aggregation of these details into the great powers of mind, nature, and social institutions overwhelm us individually with the sense of external antagonism and of immovable, unchangeable might.

Thus bulks and details have been worshipped, and such worship indicates the key to our prevailing system of thinking. Intricate processes have been worshipped and propitiated. Profundity has been worshipped. And the man who could flood us with a deluge of details gathered into terms of might and destiny, or who could cause the huge terms of might and destiny to appear the more merciless in a vast multitude of aspects in detail, has been regarded by us as the type of intellectual grandeur. For has he not set forth before our gaze, in bulk and in little, that we may be doubly assured of its truth, that which, in reality, is our individual notion? the notion of the multitudes? Does he not confirm our belief that we are in the grip of a remorseless fate, whose dispensations, seemingly so terribly unjust, so partial, so fickle, are as they are by virtue of a power beyond our ken and beyond our control? Thus have been set up before our minds two great phantoms (our own phantoms within us); one, the phantom of inflexible constant force, the other the phantom of capricious, supernatural will. The one phantom the philosopher, in our behalf, calls the absolute; the other phantom the priest, in our behalf, calls God.

In both of these systems of official thought, philosopher and priest have equally failed to set before us the small truth, that the universe, with its overwhelming infinitude of details, is to be interpreted in terms of life; that the least and the greatest, Destiny, Fate itself, are intelligible when interpreted in terms of man; and that man himself is intelligible when interpreted in terms of his own heart. Therefore it is for us to note that what as the loftiest philosophers have said, what the innumerable high priests have said, what the mightiest rulers have said, and what they say now, is really intelligible only when interpreted by us in terms of the secret thoughts and the overt acts of the lowliest--the multitudes.

The presence of misery in the life of us all, the working of a hidden unhappiness, point with precision to the center of things, to the fact, at once pitiful and constructive, that man's traditional system of thinking is all askew, and has been but an elaborate denial of himself.

That the philosopher, priest, and ruler, have not yet told this, is quite intelligible--the multitudes have not yet told *them*.

The huge veil that philosopher, priest and warrior have woven out of the thoughts of the multitudes and have embroidered with their own, must be drawn aside, and the inhumanity of feudal thinking, revealed. Also must be revealed the ruthless thinking of the lowest, the poorest, the most obscure from which, in truth, it draws its sustenance. The thought of the highest is, in the last analysis, but the thought of the lowest--Clad in fine raiment.

Thus it is that, with us, the simple totality of things, the sublimely coherent urge of Life, is split up into innumerable subdivisions, and these again interminably subdivided; and thus details of all kinds and sizes and shapes and colors confront us and we them. We touch them, they touch us, faintly or strongly, everywhere, all the time. They seem to be real. It is hard for us to believe any of them unreal. We come thus to regard ourselves as details, little scattered and crowded bits, in the confusion and turmoil; and we drift here and there, or clasp something blindly.

Now and then someone has talked of a unity of plan in all this. Sometimes it is averred to be a divine plan, a purpose, a providence, a design. Sometimes it is a mechanical plan, an automatic mechanism. But the plan, the process, whatever else it be, is always presented as external to us, always as something applied, or imposed upon all things and upon ourselves--something which rules us, or governs us, or goads us; something to which we must submit, as it is said; or, as is sometimes said, a "blind" force of which we are the puppets, the victims and the human wreckage. Or, as it were, it is a storm on a mighty deep, and we mere driftwood, jetsam and flotsam, stranding here and there upon a shore, or moving up and down passively and helplessly upon huge billows, within a fog, dense and utterly gloomy: a rift in the fog--we see something shining--but to see it vanish.

And men have talked about various "laws" which they say govern and compel these details, which cause these fragments to do this or that, to move here or there; and they have said:--This is the law of gravitation; these are the laws of trade; this is electricity; this is heat; this is business; such and such aggregate of fragments is mathematics; such and such is political economy; such and such is astronomy. Or they have said chemistry consists of such and such details; government, of such and such details. One wise man said: I know what some of these human and other details mean:--They are products of the law of natural selection, they are the survival of the fittest. Another wise one said: I know what each and every detail means; they were all made by the law of Evolution; they show a progression from simple to complex, from homogeneous to heterogeneous. Other men have said: We know better than others what all these details and all these bulks mean--they are the will of God, and if there be misery and suffering it is because man was born in sin. Others have said: This is the struggle for existence. Others have said: The Lord giveth and the Lord taketh away. Still others have said: This is the cause and effect. And yet other men have said: This is the law of supply and demand. But whatever they have said, each man has plainly meant that there is something external--that there are really but two details in the universe, one is matter, the other, force--the one detail is active, the other passive. In talking about these two details men have worked many variations, and have built up strange structures of thought--all external. It is true that once upon a time a man said: Man's salvation lies within himself alone:--He needs neither God nor priest. That another man said: The Kingdom of God is within you. But these statements were obscure. They were not scientific, as we say; nor logical. Moreover, they were, both, oriental; thus, for us Westerners, they could contain little if any suggestion of practical interest. They belonged rather in the domain of poetic fantasy; that is to say, from our point of view, unreality; and the sayers--visionaries.

The genius of the western world is practical, logical, matter of fact, direct. Truth, with it, is a material thing--something tangible, something that can be taken apart and put together, just as force is tangible and strong, just as matter is real and solid--so is the western mind solid, forceful, direct. The western mind formulates, lays down laws, rules and regulations. It subdivides, systematizes, organizes, dissects, analyzes, synthesizes. It wants results and wants them quickly. It looks upon things as they are, deals with them as they are, accepts them as they appear. It looks upon men in the same way. The western mind is mobile, restless, aggressive. It loves force because force is something it can understand; it loves matter, material objects, because it understands them. The western mind is ambitious, proud, dominant, disdainful, imperious. It loves obstacles and loves to overcome them. It is assertive, militant, extravagant, full of fire and zeal. It is ever drifting toward the defiant and grotesque. It is at home in turmoil, and loves urgency, and stress, and chance. It loves to build up, and tear down, and build up again; it loves change, novelty, progress. It loves to destroy. It lives on excitement, on feverishness. It is always approaching exhaustion, and insanity. It loves to hide behind externals; it loves parade, and show, and brilliancy, and shallowness. It hates calm reflection--it has no time for that. It is in a hurry, it cannot brook delay--the farther west, the more are these traits in evidence--the more insensate the turmoil. The western mind proceeds by trial and error--it loves to experiment, it loves to play with fire--It hates prudence, it despises foresight. It trusts where it should not [and distrusts where it should not.] * It concentrates on the immediate and the matter of fact. It sees only the surface of things and is intoxicated--in our land--with a rank and arrant optimism coupled with an incredibly frivolous cynicism, a strange insensibility, fatalism and inertia.

Ramifying through the interstices of this ferocious, flocculent western thought, but having no actual contact with it, is a gentle, sweet, altogether lovely and serenely beautiful oriental conception, to which we give the historic name, the Christian teaching. Between it and western thought there is a certain interchange of influence, such as electricians call induction, that is, a passage of influence through the intervening social atmosphere. It is mild, and small in quantity, for the arrogant western intellect is nonconductor of influence of a spiritual nature. But in the western heart, this gentle current finds a certain response which in turn induces a slight perturbation of the western intellect--tending in a degree to regulate its sinister energy which otherwise would rush on to unheard-of extremities of madness--to the finality of savage egomania.

So the western thought, in its distrust, fear and contempt of the great life, in its fanatical resolve to deny the great life and exist boastfully madly apart from it--has reared a Church and many churches wherein to imprison the Christ, that His real voice may not be heard abroad. So, in an immense dungeon of forms and ceremonies, he is shut up. Indeed it requires the power of a great hierarchy and an army of priests to keep the little voice duly muffled. Vast piles of stone to hold it shut in--Huge armies and fleets to prevent its escape--strong governments to legislate, police to stand close--lest it escape into the world. Lest the little voice reach the heart with its infection--lest the power of gentleness prove a contagion among men. So the bells peal, organs suspire harmonious volumes, choirs praise, priests lift the Chalice, the people bow on bended knee, the soul pours out its praise, in adoration of the great God of heaven, and with one world-cry, on Easter morn, all say: "Christ is risen!"

Find him! The western intellect is a thimblerigger, a truculent cheat, a charlatan. It has the same love of man on Easter morn that the wolf has for sheep on Easter morn. And the complicated theatrical performance means as much in practice to the man of the west as it does to the wolf. Were he to avow his true religion in his rites, it would be in official form what it is in the huge and startling reality of the ritualism of every day--human sacrifice to the Golden Idol, blood in streams, and an orgy of self-glorification. The westerner is a madman. What he calls his reason is a blight--a disease. What he calls his civilization is intricate cruelty, and an

* From Norman copy.

elaborate denial of man. The westerner is a huge giant with the beak of an eagle. He is predatory from tip to tip. He lives upon prey; and if there be not living prey--carrion will do.

So the whirl and the drift and the complicated bombardment of details and fragments and externals goes on day by day, hour by hour. It is a human chaos within the tranquil cosmos. A vast turmoil devoid of an effective center of gravity. It is the insanity of the conscious intellect which believes all things external to it, and itself external to all things, and solitary. It is the limit of segregation, the separation of individuals. Priests, philosophers, economists, have shouted in the din: Let us unite our self-loves, into a completely organized selfishness, then our little detail will become a big detail. There is power in numbers, in union there is strength. So, this is the remedy!--And so the quackery has gone on and goes on, day by day, and hour by hour. Then comes the social reformer, saying: "I have it! The neighbor is bad, he is selfish, murderous, tricky; he doesn't play the game fair--let us reform him." And we shout in chorus--"That is so; the neighbor is bad, let us reform him, he does not play the game fair." And so the neighbor says: "My neighbor is bad, and you must reform him, he does not play the game fair." And so goes the modern moral game of blind man's buff, and there has thus come into active being a notion of general acceptance, that the neighbor needs reforming--he is getting so bad that we, individually, (always individually) are getting the worst of it. He is too treacherous, too perfidious--there is a limit. So the search for externals, for applications, tonics, stimulants, correctives, anodynes, sedatives, soporifics, goes on busily, vehemently,--as far as the neighbor is concerned; for we now know that it is all the fault of the neighbor--he is very bad. Meanwhile Life, and the call of Life and the claims of Life we continue to deny as before; its still voice is lost in the hubbub of our words; and thus we banish the simple, the clear, the plain, the near; for we are educated on the intricate plan, the fragmentary plan--and to this plan we give the name individualism. Meanwhile, in our inverted way, we ignore man. For in our philosophy the individual is external, a thing apart from us, as individuals, and we, as individuals, things apart from him. In our philosophy he is an abstraction, not a man. For we believe in the actual existence of abstractions, they are our delight, our refuge, our pipe dreams and our highly prized fetishes. They form the basis of our intellectual method. And so we talk to the abstract man concerning abstract truth, abstract justice, abstract good, abstract rights, abstract reasoning, and so on. We believe that an idea exists apart from man; that the cosmos is tenanted with segregated ideas. For we are superstitious; we still believe in ghosts; we whistle while we walk through the graveyard we call our philosophy. And thus we make success in life artificial--failure normal. For with us the husk is the thing, not the kernel; and thus it comes about, for it can not be otherwise, under our system, that our intellects are slaughter houses, and our intellectual output is embalmed in hypocrisy and cant.

And thus while we furtively know that there is a simple explanation of our chaos within the cosmos, we as craftily avoid it; for we have a dread that it is the beneficence of Life--and therefore we fear it. We suspect it may be a living truth, not abstract truth, and therefore we hide from it--therefore we retire into our sanctuaries and draw the veil--for we feel safer with our secret thought, safer behind the veil of our fictions, where it is quiet, where we individually may have solitude, where we believe that we are inscrutable and inviolable--where, we are convinced, no man can penetrate, because we believe we leave no trail.

The explanation which it is feared may be true, is true: it is a human reality. Intangible, unintelligible to a philosophy founded upon abstractions, it is living and breathing to a philosophy which deals with Life, has Life for its inspiration and its suspiration, which exists coextensive with Life and is Life--a philosophy which affirms the creative impulse, the earth grasp, the free will and the unequivocal responsibility of man to man.

CHAPTER 4 THE MAN ON THE STREET

You cannot buy a man for money. When you pay the money, it is not a man you get in return for it, but a will-o'-the-wisp. The man eludes you. He cannot help it. So, when you bargain with a man that he is to sell his neighbor to you, sell as many of the people to you as seems possible, you cannot secure what you think you are purchasing--he cannot deliver the goods; he delivers moving appearances to you, and you accept these shifting appearances as permanent realities. The people remain; for the people never sell themselves--they give. They give of themselves with a profligate abandon, which you perhaps have failed to notice.

So, when a man has risen high, as it is said, by his own efforts, as we say, and by what is called corrupt practice, he has at the same time achieved an illusion. He believes he has bought, and that thus he really owns; that what he has is tangible,--solid. But it is not so. What he has is thin air and the fabric of a dream. It thus comes that those fictions he calls property, vested rights, the law, the constitution, the government, the army and navy, which seem to him so vivid, so real, so positive that to affirm otherwise seems to him preposterous; which seem to him so secure on their foundation, so solid, stable and lasting, rest, in reality upon a foundation more tenuous than air, as abysmal and elastic as life, and moving, now swift now slow, in response to the creative flow of the all-life. For this foundation is the thought of the people; and that--you cannot buy, cannot own, cannot hold; its simplest characteristic is momentous, irrepressible, irresistible change. It cannot sell itself. It must, in the very urge of its life--give itself.

It has not occurred to such man, so buying as he believes, to investigate the nature of the foundation, because it has not seemed important to him to search for man, and in so searching, locate himself. He has thought of "the people" and spoken of "the people" in the customary--and therefore inverted--way. The fact that the people have dreamed, and have given birth, out of their life to the printing press, the steam-engine, the telegraph, the ocean cables and many another vital, spiritually concrete, thing, calls up within his mind no suggestion of an immense reservoir of creative life and power within the people, and what such reservoir of power may mean when its flow is further released. It does not loom large in his mind that all historical and present forms, ceremonies, and institutions are but indexes, more or less ephemeral, of that vast human creative power. Hence it is consistent that he will fail to understand himself as but a minor creation of the people--at once a trifle and a trifler. He perceives what he calls facts, but does not interpret the life of the facts. Yet if he will inquire a little, parting company for a while with his laws--his constitution, his text books, and use only the simple natural mental powers that every man has, literate or illiterate, he will scarcely fail to note, in due time that, however hard he may have tried, however successful he may believe himself to be in the effort, he cannot, in fact, by any possibility, separate himself from the life-grip of the people; that such prior belief, however real it may have appeared to the fixed focus of his eye, was and is but an intellectual mirage.

If then, he push inquiry a little further, still using merely the ordinary thinking powers, the ordinary eyesight and hearing--only getting closer and closer to actualities, he will begin to perceive that, beneath the overlay of surging ceremonials and institutions, lies an intensity of creative energy in the mass of the people--beneficently creative, destructively creative

--which may at first strike terror to his soul when he actually confronts its elemental power, but which will at once surely tend to re-arrange his established notions of things--the shadowy text book, military and priestly notions which he shares.

If he looks still nearer, he will become aware how small a part of the creative life of the people has as yet become conscious within them; and he will note, by certain movements, that that power, now slumbering, is self-preparing to awaken; that the immense torpor of the ages is about to pass.

It is little to be doubted that such suggestion will seem to such man fantastic. And if he were today to ask the man on the street, the latter might agree with him, probably would; for the man on the street not having sought man--knows nothing of man. He thus considers man quite an ordinary proposition; subject to such and such laws, and so on; more or less fortunate or unfortunate, etc. For the man on the street believes himself practical, business-like; is quite sure he is no visionary. Yet he is exactly what he says he is not; he is a visionary, unbusinesslike, a dreamer of imbecile dreams.

The man on the street says, Money talks! So it does. It says things he has never heard. Things which surpass his imagination. And the man on the street also talks, alas; he scatters words like a prodigal. But the real man within him remains inarticulate, dumb--seeking seeking some sign-language in the man's doings. For the man does not know how to utter himself, he has not heard of such things. How should he know? He does not listen, he has not inquired, still less has he felt the need of listening and inquiring--it has not occurred to him. For the man on the street walks, unsuspectingly, within the confines of a world-trap, a human rat-trap of fictions which he calls business, real-life, education, and other like names.

But suppose the man on the street, momentarily awakening, were to ask the first man he meets: "who are you? what are you?" The man accosted cannot answer; he does not know. He, likewise, has not searched for man, even with man at his elbow; hence he cannot know himself. He has always more or less vaguely taken himself for granted. He has taken everything vaguely for granted. To suspect the vagueness and to search through it until he find definition, would be a thought to occur to him last, if at all.

And suppose it suddenly seemed strange to the first man that the second can tell only his name, age, occupation, nationality, and so on, and can add thereto merely a statement of his business, his property, his beliefs in a certain form of religion, a certain form of government, and so on and so on, (his traditionally acquired views which he has accepted as currency) and suppose it simultaneously occurred to the man accosted, that his answer consisted merely in this string of conventional details, and this tacit mutual assumption of bulk and importance and finality, and that, as a matter of fact, he is at a standstill for a simple direct answer to this simple direct question--he might feel uncomfortable for a moment, consider the question curious, quaint and rather queer, and the man asking it decidedly "queer." But it would scarcely occur to him that there was something within him, which, for an instant, wished to answer; but could not.

Of course, the man on the street would not think of asking such question, for he, too, takes himself for granted. He takes everything for granted; and the neighbor takes him for granted, just as he is; and all the people take him for granted, whoever and whatever he is--and the man who buys him takes him for granted; and the man who sells him; the man who robs him, the man who swindles him, the man who betrays him, the man who poisons him, the man who hangs him by the neck, who cuts off his leg at a grade crossing--They, all, take not only him for granted, but also take for granted, in just the same way, his wife, his children and his grandchildren--just as he takes for granted all other men, their wives, children and grandchildren--He will kill them if he can. For when he says "money talks" it is the same as saying, "I will kill them if I can." And yet the man will consider murder, a shocking word, if used in a restricted sense--so much is he self-hypnotized by words, so little does he feel that words expand and contract like muscular tissues, so little is he conscious of simple realities--this man on the street, this turbid half-alive dreamer--who cannot answer the simple question "who and what are you?" who has been to school, has received an "education," as he absurdly calls it, and yet cannot answer the plain, pertinent questions, who and what is the neighbor? who and what are the people? This man who would be scandalized were you to call him ignorant, yet who can give not even a fairly intelligible answer to the simple sharp questions of most searching import to him and to us all-- What is Life? and what is Man? What are we here for? His answer, if answer he attempt, will beg the question; it will be artificial, conventional, --worthless, because it will not go to the quick.

And do you assume that it makes the slightest essential difference of what walk in life the man so questioned may be? Do you assume that folly is confined to the illiterate? If so, you, in turn, have not used your eyes and ears, in your far look and your near look upon humanity.

If you think this is not so, ask widely; listen attentively; and you will hear as answer a consistent miscellany of falsehoods and half-truths that correspond with the half-death, half-life, of the man in the pulpit, the man in the underground galleries of high finance and politics, the "constructive" statesman, the judge on the bench, the editor, the lawyer, the typical man in the private office, the college professor, the social parasite, the social reformer, the mechanic, the laborer;--all will give essentially the same garbled answer, guided by a wayward impulse, fostered in a common superstition-- and couched in essentially the same terms--which mean exactly the opposite of what they say,--for what they say life is, such is death. Sift all these answers through each other, they mean the same--they mean Feudalism.

CHAPTER 5 DANCE OF DEATH

A Child's Tale

Long, long ago, in a far-away-Land, a poet wayfarer told a child's tale, which ran along thus:--
Once, in a winsome land I know, were two little ones.
Forth they went, for sun was shining, meadows bloomed.
They came upon two beauteous flowers--alike, and gleaming side by side.
The gentler child enraptured said:--
Ah Ha!--A Ha!--
Let us wish to be flowers!

They sat in the meadow and wished:--
The listening breeze stood still;
The children changed to a shimmering mist
That hovered and swayed
To-and-fro
And changed,
And changed;--
'Till lo!--
There were two
New flowers of the field.

    *   *   *   *

The breeze went smiling on, carrying so delicate a new burden that two butterflies thereabout floating, came near,--they sipped. And one, the more resplendent, sighed:

    *   *   *   *

"How strange!
I seem to feel a new life!
And I'm dreaming--
A child floats--
How sweet were they!
Ah, Life,
O, Joy,
How sweet 'twould be!
O, wish it might be!
For thee and me."

    *   *   *   *

Again came the stillness. The wayfarers of the scented air, fluttering, became a mist of many colors. Floating, slowly, swaying through grass and flowers, it then stood still; faces quickly glowed within, and bright eyes danced, and soon, there, were the children as before.

    *   *   *   *

And the sister said:--
 It seems to me
 I have been a flower
 And a butterfly!

    *   *   *   *

The brother whispered:--
'Twas so with me,
'Perhaps 'twas a dream!
Let us tell it at home!
But the sister asked:--
"Will they understand?"

* * * *

So the tale was told;
And the father beamed:--
"Beloved, it was not a dream.
'Twas but this morn,
Our own and I,
Saw two eagles
Far in the blue!--
And we gloriously wished:--
And lo, we were high in the air!
Proudly winged!
Floating! Soaring!
Forest and field, spread far below!
Near, wide! we sped!
Our souls knew the glow of the great clear morn!
Soaring, gliding, we came to our home!
'Twas not a dream!
It was Life!!--that smiled, on our desire!

* * * *

And they told friends, who said, it was not a dream for the like was theirs that day, when smiling Life returned their smile.

* * * *

And so came dusk; and the household dreamed new dreams.

With gleaming dawn, friends passing, saw, where the house had been, two lofty trees and two saplings.

Saplings and trees rustled soft in the breeze, as the friends went their way.

* * * *

Again a dusk, and again a gleaming morn; and again the friends passed. And, there--was the home of gladness! There, father and mother. There,--the children, playing before the door--in the sunshine!

* * * *

Then the story teller, the wayfaring spinner of child's tales, said to them gathered about him at the high-noon hour within the cool of a spreading tree's grateful shadow:--How great is Life!

* * * *

Returning to their labors in the fields, they mused on the tale of the dreamer, which stirred in their hearts meanwhile.

* * * *

The story was told long ago, in a strange tongue.

A Tale O' the Moor

Hundreds of Years after, in another land, a story-teller told a grown folks' tale, by the flickering fire of a chimney's hearth. It ran like this, for the night was drear:--

Hush!--what was that?! Heard ye the wind sigh? 'Twas surely a lost soul that wailed! Full many a ghost must be abroad this night!

I know a graveyard where the dead are troubled by their sins. Strange things come to pass there, mad things in the dark o' nights are seen by hapless wights; and many a wail is heard,--for 'tis a dreadful thing to die in sin.

'Twas but the other night, the very night of Holy Agnes, that a wayfarer wandered there in the dusk. He lay him down and slept, not knowing where; and they say he must have had foreboding dreams; for they say that just at midnight hour he sat up dazed:--and there were strange lights glowing pale in the ground about him. It was so still he heard his heart a-beating; so dark, he could not see his hand; and all at once there came moans:--and it was then so still that he could hear his cold sweat dripping.

And then the lights began to rise--all in a ring about him; and quick a skull grew out of the ground beneath each light. And then there came a wail!--and it was still; and the wayfarer sat frozen:--(Hist! how the wind blows! 'Tis a baleful night!) and then came a shriek! and the skulls rose higher; and ribs rose up under; and the lights rose higher, and arms of bones came; and low cries began, and swelled into a plaint, and died away:--(Hark! How the owl cries--how unwonted wild!) and the bones of the dead grew up and up,--and there were just thirteen!--(may Christ have mercy on us)--and the one was very tall, and the one was very small--and the lights grew brighter blue, as the bones began to sway and rattle, and the air grew chill. Then a gust of wind rushed by! And the big one beckoned quick:--and they all jumped into a dance! And their bones clanked, and rattled, hard, and hard, and hard:--the bones of the little one went shrill, and the bones of the big one ground deep and creaked--while groans and sobs came out from everywhere:--(The owl! What bodes the night?--'Tis a new warning cry he makes!--and your faces,--they're so green and pale!-- 'Tis a mad night!--Your eyes glow so they fright my soul!) And *faster* and faster they flew, and the lights grew brighter blue and curled:--(What's that?!--No--'Twas but the moon broke through a cloud--'Tis gone--How it caught my breath away--) (They say the little men come out such nights in the dell)--And faster and faster they flew; and madder and madder they swung and toed; and all the dead sat up in their graves, to look on--some with the flesh still on them--and the wayfarer cried out, and fell flat-- But on they danced, and swayed, and reeled; and the little one jumped on the head of the tall, and rattled so shrill that it cut the air:--(Mother of God!!--'Twas the door that blew to! Look ye not so wild!!--or I'll not go on!) and the ground swayed, and the last grave broke open wide, and a stench spread thick; and their skulls wagged so fast 'twas but a haze, and they jumped so fast they all seemed one, and the air was so thick with screams there was room for no more:--(Mercy of God!!--'Twas an awful lightning crash!--In God's name sit still!!)--so wilder they went; and all the groans and cries fell fast and slow, and rose again, and all their bones caught fire, and the smoke became a black thing, like a bat, and great green eyes that blazed:--('Tis God's truth 'twas so--may the blessed Virgin strike me dead this hour if 'twas not so!)--and madder than ever they went, and crawling things were coming out of the ground--when!--God be praised! A cock crew!--and there was nothing to be seen or heard!--

And while it was so still, the dawn broke gray; the sun came up red; and was turning white, when some passed on their way to early mass-- and they saw the wayfarer stark! and crossed themselves, and told the holy father:--(For well they knew it was the Devil's Dance; and 'tis well for us to know, lest we be stricken, by mischance, at dead o' night, for 'tis the souls of the damned--them that are in the torment that come back; and woe the sorry wight they catch among the graves! 'Tis blessed we are that we know their ways, for 'tis an awful thing to be dead and buried under the ground, with souls unsaved. May the Blessed Virgin watch over us, and keep us from the wayfarer's fate!)

* * * *

And the huddled group sighed and swayed, and became shadowy in the dying embers' glowing, by the chimney-side; with nought between them and the powers of the dark, but a roof and a wall--on the wide bleak moor--a roof and a wall to shelter from the night-storm and the owl's hollow cry; a roof and a wall to shut in and hold tight their terrors; to lock up, in the hearts of these grown children, their fear of the dark and its deeds.

Interlude

But we of a modern day! we have no fear of the content of the night. Still less do we dread the day and its deeds. Still less do we love the child and the sunshine. For if we loved the child, and what is good for it, what is precious in the soul of the child, would we seek as we do to kill it and its all? Or do we kill because we love? Because we love, better, a something that has come up out of the darkness and the deep of the earth-- A something that now gleams, by night and by day, with baleful sallow light--hovering over countless dead men's bones--rising, phosphorescent, from the last resting place of the suicide, the maniac, the rich, the wrecked, the impoverished, the broken, neglected and despised? Rising sepulchrally, with each dawn, to join with us in a *danse macabre,* while a siren-song lures and appeases; and the breath of peace blows softly:--and the wall and the roof of our great house-of-words save us from the harm of the wistful cry of the hovering life without, in a broad, fair, smiling land--A wall and a roof that hold tight within, our fear of Life and its passing gleam--our fear of a door blown open wide by a breath of Life--we haggard, grown-children of a day--Huddled, shadowy, in millions, while fast-dying embers of manhood, and of worth--pass into ashes.

Do we emerge and kill for the love of the Kill? Do we kill for love of Death? For killed we have, for kill we do, for kill it would seem we must!

It is the vivid occupation of a busy people, the deed of a practical day. The thought of a Christian world. For kill we do:--and little else we do. We kill in countless ways--by countless thoughts--through countless deeds--deeds hidden, deeds open,--thoughts hidden, thoughts open,--it is the same--by day and by night--in a dance of death.

DEMOCRACY: *a man-search*

We kill the weak, we kill the strong, we kill the ill, we kill the well. No child too young to begin on, no grave and no reverend man too old. No man too high, no man too low, none too pure, none too corrupt:--We, the people, we the hour, we the desire, we the thought, we the act: Kill: where, when and whomsoever. If there show a sign of life, we, according to our cunning or our power, our cowardice or our lust--seek to destroy!

No! We have no superstition--our broad land is filled with schools.

No! We are surely sane--we seclude our demented--are not our madhouses overflowing?

No! We are not inhuman--we never grind.

No! We are not cannibal--we do not devour our kind. We do not gnaw men's hearts.

No! We are not secret--all is open to the light and air. We never hide, we never mislead. We have no thought withheld--no thought behind the thought we aver. We are frank and clear, straight and true, clean and sound--all men may know. We have but one wish--the desire that all may share the fullness and beauty of life,--This wish is supreme in each man's breast.

No, we are not heathen--we do not worship idols:--nor do we conjure by signs.

No, we do not crucify--That was done, once and for all, nineteen centuries ago, to our deep grief. How different would it be, were He alive today! What joy would be ours to greet Him!

How can we go amiss?--our common conscience holds us true to the life-line.

How could we fail to see? With our sharp eyes!

How could we fail to do!--With our keen wit and will!

No! We are not victimized by self-deception--for are we not the enlightened of the earth?

No! We wear not masks--our countenance is open.

No, we evade no law that we have made--else why make a law--are we not free? Could we not repeal any law manifestly unfit--are we not free?

No, we never bribe--why should we? We never harm the young--why should we? Are not they the race to come?--and what are we, if not preservers and preparers?

Would we poison a man's mind?--Scarcely. Our native intelligence would automatically keep us, one and all, from that. The dire results would be too easily foreseen.

Would we betray and rob the widow and her child? Clearly not! That would spread a moral leprosy among ourselves. Our practical wisdom would keep us from that.

Would we poison the food of others?--Perish the thought! How could we make unsound bodies and hope for sound minds?

We would perhaps poison for money? Perish that thought! We value money only for its sane use. Do you think us mad?

We fill our cities with murk, and filth, and slums, and ugliness and degradation?--What an impression! Do you think we would kill the sense of beauty in its very birth in every child? Do you think we would contaminate our own minds with a sordid, nameless gloom? Say that to savages, but say it not to us. We are free-born, free-living, fully conscious, creative; the self-poised of earth.

We spend most of our money for drugs, liquor, warships, and the luxury of supporting a gang of huge parasites and pirates? What a curious suggestion--we would soon go to perdition if that were true.

The bounty of earth alone keeps us going? We are rotting with evil thinking? We are standing on our heads? We are prematurely old? How grotesque! Ask any man you meet--you will find him sound, clear of mind, serenely seeking the good of all, and his part therein. Look at our body of laws!--are they not simple, organic, creative, clear? Do they not anticipate and draw forth the amplitudes of life, and the manifest destiny of people and Land? Look at our Constitution!--the basic document of our national life, the fundamental organic expression of our individual and collective hope! Does not that superbly human and luminous document state in clear implicit and explicit terms, that, henceforth and forever, man--any man--shall rank above material possessions; and that each man shall be free to create, out of the zest of his life, out of the hope of his life and its beauty--that none shall be denied? Have you thought of that?

We are a vast herd of maniacs, each running amuck?--That is too much! Have we not manifestly searched all history, all philosophies, all religions? Have we not closely questioned nature? Have we not looked calmly into our own minds, our own hearts, our own spirits? Have we not searched, that, so searching, we might find and know wherein man, in the past has unwittingly erred? Have we not had our most earnest, thoughtful men engaged in formulating our aspirations--the life of a people--in simple, plain, intelligible terms--terms easily understood and grasped by all? Had not the world a long and bitter struggle? And had not we our struggle, ere we found this simple path, this plain, inspiring way of life? Now look abroad over our fair land! You cannot find a man who does not know what the Spirit of Life signifies for him and for all. That is how and why we have become so truly great that we are truly simple--and we have thereby caused the thought of the world to change, for that was our manifest mission. For we are just--and know that as we think so we are--and thus is our destiny at last come into our own hearts and hands--where it belongs--and shall remain!--by the power of our living thought.

You say we are a crowd of sneaks and assassins?--that we kill our honest; that we kill our true; that we kill the sane--believing them mad? That we exalt our corrupt because we are corrupt--that we exalt our thieves because we are thieves--that we exalt the unscrupulous because we are unscrupulous. That we worship shams because we are shams. That we set up a straw honesty because we are straw men. That we lie because we have no use for truth? That is dastardly and absurd! You say our civilization is a brutal bluff? How unreasonable! Have you considered our exports and imports, our bank clearings--our savings deposits, our crop reports? Have you studied our statistics? Are you familiar with our great party organizations, our municipal politics, our state legislatures, our great national system of representative government, our establishments, our gigantic railways systems, our stupendous financial enterprises? Surely you have not! or you could not speak thus! Have you examined our superb system of public schools, our many colleges, seminaries, universities? Have you walked through our Libraries, our Museums of Art and Natural history? Have you examined our hospitals, our orphanages, our varied benevolent institutions, our manifold charities, our social settlements, our religious institutions? Have you stood before our great monumental buildings, our towering office structures, our giant stores, our colossal granaries, our sumptuous hotels, our warehouses? If so, then surely you should not have failed to see the reasonableness of our prosperity and the prudent caution of our ways! It is not we who have killed--It is the unfit who have failed to survive. It is the improvident who have come to grief and so die of want. It is the ignorant--who have fallen of their own wayward weakness, by the wayside, and have perished there;--none could help them:--They would not help themselves. It is the unworthy, alone--who suffer. It is the foolish, vain, or visionary--who die of broken hearts--death comes to all--comes many a time as a bolt from the sky--We must all die. Those, only, lie in the potter's field, who, necessarily, were outcast. We may not prevail over fortune and fate! Destiny is ours, but not Fate! The ways of Life are mysteries past understanding; and so are the ways of death. Deity governs all according to his will--and with a wisdom illimitably far beyond our feeble grasp of understanding. To decry a civilization is not to amend it--what we have achieved

is the earnest fruit of long struggle onward and upward, guided by the filtered wisdom of the ages. We have had the wide world, and have drawn from the deep well of its experience. These lessons we have used with such skill as we have; above all, we have applied them in fortitude, in loving trust, in hope, in confidence in a Supreme Being whose guidance and whose fatherhood we have ever sought, and of his Son, in whose footsteps we have followed as best our feet could find the way. We are but trustees of that we have. We have acted, each, according to his light. What more can we do? What more should we do?--
    (Ah, Ha!--The pious leer!)
    O,--Ho!--Ho! Ho!!--Presto--

The Dance of Death

And still we kill and still we pray
And still we grind and still we groan
Round and round
In a circle of words
A shriek of words
A hum of words
And a rattle of words
And to and fro--
And in--and out--
And up and down--
We circle--around--the man at bay!--
The luckless wight that falls our way!--
The man who thinks that we're not here!
Ha--Ha! Ha-Ha!!
We burn--we burn!--
Joy unconfined!!--
The smoke--ascends--
The pale lights gleam--and weave and toss--
And jiggle--and bob--and
Shrilly the rolling dance goes on--in
Our graveyards--joyous--gloom--and glare!
Full long ago,
A cock did crow!--
What ho! What ho!!--
A man--they nailed--
Upon a cross--

DEMOCRACY: *a man-search*

It is our gain--
It was his loss;
It was--his loss--it is--our gain--
And this-we ever-scream-aflame!--
Aglow!--aglow!
We burn--and turn--
We jump--and roar--we
Tear and bore--
Our bones--go thump--and hump--and plumb--
They point!
Now up!--
Now down--now here--now there--
Now in--now out--
Now every-where:--
It is--the man!!--
The foolish man--who
Came too near--where
We--could hear--
He smells-of flesh--red blood--white life--
He fills--our bones--with glee--and
Strife!
And strange--things
Crawl!
And Men--long dead--
Arise--from bed:--while
We dance--and scream--
And burn--and turn:--
There is--no cock--to crow--a day!--
And night--is here--and
Night will stay--
So let us pray!--
So let us pray!!
Ha Ha!--Ho Ho! Hee Hee!--Hah Hah!! while
We twist--and turn--and
Merrily burn!!--
They nailed--the Christ--upon a cross!
Hi--Hi! Ho--Ho!--
Aye, faster go!--
Why dance so slow?--
The damned--are merry--tonight--we trow!!--
A black-cloud floats--a

DANCE OF DEATH

Green eye gloats--
It gleams--and glares--Hi!--
Faster go!
Hey!--faster we go!!--and slow--and low--
And quick--in pairs--
And one-and all--and
Short--and tall--
And thick--and thin--in racket and din!--
Dance fast!--Dance fast!!--
Too slow!
Too slow!!
Dance fast--Dance fast!!--Too slow!--Too slow!!
Hi!--Lazy bones!--
Dance fast--ye drones!--for
A man lies here! of blood--and bone!
Alone!--Alone!!--Alone!!!--Alone!!!!
Didst hear--his moan?--
I drank--his groan!--
High Christ--upon--the cross--was fixed--
He with--the money--changers--mixed!
So he--was trixed!--
So he--was trixed!!
Hi!--Faster--go!!--
A crown-of thorns-upon-his head--
And much--he bled
Hi-Hi!-Hi-Hi!! Hi!!--Hi! Hi!!!--
He-he!--Ho-Ho!!--Ha-Ha!!--Hah! Hah!!--
Hah!! Hah!!--Hah!! Hah!--Ha!Ha!--Ha!Ha--
A spear--they passed--in-to--his chest--
'Twas them--He blessed!!--Ho-ho!!
Ha, ha--ah,ha!--Ha-Hah!--Hah!! Hah!!--
His hands--were marred
His feet--nailed hard
Ho Ho! Hee hee--hee hee--hee hee--
The Savior of Men--
He was--
They said--
Hee hee--hee hee--hee hee--hee--
Yo! Hah!!--hee hee!
See, See!--The Man!!
'Twas what--they said

DEMOCRACY: *a man-search*

Aye! sing--of roses
White and red
Aye! Sing--of bliss--and
Think--of this--
We happy dead--
We jolly wights--
That sleep o' days--
And dance o' nights:--
And naughty girls--
We give--them whirls--
Jolly Roger--Ho!!
And Yo!
And toe--and
Thrust--and throw--and let--them go--
Sing ho!--
Just so:--
And parsons dear--we give--each year--
Hah! Ha--he, hee--
Ho! Ho--You know?
And charitee--sweet charitee--
Hee hee!--hee hee!--hee--hee? hee hee?--
We laugh--and leer--and swill--our beer?
Go slow--go slow!--
Ho Ho!--Ho Ho!--
Too true--too true--but
'Twill--not do!--
We will--not dance--we shall--not dance!--
'Twas all--a trance--
'Twas all--a trance!--a
Trance!--a trance! a trance!!--a trance!!--

* * * *

For 'tis yellow true--
And too mellow true--
That we dance--
Just by chance--
Who shall say--to us?--
(Who shall make--a--fuss,):--
That we do--
Just what we do--

Is quite true--
'Twixt me and you--
(But, 'tis not--wise--to say such things aloud!)
So hush--I say--ah!
Come this way--
For we--are proud (Speak not so loud)
Our hearts would break--were known the fake--
(And quake--and quake!--and quake!!--and quake!!
All things would go!)
So, talk low:--
(A word, will do, if whispered, here, and there,
With nicety)
But, in the light?--
Be careful--pray--
For it is day! you know--
(And some may see and hear and sneer and say!
    Some man you meet--
    Out in the street--
(Might get to thinking--rather hard and--disagreeably)
    And it would be
(Scarce wise to set his eyes on things he has no business whatsoe'er to know)
    Say!!--
    Come here!--
(This daylight business is played out!)
    Don't you know?--
    If you--tell stories--make them nice-
and clean--and clear--and sweet--Good--for the young--you know. And end them decently, and helpfully, and hopefully, and happily:--Say! Listen! Stop them in the middle--best of all just don't begin--For all this putter pother is but wasted breath--Things are going on all right--and will come out all right, ssh--(In the end)--(In the end--you know) If you must tell a story:--Tell it well--and true!)

              Then hear

A Traveler's Tale:

    A man's tale! A story that might have been heard if one were there. A story told by a wayfarer of the world's highway! Told in tranquility; in a spot not on the map, maybe--but surely open to the earth and air and sky.

DEMOCRACY: *a man-search*

Arrived in his native land, he sought accustomed quiet; for the ripeness of reflection was upon him. So, with friends foregathering, in a sequestered garden, filled with mottling shadows, gay flowers, and intertwining of arbor and vine, within the enfolding mellow light of declining day--he thus began:--

* * * *

I have returned at last, my friends, wanderer that I am, from a long sojourn in a strange, far-off country, where, singular though it may seem, men think and act in a closed circle of inversions, and falsify in unanimity.

The country--a vast expanse--is fair to look upon; well watered, fertile, rich in every form of nature's bounty. All aspects of this land are on a scale simple, broad, impressive:--great plains, prairies, mountains, rivers and lakes--and a long, double-frontage on the seas.

It is a land of four seasons, which successively spread their flowing influences in a simple and impressive rhythm; and the land responds to the seasons in as simple and gracious a way--forming thus an ever-moving picture of impressive, satisfying beauty.

Famine is unknown. The broad-flowing land is crossed and re-crossed by railways, telegraph and telephone lines, and many and varied other means of communication, and interchange. Nearly all the people read and write; and daily papers, magazines, and books are sown broadcast, like winged seeds upon the winds.

Moreover, the land is dotted o'er with free public schools, especially founded and maintained for the education of the children; and seminaries, colleges, technical schools and universities for the training of young manhood and womanhood are numerous.

It is, indeed, a far-flung, sumptuous, inspiriting land; and so situate, in its large serene isolation, that it may be at peace, if it will, in tranquil strength.

The activities of its people are varied and commensurate. Huge sections of its population are engaged in the art of agriculture, in the pursuit of commerce, and in the development of industries--all on a basis of diversified immensity. The energy of this people is intense, quick-witted, practical and material. And there are, in all, some eight millions of souls. The form of government is called by them democratic; specifically, as they say, a government of the people, by the people, for the people. There are not acknowledged social castes; speech is asserted to be free; and religious tolerance is universal. The representatives of the people, that is, those to whom the exercise of political powers is delegated, are elected by a universal male suffrage; every citizen of twenty-one years or over, having an unqualified vote. A single language is in use throughout the length and breadth of the noble land. Local divergences in usage are so slight as to be quite negligible. Never was a great multitude placed in so free, so expansive, so adequate, so bountiful, gracious and simple a setting. Never, to receive and nurture a vast people, were Nature's preparations so benign, so inclusive, so unspeakably gracious.

This land is known to you, no doubt, under its politico-geographical name: The United States of America. But the nature of its people--their thoughts and their acts--is a singular enigma, of compelling power to engage the thoughtful and searching mind. For you might--and rightly--infer that a land so noble, a people so situate, so completely equipped with all the instrumentalities of advanced civilization, would surely bring forth out of themselves, life-results of simple noble, strong and fruitful harmony. Yet the precise opposite is the case; and it is this singular, nay, startling paradox that I wish to illuminate, because it is so impressive an object lesson of a people gone astray through neglect and disdain of a lucid guiding principle; or, if I may say so, through its failure to evolve a sound philosophy of simple things, and a sane ideal.

When I went abroad in the land, I early noted its fair face, but as quickly observed that its cities, of which there are many, were blemishes thereon. This strange contrast impressed me at once and deeply, and awakened a mingled feeling of curiosity and doubt. This perplexity was further increased and at the same time made more elusive, as I began to discern, in the throngs upon the streets of these cities, an almost universal type of face; a face with features singularly decomposed, disorganized and sordid, and that the bodies carrying these faces walked and moved with a rhythmless irregularity--devoid of elasticity and cohesion.

The fair, youthful land, and the decadent faces and movements seemed to me in sharpest contrast; a juxtaposition and divergence that caused me not only to wish an explanation, but as well to resolve to search it out. For land and face, each in its opposite way, spoke eloquently and persistently to me. Further, there was in the faces of these people an aspect of absence. They seemed devoid of radiance; the eyes neither lustrous nor clear; the complexions sodden. These observations filled me with a haunting sense of sadness; an intimation, as it were, that something within the desires, the thoughts, the ideals of this people must be deeply awry--thus to afflict them. This impression quickly grew into a firm sense of certainty. But how to search, I knew not.

However, I determined to mingle freely with them in hope of finding a clue, a thread, as it were, that might lead somewhere.

I met many of them, in almost every walk of life. They were affable enough, in a way, although somewhat brusque. But in the very affability and good nature, in the very brusqueness--sounded a note that arrested my attentive ear. Why? I inquired, should they be thus both superficially brusque and superficially affable? There was a false note in it all; as though, in each case, the real man were not speaking; as though the real man was in hiding; and that these seemingly frank, open people were in reality secretive. This latter impression seemed strange enough; for what need was there to be secretive? And then it occurred to me, as by an inspiration of the moment, that their real life must be quite below the surface; that the dominant impulse, the first, and really controlling thought, must be insidious, and might, perhaps, be found behind what I had come to believe a screen of institutions, appearances and manners.

I listened much to the talk around and about me, and caught in it strains of manifest falsehood and specific truth. I observed, after a time, that nearly every man I met had two systems of speech; the one rather flat, formal and colorless, the other surprisingly forceful, compact, vivid and direct; and that he passed with a significant, almost unconscious freedom from one to the other. The former repelled me as much by its imitative sophistication and inadequacy, as the latter attracted by an ardent, almost youthful reach and force of its locutions. Somewhere between the two, I thought, might lie the center of gravity of their minds--around which all the verbiage would be found to resolve, like a stream or cloud of fragments.

The more I mingled and talked with them, (keeping always an eye on the great fair land and the magnificence of its equipment), the more I seemed to sense their lives. And the more I sensed, the more the sensing suggested a something furtive, fugitive and yet abiding; hidden, open, attractive, and repellent. I soon began to surmise that these people were, in fact, leading double lives--one, as a concession to appearances, and one for the sake of a something else. That *else* was what I resolved, then and there, to search out. For I had become convinced that on a "show-down," as they would say in their terse fashion--an untranslatable expression signifying a revelation of the actual facts--there would come into view an element of sinister and somber reality.

I had noted, early in my search, that these people, individually and in mass, were significantly wanting in a sense--properly so called--of the spiritual life; and equally devoid of a sensibility concerning the true meaning of Nature, and of man's place therein. Concerning these two great, simple aspects of life, their minds seemed indeed empty, and the vacant places usurped by a frivolous cynicism, and a most repellent form of cant.

When I had begun really to appreciate the bearing of these aspects, I sought again--this time with a deeper-seeing eye--the faces in the streets;--for all classes of people are on the streets, and move by one in shoals.

These faces ceaselessly haunted me; and I became ever more perturbed; for they seemed really less living than dead:--and this--in a fair, noble, prolific land. And I said to myself: These faces, these movements are telling the truth!--Whatever that truth may be. And, what seemed stranger still, everyone appeared to take these faces for granted--no one remarked them; no one sought to interpret them; no one deemed them paradoxical and uncanny. And thus came into my mind a suggestion that these people generally, and in reality, tell the actual truth concerning themselves; but do so unconsciously, in ways, only, that they cannot control, because unaware of them.

Then I noted the buildings which lined the streets--and found them just like the faces. And concerning the buildings, likewise, no one made any comment; no one sought to interpret them, no one suggested or sought an underlying explanation common to buildings and faces. And so it was with many many things I noted. These things, these aspects told me truths--truths which the people themselves did not utter in words; truths the very opposite of what the people, particularly the better educated, set forth as their assurances and avowed beliefs.

Then, with these accumulating impressions in mind, I began to look into the personal habits of the people. I soon became aware that they ate too much, drank too much, over-stimulated recklessly, and consumed quantities of drugs of all kinds for all manner of purposes, in what seemed to me a universal suicidal dementia. And this held true of all classes; the variation being merely in externals--in the mere place or fashion of the doing. An excessive tax upon the digestive, the nervous system, and hence upon the brain and the senses was of course inevitable; and I began to see from a new angle, one reason why these people could not perceive the beauty and clarity of simple things, nor think in a straightforward way concerning them. Nor was it a surprise, upon further probing, to learn that these people suffer from anxiety, and from every variety of self-induced disease--functional and organic. A curious index of the prevailing physical decay and shortness of life compared with that of normal health and length of days, I found in the enormous business of their life insurance companies; even while that business pointed to a more far-reaching social illness--some other, deep-seated cause, that made men's lives unstable and brief.

I found further, that, among them, listening, in its finer, simpler aspect is a lost art; that they listen avidly to whatever implies immediate, individual, selfish interest; to all else they are uncomprehending. The further I went, the more I became startled by this inertia; and as yet--I have barely pushed through the surface of things. I felt that, while approaching, I was still far from the real thought, the propelling motive of the people. Motive, I said, there must surely be--for in all the diversity I began to discern a slowly and strangely growing cohesion and unity:--a unison of significance even, in the very paradox of land and people.

The discovery that their foods and drinks were widely adulterated, and inoculated with quick and slow poisons, that even the milk given to infants was all too frequently a deadly poison, came as another shock--a shock so startling that it immediately gave point and definite aim to my inquiry.

Hence I immediately searched out their mental food, as well. I looked first for the philosophies and the theories of economics, as being most significant. Of these I found that they had created not one that met with general acceptance. That, in stale fact, their philosophies and economic doctrines had been taken by them from the European civilization and culture, and were and are therefore, in their very nature, a monarchial and feudal dead weight upon a naturally free people. For the virus of feudal culture cannot be otherwise than an insidious and deadly poison to the minds, bodies, hearts and souls of a people really wishing and seeking freedom.

Now then, I said, here, at last, am I upon the track. Here at last are two, strong, pivotal facts: First, this people, alleging itself to be free and democratic, has failed to utter out of its life and its beautiful land a valid statement of Democracy. Second, this people, asserting its freedom and democracy, has inoculated itself with a feudal taint which runs in its very blood and thought--and hence inevitably in its acts and their logical consequences.

Further, the feudal taint had existed from the beginning of this people, first as a scattered population and then as a nation; and among its historical sequences had brought forth a terrible curse in the form of millions of imported black slaves, an ensuing gigantic internecine war, pathetic in its waste of human lives, and its aftermath of progressive corruption. Never has the ancient doctrine of feudalism wrought such unspeakable havoc among a people--never have the effects of its disastrous, devastating virus been shown on so great and so obvious a scale. These people boast that they have no plague no famine in their land, unaware, the while, that their very feudalism constitutes both a plague and a famine, as widespread as the land, and which, like a malignant and unspeakable disease, attacks at its very root, its very beginnings, the health, the thought, and the social usefulness of every man, woman and child of the eighty millions.

That was enough! With a feudal philosophy, a feudal doctrine of economics, and a feudal religion as guides, the rest of the way was clear, and the investigation dwindled to the semi-perfunctory, for me;--a mere matter of mechanically following the inevitable drift of consequence into multitudinous detail.

It thus became clear enough what the secretiveness meant; what the superficial cheerfulness and brusqueness meant; what the typical face on the street meant; what the buildings meant; what all the talk meant; and whence arose the inability to see, think, and talk straightforwardly.

With the veil of feudalism drawn aside, and the [quivering facts laid bare] * it was all plain enough; and the hideous face of the reality looked into mine with awful nearness, and with the veritable aspect of a fiend.

Now it was all clear. Any man with this clue could instantly interpret, one by one, and all at a glance, the vast congeries of facts which at first so puzzled and bewildered me. Now it was plain, now it was but too plain--that seeming paradox--how a fair land, a most lovable land, the very acme of Nature's goodness, bounty and beneficence, had harbored a people in sweetest hospitality, as it were, only to see that people make a very hell on earth--a maelstrom of corruption--a wilderness of stealthy murder--a dark jungle of betrayal of every normal heart's desire, of every pure and wholesome aspiration.

Now it was clear how the sacred name of Democracy had become with them a mere empty word to cajole and conjure with.

This is what those faces mean that I saw drifting by me in the streets. This is what those lack-luster eyes signify; this is what the fatal absence, the lack of radiance mean; and as well the decomposed motions of those bodies, as they moved like dreary inconsequential phantoms, dazed, vacant, as in a trance, passing in a pitiful dream through a beauteous world, a marvellous world of life--passing all unconscious, all unseeing, all uncaring, all unheeding. Truly my heart turned faint as I saw them, day by day, moving their devitalized bodies and their gray, poisoned minds. No sadder, no more tragic spectacle is to be viewed in the wide world than that of these dreamers of putrid dreams, floating, like unwelcome dregs,

* From Norman copy.

within the lovely dream of Nature's soul. Now it was clear what the city meant for them--clear why it was so unspeakable a blemish on the fair land. Now it was clear why human life, with them, was held cheaper than the dirt in their thoroughfares. Now it was clear why they could not withhold the poisoned cup even from the child. Now it was clear why and how the powerful and eminently unscrupulous few were growing richer, while the weaker but likewise unscrupulous many were passing into acquiescent slavery--for, historically, their black slavery was but the prophet of the present white serfdom.

And then I inquired in amazement, What do all these schools colleges and universities mean?--what do they teach? And I found in accordance with the prevailing feudal law, that they taught a little of everything official and conventional, and nothing whatsoever concerning the realities of life--not one word concerning those simple, easily understood truths, the wide diffusion of which is essential to the health of the social body and mind, essential to all,--to every individual--if he and they would live.

It was the same in their countless churches--what was preached, carefully abstained from mention of the integrity of man, his normal and upright place in the integrity of Nature, his normal spiritual relation to his neighbor and to the vast, silent integrity of the Spirit of us all. The preachers were mere social parasites, kept by the well to do and the rich, like so many kept women. Now and then, if one of them, by chance suffered an access of manhood and spoke aloud, he was ejected bodily, and branded as heretic to the church and to the feudal God of the church--because he had dared be loyal to man and the God of man. Hence, in that fair land man is honest at his peril--he speaks truth at his peril--and every man's hand is against every man. What wonder that a civilization whose basic motive is betrayal, should now be swiftly moving toward that reckoning day which Nature had ever exacted from those who betray her?

I should not trouble you with further details; let the broad sketch suffice; for I wish to move on to consideration of another and, to me, highly important nature. My further immediate studies, concerned merely the wider and minuter ramifications of the man-destroying doctrine of feudalism, in action, and the mask of hypocrisy under which it is carried into effect in its more intricately cunning and its larger workings. The theory is very simple; it is this:--Confidence is a necessary prelude of betrayal. If the betrayal becomes at last, through carelessness or over-sureness, too evident, and the confidence which is the real working capital vanishes, then a new and more cunningly contrived form of confidence must be devised in order that a new betrayal may successfully follow. This is repeated ingeniously and continuously throughout all forms of financial, commercial, industrial, professional, educational and political activity. It is the basis of what is called by them the "system" and the first move in what they call the "game."

The key-note of the active, aggressive American life is commercialism. And this means, that, underneath the huge and tangled mass of their nominal laws, is to be found the real, the guiding and controlling basic law, namely the law of dog eat dog. And those who, in their dealings, follow this law unswervingly towards its logical limit--become their great, their eminent. And these are thus exalted from the mass because they typify the ideal, the very heart's desire of practically every American in active life. Thousands upon thousands are yearly broken by this law, and go down and down; while the few of greater daring, the few who stop at nothing, as gradually, but with ever increasing swiftness go up and up. And thus is approaching ever nearer, daily nearer, that most dreaded of human antithesis--the two contrasting and mutually explanatory phases of the single and unitary feudal law--the enormously rich and the pitifully poor:--That age-long historical picture of splendor and squalor, which but makes visible and palpable, the ideal of selfishness which all have held in common.

Does it not seem as though Fate had made a most cunning trap, that it might end, in one huge enclosure, the vast and frantic urge of western civilization--lured thereto by the compelling odor of gold--the little bait with which their mighty trap is baited! Their hour is seemingly at hand. How this people will meet its crisis, fills me with profoundest apprehension and concern. For I discerned things in them, little aspects of their lives, other than those I have mentioned; things that call up, now, vividly before my mind's eye a strange legend of the European middle ages. It had to do with a romantic and pessimistic view of life, as held by the common people --of a sense of despair and a helpless fear of both life and death, coupled with a superstitious horror of the night. Briefly; it set forth the fate of a luckless wayfarer who, in the heavy dusk of nightfall unwittingly wandered among graves in the consecrated ground of a church yard, and there, lay down and slept. The people believed, in those days, that their God lived in a great mansion in the sky, much as their feudal lords and overlords lived on earth. So they provided a house for him, to which he might come when he wandered on earth; and adjoining this house or church they buried their dead; and the keeper of the house was called a priest, and this man was on familiar terms with both the God and the people, and acted as a go-between; all of which seems curious enough now. According to the popular myth, the sleeping wayfarer, suddenly awakening with a start, exactly at midnight--which was with these lowly people, a mystic hour, fraught with dire potencies--found himself surrounded by thirteen hideous skeletons, which had arisen from out of the ground, and had begun a wild and mocking dance about him. Terrified--because he had long heard of such things--he quickly died of shock; and it was told at many an humble fireside, that the things--thirteen because of their Savior Christ--the son of their God--and his twelve disciples--one of whom, it would appear, betrayed Him,--danced on and on, ever more madly, until they caught fire from the friction of their rattling bones. And there was much more ado of the same sort--as becomes so seemingly trivial a tale.

So far, so good. It was called the Dance of Death. But that is not the thought--nor the hope that hovers within my spirit, like an azure butterfly; that same fairy wayfarer of the scented air which the imaginative Greeks called Psyche, and thus delicately symbolized the spirit. It is the second part of the legend which specially interests me, because of its present suggestiveness and fitness concerning the American people. For it seems that, when the dance was at its maddest, just at the first faint approach of oncoming dawn--suddenly a cock crowed! the dread phantoms vanished; and a new day came on apace!

It seems to me, now, as though the crowing of that cock at dawn, the ringing, jubilant, awakening voice of chanticleer, must have stood, within the darkened minds of those past and gone people as a symbol of hope, as a neighborly but mystic herald of a brighter day; of the reassuring dawn of a coming day that might be theirs, and, perhaps, would come to pass, if not for them, then for their children, or their children's children--a clear way out of their agony, their darkness, their helplessness.

It is evident enough that the American people are in the maddest pitch of their Dance of Death; that they have killed their man, and will soon be aflame with friction. But!--and this is a momentous, a wistful but--will a cock crow for them a shrill new day? And will the hideous orgy be gone? I do not know. Nevertheless, before I left their land--ah, such a land! --a land made for freemen!--I had begun to ponder, vaguely, something of the sort. For when I had done with my studies of their feudal corruption, believed myself at the end, and looked forward only and surely to disaster, my thought, one day, in its musings, left the people and the cities, and reverted to the far-flung, joyous land--in the midst and amplitude of which I was, in the open air. And I then and there felt a strange, dimly awakening consciousness arising, within me, like a whisper, from without, that disturbed the solidity of my conclusions. And I said:--It cannot be! There is more beyond! I have not looked deeply enough, nor affectionately enough. So fair a land cannot forever be burdened and betrayed by such monstrous, inhuman thinking. It is not the end! It cannot be! It is against Nature-- even though it test to the breaking point my faith in Nature's kindliness: a faith which I have deemed so serene, so secure. Even though it test my faith in the serene and mobile ever-present God of Life--a faith in which, so long, you and I and all our people have lived and loved--a faith so integral with our lives and our deeds:--That abiding and consecrating faith which made us useful one to all and all to each. Even though it shake my faith in man--that faith which is the inspiration whereby we create, and whereby alone, we may continue to create in the fullness and the joy of living.

Perhaps I undervalued the goodness of their hearts? Perhaps, in my own ignorance, in my own insensibility, I laid to malice that which may be justly traceable to ignorance alone--an ignorance of grown children, untrained and untried in the real vigor, the real purpose of living; undisciplined in the affirmative and aggressive utterance of their truer powers of thought; of that unitary, cohesive thought and action which must exist purposely and solely to create, sanction and sustain a beneficent integrity of all the people, to the end that they may live in the fullness of their days and proclaim the open, lucid utterance of their individual and collective life. Alas! they do not seem to know, even to suspect--that this is happiness!

And yet they have the mental powers. They have a sufficient physical equipment; they possess a land exhaustless in its supporting power. If, in their mad dance they have turned the use of all these agencies into abuse, may they not--if the cock cries--suddenly transform abuse into use? Who knows?--in fairness I must ask, who knows?

Perhaps it is not for me to answer. Perhaps my foreign eyes are too dull to see so deep. Perhaps the truth was on the very surface and I could not see it. Perhaps it can be only one native-born and close to the soil and the people, who may be near enough to see clearly and say clearly that which I can only surmise--even as I feel the surmise to be the child of my hope. Who knows? I recall that I heard voices there, crying out in the wilderness.

But this I noted, and now well recall:--No people put thought into action so quickly as they--when once they *see!* This is their inspirational force, their true power--derived from the land--a gift they have used in material concerns, but lamentably have neglected in all else.

But this I do know. A psychological hour is now approaching the entire world of mankind. It has been eons in preparing. It is immanently near. Its coming is world-significant. It can delicately be felt in the air--in the world-atmosphere of the spirit of man.

This hour will come--and it will pass. If it is not seized and held, America will sink into the morass of its corruption--and man will perforce begin anew the long, long wretched struggle, and perhaps may be doomed to wait unnumbered ages for such a pregnant hour again to come.

But, if it be seized, as it moves, the American people will change, and rise at once, regenerate! to become the greatest, noblest people the earth has known. A people that the vast race of man, from the beginning onward, has prophesied and looked and waited for. A people that long-yearning time has waited for. A people that a long-yearning, long-loving, long-creating and preparing God has waited for. A truly Messianic people--a veritable incarnation of the Great Life--the Great Spirit--an inspiration, a joy, a hope, a promise and a pledge to all the illusioned, suffering and aspiring peoples of the fair round earth.

What will they do? With their great earth-grip, will they also at that psychic hour take a great grip on the Creative spirit? And thus cease, once and for all, to be victims of Destiny, and, so, *create* their Destiny out of the heart, out of justice; and, so, hold it, safe and secure?--Or--will they miserably fail?

I do not know. I merely know that it is in their power to do as they shall will--if they but see! And that, in them all, is the unused power to see. For that is the simple and great gift resident, latent and aspiring in the heart of every man. His God implanted it there in the beginning; and, since then, has waited, oh, so long! For man has denied Him face to face--knowing not what he did--for he saw not the living and radiant Spirit so nearby. He would not listen to the prompting whisper in his heart. He dared not trust the calm assurance of his soul. For man feared to be betrayed--and so,--betrayed. Because he knew not that The Spirit is incarnate, not in the one man alone, but in all men.

If, when it comes to the psychic hour, that floating spiritual hour, the American man, by an inspiration as ineffable as it shall be divine, and clear and near, looks into his own heart, he will see all and know all; and will be born anew. If he denies that gentle and approaching hour, hovering in the flow of life, and come to fertilize his soul, it will not plead again, it will not wait; but will pass on, silently as the light; and then farewell to hope, for centuries to come, perhaps forever; for, then, European civilization, now trembling will come to its sure swift downfall. And this will be the end. For the savagery, unloosened, will become brute real, instead of artificial; and, in their mad and sanguinary orgy, they will vanish exhausted, from the earth, to join the fading caravans of the past, moving into the abysmal dusk.

I do not know. The thought fills me with keen foreboding--only to burst into effulgent light. But I hope!--with all the ardor of the love I bear mankind.

Meanwhile, my friends, I fear I have fatigued you with this long-spun tale.

Perhaps it is my love of the fragrant earth and the open sky that has drawn me so strongly to that far away people, and which keeps them ever in my thought.

Perhaps, in a measure, it is the pendant picture of our sunny land and our own strong, sunny people! For, over there, so many of the children sadly are hidden away from the face of mother earth, from the sun and the sky, from the delights of childhood's hour of wishing and becoming; whilst here, of immemorial yore, our children pensively and laughingly have known the flowers, the birds, the trees as friendly companions in freedom, and in the beauty of their hearts' desires, as they have played in the sunshine, before our peoples' doors; while those that bore them and cherish them, have worked in peace, in strength and good will, carrying the hearts of the children in their own; while, ever and anon, some wayfaring teller of child's tales, some poet-spinner of gossamer webs, weaves an airy fabric of humor and delight, to reassure them in their faith that Life is not a mystery but a smiling presence clear and sure.

Behold: The crescent, yonder;--sinking through the boughs!

The air is still.

Thus, in my heart rests hope, new-born;--and gleaming as the silvery moon.

Ah, may the hope, the dream, the wish come true! [For it is to my soul as the music of one now hid] * in the nearby dewy wood, striking quick a harp of many strings.

Such harp is the heart;--when truly known.

And wise is he, who touches all--with a firm caress.

Is it not so?.

Surely, Life is convincing--in that it loyally gives and receives.

And this, my friends, is all that is real.

* From Norman copy.

CHAPTER 6 THE GREAT CITY

Enough of fairy tales: Let us again go forth into the world of men. To see them there as they are. To come upon the lurking thought. To see men pictured forth before our eyes; to see men in living dramas.

For unrecallably have we set out, you and I, as searchers of man. Having eyes we cannot fail to glimpse him. Having ears we cannot fail to hear him. Having sensibilities we cannot miss the trail that leads to him. Hence we shall not be denied.

Behold: This is the Great City! Murk fills the air. Would you know what the people think here? *That!* is what they think; therefore it is here! So stands the picture forth before our gaze: In it the brutal fact, murk, stands face to face with the brutal thought, murk; here in the open; not now in hidden sanctuary of any one, behind the veil of each, although it is there also; but now before the veil, in the open; where you and I may see, where all may see a thought at work! Where each man in the great city may see the picture of his secret thought and his open deed, painted dark against the sky and gloomy upon all things under the sky.

Had you thought all pictures garnered into galleries? Come forth out of yourself! Be disillusioned! Awake! The *telling* pictures are in the open. They cannot be hidden. Who can hide them? They cannot be obscured, explained away or denied. There they are. Anyone can see what they mean.

This is the Great City! Behold, filth in the streets! Would you know what the filth means? It is the people's thought. It is their *desire!*-- else it would not be here. The filth is of a piece with the murk. The two thoughts, the two things merge into one thing, one thought, one picture:-- one pessimism.

You say there are practical difficulties? Come down from your high horse. This is an expedition on foot. Stay here by me, with your feet on the ground, and look *straight* at things, so that things and thoughts may look *straight* at *you!* and connect up with you, and you with them. This is the first step toward the open eye; and the open eye is the first step to the seeing eye. You shall not evade nor shall you quibble. For men have evaded and quibbled these thousands of years, just as you are proposing to do. They refused to see straight. You propose to refuse to see straight. But it won't go. The time is past for that.

There are difficulties. There is one difficulty; and that *one* is practical indeed. That one difficulty *concentrates in you.* You are the obstructionist. It is *you* who create the difficulties that you now evoke and invoke. To conjure difficulties is your carefully trained talent; but that *one* difficulty you avoid and evade. For you dread the truth. You dread to find it in the open, pointblank and plain, where all may see. Above all you dread lest others perceive that identical truth in you.--*Just where it is!* Hence you parley; and palaver and pull wool.

That one practical difficulty which concerns you directly, individually, is precisely the one difficulty around which all others revolve, as on an axle. Have you ever seen a wheel *at work* without an axle? No? Yet you see all these practical difficulties *at work*, and do not see, or rather do not wish to see the axle; at least you say you do not see; and meanwhile you bewail the state of affairs and the iniquity of the neighbor, or else you prate of prosperity, which is merely stating the same thing in a different set of words. In each case you avoid the issue, which is neither prosperity nor iniquity but *yourself! and your secret thought.*

But I know the axle. And where do you suppose I found it? Do not waste time in guessing.--I found it in *myself! Therefore* I know it is in you, and in us all. For you and I are alike. All other men are like us. Therefore you and I shall find it in them all.

You have heard it said that clothes do not make the man. Neither do clothes hide the man. And whether the clothing be of cotton, wool or silk, or whether it be woven of words or thoughts or deeds shall make not a whit of difference with us, for we shall see the nakedness of the thought and the act. They must and shall stand bare before us.

This is the Great City. It is the crux of things.

Men are crowded here, hence they must be put to test.

We see them better, here, than scattered sparsely over the land. We see them in their bulk. We shall see better what they create! We shall see the direct consequences of their thinking. We shall see the axle-thought at work! turning the other thoughts about itself and making them work! And we shall see men clinging to the rim of the fly-wheel, men on the spokes, men hidden in the axle--as the wheel ponderously turns, day in day out, night in night out. And we shall see the iron truth of it. And this truth shall suddenly become alive and jump into a horrid, kaleidoscope smear, before our eyes. So will I make the iron feudal truth without* you, within me, within us all--jump out alive!--stare at us, whine at our hearts, and look formidably into our souls--face to face in the open. The darkened soul of the Great City shall confront our own--like unto like.

For had I not found this truth in myself, I could not have found it in you. And had I not glimpsed it in the Great City, I could not have found it in myself. For what I saw in the Great City was the soul of its people confronting my own, like unto like! And I could not escape! There was nowhere to go but that soul would follow mine and inhabit it.

Hence I know that in the Great City men now see dimly in the daylight. See things human with untaught glassy eyes. They see not their fellow men because of the Great pestilential City they have created. They see not the City they have created because of the crowding and surging pestilence of their fellowmen.

But, just so sure as the men living in the Great City and continuously creating and sustaining it as it is, *once see it as it is!* and their fellow men *as they are,* within it; all the men, women and children within

---

* The word *without* though it also appears in Norman copy, probably should be *within* to conform to the meaning of the sentence.

it; as they are--two millions of them in all (What Power!!)--they will, that hour, begin to destroy it, and to remake it.

As it stands today, they see men of all kinds, everywhere, and do not know what they are. They see the city, everywhere, and do not know what it is!--For they are, one and all, insensible, in the world-old trance of Feudalism! Hence they wander, phantom-like, and create, phantom-like, unheeding a crowded world of realities within they move as wantons, even as they jostle realities, look squarely at them--and see nothing.

Behold! This is the Great City! How many hearts break daily here? Who knows? Who cares? What other useful end can there be for hearts, in the Great City?

What sorrow is here in the Great City? Who knows? Who cares? Do you care? Do I care?--provided it be not our sorrow? And if it be our sorrow do we not think the Great City heartless indeed? Does it not weigh upon us like iron; does it not seem monstrous, and stone cold? And who cares about our sorrow? Why should anyone care? Are we so different in thought and act that our sorrow particularly signifies? Why complain, if we would receive and have not given? Why curse?--when we have helped create the gloom? Let us then accept our logic. Let us not whine--if we cannot see and think and feel and act to better purpose than to create sorrow.

How many poor are here? Who knows! Who cares! Do the poor themselves care? Do the rich care? Do we care? Obviously, graphically not. For the poor are here; the poor, the demented, the crippled, the criminal and the outcast, are all here in the Great City. They are our thought, our deed-- as well as their own. And are the poor therefore white-winged and as angels? Or are they the sinners, and the rich they favor,--white-winged and pure? No! Poor and rich, the broken, the demented, outcast, criminal are, all, just like you and me! There is something interchangeable in us that fits exactly with them all. That something is a *thought!* It is the *Feudal Thought;* the axle-thought of all civilizations of the past and of today. That thought which has been hugged secretly and blazoned openly by the Man of the Past--and which we hug and blazon this day. Only we mask it. We call it, good-times, or hard-times, as the case may be; we call it by every name but its own. We even call it Charity; we even call it Religion! We even call it Philosophy! When you get down to our last thought--it is the same in all. *Therefore!* things are exactly as they are! The conventionality whereby one man is called a priest, another a pauper, this one is called an economist, another an imbecile, one a scholar, another a thief, one a senator, another a blacksmith, does not make an iota of difference when we come to deal with the simple, the obvious and the fundamental in man,--stripped of all subterfuge, casuistry, sophistry, fine language, fine art and fine nonsense, and scientific self-deception.

Thus do we see ourselves pictured forth in the great city. Anything and everything we see there, is ourselves.

All the people think in terms of murk and filth, wealth and poverty, crime and misfortune, and the rest of the long list? And there is the thought, pictured for you, point blank, in the open, where all may see. The smoke, the filth, the rich, the poor, are merely parts of a great picture --the picture of the Great City. The picture itself but the open showing of our one thought *at work!* continually painting fleeting and permanent pictures for us all to see and heed.

Had you thought the many pictures and the great picture not here because you had not noticed? Do you think, now, that they will vanish if you disclaim them? Do you think that ever again you can draw a veil of words to hide them? Not so! That is the pedestal on which you have long stood in an illusion of wordy, fanciful isolation. On that pedestal, in that isolation you shall never again stand. For I shall cause it to dissolve--and your feet shall come to the earth.

From now on you are to remain with me on the level! (It is "high" enough;). You shall keep your feet on the ground, and you shall see with a clearing eye. For I will unroll picture after picture before you. Pictures all real, all so different and yet all of a kind; For they will be views of the great moving panorama Man himself has painted, as, from the beginning, he has spread, in many colors, the many scenes, some sombre, some gay, vivid, tremulous, revolting, inspiring--spread them all upon the fair Earth; has drawn and painted them all out of the dream stuff of the single thought wherewith he has driven himself, like chaff before a whirlwind of his own, on the path of Time and Destiny:--The soul-disturbing thought of self--the abandoned ego!

The Man of the Past thus has helped paint the pictures we now see. Therefore he shall go with us, a shadowy, but real companion, as we walk the streets of the Great City, seeking realities, seeking the how and why-- seeking ourselves therein!--and seeking beyond!

Now you, in your list of practical difficulties, complain of corrupt politicians, in the Great City--shoals of them. Now who has corrupted them! Did not you? Did not I? Did not they themselves? Have not we all? Have they not accepted corruption because we asked them to, because we set them alluring examples, because we sanctioned them, because we drove them, willing, unwilling, or hesitating, or wishing, though they might be? Were they not, in fact, as chaff before the silent whirlwind of our stormy heart's desire, our secret predatory thought, within our multitudinous sanctuaries of one? That sanctuary of the poor man as well as the rich man, that sanctuary of the ditch, the coal mine, the railroad yard and the mill, as well as of the pulpit, the altar, the university, the editorial chamber and the private office? Are they not therefore a picture of our thought? The thought of all the people? Look at them near and square, look at them as brothers; not on terms of superiority or inferiority as you would like, but on terms of likeness, as you must! Look near and searchingly; get up close! Are they not your very image? Can you not see clearly the thought you hold in common with them? Does not that thought join your hands with theirs in fellowship?--those whom you affect to despise? Are they not your secret thought *at work* in the open? whoever you may be, rich or poor, or in between--or in any walk of life!

Do you suppose that because you have held up your hands in pious horror and have bellowed or squeaked in protest, that you are immune to responsibility? Do you assert that "righteous indignation" is other than a farcical phrase? Search your memory from the cradle up! Test your life-thought with acid reality. You know! I know!

Do you suppose that because you have remained sadly silent, that you are immune? Do you suppose that because you have pitied the depravity *of others* that you are immune? Do you suppose that because you have led an "upright life," as you call it, that you are immune? Do you believe yourself immune because you place your trust in Jesus and the feudal God, and the Sunday school, and heaven, and all the rest, and are of the elect? Do you really believe that you can thus escape the shrill call to personal responsibility and accountability here! The cock-crow of dawning Democracy! That cry which shall awaken men to realities!. That cry which shall awaken men to you! and to themselves!

If you have so thought, then you have another thought coming. A thought that I shall lead to the threshold of your door and cause to enter your soul. And there it may grow and amplify until it brings you to a genuine and willing utterance.

If I hold you in the hollow of my hand, it is so because you yourself have revealed the closed circle of your thinking and the narrow boundaries of your sympathy--and in the so doing have revealed to me my own, and thus have shown me the way.

But do not fear. For if I shall show you many pictures, and explain them all clearly, it is to be solely that you may see at last how it must have come about that all the little pictures and the great picture are your true portrait--the likeness of each and all of us.

Rest assured I shall not assert you are essentially either worse or better than any other man. For the tie between us all is indissoluble; and the responsibility is universal as well as specific, joint as well as several--and so is the hope!

And if I remove from you the garment of your hypocrisy, I will also remove your humbleness, and banish your fear of Life. Because I will reveal Life to you in all its sweetness, grandeur and regenerative power. I will outline to you who and what you really are. So that, henceforth, you will walk the streets of the Great City or the pathless open fields alike, companioned by a new thought that shall have grown within you--a thought that will be not entirely of self, and will have parted company with murder.

Be not irresolute. It is yours yet to pass through many a gruesome scene, to view ever deeper and nearer the tragedy of human life. The bitterness of its folly. But, in due time there will appear an imposing parting of the ways. And then the choice will be left to you. Your sanctuary of one will then have become enlarged to the size of the great round Earth. Then! --choose you must! Men will know your choice; for you will be in the open with them all. And before that time I shall have made plain to you, plain as daylight to you, who and what they are.

Meanwhile there is no escape. You are surrounded in advance. The circling investiture of circumstance is historically closed. Nor shall I need to send you the conventional invitation to capitulate. It will not be necessary. For I will cause your citadel to dissolve--leaving you alone in the open. And then I will cause the investing army of your own phantom thoughts to dissolve--leaving you alone in a new, fair world. And then I shall, myself, dissolve--leaving you alone with your own spirit--as a freeman should be.

As together we walk the streets of the Great City, roaming here and there, passing a mansion on a boulevard, and then, elsewhere, passing sweat-shops lining streets not called boulevards because not respectable enough, not well enough paved, not tree-planted and grass-platted, vacant of fair equipages going and coming, and children prettily dressed; but crowded with other things, unseemly; do you believe there is no connection between the two pictures, the two realities? Do you think there is really not a modern ghost, making a modern trinity of our one, ancient, persistent thought? Uniting parent and offspring in one? Is not the sweat-shop the parent? Is not the mansion the child? Does not the man in the mansion know it? Is he not content? Is not the mother on whom he sponges seemingly resigned? Is it not fate! Have we not been told that an all-wise providence has thus arranged for the good of all? That it is through the benevolence of the rich that the poor are given work? That were it not for the Charity of the rich the poor might sometimes starve? Have not the poor long drawn inspiration from this comforting thought? Did not the poor create this thought out of their sweet, sad dream?--as they have created all things? Is it not also our thought? Are we not, all, agreed? Is it not therefore our portrait, one and all?--this little picture in the great city!

And thus, ever unfolding, as we cross and recross many paths, appear picture upon picture, revealing in vibrant form and varied coloring the multitudinous aspects of a single thought the people hold and stand for:--some in overwhelming contrasts, others blending into a gray insipid monotone. Pictures painted not by artists, so-called, but by ourselves--by all the people. Pictures, without frames, conjoining, interblending to form a huge, graphic image of the totality of our thoughts, and the singleness thereof as interpreted in our complicated, tangled and thwarted lives.

It may have been your habit of mind to consider drama as occasional; episodic; an artful presentation merely, as set forth on a stage within an isolated house called a theatre; and more or less well done, more or less inane, as the case might be. That is but a little truth. The broader, unescapable truth, is that you are ever in the midst of a drama; a drama in the open. You are both spectator and actor therein. It is the drama of the Great City. This drama is unfolded within the action of the greater drama of Land and People. The drama of Land and People is in turn enfolded within the greater drama of the nations and peoples of the Earth. This latter drama is but the tidal continuation of the still greater drama of history; and the urge of it all sets forth the stupendous and pitiful drama of Man,--moving passionately through the ages, and as passionately moving today; ever-seeking, ever-thwarted Man! It is this great drama of the soul of man that we are slowly to unfold. It is the background, the vista, the ever pressing drift, now nearing culmination for weal or woe, on which we must set our gaze, and concentrate our hearts and minds. It is the one drama! and in it man (the spirit and summation of mankind) the sole actor, has moved and moves in solitude through the great wilderness and teeming world of nature, through darkness and light, ever, in a darkling dream, seeking to know man, seeking to know God,--and tragically unaware! unaware!

And thus, in the drama of the Great City, are enfolded lesser and lesser dramas,--dramas growing ever acuter, more poignant, more intimate, as they grow ever, but in seeming, only, smaller and less significant; dramas innumerable in the open, dramas of the day and the night. The lesser drama keys to the greater drama, the greater a key to the lesser, and the least. Dramas, without end, within a roof and a wall. Terrible and subtle tragedies behind closed doors; behind the door the breath of Life has blown to, to hold in tight the sordid and calloused soul--the wrecker of thousands of his fellow-men; to hold in tight the terrible, the solitary drama of one, bitterly alone behind the door that Life has blown to in disgust with man.-- A flash! and it is done! A drama of the wretched home:--Enter the man, drunk unto mania, surly, irritable, A surging word of reproach; an oath and a blow; a woman prostrate, huddled screaming children; a maudlin interval; and then a man, outstretched, snoring on the floor in the night stillness, in the sanctuary of one home, behind the closed door, behind the veil where we are told we cannot enter because there is no trail and all are safe in solitude.

But there is a trail. It leads from the forlorn home direct to the workingman's saloon; and there it parts in two straight lines, running, one to the brewer, the other to the rectifier--both poisoners, both cowards--(they both struck the woman). From the wife beater, beaten wife, children, brewer and rectifier run lines straight as the crow flies to you and me (we also brutalized the man, struck the woman, terrified and degraded the children), and from us, they run straight to every man, woman and child in the land--and come back to us; and between all the people in the land they cross-connect, and connect us in endless combinations.

Have you deemed the inter-relations of human life and civilization impossible of precise definition? Have you agreed to be thwarted? and that the aggregate of human life is a mere blur, a smear, all grays except a few bright spots for the favored,--and that there is no simple definite meaning underlying it all?

Do you think there is no center of gravity? No definite direction of urge, merely because the man on the street seems commonplace to you, and you to him? He, the practical man; you, the practical man--inane dreamers both--visionaries, spending your lives dreaming difficulties and hence creating them--never dreaming a solution.

Awake! The hour is drawing near when all this must be changed --or we undone!

Wake! Be a man! Do you really deem it incredible that all these varied, endlessly flowing and intermingling pictures and dramas, have sprung, and can and now do spring from a single thought all men have held in common, and have not ceased to hold? Do you really believe that violent opposites cannot contain the same truth? Do you really consider differences more significant than similarities? Have you been betrayed by words, not knowing the meaning of words?

Are you then the closet-philosopher, who has spun a theory of thought, but has not gone abroad among men in the world of stress--where he might clearly see that acts, and *acts alone* identify thoughts. Where he might see the mind, the heart, the soul of man clearly, indubitably set forth in the actual pictures and the actual dramas of man's individual and collective life? Open to the view of all--even to the dull, dreaming, inconsequential, frivolous philosopher of abstractions!

Why should we bother with the rubbish of abstractions when we have the palpitating living thing? Why should we take a tortuous and obscure way, which never arrives, when there is a clear way straight from deed to man?

Awake! Let your heart expand until you become aware that you are not alone! Until you become aware that between you and every human there is a thread of thought connecting all together. Binding all--brain to brain, heart to heart, soul to soul, body to body, life to life. A thread more ethereal than gossamer, stronger than steel. A thread we cannot break, a living thread from whose band there is no escape--and yet a thread which may transmit a new universal impulse that shall prove our salvation.

Had you thought it possible really to isolate yourself from your fellows? To evade and deny the tie? To evade and deny your responsibility, your manhood? You cannot! Along these delicate threads, these live wires, I will pass like a current, and, entering intimately into your secret depths, will shift your ballast; and you will feel the awakening shock of an enlarging consciousness as I bring you to an even keel.

I will search your mind as never mind has been searched. I will search your heart as never heart has been searched. I will search your soul as never soul has been searched. To me you are no secret. To know you I have merely to look at any other man, high or low, rich or poor, in the ditch or on the throne of the vicar of God on earth. And if I look at a thousand men, I shall see but yourself in a thousand occupations or situations, the same You--called by a thousand other names. So shall I place you, at last, squarely before yourself and before all--in the open, and in secret, whoever you are, wherever you are, and whenever you are. And I shall set humanity square before you in the open, and in the secret longing. Square in the daylight--face to face!

As we walk together in the heart of the Great City, is there aught greeting our eyes to suggest or even hint the nearby presence of a noble Lake, the teeming prairies, green and radiant, half-encircling the Great and gloomy City? Do you think the picture of the City one thing, the picture of the fair broad water and land another thing? The drama of the City one thing, the drama of the open another?--the drama of the open air, the open sky, the open waters and the open land! Do you perhaps deem them paradoxical? No. Undeceive yourself! Open your eyes! The two pictures are but parts of a larger; the two dramas but responsive and coordinate scenes of a greater, simultaneous drama:--Picture and drama the same; and, together, merged into one living image, which marks us, as with a fateful and monitory finger; and then moves to the one thought within is* from which the mirage of a seeming paradox has come forth to obscure the city and the open.

Spare your explanations, your excuses, practical, sentimental, historical, scientific, benevolent and what not withal. I have listened to the chatter for many a year. Patiently I have read on page after page of many a book, endlessly, concerning an exquisite and delicately rapturous difference between tweedledum and tweedledee; knowing well, in decency that the real proposition (so deftly set aside) had nothing to do with either tweedledum or tweedledee, but vitally concerned you and me! Over and over I have seen the hair split into a thousandth part, and, meanwhile, I have seen simple men DO!!--simple things--and do them well!

Thus have I come to know to my sorrow and waste of time the inanity of the wise, pious, wordy, over-educated poseurs--and their joint and several inefficiency. By way of compensation I have learned their lesson.

But they are busier than they opine. I shall show you in picture and drama their color, form and movements. I shall show you just how, why and where they fit into the scheme of the little dramas and the great drama. We shall run along the live wires reaching to them, and binding them to us all in the fierce, disconsolate and impassioned stress of real life. That life, calling, calling,--calling!

So, too, in the drama, shall appear the man on the street. He *says* he would not do certain things. But in the great drama I shall point him out to you in the act of killing by thought, by word, by deed, by indifference, by indirection. We shall run along his wire like Nemesis! Because he is a liar, a thief, a scoundrel and an assassin--and because he has declared his religion to be his most precious possession--Because he has been benevolent and charitable with the loot of his murders. I shall show him to you sitting silent, or wandering like a madman. And in the great moving picture I shall point out to you, as therein clearly set forth in

---

* Obscurity. The context suggests that this is probably a typographical error and should read *it*.

sharpest definition, just what the word "practical" means, as used by him; just what his word "business" signifies; and just what "economy," as he understands it, signifies for him, for you, for me, and for every man, woman and child on earth. No doubt he lies; sometimes even to himself. But the lies, the hypocrisy, the turpitude, the concealments, avail not. For, unwittingly, the man on the street, he who is no dreamer, no visionary, who believes himself no artist, no poet, is painting on the great picture, his great and little share, and revealing there, with a precision unattainable by him in conscious speech, the startling truth concerning himself and us all --where we may see.

What a curious notion men have, concerning themselves, their thoughts, their sayings, their doings; with what a curious hebetude they minimize and maximize their parts in the roaring farce, the vaudeville, the melodrama, the tragedy of the Great City and the far-flung Land. How like semi-mechanical figures they go this way and that, not dreaming their dream is come true; not surmising that daily, as a sheer reality, it mocks them, jeers them, warns them, ridicules them--and seduces them into dreaming anew!--And yet no one laughs!

Think of a civilization, a city, a land in which men are honest at their peril, and speak truth at their risk!--And yet no one laughs! No one smiles.

Think! of a civilization in which the predatory, the relentless, the parasite, the saintly, the feudally benevolent pull the wool over our eyes-- knowing us for the sheep we are!--And no one laughs! Preacher and teacher pulling the wool over our eyes--and their own. All of us eagerly pulling the feudal wool over our own eyes--And not a smile!--all serious and fanatic, in a vast silence, and emptiness of sympathy. Truly our feudal denial of reality has at last undermined not only our sense of human tenderness, but even our sense of humor. Thus no one weeps at the dream come true.

Had you supposed that the poet, only, could see such dramas? Only an artist paint such pictures? Do you still worship genius as a fetish, and still consider it a thing apart from the common? Undeceive yourself! Unglue your eyes! We are all poets--every one of us. All artists. All geniuses. Only--we deny it; we decry it; we say it *cannot* be so! And *why* do we deny it! Primarily, because we are cowards. Broadly, because we deny any and everything that is real; narrowly, because we decry anything new--we revile anything true--we ridicule anything that is broadly sympathetic--and, most conclusively, because we persistently mistake our reverse-sight for insight. Under the age-old stupefaction of our feudal education and training we deny life--and affirm death. We lack a knowledge, an insight into the simplicity and naturalness of that illumination that is called genius, merely because we have no use for it. We do not know that it is a universal quality resident in all things, and neither more nor less mysterious than the open air, the sky, the land, the water and--the neighbor. Genius is the simplest thing in the world. It is the only simple thing in the world of men. *Therefore* it is common, to all men. Now if you can even partly dissolve and reshape your notions concerning genius, you will have taken the first step toward an understanding of man; and toward a perception of those latent powers within him which it is the function of Democracy to call forth. Genius is the simple unsophisticated power to see, hear, and feel Life! Therefore genius in Man is nothing other than the historic aspiration of Democracy. That deepest, simplest instinctive aspiration of the human heart, which has glided through every form of Feudalism;--an impulse so small, so simple, so persistent, so integral with the spirit of man, that it cannot be exterminated. It is that one, little thing, in all the people, which you cannot fool all the time. Of all our imbecilities, the suppression of genius is the most pathetic, deplorable and utterly inane.

Burdened with our darkened and grotesque notions concerning genius (which is equivalent to saying our obscure notions concerning the beneficent All-Life), is it to be wondered at that we deem great things (as we call them) difficult, and great men (as we call them) necessarily rare?

Have you ever stopped to reflect that the education you have received in school, college, University, and are still receiving in the greater school of practical life has been and is Feudal?! with all the manifold inversions of human thought that that word, that reality, contains and breeds? No, of course you have not. How do I know? *Results!!*--results set clearly forth in the pictures and dramas you have made and are making!--you who are no artist, no poet!--Yet have the power to paint most startling pictures, and create most revolting and heart-rending dramas! I don't bother to look at you, or to talk to *you;* I look at the insane, the destitute, the criminal, the vicious, the corrupt, the restless, the tuberculous, the anaemic, the outcast, the criminal rich, the financial rottenness, the political rottenness, the poisoning packer, the treacherous lawyer, the unscrupulous business man, the timid and hypocritical priest and preacher, that you have created and are sanctioning this day!--out of your feudal thought. Is it to be wondered that you are a hypocrite?--(and it doesn't make the slightest difference whether you are a conscious or an unconscious hypocrite--the *result,* in practice, is the same). Is it to be wondered that at times you look upon men as through the ravening eyes of a wolf; and at other times through the timid and flattering eyes of a cur? Is it to be wondered that hate, envy, malice, vengeance, jealousy, greed, anxiety, pessimism and, at times, despair, have a home in your soul? Is it a wonder you do not know who or what you are? No wonder you do not know who or what the neighbor is. No wonder you think genius is necessarily rare. No wonder you suspect nothing of the all-inclusive beneficence of nature--of that gentle power which is ever seeking to make real men, and is ever thwarted by your kind--of that life-giving power which ever faithfully and hourly is striving to make a real man of you--and is being hourly thwarted by you. No wonder you have neither sought nor found man! And still less wonder you have neither sought nor found, nor had curiosity concerning that Spirit of Democracy which for so long and with such patience and wistfulness, has waited, until you be ready, that it may enter and illumine your thought, and establish therein the consciousness of your integrity. No wonder, instead, that you slammed the door shut in its face and sordid terror (lest this Spirit of Life enter--lest the genius of Life--the power of Life enter--to make you human)!--slammed the door that you might be alone with your darkened egoism within a roof and a wall of self. No wonder you have so heavy a countenance as you walk the streets of the Great City--alone, bitterly alone, helplessly alone amidst the shoals of faces, among the half-humans, the feudal humans--who are moving swiftly or slowly towards nothing whatsoever but graves. Because brutally they have struck kindly and smiling Nature in the face--in return for her smile. No wonder you cannot see these faces, ghostly and pictorial as they are, dramatic as they are, eloquent as they are of the feudal thought you and they have held and hold in common--and which your forebears and theirs held in common--The feudal thought which wears out the heart, unbalances the mind, devastates the soul and wrecks the hopes of mankind. That feudal thought which has brought hitherto civilizations to decay; and is now, swiftly disintegrating and inflaming our own. That! is our Crisis! That is what our Crisis means! That is what makes a terrible reversal, revulsion and cataclysmic revolution, not only possible, probable, but imminent. That is what renders imperative the prompt liberation and diffusion of the aspiring spirit and the kindliness of Democracy. That spirit, so long thwarted and denied utterance, that it has accumulated intensive explosive power within the subconsciousness of men. That is what the printing press, land lines and ocean cables mean, in the last analysis. That is what the teaching of the Nazarene means in the last analysis. Our hour is on the wing. Democracy is at last about to be born. Whether in anguish, alarm and terror, or in peace, reasonableness and joy--remains to be seen. But one thing is palpable: our equilibrium is unstable. It is trembling delicately in its balance. And, soon, we are going--one way or the other. It is high time that you get busy thinking about realities. It is high time you begin to understand what this prosperity of ours means *under the surface;* in the pictures and dramas, in the open;--(and in yourself)! *This* is the thought you will want to take with you into your sanctuary of one, behind the veil. This is the thought that will cause the feudal mighty to dissolve as though they never had been. You had better get busy forgetting your "practical difficulties!" and learn how simple, how masterful, thought and act can become, when you will them to become so. How quickly problems can be solved when we make up our minds that they shall be solved.

It is then equally no wonder you deem benevolence and charity sweet and lovely things; no wonder you do not see that these two fetid-sweet feudal words are but the names of two ghastly, grinning skeletons in the ring of our grim and ponderous dance of death; and that you and your kind, (all of us--feudal) are but phantoms joining with them, hand in hand, clattering, running and clamoring around and about dazed and momentarily terrorized manhood; and that all the fine words, all the fine deceptions, are but a weird and sombre song of the Modern Crucifization.* No wonder you cannot see that what you call Business is the name of another such phantom; and the laws of trade--as you call them--others; Industry--as you call it--another; and society as you call it--another; the rich man--another; and the poor man--another. Can you not hear them all?--like the murmur of a keen wintry wind driving through a bare forest--singing the song of the Great City? Can you not hear it? It is roaring on, day in, day out; night in, night out; in the churches, in the asylums, in the jails; in the mansions, in the shanties; in the pest house, in the hospitals, in the police stations; in the mills, the factories, the ditch, the marts of trade; in the hotels, the theatres, the boarding houses; in the sweat shops, the rear of saloons, in the private office, in the newspaper sanctuary, in political committee rooms:--Everywhere--anywhere! Ceaselessly!--Here in a whisper --there it passes in a wink, a nod, a tip, a sign--there amid clangor and clamor, and bustle and hustle, buying and selling, hooting and yelling--There it is! For you to see! For you to hear!--in the Great City! In the Great City where you and I are walking side by side, looking into the faces of the passers-by; observing the traffic in the streets, and over the streets, and along the streets; dropping in here and there and everywhere, by day and by night, only to hear the same song with its endless, teeming variations in pitch and key and intonation and volume--in smooth flow, in rabid dis-

* See also p. 252 where *crucification* appears. The word *Crucifixion* also appears in text.

cord--in fine words and ribald words and crude words--in pious prayers and in strings of oaths--It is always the same, always with the same refrain --The Dance of Death and the Song of Death! For we are indeed a busy people--none busier--We have no time--we are greatly occupied--And business is business--so we say.

And do you think the Great City really is alone, in a gloomy isolation? Alone in its murk and jargon? Not so. There are filaments. They go forth from its engorged and inflamed nerve centers:--Ganglions quivering with incessant messages that flick out to the land and come in from the Land--Ties to other great cities, to smaller cities, to every village in the far-flung Land--Ties to the whole great World of Land and the Isles of the seas. The Great City! It is as a man--created Monster--shuddering with the load of traffic in and the burden of traffic out; traffic following the gleaming, parallel threads, far, far throughout the Land, and coming, far, from everywhere, constantly approaching, nearing, and arriving. And the monster groans and sighs. Ever pregnant, as it were, with its one darkling need, it brings forth, every day, the infinitude of things of which it dreams --such as they are, and they live for an hour or a day, or they are absorbed and elaborated into its tissues and further irritate and inflame and engorge and impoverish and congest, and dull its semi-consciousness; as it grows and waxes huger, and becomes heavier and heavier upon the Land and the People:--Broadening, elongating and holding within itself multitudes--a fantastic and passionate mass. The Great City is shaped Titanic, rough, and hulked in a human semblance. Its passion is a mystical, distracting, devastating urge and confusion:--Bewildering, vast, oceanic to those who do not see --but heavily feel--and lament, or curse or flaunt. Clear and gross enough to those who see that the monster is without a definable brain--and without seeing eyes--bringing forth blindly, struggling turgidly, quivering and working without a clear thought--A Caliban in the Midsummer-night dream of a new century, in a Land magnificently fair and filled with shimmering and hovering gayety and beauty and wistfulness and delight--and a winging spirit of the Land, that laughs it to scorn, because the Monster does not yet know how to wish to be glad.

No! the Great City is not alone. It is in purblind touch with the world; and the borning thought of the world disturbs it. Within its massive bulk a consciousness is struggling toward the slowly envoluming light of a dawning day. That is all. And the seasons sweep over it in untiring succession. And the great shadow, night, sweeps over it silently. And the great orb of day moves over it, dazzling and silent--as the Monster broods in a fateful mood--dreaming by day and by night, its inchoate and turgid dream

--in the midst of the steadfast prairie--by the steadfast Lake. Unaware, unaware!--For the Great Feudal City, the man-created monster, has not yet dreamed of man.

And there are other great Feudal Cities in the Land. One lies in the East near the sea. It is the Great Feudal City of the little feudal pennies. It is stark and ferocious; clean and callous. Blasé, glutted and irritable, it is ever ravenously hungry, with a dyspeptic and maddening hunger for pennies. It, also, is a monster. It has one eye that sees everywhere, that can spy a penny a thousand miles and more away, hidden though that penny be in the tall grass, in the pocket of a poor man. It may be the last penny--just one--but the all-ferreting eye detects it--and forthwith the penny begins to move toward the Great Feudal City by the sea. That is all--is it not enough? When you wake up you will think it is enough.

And there is another Great Feudal City in the east. It lies not far south of the one-eyed monster and is tied to it by cables of feudal power--surcharged with viciously crossing high-tension currents. This third city is clean and rather fair to look upon. It also is a monster--with a bland, smiling face,--which is right and proper--for, here, all treachery culminates. For, in like manner, as the little pennies flow to the City by the Sea, so all the little treacheries throughout the land, rippling gaily on in rivulets, conjoin and conjoin and debouch here and there in irresistible volume. Hence, here, in this City with the smiling face, this Capital City of the Land, the American people achieve their heart's desire--for here they are betrayed in bulk. And yet there is a truth in treachery. Hence this City is a mirror, our great national soul-mirror, accurately giving back a faithful and fateful reflection of all the people in all the land. Look into it--you will see the apple of your eye. If you do not like the image--Change! So much for Great Feudal Cities. Let us pass on.

CHAPTER 7 THE LUXURY OF THE POOR

Come on!--let us press into the thick of the Drama of City and Land:--To see in that drama, unrolling, the world-array of poor and rich; the poor and rich of all time. To hear Truth proclaim them parent and child!
Note the time-honored arrangement!
See the child!--ashamed of the parent. See the parent--looking keenly at the Great High Child! Gazing meekly in pride that, in the disdain of its own proud offspring is revealed a wish become real. The Child appears as a vivid dream come true--a thought-dream of power, riches, glory!-- a solid, sordid, immovable fact! A wall! (swine turned to rend)--an adamantine power, a fascinating power to daze, and delight, and make proud, the poor.

What a deep, ecstatic dream--so to have brought forth a Child! That Child, now on high, engloried; raised there, forced there, exalted there, by the poor; and from that eminence to shed radiance upon the poor; the radiance of a derision which takes the poor brutally for granted.

But, in the Drama, bellows Truth, saying;--The poor have ever made two kinds of children--one, flesh-born; one--thought-born; while the rich, double-sired by flesh-father and thought-father are thus double-begotten of the fecund soul-gestation of the poor.

Thus roars Truth--the Terrible Tattler:--

"Blessed are the poor in that they have two broods of children-- one rich, one poor; one to love and hold physically warm and near; one to maintain on high, far, far above the modest roof and wall wherein betimes the mere flesh-children sprawl, wonder-eyed, and grasp at the moon or whatsoever glitters; wherein the non-resistant rag doll is princess, fine lady, Queen--at the wish and will of the dreaming flesh-child of the poor;-- The child, the dream, that are to make more poor, more rich."

"Blessed also are the rich; doubly blessed, doubly rich, in double fatherhood. Having thus a flesh-sire to proclaim:--a thought-sire to ignore and hide away. To hide away in by-way, slum, modest home; in mill and factory and mine. To hide away, sprinkle over the fair land under the noon day sun, secluded in the open. To hide, all, by one enormous gesture of denial: to banish all by one word of negation:--Mine!"

And who are the poor? Manifestly those that are not rich. And as there are rich, richer and the richest, so are there poor, poorer, poorest. Out of the web of gestation and the urge of birth comes it, as set forth in the action of the life-drama, that Richest is child of Poorest--veritable Great-Offspring of slum and pit and poverty; whilst Least-Rich is child of Least-Poor,--In it, flesh-child and thought-child begin a prophetic approach and merger.

In the Great Drama the poorest are plainly to be seen *in the act* of emptying their lives--that the richest may survive;--and the richest are plainly to be seen *in the act* of receiving, with ready hand the offering of the last gasp of the poor;--even the death-rattle of the poor helps fill the great purse; even the putting of them in the ground; even their shadow-journey. Thus they depart that the rich may stay:--For the poor have not "families."

And thus in the Drama, as by magic of old, arises the unfolding spirit of its urge; foretelling, as a cloud by day and a pillar of fire by night, its tragic denouement. By the murk of the cloud and the glow of the pillar of fire is obscured, and revealed, that poor and rich, each and both, lead sinister double lives. One an open life, estranged; one a secret life of utmost intimacy; of a privacy insidious, clandestine, furtively constant--savoring of stolen sweets, given and taken together.

Ah! The drama of Poor and Rich; What vast pictures! What historic action! What unison of times and places.

Is such weakness of the poor really born of power? Or is the power but seeming, the weakness deceptive? Could, possibly, the Child be thus ingrate--the Parent-Poor thus madly doting?

Or is there a communion beneath the surface of it all? An incestuous spiritual unison--like a secret thought within a secret thought? An age-old skeleton in the closet? Akin to that skeleton at the feast of Poor and Rich, held in the great hall of their fathers in civilization; a hall, domed by the sky, floored by the earth and walled by a fateful wall of men that they have taught, and ranged like a phantom army of defense, encircling like a horizon! A magic hall--empty of all--but the Two--and the grinning one:-- while invisible Illusion whispers in the ear and dilates the eyes of the Two-- as they feast upon the substance of mirage--unaware! unaware! these Two, who feast on Glory--Even as this picture arises from the drama, hovers, and returns within its flow.

How and why has come this aristocratic fateful, gorgeous progeny? How and why has it come out of the poor? Out of the poor so seemingly barren, so seemingly unendowed with imagination? The poor, so seemingly bald and pinched in thought?

How could such excess of splendor have arisen out of their prosaic dullness? How could such great material wealth have seemingly self-gathered out of such manifest poverty? How could learning, brilliancy, and pride of place have sprung from bestial squalor, from brutish stupidity --as we piously say?

Or does the Drama indeed assert a huge inversion? and set forth the poor, luxurious!--the rich, dependent!

Is this true?

Can it be true the rich are the creatures of the poor? The poor, Creators of the rich.

The rich--recipients of alms? The poor--prodigal givers! out of their abundance?

Turn!--as ever--to the Drama of Man's Life!

The *answer is unfolding* there!

You need ask no man; it is not worth while;--The poor will not make true answer--the rich will not make true answer.

DEMOCRACY: *a man-search*

But the Drama of Man's Life is making true answer. The Man of the Past is making true answer:--To you and to me. The drama of today is making answer to the multitudes.

And the threads of life, reaching from our hearts to everywhere, reaching, far back into the twilight of man, are tremulous and beating with the murmur and current of response--seeking opening ears everywhere--ears to hear and heed the still small voice now persistently and truly answering amid the clamor and mania of denial and derision.

The poor are too hypocritical to answer. Likewise the rich. So are the learned; so are the complacent; so are the brilliant; so are the crafty.

The poor are too proud to answer. So are the others.

Great is the Drama of Man!

Intolerable its climaxes!--

Not of battle and song--not of arms and the man--not of splendor and decay.

But of the children of the poor even *today!*--mouldering, that the children of the rich may thus take root in Death. *We* have reached, today, a climax of human sacrifice--of immolation which *we*--Today,--in incredible hypocrisy--dare to hide. We, today, unabashed, dare speak of Nature as red-clawed, ravined and red toothed! We, who affirm in pride and pomp that we are above the brutes because we forsooth are endowed with Reason, and not they.

Truly the poor are strong, that they carry so heavy a load and are uncrushed.

Truly the rich are strong that they can thus long stand the strain of suicidal mania, and not collapse.

But they have not yet met these things face to face!

The mania of tradition is still with them. The crisis and the awaking are not yet upon them--rich or poor.

Truly the poor are rich. They pay the fiddler, Death, for all who dance. They beckon to all, and invite all:--

"On with the dance!" they say;

"Let joy be unconfined:--

There is much room, and a long rest--under the ground. There, where we need not arise at cock-crow:--

Rich or poor."

In the wall of Destiny, Death is the only door they know.

Truly the poor are spendthrift--They support the rich; back them in extravagance, finance them in venture, in stratagem.

Truly the proud luxurious poor have not denied themselves the things of the spirit. Pomp and glory have ever been in their hearts. Towering

THE LUXURY OF THE POOR

ambition has been their dream. Hence resplendent dynasties, sumptuous temples, magnificent castles, palaces, imperial thrones, monuments upon monuments have been their free gifts with hands overflowing to the world. The hands of the poor. On the poor, the lofty superstructures of civilizations have rested as upon a firm foundation made of human bodies. In them the great tree of knowledge has its roots as in a fertile soil. They have paid the cost of all. Paid with tears; paid with toil; paid with hunger; and consecrated with their diseases, their degradation and their obscure and long-forgotten graves. They need no monument. Every structure in the whole great world is monumental to their memory.

That is why they ever have been, and are, today--The Poor. They did not, could not, understand that such extravagance even when coupled with extremest self-denial, must surely keep them impoverished.

Thus it is a theory that confronts the poor, rather than a condition. It is their own theory, in fact. For the poor have been the theorists of all time. On their theories the entire social structure has ever rested, and now rests. The theory of might and cunning is theirs; so is the theory of glory; so is the theory of I and mine; so is the theory of a God. The theories of the learned, the rich, the pious and the mighty are mere etceteras--mere ornamental additions. How then, today, can the poor justly quarrel with those who say that their poverty is due to their improvidence, their lack of prudence, intelligence and thrift?

They therefore should heed and take to heart the benevolent suggestions of those pious, wise, and rich, who suavely counsel them to *Save!* to be sober, to be honest, to be industrious, to acquire education-- They should, indeed! Unless they prefer to remain of those poor of whom the Priestly Caste has promised the Warrior Caste that they should never be without them. Those same marvellous poor who, some day, shall surely inherit the earth--when the time comes that they change their theory; and a new dream shall thus be born of their transcendental ancient dream; a new condition come out of the old.

How introspective have ever been the poor. Ever dreaming dreams within dreams. Closely they have pondered the ways of life. Much and long they have reflected at first hand. Their thought has been the wellspring of all philosophies. Their yearnings the inspiration of all religions. To them has ever been made the first and final appeal. Their answer has ever been conclusive. In the last analysis they are the law and the prophets. They are the dreamers of the dreams that count. What they accept is accepted. What they reject is rejected. It is they who have been vain, arrogant, tenacious of purpose, intolerant of suggestion, disdainful of counsel. No one can hypnotize them. But their power of self-hypnosis is as a deep and inexhaustible well. In them is the initiative. They are the creators, the sustainers and the changers. When their thought changes, all changes, when their thought holds still, all holds still. They hold the rich and the clever on high by the mighty unremitting power of their mass-thought. Thought, so simple that the clever cannot penetrate its simplicity. Thought so irresistible that the powerful cannot understand its power. It is only the poet, the so-called genius, he of the simple amoeba-like mind, who may enter the thought of the poor--for they are of the same cosmic primal stuff. They alone, the great poet and the great poor are elemental--hence creative.

Thus behold! What a Child of the Poor is Civilization! What a glowing dream-child! How radiant;--How fair in high places! Yet the mother oft has passed timorously in dark places; the dream-father whose name is Toil oft has bent the back, oft broken the heart in unremitting effort--that the Spirit-Child might be well arrayed, well sheltered, well nourished and well trained. For, has not the Parent ever and always wished and hoped that the Child might have a better day than his own? and rise in the world? and prosper? and become great, wise, powerful--and fill the soul of the Father with pride, joy, and a reflected glamour?

Has not the heart of the Father ever yearned for a glorious Son? Has he not ever deemed himself expressed, compensated and comforted in such Sons? And has he not ever desired in his soul--a fair daughter? A radiant daughter? Has he not ever spun out of the mesh of his heart a slender thread wherewith he wove many and many a fairy tale? Has he not dreamed many a dream--Hoped many a hope--longed many a longing--yearned many a yearning? Truly he has, truly he does--this timeless Father --The timeless Poor.

From the beginning, the Poor have been the pristine dreamers of dreams. Close to earth, they have exhaled the delicacy of the Earth-life; and have brought forth out of their earth-fertility, out of the mystic solidity and power of their teeming mass-thought--the wonders the man of the past beheld, the wonders we behold!

They have dreamed what they have believed a lovely dream. To them it has been intimately, fanatically real and true. Beware lest they awaken--(or hope that they awaken) and find it less lovely. Lest--(or that)-- the self-hypnosis pass. Lest the illusion burst like a bubble, and be lost. Lest the illusion of illusions that has enslaved them be gone--Lest the *Feudal Illusion* vanish!

Has not man lost illusion after illusion; and has he not clung to those that remained? Does he not at last lose a last illusion?--Even though in the loss of the last he creates anew? Is not man in thrall to his illusions?--are they not his most deeply cherished possessions? Have not the rich their profound, their startling illusions?--Are they not moving toward the rupture of the last? Have not the poor their illusions? Are they not now likewise moving toward the rupture of the last? Is not the last illusion of rich and poor identical? Will not the awakening be mutual, and--simultaneous? Will it not be a world-shock?

The Drama-Voice says it is so. The Drama-drift is leading toward that inevitable world-collapse and awakening--irretrievable loss of illusion of rich and poor--and the new gain of both--as out of the old dream a new dream shall be born to both--and its spirit take on substance and form of regeneration.

This is the sonorous new song that the Voice of the Drama now sings. This is what the swift-driving action of the Drama means--the Drama of Poor and Rich--within the world-drama of all the Lands and the seas and the peoples of the earth, and under all the skies.

Surely the drama of our present real-day life sets forth convincingly that the poor are very kind to the rich. That they have pampered them; indulged their every wish, their every whim, their every distracting ambition; and hence utterly have they spoiled them--yea ruined them, perhaps beyond redemption. So infatuated have been the poor, with their own dreams, their own ideals of might and power, and splendor and glory, world without end; so enwrapped are they in their dream, that they do not dream it as a dream. They believe it all real and separate from them--this power--this glory--this disdain--which was in the beginning, which visibly is now, and which seemingly must and should endure.

For, in their last illusion, the poor believe that Fate has reared a wall. That Fate has made rich and poor to be apart--unaware that they themselves are Fate! That with a breath they might blow down the wall.

They, the poor have long looked into the stern, visage of a Phantom guarding a door in the wall they have reared. Thus have the poor looked at themselves unaware. It is they who have cried aloud, from the beginning; whispered, murmured, sighed: "What is the use?--What is the use?"--and have broken their hearts against their own wall, saying: "It is the will of our God!" They;--unknowing, unaware, that, in power and pain, in the durance and travail of their dream of dreams, they had made even the Gods! and might, as with the touch of a hand, with the breath of a wish, cause the door in their wall to swing of itself open wide.

Yet so illusioned, so indulgent are the poor, so anxious to please, they give to their rich grown-children many toys, many playthings. They have in this generation said to the Dream-Children:--"Here are the railroads, mines, ships, telegraphs, newspapers, banks: here are mountains of ore; here are Great Cities; here are forests; here is much money. Play with these things; be happy!--lovely apples of our eyes--Majestic ones--noble ones --incomparable!"

And the grown children, the Spirit-Children of the poor have played with the toys; have made playthings of the banks; railways; forests, mines and mills; have quarreled, scratched, screamed; have made a wreckage, disorder, twisted broken and snarled mess of them. They have become angry, purple, fierce, brutally lustful-looking--have the adorable Children of the Poor. Have come to confound their nursery with the real world of men and things. In their world of illusion they seem gigantic to themselves. Quarreling, midget-like in the pockets of the poor, they seem less great to us. Looked at close, they confound with the dirt.

It all seems mystical; paradoxical; it all is unitary, simple, plain. The feudal thought ever held in common and now held in common by poor and rich, has ever made and now makes the two one. In the feudal scales the rich and the poor are exactly in balance:--It must be so, If the poor become poorer the rich must become richer. If the rich become richer the poor must become poorer. The feudal system has its logical inexorable moving equilibrium between poor and rich. The center of gravity is the feudal thought--the first-thought of Self, the dream of glory.

Nor are the rich the only costly children of the luxurious poor. There is also the priestly hierarchy; that graded series of fair, fairer and fairest children; of noble, nobler, noblest children; wise, wiser, wisest; crafty, craftier, and craftiest children; children grown out of the heart-love, the God-love, the solicitude and anxiety of the dreaming spirituality of the poor; out of the sacred God-search of the poor. Children lifted tenderly by the poor and exalted by them out of their mass--high, higher and highest-- from the beginning, so unto this day. The Great Church was the Great Child of the poorest of the poor. Its splendor, wealth, pageantry and power grew up out of the soil of the luxurious fear, the luxurious hope, the luxurious self-denial--yea the luxurious self-effacement of the poorest of the poor. It was so from the beginning. It is so now. It is so set forth in the Great Drama of Life. So the feudal poor, the feudal priesthood and the Feudal Church have held in common, have worshipped in common, and now so hold and worship a Feudal God who came true out of the longing, wistful, trusting, fearsome dream of the poorest of the poor.

The poor have ever said to the priest: "Let not the Good God get away, O, holy father!" and the priest has ever answered: "I will not let

Him get away if you are faithful children! Give me pennies!" And the poor have said: "We will give thee pennies, Holy father; only let not the Good God get away--he is our hope and our salvation--for we are weak, we are poor, and so dependent on his mercy, grace and loving kindness!" He will bear our burdens, will he not? and the priest has ever made reply: "I will not let Him get away; he will bear your burdens, if ye be not unfaithful to The Church:--Give me pennies!"

And out of these pennies of the poor, as by a veritable lamp of Aladdin, grew the vestments, the churches, the great cathedrals, the palaces, the monasteries and the precious lands. For the poor feared lest the Good God, which they had created, forget them and leave them in a darkness and a helplessness of solitude. They saw not the wall of priests they themselves had built to separate their God from them. Nor saw they the God of the Hierarchy--behind the veil! For the priest smiled not before the veil! Thus how should the poor know there were many veils.

Nor are the rich and the priests the only costly children of the luxurious poor. There is the aristocracy of the learned. The dainty learned--the wise Thought-Children; they of wrinkled brows.

The poor had dreamed there was much to be known. They had thought that knowledge of power must mean power of knowledge--for the poor see all things upside down (so do the rich and the learned) (It is soldiers and priests who see things profitably straight.)

And the grown Learned-Child said to the lowly parent: "I would write a book--but I need a Great Library; for knowledge is in books. And the poor replied: "With our pennies not only will we provide a library and many books; but we will surround that Library with a University--for we, helpless in our ignorance, and little understanding, would foster learning. So we shall build for you and endow for you. For recompense write us one good book. So in time the Learned Child said: "Here is a book: it came from my brain." And the people said: "It is wonderful;--we cannot understand a word therein. Was it writ for us?" And the Learned Child said: "No, not for you. It was writ for great men like myself. It deals with thoughts and things that can not in the least concern you! I would surely lose my caste were I to write a book for *you!* It would have to be so simple, so poetic, so true that, surely, it would meet with the derision of my kind. They would deem me insane; would scourge me from the great house of learning, and thrust me forth into your outer darkness." And the poor said: "It must be so; for we are very dull and near to earth. We would not have it that you meet with the scorn of your kind,--leave scorn to us; for you are our great, revered and splendid Guide. And in you we trust--you know what is good for us; we do not." And it seemed not to occur to the grown-child-philosopher to wink his other eye. For he had lapsed into abstractions; taking himself seriously, but taking none other seriously. Moreover he cared not for wealth and the usual and customary God. He sought a God of transcendental vacuity. A God which he and his kind called the Great First Cause, the Infinite, the Absolute or something of the sort, implying possibility of a detached or detachable abstract Idea--something to play with in the Kindergarten of the learned: As to say: Ah ha! Let us wish the chair to be a horse--and forthwith it is a horse. Thus the Learned Children made Gods at their pleasure; while the poor made the Gods that count! The learned, unaware, the while, that the poor are the real idealists; that they are absolute in strength, infinite in resource, and the social Great First Cause. The great first cause from which the learned, in their illusion, believe they have detached themselves, and can remain detached, unaware that their Great First Cause, their Infinite, their Absolute, is but the reflex of a feudal-thought image of the poor--working *up* to the learned.

The poor deem themselves hard-working, practical people. The learned philosopher thinks them so too. Hence neither knows the other. Yet they are each alike--alike as two peas in the pod. They both hold in common the same feudal notion concerning knowledge and understanding. Hence the philosopher is as unpractical in his way as are the poor who give him food, raiment and shelter. Unpractical, in that neither has sought Man. Nor have they sought him jointly. Hence the hitherto futility of coupled poverty and learning. Just as the hitherto and present futility of coupled poverty and riches.

Nor are the rich, the priests, and the learned, the only costly children of the luxurious poor. The brood enlarges, there is especially the glorious company of statesmen. The Statesman-Child, put forth of a dream of justice and war, dreamed by the poor.

And there are other expensive children--Great and austere and beaming children--eminent feudal children of the feudal poor:--Merchant Princes--Captains of Industry--Eminent Counsel--various magnates--huge parasites--and the rest of the motley feudal crew--"self-made," dreamed, created, exalted, sustained; clothed, housed, fed, and provided liberally with funds by the lavish poor:--penny by penny--millions upon millions of pennies; half pennies, quarter pennies; hundredth pennies; pennies, split into the thousandth part; split finer than the hair of tradition. All for the good and wise children.

Passing strange! These children take themselves seriously; they ask us to take them seriously.

Stranger still!--The Great Drama is busy with them now--very, very busy--busy with all the dream-children of the Poor!

Strange!--In the Drama of City and Land, masks are falling. Iridescent veils are lifting, one by one. Demi-gods are dissolving. Respectability is collapsing.

Strange!--The wall that Fate has reared is faintly trembling. Strange!--it feels the first faint breath of early dawn--the wavering impact of the rays of a Sun not risen! The Sun of the heart of a people.

Are there watchers on the towers?

What say they?

* * * *

Such is the Tale of the Poor and their Dream-Children. Told in a passing hour.

So much for the unfolding drama of City and Land.

Let us push on--push on!--

For we begin to hear the Man-cry! within the jungle of civilization. The faint, far cry of the past, the swelling cry of our day.

CHAPTER 8 A WORD

Remember: we have been coming face to face with things as they are! Our search deals directly with the facts of life. We are casting aside conventions, traditions, labels, mock-shows, and make-believes. We are gradually penetrating the artful allurements of man's selfishness to find the core of his savagery--and to seek a sounder core within that core.

Remember, we are not dealing in sentimentalisms; nor are we moralizing; nor do we recognize conscience, or the Sunday God as guide; nor the Money God; nor the Property God.

We seek the facts of life--to lay them bare. The facts of man's life are his dreams, his acts. It is what he dreams and does that counts and costs, not what he affects, upon notice, to think or believe.

A WORD

In the last analysis his acts are brutal.
So are his pretenses flimsy.
Our civilization is a form of intricate savagery.
That savagery is nurtured in a single, simple principle.

That principle we shall find, isolate, and, disembarrassing it of all the beauty, sumptuousness and splendor of the civilizations which have enveloped and now envelop it, which have hidden and now hide it, we shall make it plain to see. It is a small thing in its inception; smaller than the scriptural grain of mustard seed. We will make it as plain, as it is big in practice.

Just as the universe pictures to us an expansion of the principle of gravitation; that principle which, we say, animates not only the great suns, but every tiny particle of earth and air--so the principle which animates our civilization is apparent everywhere in everything. In obscure men and minute details, in great institutions and conspicuous men, we shall find it at work *making facts!*

So let there be no manner of doubt as to where we are going.

Of sentimentalisms and of academic theorizings the world has had so much that it is sick of both and knows them both to be nostrums. They are merely ways of turning our backs upon the reality, man, the neighbor.

As to our religion--the so-called Christian--a mere ecclesiastical institution--the world is coming to know that also as a nostrum and a delusion; --another way of turning our backs upon the realities of thought, things and man.

It is apparent that the world knows little of Justice. Because Justice is insistently concrete and deals with actual man. But the world has held Justice an abstraction, man an annex thereto. Thus again, we have turned and still turn our backs upon appalling injustice, because we hold an abstraction to be more urgent than man.

Hence has arisen, by the consent of all, and through the work of all, the overpowering Institution of Property. This institution men have made sacred above gods and man. Toward Property they turn their faces, as they turn their backs on man.

Under its prodigious accumulating weight and prestige, common men have sunk ever deeper in the sandy road they travel, not knowing what burdened them, not knowing their own worship of property created the burden.

They have panted ever harder, feeling a lessening life in the air--not knowing why.

Believing their own small, individual savageries to be natural and right, they have thus lost the key to the great and growing savageries. For they have not apprehended the fact that, also Justice is a small thing in its inception, that all big things are small in inception.

The average man has both underrated and over-rated himself--and all others.

He has no sense of proportion--no judgment of distance. To him perspective does not exist. It is too much trouble for him to see straight.

He has no standard of values, other than a money standard, which he holds so close to his eye that it eclipses all else.

He believes powerful things must be large, and great things big; of insidious things he is unaware. Of the insidious nature of his own thoughts he is especially unaware. Of big or little things near to him he does not divine the real significance--nor of things far--either.

He is boastful of the worst that is in him.

Ashamed of the best in himself, he turns his back upon it;--but others see what is decent in him.

The average man discloses all men.

He carries a pocketful of excuses.

He carries not one genuine explanation.

He advances not one basis that he dare apply to all men and have all men apply in rigor to him.

He is a coward, this average man.

Pushed to the last analysis he lives that others may die.

But he says that is not so; he says; "live and let live." That is one of his dastard lies. He has no thought so to live that others may live. He is too passionate for that. His mouth waters too easily. He whines with hunger at the mere thought of power. The vision of money makes him demented.

Let us have no illusion in this matter. We shall not heed what men say. What they say is unworthy of our credence. We shall see with our eyes, what they *DO!*

We shall not ask them. They would lie; coarse or dainty lies, as might be.

But we shall certainly ask the great drama of things visible.

It will not lie--because it cannot. A pine tree cannot lie and say it is an oak, we can see it is not. A crow cannot lie and say it is a song bird; we can hear it is not. Ice cannot lie and say it is warm; we can feel it is not. No man has to consult a philosopher to make sure that he is hungry or athirst; he knows!

So much for the acts of man. Anybody can see them.

Now as to the thoughts of man. That is a similar matter. Men have not been taught to think straight. They have been trained to agree that they think straight; which is crooked training.

The average man not only does not know what he really thinks, he has as little conception of the influence of his thought upon others. He is cock-sure in the belief his thoughts are his own and cannot escape from him, unless he so wills. He little suspects that his real thoughts flow away from him in spite of him, to reveal themselves in his acts. He therefore as little suspects that he cannot make a move that does not constitute a record --his biography--his autobiography--somebody knows! He does not seem to care how his thoughts damage others--thousands of others who have never seen him and may never. Damages them to their deadly hurt; conscious or unconscious of the source of the hurt though they be.

He thinks the mean little thing he does (as he believes in secret) can do no harm. He so thinks because his mind is untrained to see big things growing out of little--although the growth takes place before his eyes; although the growth takes place out of his own thoughts.

Hence when he sees big things looming before him he is unable to trace them to their real origins in his small self, his small thoughts, which he deemed so secret--which he was sure were so small they could do no harm. That is his illusion--out of which grows his other social illusions. That is his crooked way of seeing and thinking, out of which, before his very eyes, grows a crooked civilization.

He preens himself that he really is alone in the world--that there is not such another--That is his ego-mania--out of which grow other manias.

He cannot believe that men are all alike. He believes himself the one exception--the one just man--the one man whose wrong can do no harm.

Hence he will not see himself in others--and is thus socially blind.

This is his hypocrisy!--out of which grow other hypocrisies:--The average man!

For, the man who will not see himself in others and will not see others in himself, thereby refuses to see anything worth while. But he emphasizes his own lunacy. He is not yet a man.

Still less then can he see himself in his larger social surroundings-- and that failure shuts him out from understanding.

Were you to tell him that each man hung on the scaffold is himself hung in effigy, he would call you far-fetched and fantastic; unaware that it is he who is fantastic; while the world pays for his fantasy because it shares it, and justifies him!--to the manifold cost of all.

Select some man famed for his "responsibility," as we call it; say to him that in the shocking reality of life, he is irresponsible.--He will deny it with specious anger or guile; because he, like all, believes himself unique--he suspects, and is ready to admit that he is the only just one.--He firmly is convinced that he is not like other men. Only once does he say he is like other men, and that is--when he is found out.

And if you hold up to him, a picture of real life, he will say: "What of it? I know all about that! I take the world as I find it--I did not make it;" unaware how much of it he has made, just as it is; not knowing always how or why; because he has not been trained to see, think and feel straight--and hence not caring to enquire. Especially is he complacent because the world of men tells him he is right. For that world does not see straight, think or feel straight--for reasons.

In our man-search we shall have naught of personal opinion, naught of prejudice--naught of malice.

We shall seek the facts in the drama of real life--for the soul of that drama knows neither opinion, prejudice, nor malice--any more than does a pine tree in its forest, or a fleeting cloud on high.

We shall search out the soul of man, which is both less and greater than has been supposed.

Thus nothing shall be too large for us, nothing too small. It is as easy to see a mile as a yard. As easy to look down as up--as easy to hold a feather as a pebble, as easy to see one color as another--as easy to feel right as to feel wrong.

In the great world-drama not a thing is insignificant. The small is wholly as meaningful as the big. There is just as much of the spirit in a passing smile as in the whole history of man and his institutions.

It is to this Spirit we must get as close as the All-Life is close to us. We must become aware of it, just as the All-Life is aware of us. We are to make it our own. That is what we are here for.

We shall give the man who says he takes the world as he finds it, who avers he did not make it, a touch of wrath. For in no other way can the hide of his complacency be loosened. Thus shall we usefully be wrathful toward ourselves, and loosen our own hides.

We shall show, to him and to others, where he fits in; the exact nature of his influence; the virus of his irresponsibility, the portent of his social madness. So shall we again be useful to ourselves. So, step by step, shall we illuminate ourselves to ourselves.

We shall crack him, so that he will fall apart and we shall see his kernel. And thus shall we see our own kernel too.

A WORD

We shall show him, busy, in the drama in his actual role--that of a traitor to mankind.

He stands for what is worst in you and me. To know him we have but to regard the meanness in ourselves. If we tap him and he sounds hollow, it is but our own hollowness we hear.

For we all have bred rascality, and we have all chattered practical difficulties.

And the man who seeks to be honest, who would be just, who has not parted company with human feeling: He, also, shall we set forth. In the great Scheme of Life, we shall show to him and all, who and what he is OO* and why he has not counted!

He stands for what is best in you and me, and in all. To know him we have but to regard the best in ourselves and seek to understand why it has not counted--why it has weighed as but a trifle, in the feudal scales. Why, in short, we have been unwilling it should count.

Our task is large, but simple. We are to seek and find man past and present, at the center of his environment; and concurrently to behold the environment expressing each man. We are to seek and find in the past and present the thought that has created and which sustains the environment, while disclosing the how and why of it in all men, and to all men. We are to locate man, not only in history and in other lands, but here; today; this hour--face to face--shorn of equivocation, shorn of the last shred of hypocrisy, and not a refuge left.

We have gone part way; but our circle is far from closed. Man, the agile and resourceful, might easily escape the line we have thus far drawn. It is for such daily "practical" needs that he invented sophistry. These daily needs to betray himself are the chief excitant of his guile.

But his wariness shall not avail, nor shall his silence, nor shall his furtive shyness.

Keen as are his feudal scent and hearing, he yet mistakes the direction of the wind.

For we are of the day and of the hour.

All horizons, all heights and depths and reaches now are ours.

And ours is the Vortex-Land.

* Obscurity. The context suggests that this is probably a typographical error and should be the punctuation mark -- which occurs throughout the text.

GROUP III—THE MAN OF THE PAST

Chapter 1 Historic Sketch
Chapter 2 Feudalism
Chapter 3 Democracy
Chapter 4 The Multitudes

CHAPTER 1 HISTORIC SKETCH

Spirit of Eld!!
Lo, quickly appears the Man of the Past! He of the spirit! To touch our hearts, that we, in spirit, soar through his domain.

Lo, from the heights it seems but yesterday the Hun drove before him the German hordes in foaming waves upon Rome! It seems but yesterday the Saracen, sword in hand, Allah in his shout, swept the Mediterranean south-shore like a fire.

It seems as yesterday an image arose in the minds of men, of a God slain for them on a cross.

It all seems modern; much in the foreground; and all open, on the sunlit, storm-swept plains of the story of man.

Purple and white-capped as mountains, arise a silent range of civilizations hiding the real past, except here and there in glimpses through its vistas.

Behind all this foreshowing, as a supernal depth, abides ethereal Nature, serene, fecund; flowing within the sweep and immensity of Life.

From its enveloping, a semblance of man once upon a time came forth as a little thing. A bit of soft stuff inspired by the Power of Powers. A little one, a mite, searching, seeking; patiently, sturdily; incessantly, ah, so clamorously aspiring.

With what swift glance are we aware that the Man of the Past and the Man of Today are the same and one. Imagination at a sweep bodies him forth totally as Aspirer, Wanderer, Seeker.

Yet how long the career; mostly behind the veil, for us; and how slow, how tedious! Painfully has he taken step by step, now exalted in illusion, now depressed in collapse. Now despairing, now hoping; ever hoping. Hoping then, as man hopes now.

What a setting for our Man-Search!

How unitary is he with it all! The same voice, everywhere, ringing clear, fainting away.

So unitary, and we with it, that there seems, in our mood, no background, no foreground; but a heightening glow of fusion into a single, purposeful Personality centered in the Universe--no past no future--only a moving Now! A soul!--A Spirit! A visible world-man with eyes that gleam, with heart that throbs--a world Spirit that would be free! That would come to its own! That would come to its Earth!

And anon, before us, how this living presence, this solitary one hovers, floats, shimmers, darkens and dissolves as a world-rain; each drop a human--toiling, grasping, struggling. Blindly, hatefully, wearily, laughingly, tenderly dreaming and hoping; dreaming and fearing, dreaming and hating; dreaming and loving; and ever coming the new son of woman; and ever going,--to sleep within the earth--that others may pass over, forgetting him. Pass over him in multitudes, to sweep here and there in eddies, currents, whirlwinds; or to crawl in a huge spread; each horde a myriad of specks; each speck a man, woman, child; each carrying hither and yon, and to and fro, a brain, a heart; a curious enquiring brain, a strange, kindly, tempestuous heart; and each--a Soul! Each proclaiming a God of Gods--from the beginning.

Meanwhile man overran man. For might was right.

* * * *

Thus men congregated, master and slave, in massive nations, in the long-ago.

When the record of history lifts upon the opening act of his authentic drama, we behold him civilized, adhesive, clinging to himself, busy with his practical needs and doings, but enmeshed in his thought; the thought which has mastered him, but which he has not mastered--for he knows it not.

So strides he through history--the unmasterful man, the weary slave with many masters, without and within; the weary master with many slaves without and within, and many lustful masters within and without.

Each man a slave to the image, the thought which holds him in leash; drives him with resistless power.

An image, a thought which ever menaced him as Fate; Destiny; Nemesis. A thought borning progeny in a leviathan dream, amid the quicksands and pitfalls of reality:--For he saw not.

* * * *

Thus in the near background loom Chaldea, Babylonia, Assyria, Egypt.

* * * *

Thus in turn each such nation seems but a single man; as an urgent man of temperament, imagination, will; with an heroic readiness to enter the arena with Fate, in hope to conquer.

Behold each, in turn, going down before Fate! Yielding to Destiny! Passing into the tomb of the nations. Borne there amid pomp and the mystic rites of the Gods that failed!

But lo, each, passing, left a testament to mankind. Each made a bequest wherein we, nameless and unborn, were made legatees of great thoughts, great poems of man; of vast material and spiritual monuments to his memory. These were left by them for us to cherish; and to enquire of these most earnestly why Man failed in his contest with Fate. To enquire what the thoughts, the poems, the monuments really meant and mean. To interpret the mind of the Man of the Past by the records he himself set down enduringly.--His own story of his own life, wrought with his own hands out of the fabric of his dreams.

* * * *

Such is History. It is not what we say; it is what he said--in what he did--the Man of the Past.

These men, our predecessors in hope, struggled ceaselessly, however unwittingly, that we may be free.

The Man of the Past sums all our prior struggles to be free. We and He--are now and here in conjunction. For then and there--is now and here.

Great is the Man of the Past!

In him is compressed a drama of such dire intensity that poignantly it thrills the heart, allures the mind, and lifts the soul in its Freedom-Search.

With him we walk side by side in his day and stress; knowing him bodily, looking into his eyes as into eyes of man today. Knowing his enthusiasms. Hailing him, brother, alter-ego, ego-, across that span of years which vanishes at a gesture, to become here and now.

Thus, in spirit, are all the men of the past ourselves. Verily we are alike. In them we feel not only our own being, but how much the seemingly frail fabric, man, may endure and not be utterly crushed.

They of the past are our sound guaranty of endurance and power. They of the past but require interpretation, to be plain.

It is thus they inspire us to new courage and the dauntless undertaking of great, new, simple, things.

Their resplendent failures simplify our program, and now point the road at the parting of our ways; a parting of which they knew not in their days--and perhaps could not know; for they saw not, as we see not.

Whereas, at the very point of the parting of our great ways stands now before us an inspiriting presence, becoming ever more readily understandable when we come awake to a consciousness of the essence and simplicity of our modern power.

If we shall show results, in our new way, as the Man of the Past showed prowess in his way, we may well be not ashamed.

Before him ever stood a phantom by a door that would not, could not open.

Whereas we have but to avert our eyes from this same phantom at which we still gaze with fascinated vision, to behold the presence of Life!

He faced Death much as we do; perhaps with greater unconcern.

He faced the All-Life much as we--but not in greater fear.

Man's fear of Life is his subtlest fear.

His fear of Death quite secondary.

Some have said that man is resolvable into a fear of pain and a desire for pleasure. That these guide him; impel him.

What gives pleasure or pain man knows, in a way. But that which gives neither pleasure nor pain he ignores.

Man, standing with outspread arms may touch Life and Death with his finger-tips, and may feel sure of each. But midway and beyond lies that which is neither Life nor Death:--A unitary Spirit of whose reality each is an illusory aspect.

This spirit, silent and nameless, is the Power of Powers--too gentle to be felt. Its search is the God-search.

At the parting of the ways of the Man of the Past stood Death.

At our parting of the ways stands Life.

He of the past looked one way.

The silent and nameless Spirit slowly is turning us that we may see if but we choose.

This turning now heralds the regeneration.

We as a people will not call it such; for it will appear to us vividly as catastrophe.

So, for the Man of the Past, Death was a phantom, saying, "What is the use?"

* * * *

What historic power is ours:--That spiritual power of Modern Man to annihilate time and make himself one with the Man of the Past. To enter into his mind, his heart, his soul. To take him by the hand and lead him in a moment through the centuries, to the threshold of our doors. To draw him into the sanctuary of our inmost thoughts, that we may commune with him in spirit.

This is a modern power. This is the historic version, that winged spirit of sympathy whereby and wherewith we may meet the Man of the Past anywhere, at any time, through the long flow of the Ages, through the length and breadth of lands and seas--At any moment to greet him!

What power is now ours to see, to hear, to do!

This is what COMMUNICATION has come to mean for us.

This is what the power of Listening has come to mean.

This is what the power of Feeling has come to mean. It is the modern Clairvoyance--the seer-sight. It is the superfine listening and talking of the printing press, the land wire, the ocean cable. The talking of words grown new with meaning. The listening to new meanings. The charging and expanding of ancient words with modern purpose.

What power is now ours--To Grasp!

What power to choose!

What power to cause Fate to vanish!

What power to cause Destiny to withhold his hand.

The power to put forth our WILL--in place of Destiny.
This is the spiritual dawning power of Democracy.

A power outpouring from the interplay of intelligence. The power of democracy is already grown greater than we. It stands before us now and awaits our awakening. It is now looking at us steadily. When shall we awaken?

* * * *

Thus may we pass, swift or slow, through the realm of present and past, moving like the spirit of the wind; now high, now low; now in, now out; now to-and-fro--now everywhere. Sweeping through lands and great cities, flowing and playing, and penetrating not only the life of the past but the life of today. Going and doing, where neither zephyr can go, nor storm can do. For we are of Spirit.

Thus may we see with new-grown eye.

Eye of a new, clear sight.

Eye of consummate sensibility.

Eye that seeks man to find him:--knowing full well that all centers in man; hence knowing man to be the key of all.

Hence are we moderns come verily to fulfill.

Thus, spread before us the civilizations of Greece and Rome, as through the limpidity of time.

Into them enters the spiritual, searching vision seeing all, interpreting all, transporting itself within the very soul of these civilizations; of these men and their hour; noting the brilliancy; the power; the fateful illusion; the internal decay; the loss of balance--the downfall--and the why and the how of it all. Great is this spiritual eye which, in its triumph, comprehends man because he is man.

* * * *

Also appears the Barbarian of the North:--The primitive founder of our western civilization. The savage whose traits are palpably writ in our own; the savage whose virtues are struggling for recognition in us. For he, of all men, had the instinct, the passion of freedom.

He was wild, uncouth, romantic, childlike; a barbarian of barbarians--aggressive--direct--cruel.

He, too, wished the Earth; and took a strong grip on it. He was the real man of the west. In him we see ourselves.

He upset the past that he found. He divided, diverted and dammed

HISTORIC SKETCH

its streams--making whirlpools of them. He made a chief-vortex of his own wild desires.

* * * *

Came also the Church, seeking man, to enthrall him; creating a vortex to draw all things, all men, all power.

Came, then, the ages we call dark.

Arose also the institution we specifically label Feudalism.

Appeared also hallucinations, ecstacies, fanaticisms, the Crusades.

Came on the seething and boiling of the cauldron to be called Europe.

Appeared a sombre mist on the north; a shining shifting light on the southwest, south and southeast.

Came fierce reactions as the mongrel civilizations became utterly hybrid--crossed and recrossed; inbred and outbred; a fantastic and miscellaneous riot of cross-fertilizations, with many slow changes and many mutants.

For there had been fierce collisions of races, tribes, clans, remnants. Tooth to tooth, claw to claw was the law in the truculent, lumbering beginnings of nations and the slow rise of monarchism.

Ephemeral empires flitted; no cohesion, nothing to cohere about. It was every man for himself, in the tumultuous struggle for personal power, within a chaotic urge that was seeking stable forms; a rough, heavy flow, with surface upheaved; in waves combining and sinking as in a storm-driven sea of men. And the sky was heavy with the clouds and downpour of superstition.

Such was the weird, rough and tumble shaping of European civilization resting then as now upon the right of might and cunning.

* * * *

Troubadors sang and sneered while monks devoured the land, nobles devoured land and people, and the people devoured each other.

Wars, wars, and more wars.

Intrigue and more intrigue.

Betrayal upon betrayal.

Murder upon murder.

Kill and let kill was the word--the logos of the time.

Rose the Church higher, looming vaster.

With increasing Church came increase of ministering beauty; song; and power, and glory.

With nobles and Kings came opulent parade.
As Church and nobles rose, the people sank,
As beauty increased, squalor increased.

The people fought, worked, dreamed, and listened to story-tellers and wandering minstrels.

In an age of crapulous romance, of fanaticism, cruelty and credulity; an age of illusive faith, renunciation, and despair of this world, slowly the nations shaped, took on semblance of individuality and suggestion of identity. The spirit of nationality was beginning to emerge from the chaos.

Slowly the tornado subsided; continuing, thereafter, an ordinary variable storm. The sky opened and closed here and there in alternate sunshine and gloom--peace and war, and war and peace.

Thus moved the troubled spirit of man--our man.

* * * *

Growing nation pressed on growing nation--the borders ever advancing, retreating, swerving, or collapsing as the greater fed upon the lesser, great gnawed at great; and least had its fangs in the throat of least; each growing nation taking on semi-solidity and a fairly permanent name. But all in a huge house, bitterly divided against itself. Truly dog ate dog in those days; for that was the law. And by the arbitrament of that law, our man stood or fell.

* * * *

Arose schisms and mutinies within the Church, whereon it laid a heavy hand.

Came also universities. For men began to wish to split hairs systematically, and to exercise the brain, as it were, gymnastically.

Came also lawyers anew; and with them the beginnings of regularity, order, procedure, and applied sophistry--the super-refinement of cunning.

Came also agriculture and commerce; bankers and physicians.

Came also a spirit of inquiry--feeling its way.

Came also the so-called free cities; the so-called Republics; and the dawning of mediaevalism; as a new consciousness began to form.

Yet still there were wars upon wars. For, still--might was right, and cunning was exalted.

* * * *

Meanwhile had re-emerged, through oppression and gloom, the original individualistic spirit of the Teuton barbarian; and men had begun thinking somewhat of freedom.

Thinking, a little of freedom, they began to create, a little, in the image of the thought.

And, the while, there were wars and more wars.

When some began to think aloud, the Church, now very powerful, and alarmed accordingly, tore them with its claws; and with its roar damned them. For such was the spirit of the hour. Such was the darkened soul of the Man of that day. Men were brutal, hence the Church was so. For the Church was but a corporate name for men in action.

The mind of the man of that day was constricted. His world was small; and might and cunning both meant right.

* * * *

The vague dream of freedom enlarged a little; clarified somewhat. It was a ferment-dream, foreboding change.

The old order was becoming too rigid, was pressing too hard, was too grasping, was strangling and impoverishing body and mind. A new order cried for shape. Men were awakening; illusions were passing. Heresy, restless mutiny, inventiveness were stalking abroad, or skulking. Men began to see new things; to form new thought-pictures; and wonder. Revolution was shaping.

Science had come--a babe in the manger.

Man began to enquire a little, and then to enquire more. Seeking, he found a little--and then a little more.

Knocking, it was opened to him a little at a time.

Man's intellect was beginning to re-articulate and shape anew.

Semi-Reason began to take the place of phantom faith and fear; it seemed hard. Here began the childhood of the modern man of the west. He was seeking a path to freedom.

Turned pale, the dawn of a new day; a day of protest of assertion, of enquiry of affirmation. The soul of man had passed its mediaeval meridian. The soul of our man.

* * * *

Now came an era of mental inversions. The intellect of the Man of the Past began to right itself concerning certain specific things.

These inversions were called and are still called discoveries. (Thus, when we awake, we will look on Democracy as a discovery; because it will seem to us first of all a huge inversion.)

Thus, a man discovered the physical relation of earth and sun. It was and is the greatest of human brain-achievements, the most prodigious somersault of the mind. The man did not know what he had really done. He attached specific importance to his deed. His world of experience was too small to allow him to know what a big thing he had in reality uncovered. For it was none other than the Phenomenon of Inverted Thinking, --the bane of mankind.

Then came mechanical inventions: the printing press, the magnetic needle.

And then a man drew aside a veil from a vast new land--a sleeping continent. (Whereon we, living and breathing today; talk freedom and achieve slavery.)

* * * *

Came also constitutional Kingly governments.

Came also standing armies, and wars and wars; for the right of might was still held valid by all the people, rich and poor, pious and scoffer, vulgar and learned. The thought held man in a harsh grip,--our man!

Then the mind of man began to grow and ramify vigorously. His free spirit was beginning to flow through the interstices of his own organized self-repression.

Came the steam engine, the power loom and their kindred.

Came also talk of the natural rights of man; and bloody revolution--ushering in the beginnings of a copious brilliant semi-modern day; a day as yet unfulfilled; for might has been nevertheless held right; and wars have not ceased to follow upon wars; and cunning has not ceased to be exalted.

* * * *

Throughout all the swirling, ebullition, upheavals and subsidences of the centuries, the mind of the European Man of the Past has struggled through darkness and entanglements, only to emerge into a fata morgana, a mirage of the Modern--the brilliant culmination of inverted thinking, and the crisis of change.

It is ours to take the bold step forth from inward darkness of phosphorescent gleaming. That vital stride which shall bear us across the threshold of a new thought. Which shall take us out, into the open air, to greet the upright spirit of a clean, new day. A day in which we shall turn our faces toward the average man as serenely as the philosophies and religions of the past turned their backs upon him, as though oblivious of his reality--and careless.

* * * *

The Man of the Past, in his way sought Justice. The way was tortuous, obscurely lighted. He could not detach right from might, nor right from cunning. He dreamed, aspired and fell. Again aspired, again to fall. But at each recurring crisis he aspired higher, and fell perhaps not quite so far. For, somehow, somewhere in his heart sang the small voice of Democracy. He heard it now and then in flitting moments. When not too busy at his engrossing feudal tasks, he heard its song--and was cheered, he knew not quite how or why.

* * * *

So, throughout the duration of prodigious lethargy, nimble-mindedness, and frantic purblind struggle of the past; throughout its brilliancy and gloom of power, its calms and tempests, its upheavals and subsidences, may you and I, standing on the peak of today, hear our story told, as a tale, by the Man of the Past. Told by the Spirit of Man now as it were alone in solemnity; now intimate and near by; at all times multiple as mankind, multifarious as his ways, manifold as his dreams--ever flowing from one into many, from many into one, endlessly interfusing within the action of that great drama wherein we are ever our specific selves, yet ever of the man of the past--and he of us.

Verily it thus seems, all of it, as yesterday, this great past, to us swiftly or slowly moving therein, borne on the broad sustaining pinions of the spirit of man--fancy free, heart free, ever searching man--our Man.

* * * *

CHAPTER 2 FEUDALISM

The most ancient of sanctioned laws is the law of the right of might. It is tacitly approved by the man of today. In his practical dealings he knows none other, except by whim, caprice or benevolence. In theory he speaks of the might of right, which, with him, is a palliative abstraction. Thus is his intellect divided between cowardice and courage, between abstract and concrete, between crooked and straight thinking, as man's intellect has always been divided:--a veritable house against itself.

The inception of the law of the right of might lies within the beginnings of a law of self-preservation at first tacitly assumed, afterward consciously and constructively formulated, and which men have unanimously agreed to call "Nature's first law," because the concept of the right of might has been their own first law and last appeal, not only in large affairs, but in the little and the littlest.

In other words, man has always held that, to preserve himself he must dominate the neighbor or be his slave; for right meant both dominion and servitude.

What may therefore be called pure or unadulterated Feudalism (that is, Feudalism unadulterated by Democracy), meant, in essence, master and slave, and was expressed in fact, in the broad compensatory aspects, dominion and servitude. That is, servitude and dominion moved about the same intellectual center of gravity, which center was none other than that conception of self-preservation in the individual and the mass which evoked the spirit of might and exalted it as right.

Hence, all the civilizations of the past, expressing as they did faith in the righteousness of this theory of self-preservation, are feudal, and, inasmuch as our own civilization is based in practice and in doctrine, upon exactly the same concept it too is feudal.

Hence equally, if in the modern movement of individual and mass thought there comes about a weakening of the notion that servitude is necessary to self-preservation, there must come with it, logically and inevitably, the notion that dominion also, is unnecessary to self-preservation. Such change of thought, therefore, if it comes, will in the nature of things, constitute the intellectual beginning of the downfall of Feudalism as a social doctrine and practical rule of conduct.

Also, in the past the spirit of cunning came forth companion to the spirit of might. Thenceforward the man of cunning and the man of might were right. Both sprang from a normal desire for power. And both became perversions of man's natural powers because of a primary misconception concerning the basis of human self-preservation. It is this weird misconception that constitutes the tragedy of historic man. To this dark tragedy therefore, we give the name Feudalism.

Out of the multitude's dream of the glory of might sprang the coarse warrior. Out of the lowliest dream of the sanctity of cunning glided the humble priest. Out of coarse warrior grew resplendent potentate. Out of humble priest grew resplendent high-priest. Therewith began an alliance between these two. For they stood for the fiercely and subtly attracting and repelling aspects of man's unstable and marvellous intellect warring within itself and yet seeking, within and without itself, stability and peace. Jealousy, envy, fear, suspicion, hatred, mutual tolerance, were the portion of prince and priest. For each needed each. Each was complementary and supplementary to the other. Each was so necessary to the self-preservation of the other that each strove to master and subjugate each--that warrior or witch might achieve sole dominion over the minds, and domination of the bodies and property of men; control and direction of the thought, the will and the energy of the multitudes. That there should be those to have and hold dominion over them for the common good was the intellectual desire and attitude of the multitudes. It seemed to them right. For to them might and cunning, force and craft, wisdom and power, glory and omnipotence were attributes with which they had as it seemed worthily to them, endued and endowed the Gods as the highest renunciation of their social powers in the hope of compensatory salvation from mysterious evil. It was indeed their dream:--their dream of wisdom and omnipotence. For to them sacrifice and salvation, death and transfiguration, were as much one in thought as were servitude and dominion--as vivid as master and man:--they seemed right:--they implied self-preservation:--it was the only way as it seemed to them. It seemed real to them--this phantom of vicarious self-preservation in the persons of the elect and exalted:--as real as it seems to us.

Thus the dream of absolutism, as an ambition and a goal, came boldly and bodily imaged forth of the multitudes to lure on prince and priest. And thus, in the dream of the lowly, came the ferment of man's intellectual madness. For the dream of force and cunning, of glory and power, of dominion and servitude, of master and man, made his world unreal.

Thus the basis of Feudalism is an intellectual conception. For, be it understood, historic man high and low laid stress upon the rectitude of his intellect. He was sure it could not fail him. He made scant allowance for the fact, that, for every position his vainglorious intellect assumed, a convincing response would arise from his senses:--for between the senses and the intellect of man exists a most curious interrelationship of mutual dominion and servitude:--just as the same subtle relationship has ever existed between rich and poor, lowly and exalted, prince and priest.

Thus it was that, in the past, the priest, in his tense secretive ambition, sought theocratic absolutism through wily shifting of the sense of certitude of the warrior, and hence the subjugation of the warrior and the longed-for control of his physical power over the multitudes--that the vicar of heaven might be prince of the earth--for the earth and the multitudes have ever been real to the priest. He alone has glimpsed the reality of power over man. He alone has understood the terrible power of gentleness. He, alone, has perceived all folly but his own.

The warrior also sought a theocratic absolutism, through subjugation of the priest, by shifting his sense of security in graft, and thus seizing upon the control and utilization of the subtlety of the priest's power over

FEUDALISM

the fears and hopes of people:--that the prince of earth might become potentate of heaven. In the view of each, subjugation was the sole evidence of power, and such power alone was deemed by all men to be at once Godlike and earth-like. The multitudes believed that man might become a God. Prince and priest knew that the multitudes could be completely subjugated only through manipulation of this idea. Each so acted. Thus came each at the throat of each, and thus was sometimes priest under-wolf, sometimes warrior, in the keen, icy struggle for dominion as acknowledged leader of the pack that preyed upon the world of men, as the world of men was ready to prey upon them.

Thus were the forming civilizations grandiose, ferocious, intensely imaginative, introspective, esoteric, mystical, verbose and drastically practical. These were the shapings of organized Feudalism, with all its mysticism of rich and poor, strong and weak, darkness and light, good and evil, exalted and lowly. For it was divinely ordained:--so all men said. Thus in our own day we believe our sanctioned ferocious civilization to be divinely ordained. Thus civilization and feudalism have been in fact synonymous terms throughout all recorded history.

It is typical of our traditional view of ancient, mediaeval and modern Feudalism (or, as we call it, the history of civilization) that we have been taught, from the cradle, in season and out of season, in all occasions, in all times and places, to see it completely in reverse of its reality. We have been taught that this phantasm was and is man, instead of being taught that it was and is man's mirage; and that by the guidance of that mirage, we might somewhere find the reality--man:--and that the man-search is the true business of men. For the institution of Feudalism worked in appearance from the top down. The show and parade and semblance of power were all the * the top. In this radiance of reflected power, the source of power, in the thought of the multitudes, was invisible. It has not been officially set forth to us that the spiritual idea of Feudalism had its being in man's self-created vision of the external and miraculous. The vision, the image, of the God was of an immensity of external power and wisdom. God was on high. Hence, with pictorial fitness and literalness, power and wisdom seemed to descend from the God--the highest of all,--to the highest of earth, the potentate and priest, and from them seemed as visibly to descend to the multitudes. Sometimes indeed, as seemed dramatically fitting to an imaginative people, the God himself descended to earth. Hence were the imaginative lowly called lowly, by themselves, and by their exalted. Hence were the exalted called exalted by themselves and by their lowly. For ex-

* Obscurity. Probably should read *at*.

alted and lowly, rich and poor, each possessed each in a marvellous bond of sympathy and union. They worshipped in common a feudal God. And the God-conception is ever in exact accord with the social conception. This same idea plainly survives and is potent with us. It still remains the intellectual pivot of our civilization. Hence with us still exists that same clandestine bond of sympathetic union between rich and poor, powerful and weak, betrayer and betrayed. Each adores each with the old feudal infatuation. Quarrels are but preludes to luxurious reconciliations. We still believe power and wisdom descend from a God, we still believe in the miraculous and in magic. We have not yet learned to identify power and wisdom with ourselves; hence we fail to understand that which is very plain and specific, namely, that force and cunning are but social perversions of our own normal power and wisdom. Hence our thought has remained basically feudal; and our Democracy thus far is little else than a vague, wistful dream not yet grown clear enough to come true:--because we are not yet ready, in our drowsy and luxurious heaviness, to make the required intellectual inversion of our traditional concept of the right of might and cunning.

So the man of the past created his civilizations in the image of his thought, and in the same identical image created he his God. His civilizations, in their flowering thus became the picture, the drama of that idea or thought which he conceived to be most profoundly spiritual, most real, most solid, most nearly everlasting.

Hence, while Feudalism arose in fact out of man's most simple selfishness, it became in its times of glory a marvellous sublimation of that same selfishness. It became, indeed, transfigured into a vast and opulent poem of ferocity, cruelty and cunning--the apotheosis of plunder, graft, extravagance, splendor and abject misery:--and a riot of duplicity:--exactly like our own.

Surely Feudalism was and is a simple and absorbing passion of man. In it he has glaringly displayed one phase of himself--his abnormal ego.

But a new passion is about to arise within the soul of man--the passion of Democracy--which shall inspire his intellect to set forth in unexampled clarity and spiritual beauty that still simpler phase of himself which, during all these ages, he has, in fear, himself kept submerged--in his normal ego. For the passion of Democracy is the passion of the modern world-shaping consciousness of man: the consciousness that power and wisdom reside in and arise from the multitudes; the consciousness that man, normally, is simply unselfish; and that, in the reasoned exercise of that unselfishness, lies the sublimity of his spiritual power, his simplest and cleanest manhood.

So viewed, Feudalism has been man's stupendous, world-old phantasm; his witching mirage; the eidolon of his fear of the All-Life; his altogether pathetic failure to find the simple and sound foundation of his own nature.

Under the sway of the spell of the Feudal illusion, under the powerful thrall of its gorgeous and miraculous and miserable dream, the world of men still sleeps within the great world of Reality.

Verily no passion of a God could equal the passion of man. It is incalculable. Nor has man yet invented a God that could suffer as man has suffered, or aspire as man has aspired. Feudal man indeed curiously underrated his intellectual powers, and, therefore, caught but fleeting and flitting glimpses of his own integrity.

Such is Feudalism:--The great shadow of man's intellectual self-eclipse. The great veil, which he has drawn before the countenance of Life. The opalescent and glamorous mist with which he has obscured the dream-clear purity of vision of his own spirit.

Thus how closely are we of today drawn to the man of the past. In what bond of affection are we. How visibly is he of us; and how noteworthy are we dreaming our new dream of Democracy within his ancient dream of Feudalism. To our dawning and clearing world-embracing and timeless sympathy how vivid, how real is he, as we vision him forth in his long ago!

CHAPTER 3   DEMOCRACY

Notwithstanding the law of predatory and subservient self-preservation is the most ancient, and likewise the most modernly sanctioned of man-enunciated laws, it is a pressing truth that Integrity ever has been and remains the valid law of the cosmos:--that cosmos with which, in spite of his favorite beliefs and unfaiths, man is so integral that in no sense can he get away from it.

That is, while man's intellectually formulated social law has sanctioned might and cowardice because he believed them right, the vast and friendly domain of nature within which he has moved and moves has ever set forth the oneness of all things to be right.

The inception of this law, principle, or urge, or spirit, of integrity

--this most ancient and modern thing in the cosmos--dates back not only through man's intellectual law of selfish self-preservation, but, indefinitely far beyond that to the primordial law, aspect, or urge of self-creation. That is, as we fundamentally and conjointly among all the peoples of the world understand such things, it is the law of oneness of the infinite Spirit, or that, to which we, and all peoples of the past, have, under varying synonyms, given the conventional name, God. For the term God, or its equivalent, has ever stood, among all the peoples of the past, and really still so stands with us as a symbol of what we mean in everyday language by the term, right, or integrity. That is, reliability, safety, security, balance, equipoise, peace, certitude; or in language of wider horizon,--wholeness, creative and preservative power, wisdom and goodness.

It is of the profoundest and simplest instinct of man that he has ever clandestinely as it were, felt himself at one with the integrity of all things; that he has surreptitiously and furtively felt and known himself to be co-continuous with the vast primordial, spiritual integrity, and it is precisely of this deeper faith of instinct, that man's feudalism has been a prolonged intellectual perturbation. And in this perturbation, this aberration, is bound up the drama of his sorrows, and his bitter discontent with life.

Man's turning toward integrity was but an episode of his indolence, of his ease, of his meditative solitude, of his temporary safety. But the moment he set eyes on the stranger (the other man) presto, all was changed, and the calm of universal integrity was dispelled by the storm of seeming individual diversity. For, lo, this other man, the neighbor of earth, was forsooth a stranger, hence an obscure enemy. And yet man has also ever been more than ready to welcome this stranger, if but he dared; for in him, also, he has perceived an obscure friend. Thus are seen the original urges of Feudalism and Democracy. Feudalism has ever been the urge of that phantasmal fear or lust which regarded the other man as enemy or prey; Democracy ever that urge which regarded the other man, the stranger, as friend, likeness and equal. Hence, in the historic drama of the civilizations the sane kindly and original urge of Democracy ever has been the victim of the subsequent fiercely treacherous and destructive delusion and mania of Feudalism. That is, Feudalism in essence, has ever stood and now still stands for man's mad intellectual treachery to mankind, Democracy for his fidelity. The one tends toward spiritual disintegration and the betrayal of the heart, hence toward social downfall, and the other toward social strength, stability and wholesomeness.

So it is with Feudalism and Democracy, and so have these twain ever seemed to war within the being of man, and thus has man ever kept his intellect and his heart estranged. And thus has man oscillated in his career, now coldly intellectual, now feverishly emotional, now fast, now loose, now honest, now dishonest, now rich, now poor, now victor, now vanquished, now eminent, now obscure, now virtuous, now vile, now hero, now dastard. Thus during all his career man has known no balance but the beguiling equilibrium between his cold lust and his hot lust. It is true that in the cold bursts of his asceticism and the hot bursts of his abandon, man has equally achieved marvels--marvels of intellect, marvels of emotional crisis and of physical accomplishment. But it is just as true that he never knew where he stood. His feet have been off the ground, and his head and heart have separated and wandered anywhere and everywhere. For he ever thought himself a law unto himself--which was actually right, but passingly wrong. In man's sane social balance, it is strictly fitting that he be a law unto himself, for in such poise he recognizes and acclaims the fundamental law of integrity; but in his feudal unbalance, (really his feudal insanity), when he declares himself a law unto himself, it is but to declare himself anarchic to the primordial law of integrity. For it means simply this: that he wishes to apply a law to himself of his own fantastic devising--he forgets that there are others. But the real man, the sane man knows that no law can apply validly to himself that does not in equal and fullest measure apply to all others, and this corrective thought must tend at once to bring into equilibrium his overturning and collapsing intellect which has led him into the ghost-like supposition that a social law might be found, applicable to him alone, and not equally, unequivocally and fully to all men.

Thus are the appeals of our modern predatory great ones, to a "higher law," both right and wrong, both fantastic and normal. Wrong intellectually, right in this that the predatory urge is, after all, but a profoundly obscure desire to be of use to others. It is but an intellectual perversion of the normal activity of the brain:--the decay of the real ego.

There is a fundamental urge in man which causes him to hunger for work, which causes in him a deep desire to give his whole life-energy to the service of his fellow men. And this urge is clearly discernible to the sympathetic eye, throughout all the history of Feudalism. In other words, man's heart has always been right. All his confusion has been wrought by his vanity and absurdity of intellect. The splendid urge of his imagination and his will has been misconstrued by him, and it is his own intellect that has prepared the pitfalls into which he has sunk, even as he believed himself on the scent of something socially real. It is not that Feudalism represents what is bad in man's heart--for there is nothing bad there. It really represents the instability, the incertitude, the perplexity, the bombast, the stubbornness and, alas, the cowardice of his intellect.

If you wish to know how true and trite this is all set forth in the reeking feudalism of our modern democracy, you have but to touch with your fingertip anywhere--no matter where. Try first the places in which you are convinced it cannot possibly exist:--There you will find it in its over-ripeness. Touch with your finger the high places, the sacred places, the choice places, the pure places, the reputable and eminent places--you will find it there--but you will find it everywhere else--in the obscure and lowly places as well:--and you will find it, equally, throughout all the past.

The feudal desire to do "good" to others is the righteous as well as the wicked man's delusion; for he has omitted, first, to take account of himself. He believes he is really a law unto himself. Truly he is; but not unto himself alone.

It is not because men are essentially vicious, that they are feudal, it is merely because they do not clearly understand the essential and concrete nature of their relationship to their fellows, to the earth, and to the spirit of integrity.

The discernment of this spiritual relationship is therefore of the essence of Democracy:--for Democracy is the New Way. And the unfolding of a law of self which shall likewise be the integral law of all, is the manifest mission of the man of today. Else why regard with such wistful interest the man of the past!

It will be seen therefore that what we are here choosing to call Democracy or The New Way, is but the ancient primordial urge within us of integrity or oneness. And it is this very urge of nature (Nature's true first-law of preservation), that is awakening within the heart of modern man the desire to seek a fundamental law of social integrity or oneness, wherein each man shall be truly a law unto himself. For that basic law shall imply the liberation of his free creative and integral spirit. It shall be an organic law, or human utterance, not for one man or a few men, but for all men.

This is of the essential nature of Democracy. For Democracy and the oneness of all things are one. Thus, even within the depths of historic feudalism, one perceives the primal urge of man's spirit toward Democracy.

So, if feudal man has been a wanderer and a seeker, far from himself, far from man, far from the earth and far from his God--Democracy is but his home-coming.

The tragedy of the man of the past lies in this, that his unstable intellect led him to believe that his normal power consisted in dominion over his fellow men; that is, in the right and therefore the rightness of might and cunning.

It obscured to his common sense the manifest fact that cunning is but the perversion of a normal desire to accomplish useful and beneficent social results, just as force is but a perversion of man's natural power to create social integrity, beneficence and peace.

Thus, since Feudalism has for foundation and superstructure a false attitude of the intellect, and as its entire fabric of thought, in all its aspects of institutions, manners, methods and processes is becoming daily more clearly artificial, futile, extravagant, mischievous and cruel, it cannot longer stand as an intellectual proposition, but must crumble and fall before the searching powers of modern critical and creative integrity of thought. Its phantasmal conception of the dual nature of man must vanish before the increasing light of our clear and radiant conception of man's reality, the inexhaustible fertility of his powers, and the vividness of his integrity.

In the course of Feudalism the head was wrong, the heart essentially right.

In Democracy both head and heart are right.

Thus throughout all history the vast phantom of Feudalism filled the Earth and the Heavens.

But today:--The free spirit of man draws near!

CHAPTER 4 THE MULTITUDES

It is said that human nature always has been the same. That is true. But it has not been pointed out with suavity and persistence that human nature has ever expressed itself through two significant phases or aspects, which, by whatever name they hitherto may have been called or miscalled, we are here for most pressing purposes of reinforcement naming the feudal and the democratic.

To be sure, much has been said concerning good and evil. Variously it has been assumed that good and evil are abstract external powers acting upon man while independent of him, yet he not independent of them. And yet good and evil manifestly are man himself appearing alternately in two phases or modes of himself, both arising from the same radical or root of self and readily explaining him, even to himself--would he but pause and listen.

There is no dualism in good and evil. Man merely has thought there was; it has been his spectacular divertissement. There is no dualism in the cosmos. Man flippantly or solemnly has thought there was; it has been his opulent dissipation. The universal spirit is integral. Hence is man integral. The belief in dualism has been man's specific self-poison secreted from his luxurious fear of seen and unseen Life; his turning in upon himself as a lover of himself, now in panic of incertitude, now of certitude. He would not let himself alone. He did not know how to do so in a quiet way. In this belief, therefore, lies the kernel of his philosophy of despair:--his extremest, most tranquil and most solitary luxury:--the epitome of his self-complacence, his self-pity, his self-love, his self-aversion and his self-absorbed, intellectual disdain of his own manhood. He would not accept it: --always he made a mental reservation:--a terrible protest when self-driven to extremities.

Feudalism has ever been the potent expression of man's illusion of dualism. In it are involved the coupled and dual notions of Master and Man, of Rich and Poor, of Good people and Bad People, of good God and bad Devil, of Vice and Virtue. So vivid have such mental images seemed to man, so real, so specious, so certain, so right, so changeless, so graphic, so sharply projected upon the screen of his outer world, so God-made, God-ordained, stable, eternal, God-sanctified and God-engloried; that man has not ventured to doubt his senses; has not presumed to suspect their abject and affectionate servitude to his domineering and profoundly unbalanced intellect. Hence he has said: whatever is is right--it must be right because it is.

Thus out of the self-imposed dualism of man's egregious and little-understood intellect sprang Gods of caprice, by turns cruel and kind because feudal man, that is, dually imaginative man was so. Also sprang out of the mournful fatality of his prefervid dualism Gods utterly removed from him. Out of it sprang likewise the bird-like notion that man's soul was separate from himself, even as an eagle and its nest;--a something that had come silently and formidably from the air to inhabit his body conveniently as a house. It seemed to him obvious it must be so; for man in his insistent dualism has been profoundly phantom and most curiously a dreamer and a fanciful image-maker. Therefore always was there a double; always were there two things, not one thing. Hence was his own single thought divided against him. Hence could he not find himself to know himself:--because he was divided against himself and in conflict against himself, in mutiny against himself, in rebellion against himself, and in conspiracy with himself against himself. Still less could he find and know the neighbor--who is but himself. Hence was he divided in his thought against the neighbor, and strove, mutinied, rebelled and conspired against the neighbor. Hence was his thought troubled and phantasmal concerning the relationship of himself and the neighbor, and therefore concerning all other things and all other Gods, and especially concerning his own spirit, his own integrity. Always, therefore, the bewildering and agonizing notion that there was something external and estranged from man. Always the notion that there was something internal and still estranged from him, flattering him, placating him, imprecating him, discrediting him, watching him, intriguing, conspiring, ready as a wild beast to overthrow and destroy him, and yet strangely fearing him and as strangely docile, willing to be slave. Always the notion of two great powers without: Good and Evil. Always the notion of two strange, furtive, abysmal powers within:--Good and Evil. Never the notion of one power without and within:--the All-Spirit, man himself! Under the domination of so arrogant, so melodramatic a fear, hope, distrust, frenzy of incertitude and frenzy of certitude which man so avidly harbored, how could man find man? How could man emerge from his feudalism? From his petulant, fickle, abnormal ego?

It is to this very notion of dualism, this supremely drastic notion of the phantasmal, external, theatrical nature of good and evil, that there was given the sharpest cleavage, the most precise, superb, mystical and elegant separateness by the brilliantly constructive minds which absorbed the notion of loneliness and strangeness and companionship from the people, the multitudes, the lowly, and reared of it vast verbal and ceremonial edifices in philosophies, religions, governments and wars. And yet man ever truly strove to find man. But he believed the neighbor double, while man is surely single; hence he failed to find. And to this failure of the multitudes and of their chosen exalted, the warriors, philosophers, the poets, artists and priests--to this colossally simple failure--we give the name Feudalism. For in it is summed up the breaking of the hearts of the multitudes carrying with them their exalted, in a veritable surf of tidal urge and ebb against that wall of their own uprearing which they called Fate, or God, or the Gods, but which they never called man. Thus through the ages has the notion of good and evil obsessed and distracted the minds of the peoples of the world,-- the exalted, the multitudes, the lowly--earth-creepers, heaven stormers, hell-evokers all, in a liturgy and litany, in a paean and dirge of self-denial--of denial of Life and of man's reality--as they pursued the dual ghosts. For most surely they believed good and evil to be spirits, even as their forebears had believed the darkness and the light, the night and the day to be powerful spirits inscrutable in their great lairs, and coming forth potent for weal or woe. Such is man in the dark side and the light side of his marvellous, fruitful and prodigiously active and fertile imagination. It is in amazement therefore that we regard man when we begin to get a glimpse of his natural powers; and it is with awakening amazement that we regard the multitudes of earth when we begin to realize that it has all come from them; that what they sanction is sanctioned, and that, per contra, not a solitary institution can exist, not a government can exist, not a church can exist, not an army can exist, not a formal God can exist that we do not sanction. Hence it is the multitude that have ever been the primal social power, because the multitudes stand for the individual in mass, and because the multitude itself finds its own center of gravity within its own mass-thought. The mass-thought of the multitudes has hitherto been animated by the conception of dualism-- by the notion of light and darkness as powers, by the outgrowing notion of good and evil as powers, by the notion of a terrible disturbance within the soul, by the notion of complete incertitude and caprice, by the consequent notion of fear and the consequent notion of escape from the bondage of self into the free and open field of servitude or dominion. For to the primitive minded, superstitious and phantasmal man servitude was a form of freedom; that freedom from self-struggle which came to him through yielding obedience. So yielded he obedience to his Gods. Also, dominion seemed to him a form of freedom; another way of escape from lonely self-struggle and self-slavery:--an escape into the open world of conquest, and of creating out of other men a host, an army of offense and defense, that he might carry his struggles into a greater, higher world than his little world of inefficient self:--That he might secure the freedom of glory and power visibly, that he might dominate visibly the terrible powers within and without and be secure; that he might aspire even to emulate the powers of his gods; that he might indeed perhaps himself become a god on earth and thus achieve complete freedom. For man ever has searched for the Gods, has striven to emulate them, to rival them, to dominate them, has conspired and rebelled against them. For man in his heart ached for freedom; for man in his intellect keenly sought freedom--the freedom of dominion or servitude. Also in his heart he wished peace, the peace, the tranquility of a complete dominion or a complete servitude. Also in his spirit he wished peace and freedom:--the freedom of Death or of Life; the peace of a death everlasting or of a life eternal. Thus were the fears, aspirations and conduct of the man of the past essentially the same as the fears, aspirations and conduct of the man of today. But turn his dualism of mind into singleness of mind and you turn Feudalism into Democracy.

The incertitude, the lack of confidence of the multitudes of the past made them timorous, modest, bashful, self-deprecatory, self-abasing, self-effacing--and prodigiously generous, amazingly fluent of heart; quick to anger, quick to anything and everything and likewise slow to anything and everything; hence active minded, suspicious, crafty, fickle; hence slow minded, docile, swinish, contented. Hence resenting change until excited; hence insisting madly upon change when excited. Desiring mostly a change in moods rather than methods. Reviling the rulers if the rulers were tyrant, blessing the rulers if the rulers were lavish. Reviling the Gods if the Gods failed, blessing the Gods if the Gods fulfilled. Such is feudal man, today and then; such the multitudes then and now; such the exalted, the chosen. Such was master then, such is master now--and such is slave. Names change, the names of men and gods, of institutions and processes, methods and customs and manners and clothing; but what was feudal then is feudal now, and what is feudal now was feudal then. It is all the same; for men are all alike and have ever been. The American slave is the Egyptian slave, the Russian slave is the Egyptian slave, the German slave is the Egyptian slave, the Chinese slave is the Egyptian slave. It is all one; and the masters of today are the masters of ancient Egypt; it is all one thought, one motive, one impulse, one urge, one phantasm held in common through the ages by the multitudes of earth and so held in common with them by us, of today.

Thus have the multitudes been ever arrogant and bashful, keen and oblivious. Ever stupidly and sturdily trusting, ever sturdily and profoundly fickle. Thus have they ever stood amazed before their own creations, believing them the while the work of powers on high. Thus have they stood dazed and timid and diffident before that which they created with their own hands and feet and backs, out of the sweat of their bodies and their dreams. Thus have armies impressed them--as though vast glittering armies were not molded of themselves, by themselves,--the multitudes. Thus have temples and palaces and dungeons impressed them, as though temples and palaces and dungeons were not made and dreamed out of the abodes of the thoughts of the lowly, and thus have governments impressed them; and religions; and luxury and pomp; and the appalling pride of caste; thus great engineering works; thus great poems, and the sciences. They all seemed miraculous, divine; they were all simply and intensely human, ineffably of the multitudes, universally of man's spirit. They all arose out of the dreams of the multitudes, from out the fertility and fragrance of earth, and floated on high into the light air of their wonderment, even as vapor of earth's moisture arises and forms in feathery and towering clouds in the firmament. Who would suppose that such cloud-like civilizations could arise to the heights from the sweaty dreams of the forgotten and discredited millions of the earth; surely not a feudal dreamer; surely not a Pharisee.

So, has man, the earth-creeper, been abashed and easily confused, because he knew not himself nor his powers. Hence he has not known the nature and the power of his dreams, nor how surely they come true to his multitudes, whatsoe'er the dreams might be. Man's lowly and resplendent feudal dream has come true as a likeness to him through the ages. He is now softly dreaming the dream of Democracy. It will shape within his image-world, earth-man that he is, and come vividly true to him in the ancient, primal and ever-youthful power of the earth's wistful multitudes. For, lo, it is the dream of the infinite spirit of Integrity shaping true through the aeons. For man is the dreamer. When widest awake he most vividly dreams --and most dramatically acts his dream. And when fullest awake he is nevertheless and always most profoundly asleep and dreaming within the dream of the All-Spirit, as a part thereof. But man seldom awakens--even for a moment:--such dreamer is he! Truly what a spectacle is the drama of man, the lowly creator! and, behold, before him outspread, the multitudes of his Works and his Gods on heavenly high and on the fair Earth. Truly, the Man-Search is worth while.

GROUP IV—DREAMS

Chapter 1 God-Search
Chapter 2 Man-Search
Chapter 3 The Nazarene
Chapter 4 Story of the Church
Chapter 5 The Dream of Power
Chapter 6 The Span of Life

CHAPTER 1 GOD-SEARCH

The dream begins--the God begins.
The dream unfolds--the God unfolds.
The dream fades--the God fades.
Changes the dream--changes the God.

* * * *

Most passionately the man has sought the God. He needed. Out of the depths of his being he desired. In daily life he appealed, clung as to a straw. The God-Search has been and is none other than an unremitting need. The need of self-utterance and self-preservation of the spirit and the flesh of man. The God-cry has been the man-cry: Ever and everywhere.

* * * *

That which we today call God is a dream:
The real lies beyond.
That which we call God was for the Man of the Past a panorama of illusions fatefully shifting.
The Man of the Past sought many Gods:
He found what he sought.
So thirstily did he wish gods that he himself became those gods in his wandering delirium.
His gods were his hopes, for he must find something stable.
His gods were his fears, for still he must find something stable.
So he projected them forth from his spirit far out into his populous world of spirits, hoping thus to find an anchorage to fasten and steady him in his universe and practical world.

* * * *

The God has been the man's enigma, even as Life has been an enigma to man. And in just measure, as man has feared his own life, so has he feared his own God. In just measure as he has abased himself, so has he abased his God, his Lord, even while exalting Him. Thus has man's God, as an illusion, beguiled and betrayed man, because man feared the God which he made, and sought to betray him. It was thus betrayal for betrayal.

Out of his love, man also, in tender moments, thought to make a God of Love, and sought to persuade himself that he loved this god above all his gods. But the man's God of Love proved in his turn an illusion, and loved not man, because man esteemed not man. How could it be otherwise?

* * * *

Thus a guardian God arose on high out of man's passionate fertility: --the radiant God-child of man. And thus were the many ardent, heedful gods, children of man's intimate longing and need. So were his fateful gods picture-children of his fateful spirit. So were his practical gods offspring of his workaday needs. For man, himself a grown child, could not abide alone. He was too frail, too sensitive. He needed the companionship of a God. His soul cried for fulfillment, for surcease, for conjunction, for rejuvenescence, for self-recreation; for man wished to live.

* * * *

There is a God not made by man.
This God man has ever sought, shall ever seek, in spirit,

Approaching, receding,
World without end.
This God is a dream.
Our deep dream is this God.
This God is a wish
Flowing in Life.
To us Life is a dream;
Flowing in us.
Our dream we call the Soul.
Hence the soul dreams its God.
So a God comes ever true to the dream of the soul,
Whatsoe'er that dream may be, whatsoe'er it shall be.

* * * *

Man has stood, in meditation, solitary, in his universe--not knowing it to be his.

In perplexity and in soul-awe he has cried: "Help Lord! Thou art my present need! Send power to know!"--and there came for answer a silence.

And man has tilled the ground with close industry and care; and the drouth came; and he cried: "Help Lord! Help--Lord!! Thou art my need. Send thou now rain to earth!"--and the dry winds blew.

And man has met his man in battle array, and has cried in hope; "Help Lord! Thou art my present need. Send victory thou Lord of Hosts!"-- and the slain covered the field, as the great went down.

Thus the great God, SELF, replied to the dreamer of self. Answered, with a silence; a silence the man of despair could not understand-- for he knew not himself. Hence he bethought him angrily to make another God--or yield--or blaspheme his God, in grief, and re-create him in agony of hope.

And man has met man in battle array, and has cried: "Help, Lord! Send Victory!!"--and Victory came down among the slain and perched on the peak of the banners. And the man said: "Great is God!"--found him good--and bethought him to keep the God.

In moments of peace and plenty man has said: "The Lord is my shepherd, I shall not want."

In hours of alarm and rage he has cried:--"Awake, why sleepest thou, O Lord?"

Trusting not man he deemed his God untrustworthy, fickle--a capricious God with personal aims, that needed watching. Not knowing man, how could he trust man? Not trusting man, how could he trust his God? For all men, and all their Gods, are alike.

Cried the Prophet of Old:--

"Thus saith the Lord: 'Cursed be the man that trusteth in man, and whose heart departeth from the Lord.'"

Thus loomed and was worshipped a mirage God. And man, fearing Life, put not his trust in man, but asserted the wickedness of the neighbor's heart--hence affirmed, in vainglory and illusion, the folly of his own.

Hence was the God a treacherous God, which at the last betrayed His people into bondage--because they trusted in him, who could not trust in each other. The God was of them and their illusion.

Hence the Prophet of Old, cried, in revolt, to his God:--"Why is my pain perpetual, and my wound incurable, which refuseth to be healed? Wilt thou be altogether unto me as a liar? and as waters that fail?"

To soothe his sore need the God replied:--"I will deliver thee out of the hand of the wicked. And I will redeem thee out of the hand of the terrible."

Thus the prophet, with the balm of illusion healed the burn of illusion, in that sad exile whereof it is writ:--

"By the rivers of Babylon, there we sat down,
Yea we wept,
When we remembered Zion.
We hanged our harps upon the willows
In the midst thereof.
For there they that carried us away captive
Required of us a song;
And they that wasted us
Required of us mirth, saying,
Sing us one of the songs of Zion.
How shall we sing the Lord's song
In a strange land?"

* * * *

Thus intense man made an intense God out of his self-infatuation, to whom he poured out all his covetousness, longings, rage and grief; his adoration, his jealousy, his hatred, his treachery, his ambitions; his dreams, his ardent desires--his every thought. Thus intense man picturesquely and passionately worshipped his ego, and communed with it, for man, since the beginning, has talked to himself and listened to himself.

And yet with what curious deprecation the psalmist sang:--"The idols of the heathen are silver and gold, the work of men's hands. They have mouths, but they speak not; eyes have they but they see not: They have ears, but they hear not; neither is there any breath in their mouths. *They that make them are like unto them; so is every one that trusteth in them.*

* * * *

Thus is the God-idea ever a mystic symbol of the Man-idea.
The pure God is ever the pure man.
The dream-God is the dream man.
The Lord God is ever the pirate, the plunderer, in action.
The over-wise God is ever the priest at his work.
The political God is ever the intriguer in his mess.
The property of God always has slaves and lowly ones.

For man creates no God greater than himself:--He can utilize no God better or worse than himself. That he can create and utilize such a God is a figment, an illusion. Let there be no mistake concerning man and his Gods. For the Gods are as plain, as simple, as phantom, as man.

That man has created great and beautiful Gods, sets forth man's great and beautiful powers.

When man frankly worshipped the storm as a storm, he was wiser than when he worshipped the storm as a spirit.

When he feared the night as night, he was truer to himself than when he feared the night as a spirit.

And when he worshipped the sun, as the sun, he was simpler, more thoughtful, more sympathetic, than when he worshipped the sun as a God. But he thought not so; for he, extravagant and over-anxious, neither grasped nor could understand the simplicity and beautiful clarity of his own powers.

Thus as man became more and more sophisticated, his God became sophisticated, secretive and withdrawn.

When man was direct with his God, his God was exactly as direct with man--neither more nor less--for the God was exactly the man.

When man is phantasmal in his intellect, all things react phantasmally upon him. When man shall become lucid, all things will become lucid. When man shall become natural mentally, all things will become natural to him.

So powerful is man's thought that, as he thinks, so the universe reacts upon him. He calls the Universe to himself: Evokes it: It replies. Thus man creates a Universe by the power of his thought. For no universe can exist for him other than such universe as he is willing to select and approve. And likewise, no God can exist for him other than such God as he willingly prefigures in expectancy and welcome. If he creates a God of Hell it is because such God is welcome to his thought, and he embraces such a God in clamorous unison, for his purposes of wrath. If he creates a Prince of Darkness, it is because he wishes such a Prince. Man's thought is powerful beyond the present willingness of that thought to conceive itself. He does not know himself--so eccentric, and hot, and cold, and furious and weak has he been. He has as yet but a glimpse of himself. In his sublime innocency he has told how the God has made revelation of Himself. Let us reveal man to man. Let us write the poem of man: The hitherto unwritten: The poem of the primacy of the Man-Child. This is the modern revelation--The Logos of our Time. For such is the Man-Search--the Poem of Man--in his naked mentality, in his supreme desire to fructify and create with his passionate, virile, impatient intellect. Such is man--the dispenser of power. And such, when calm, is the greatness of man: Passionate, intolerant, arrogant and imperious man--in his desire to overcome the Earth, to breed great children from his brain. For man is the brain of passion, and his hitherto most passionate and daring outburst is the creation of the gods. But man must be calmed in his energy, and the torrent and flood of his thoughts diverted to the lowlands. Thus will man become sane through relief. Man, the wanderer, the seeker, the poet, the aspirer--creating gods as a wayfarer in passing.

Therefore:--As man became mystic the God became mystic. As man became hysteric, the God became hysteric. As man became cataleptic, the God became cataleptic. As man became a trader, the God became a trader. As man made bargains with the God, so the God made bargains with man. As man became a politician, the God became a politician. Hence, as man betrays his fellows, so the God betrayed the multitudes and the elect. As man became mighty, his God became mighty. When man was warrior, the God was warrior. When man was agriculturist, the God was agriculturist. As man began to create, so he invented a Creator-God. As man dreamed in tranquility, so he put forth a God which dreamed in tranquility. As man surmised how the Universe was "made" so he "made" a God, who "made" the Universe that way. Thus has man ever been erratic in his dealings with his God, because erratic in his dealings with himself and the neighbor. His God has been the symbol of his hypocrisy. For man has not sought a God of integrity. Hence has man's God, as a symbol, failed to create peace on earth and good will to men. For man has not wholly desired either peace or good will. What he really desired was either dominion or servitude:--Either to win or to lose. Feudal man could have no use for such God of integrity other than to beguile the multitudes therewith and thereby; and the multitudes had no permanent use for such God:--For the multitudes wished to win or lose.

Man has ever hoped that he might at once be crooked and straight; and if not both, then successfully crooked. He has not in all his history hoped to be straight alone. Hence has his God been a symbol of specious duplicity.

So soon as man desires in his heart to be honest, just so soon will he create an honest God--an image of his own integrity.

So long as man is a liar, he will have for his God an omniscient and omnipresent liar, an infinitely wise beguiler.

So long as man is himself a man-destroyer, he will have a man-destroyer for his God: A glorious and kindly destroyer, a parasite-God, one that glories in the opulent abasement of the poor and unfortunate; one that gives to those that have, familiarly, and takes as familiarly, from those that have not.

Whatever the social view is, such is the God-view. In times of master and man, the God is a mighty ruler, the man a sinful slave. In all the God-images, the social status is ever taken for granted, always was. In times of poetic imagination, the God is a poet and highly imaginative. In times of wickedness and downfall, it is the God that sorrows and is bereft of his people. Thus is the heart of the people the heart of the God; the soul of the people the soul of the God--the thought of the people the thought of the God.

This is the marvel of the bond between man and his God:-- it is the historic self-love, self-chastisement, self-regulation, self-destruction and self-glorification of man. Truly man has ever celebrated himself: in God-images of his moods and whims and passions. Endless are the aspects of his Gods. And when, at times, he has had one Great God, ruler of all the Gods, then was that God symbol and vast image of man's sublimest hopes and fears and momentary understandings.

As God-maker, Man has given us a glimpse of his inexhaustible natural powers.

Now let him try his skill and power at man-making.

Still, the God-idea has always been man's great balance; willy-nilly, it stood for his own notion of integrity--such as it was. He could not exist without it. He cannot exist now without it. There is no such thing as Atheist. The word is a misnomer, a no-fact. For he who says there is no God has merely a particular God-symbol of his own. For the no-God idea is but a phase of the God-idea. The God-idea is perennial. The God is the Ego. It must therefore last as long as man lasts--and must change as man's thought changes. It must range in beauty and clarity and power as man's thoughts so range; and likewise, it must so range in cruelty, in hypocrisy, in inhumanity.

    Therefore it is not wholly in derision that we view the men of the past as more or less futile and humorous and pathetic God-maker. Such view is far from the purpose of our Man-Search. We wish to search man in his prodigious and heart-rending follies. To find why he has broken his heart without just cause:--why he has broken his heart for a phantasm. And, further, if we here set forth man broadly to view, in his dramatic role of God-maker, it is but to look steadfastly into his ego that we may see, therein, in that selfsame creative power, the vast, unused power of man to create man in the image of integrity. It is to weigh and solidly judge his appearing power to create a new civilization in the image of his integrity. It is to balance his historic power to create *Gods* in the image of *Master,* against his evident collateral power to create *Man* in the image of *Man.* This is the very essence of the Man-Search. Hence is the God-Search the Man-Search, and the Man-Search the God-Search. They are one. And it is man, primordial and eternally youthful man, the ancient artistic and extravagant dreamer of the Gods, who is to become the modern sane dreamer of Man. Hence are we seemingly pitiless and iconoclastic; for, to the feudal imagination, with its profound and phantasmal fear of life and of the reality of man, Democracy seems indeed pitiless and destructive. To the feudal mind, Democracy seems likewise a terrible phantasm. For the feudal harbors naught but phantasms and it can harbor naught else; that is its psychic quality. Hence, saturated with the traditions of caste, it cannot grasp the sublimity and clarity of the idea of human equality. Hence, with far-focused vision, it cannot short-focus upon those powers that are clearly natural to all men, nor perceive the reach and certitude of those powers.

    Hence it is that the Feudal-God-Idea is extravagant, wasteful and futile. It is too unscientific. It costs too much in blood and sorrow, and the degradation, through folly, of man by man.

    Thus the bond between man and God is at once beautiful and terrible:--For the God-idea is the most powerful of ideas--the most searchingly potent: The most far-reaching in its action and reaction. And yet truly God has been a little thing to make so small a thing as man so much trouble. There is a grim and ghastly humor in it all. And yet he who is devoted to man, and loyal to man even in his follies, must feel toward man's many gods of many moods, the thrall of affection and pity:--a tenderness toward the God-children and the men-children who created them in the garden and the nursery of the beauteous savory Earth: Under the stars, under the sun, within the shadows and the dusk, amid the moonbeams, on desert and river and lake, on mountain peak and in dell and dale, by the mighty sea, in the sombre forests: Where the man-child was--there was the God-child with him at his call. And the two communed, embosomed both, in the sweet amplitude of Life:--and they talked to each other of Death; and what it all meant: these two children that went forth every day in the garden of the world: and what the two wished--they became: So sang they at times the song of Life--so danced they, at times, the dance of Death:-- These two, together.

CHAPTER 2 MAN-SEARCH

By the power of what light within or without, has man hitherto customarily sought man? In what light has he expected to see him? In the light of selfish self? The light of the law of the jungle? The transfiguring light of abnormal ego? Has man with open eyes sought the neighbor, or with eyes astigmatic and pre-judging? With mind wide open in welcome for him, or held as a door suspiciously against him?

Has man really sought man? Has he gone forth fully intent upon finding? Has he sought him busily, determined as busily not to find? Has man with keen calculation avoided the real man? Has he held him at arm's length? Has he erected a barrier, a wall of feeling and thought, a wall of fear and doubt and distrust and cruelty, of utter selfishness and vanity and hypocrisy and benevolence and charity, and the fiction of good will between himself and the neighbor?

If not, what does caste mean? What does master and man mean? What do wars mean? What does the so-called struggle for existence mean?

And what, then, do broken hearts mean? What means the warrior-man, what the priest, what the politician? What does the "successful" man signify for us, what the "self-made" man, what the parasite? What do rich and poor mean, what do lowly and exalted mean? What does the outcast mean?

What, then, do you and I mean? What do all men mean?

How, then, are we to interpret history? How then are we to interpret ourselves, if there has hitherto been a valid Man-Search? By what light then, within or without, are we to see ourselves, and interpret ourselves, and thus know the Man of the Past, and the man on the street?

Surely, there has been no valid Man-Search by the many, and there has been no sane, clear Man-Search by the few. There has been a man-hunt and a man-plea:--feudal man, hunting feudal man and pleading for him; and in the hunting and pleading glimpses were caught here and there of what was deemed a super-man. All of which was moonshine and the dance of death therein; for the normal man was never sought. He was assumed to be negligible and not worth the seeking.

Yet there has always been a general and a special sense of mutual aid, of tolerance and dependence. For, somehow and in some way, men had to cling together, since they all feared Life. Leadership, therefore, was desired, was deemed requisite, and was paid for. The weak and simple, and the strong but simple, paid a price to warrior, politician and priest for services rendered and to be rendered. The price was high. It bred ambition then, it breeds ambition now. It sets agoing violently the dream of power, of gluttony, of over-much of everything. It hardens men's minds so that they can behold suffering unmoved. It awakens a monster in the dream of possession. It has kept and keeps men apart, this terrible price. It evoked the dream of exploitation, this high price:--this premium set by the multitudes upon the powers of might and cunning; this prize offered by the multitudes to those who should betray them in the name of glory.

The average man is not weak. He merely thinks he is. He thinks so from force of habit, because of the grip of tradition, because of his absurdly false education, because of a varied and curious self-deprecation, an over-valuation and an over-awe of externals, an over-confidence in the powers of might and cunning, and a total misunderstanding and undervaluation of his own natural powers. For the average man will not search to find in himself the normal man.

He need not pay to be exploited under the guise of leadership. He need not foster the predatory. He need not warn the parasite.

For he is getting now a daily education in the practical way of Life. He is beginning to see something new and novel to him within the stage-setting of the social play. Its traditional hidden secrets are becoming open secrets.

To the millions of men object lessons are coming very thick and fast, and they are coming too plain to be misunderstood. They are brutal lessons. Disillusioning, and yet awakening.

You are going to the public school now. Going to the great free but costly school of real life. There they are curiously watching the veils, rising seemingly of themselves, one by one, in an impressive transformation scene, as the plain ways of crafty men are set forth so unmistakably that each average man may now see, therein, his own ways, sharply stated.

It is a new school and a good school, for it is a strictly modern and plain school which all the people are attending every day. They are learning the way the thing has been done; the magical way of doing treacherous things, the magical and glorified way of stealing, of lying, of murdering.

No man need now wear the dunce's cap.

Formerly the children, only, went to school. Now at last it is the turn of grown men also. The time has been long in coming, but it is here. The average man needs the training. His great need is to see complicated things in a simple way, that their underlying simplicity may reveal itself to him, and he thus acquire the rudiments of the great and only art of plain-seeing, plain-feeling, plain-thinking, and plain-doing.

The average man may now affirm his manhood if he choose. Such thing was not deemed possible in the past, either by himself or by the exalted parasites which he harbored in his fantasy of fear. But it is possible, now.

To achieve this he must pay the new price. That price is none other than the immediate abandonment of his own private rascality, his own private superstitions, his own particular recklessness, his own special and general irresponsibility, his absurd and destructive unwillingness to think beyond himself, to feel beyond himself and his private prejudices. It is to these vices that he is and ever has been slave, not to any potentate warrior or priest of the past, or any high financier, captain of industry or politician of the present. No man is or ever was, or ever could be, slave to another man. The average man is now and ever has been slave to himself alone, and his enfranchisement, his freedom rests now, as ever, with himself alone.

The mighty have ever been but the mirages, symbols, the explanation of the average man; the little things mentioned are the origins of the mirage. The small every-day perfidies and stupidities of men are the realities that fertilize all the big rascalities and all the big stupidities because, forsooth, men do not see the neighbor with open eyes; because, they habitually see him by and in a false light.

Man may therefore now substitute the new price for the old, if he will. Has he the nerve? Can he, as yet, see straight enough, think straight enough, feel straight enough and act straight enough to accomplish the thing in himself. Or is he still intoxicated and maudlin with the old-time luxury of self, and thus an easy victim of the beguiler, high and low, eminent and obscure, rich and poor?--for the betrayer is of all men, and all things to all men.

It is a little thing, a simple thing; but it means self-control. Has he that self-control? Can he muster the resolve? Does he see himself clearly, or is he still in fact a weakling? If this latter were true, then would our man-search be ended, and man found. It would have been proven that he is too luxurious, too sentimental to be free.

And yet we, climbing to the towers, there looking far abroad to the horizon of mankind, descending to the level ground, prying familiarly, sharp and near, we are not yet satisfied, we are still searching. The searching that men have done in the past does not suffice us. It was not conclusive, clear. We are not satisfied with their light within or without. It was not the true light of man. The modern light is better: Still, it is not clear enough; but it is growing daily clearer. It is growing white, this modern light: Much like the sunlight. The old light was weaker--more like the moonlight and the starlight.

It is our dream to see ancient and modern man set forth in outline, clearly defined; to have him accurately weighed in mind and heart, in thought and deed, and unequivocally known. To see the character of his thoughts very plainly shown: so plainly that he will know them as his own. That is our dream: it will surely take shape. It is now beginning to take shape in the world of men, for man now is being searched by man in earnest, in a new way. He is being examined high and low, rich and poor, eminent and obscure, present and past, by a new light within and without. He is being put under the microscope, his motives searched, his guiding thought searched, his acts searched, the near and far-reaching effects of his thoughts and acts searched. His attitude toward the neighbor is being carefully examined; and by what light within and without he confronts the neighbor, by and in what light he regards all men. The quality of this light is being carefully examined. We are much less impressed now, by what men say than was the man of the past. We prefer to scrutinize what they do. We prefer to asume as a working basis, that what men do and have done toward their fellow men explains exactly what they think concerning man. And on this basis we will determine whether their thoughts are harmless or injurious to men. We are enquiring thus what "the survival of the fittest" means. And thus we examine the "standard" thoughts, the "classic" thoughts of men. We put them in contrast and in harmony with acts. We must know all. All must be opened up. All the dark corners must be explored. Not a cranny left unexplored. There must be no let-up, no hesitancy, no bashfulness, no timidity, no fear of man or God, no superstition concerning man or God:--but one, single, fixed resolve to search all, to know all, to bring all into the open, to search man to the core, find that core, to ascertain its exact value, to cast aside that which is worthless, to cherish that which is of genuine value and worth, here and now, for the good of the man of today, and for the good of the man to come.

It is a serious business. It must be carefully and accurately done, relentlessly pushed to a conclusion, once and for all established, and man's real nature defined. We have had enough of mystery, of wonder and of Phantasm, let us now have the clear light. This is the new man-search, the real man-search, the new school. This is what the dawning of Democratic thinking and feeling means:--that the people are to be bitten awake, and forced to do their own thinking, by the folly, the incompetence and the ignorant cruelty of the privileged few, that the people must sting themselves awake to a realization of their own folly, incompetence and ignorant cruelty. They must become aware, also, of the value of that good within them which has been theirs always, is now and ever shall be--of that very quality which makes them men, dependable and sound; of that, precisely, which they have hitherto quite stupidly denied and belittled; of that of which they are now, as of old, curiously ashamed, because they deem it almost jocularly small, simple, negligible--this splendid urging of creative good in them:--their one sound, sane and lovable possession.

This is our dream. For there are modern dreams as well as ancient. Let us not forget that.

By the character of the dream, the dreamer is known. Let us not forget that either. Let us not be ashamed to dream: For that is all we do anyway.

There is much to dream about in our modern day! Fine new

dreams. There is, for instance, a new man to dream about. There is quite certainly a new civilization to dream about. There is common sense to dream about:--that new common sense which is, plainly enough, the beginning of practical Democracy.

And there is a new beauty to dream about. The beauty of a new day and its new doings. Its splendid new undertakings, its vast adventures. And there is kindness to dream about; the kindness of a new day and its clear new deeds as between man and man.

There is a new art of expression to be dreamed about. That new and splendid art to be of the real life of a wide-awake people, in which new, joyous and natural uses shall be satisfied, as simply, in terms of a new fitness, and a new propriety and warmth.

Let us not be ashamed. For to be not ashamed is in itself a new art for the people. And out of this new art will spring all the new arts. To be not ashamed is the very soul of inspiration: the beginning of the natural outburst of the song of man.

There is much to dream vividly about, plenty upon plenty, O men of today! The materials of inspiration are right with us and about us. It is for us to see them, for us to hear and feel them, to recognize the urge and the call and the need, and at once to do! For the new art will be the art of fittingly doing all things in accord with man's integrity and the beauty and the power of his spirit.

We do not dream enough, we moderns. We are to dream more; dream wisely, in a clean purposeful way.

We are to dream of the reality of man, of the reality of his life, of a joyous life, a full and well-lived life for him; a life that counts;--a man that counts. For if man, the real, living personality--any man--does not count, what counts?

How can a God count, when the average man does not really count?

We are thus to dream real and right dreams of human sunshine and gladness, with the joy of efficiently living and of efficiently doing, for why live if not to do? And why do if not to live? Dreams of health of body and mind; of radiant health, of health that shows in a lustrous eye. Dreams of the clean, sound, courageous and devoted heart. Dreams that count for us all--that really avail. Dreams of integrity; gentle, manly, spiritual integrity--livable, lovable and delightfully valuable to all mankind, over all the earth.

So must we dream, naturally and intelligently of man. For he is worth dreaming about. He is filled with splendid native power.

It is such dreams that are apt to make a present and a future for us; something we can take hold of with out * minds, something which shall give to our thoughts a definite aim, a clear purpose, a warm unifying inspiration and aspiration, with one clear, sane and ever in view--The liberation, development and utilization of what we are beginning to know as man's efficiency in all his faculties, all his capacities, all his uses. That is, the freeing of the real spirit in the real man. That is worth while.

Then will our dream spontaneously shape into a new civilization, a civilization that shall be true to man, and which, for that basic reason, shall be unending in purpose, inexhaustible in fertility:--just as man himself is inexhaustible in his natural powers, his splendid powers.

That is a dream worth while.

That dream, we can achieve.

It is living in us all. It is altogether natural that we dream it. It is as completely natural, as the dream we now enact is completely a caricature and a barbarism.

Arouse, sleepers, our hour is at hand!

For the multitudes are the slumbering gods,

Remember the multitudes!

In them lies the power of creation, of sanction, of denial.

In them lies the all-powerful working will.

In them is the voice that says Yea!

The multitudes of earth are awakening, like seed wheat in the springtime, they are pushing forth, from their ancient dream of the soil, the air, the forests, the seas, the mountains, the deserts. For the multitudes have been the earth-dreamers, and because of their faithful dream of the earth, they shall inherit the earth, as was said of old, by him who gave his life for the multitudes, by him who said: "I am Life."

Each man knows his heart.

Each man knows that he has the power of choice.

Each man knows that choice is everything.

Each man knows that to choose right is to choose well. It is simple.

Each man knows that to choose well is to do well.

Each man knows, to a living certainty, that to do well is the clear mission of man.

Each man knows that it is for this that he inhabits the earth.

Each man knows clearly, in his heart and his mind, that this is his sole reason for being. That thus, alone, can he justify his existence.

* * * *

* Obscurity. The context suggests that this should read *our* instead of *out*.

So dream the new dreams--dreamers all!!
Dream the dream of the awakening multitudes.
Help dream the dream of man and mankind.
This is the right road at our parting of the ways.
This is the first forward step on the new right road.

This is the law, without exception:--the law of the life of the multitudes.

The law the world of men has searched for through the long ages.

The one law of self-preservation.

The splendid law of self-creation, of self-utterance, of self-efficiency of the multitudes of earth.

So shall we dream to see a people self-created in the image of its plain and clear integrity.

Then will human life cease to be the mirage and phantom it has been and the reality of civilization will surely emerge in the image of this new thought, this new wish, this new will, this new desire of the heart of the multitudes for the whole fair earth.

This is the law which the spirit of the All-Life is seeking to awaken to conscious recognition and acceptance in the spirit of all men today.

This is the Messianic law of the world's people, which, since the beginning, have dreamed to be truly free.

We shall arrive.

* * * *

Now are we, earth-wide, awakening from the mystic dream of the past. Push on! All! Over all the earth! Push on! in the new Man-Search.

All ye dreamers dream on, work on, and the dream will come true. For it is a dream of thought, of action, of reality. It is indeed a dream of simple common sense, of simple common honesty, of simple common humanity; that is, of simple common kindness.

It is a dream to be dreamed by all in the open daylight, within the practical every-day working world of men and their thoughts and their doings.

The dream to be dreamed when we are all widest awake.

More than that:--It will be the convincing sign, the proof, that we are all awake.

Then shall we cohere over the earth as one people, with one purpose:--the good of all, the free spirit of each. That is the real Individualism. That is the real Collectivism. That is the real Democracy.

* * * *

It is now ours to invert the thought of the past. To set it right side up, right end to. We have the power because we are beginning to see straight, to feel straight, to think straight, to act straight. That was the only power needed.

* * * *

So let us dream this kindly and strong dream of dreams, supreme among all the dreams of all the peoples of the earth. We have seen something of man in his instability and folly. Let us seek to find and know him in his superb integrity, even though to find him we must walk through the valley of the shadow of death.

Man must now take an accounting of himself. In that accounting he will, for the first time, behold in himself the phantasm of the past, and for the first time will see likewise the real world of things and thoughts and men reflected within himself; and will understand it and himself.

It is simple.

It requires but the consciousness and the will.

That consciousness, that will, are becoming ours.

* * * *

Many were the prophets, poets, and teachers of yore who caught gleams and flashes of this truth. For this truth has been ever present. To see it is not new, but to see it clearly, to hold it steady, to put it to use, is the modern power. Efficiently to utilize this power, the modern modern * mind must completely rid itself of the ideals of warrior and priest, of trader, of parasite and politician, that is to say of the hitherto exalted conceptions of what these, historically, have stood for as the elect of earth, namely, the right and the power of might and cunning, the sanctity of betrayal, the sacro-sanctity of exploitation. In place of these must be reared on high in the minds of men the conceptions of the inexhaustible power and right of man's integrity:--the clearness, cleanness, sanctity, serenity and power of his free spirit, and this must be held universally true, not for one man, not for a few men, but for all men, for the multitudes who shall come thus into their heritage of the spirit and of the earth. This is what liberty means. This is what equality means. This is what fraternity means. These are not

* The repetition is in the MS.

academic phrases. They are true word-symbols of man's reality:--They stand for the intuitive and profound however dim perception by men, of the reality of what we are here calling Democracy. Truly there have been teachers and prophets. But the multitudes of the whole earth were not ready. It was still winter in their souls. The warming commotion of an Earth-springtime had not come. Hence there could have been no valid Man-Search by the multitudes; and until the multitudes should seek man, man could not effectively be found; for of what avail was it for one man, or a little coterie of men to find man? It is only what the multitudes, what the peoples of the earth, broadly speaking, think and do and sanction, that counts, that ever did count or that ever will count:--Witness the tragedy of the Christ!

CHAPTER 3 THE NAZARENE

The hand of Rome let go the floods of religions, as reservoirs pour when dams are destroyed; and such commingling of the waters of the spirit, the world had not known.

It was a time of agitation and flux, as current moved within current, and wave rose upon wave, in an oceanic unrest within the souls of the men of that day. Its spiritual vortex formed in Judea. For there, in the world of that day, lay the spot midway between the center of aggressive militant thought, and the massive lethargic religions and philosophic traditions of the Orient, the dilettantism of Greece, and where flowed slowly on, the turbid stream of Hebraism.

It was a dark world there, a world of servitude of old, a world of despotism anew, for the heel of Rome was firmly on the neck of the multitudes.

It was a dark world there and then for the inner man. A world of sombre thoughts, a world of mirages, of sorrows, that centered in the little world of Galilee--a nothing on the broad earth.

It was a dark world for the outer man. Bondage, he and his forebears had known of old; bondage he still knew. He knew his body was not his own. He believed his soul not his own, for it was time of Master and Man. The Roman ruler was God.

Long and long had caste prevailed; and the pride and the shock and the misery of caste had taken a firm parasitic grip of men, body and soul. It was a world of disgust and splendor. It was a world of sadness for the vacant many. It was a hopeless world for the many. A world of longing, of questioning, of sour, fermenting, anxious speculation, commingling in a smear of brutality, pessimism and gloom.

So huge, far-spreading, overwhelming was the sway of Rome, that the many, the multitudes, felt themselves unworthy, transitory feeble, negligible, inconsequential, unavailing.

Misery was no new thing to these vacuous, dreamy multitudes, but their sorrows sharpened now and then into poignancy under the ever-present pressure of that power whose center to glory lay far over the West, but whose hand was instant and mighty in the nearest hamlet, and fast and close upon the meanest man.

Predatory systematic selfishness and Parasitism was the official order of the day, and pessimism the daily meat and drink of the multitudes. Feudalism, in the risen power of Rome, had taken on a new aspect of stupendous expansion, brilliancy and centralization; and the mass of men was spread thin on one dead level of nullity. There was none to affirm life to the multitudes, and yet the multitudes vaguely dreamed of Life, even while the mighty they had chosen for masters, denied them the fullness thereof. Force had become supreme; and the complex and already overstrung Roman world of men was held immovable in the grip of a universal parade of power, impersonated mighty and mobile in the legions. For the legions, be it not forgotten, were men of the multitudes, who would kill the neighbor.

But Rome, the magnificent, the clean, the disdainful, let the diverse multitudes alone in their contemptible local religions. Hence, because of repression of body, because of suppression of political and social thought, men's minds, which must needs be active or die, became grotesquely sensitive to the religious emotion and its limitless world of speculative luxurious excitements and phantasmal compensations.

Such was the world of that day; for the world that counted was the world of Rome.

Into that great, sordid, orderly world must we enter in spirit. Into the little province of Palestine, and its littler Galilee, and its minute Nazareth, must we enter, with hearts and minds inclining, if we are to form even a faintly equitable conception of that delinquent * element in our social fabric and environment of today that we, from force of habit, call Christianity.

For that world, then, was visibly ripening for a new birth, a new advent. The unique repressive force of Rome itself was solidifying an aspiration in the sodden substratum of the hearts of men, even within the sanctuaries of their self-abdicating souls.

Into that lower world of luxurious despair, and of level misery, was to come a strange new word, an incredible, passing affirmation of life. A word whose message had meaning we are to weigh and ponder.

The materials of religious thought then pouring into men's minds, were of inestimable richness and variety. They came in huge streams.

Came, from the then long-ago, the stream of Vedic thought. Came the splendor of imagery of the immaculate Brahman, and his one god of mind, and that god's exhalation of the universe, and therewith and therefore of the world, and of man and his spirit, and so held in Brahmanical balance of reality by the Mind of Minds, putting forth sensation after sensation, emanation after emanation, beginning with a primal trinity, of which the Brahman was first, the warrior second and the agriculturist third. That is, the Creator, the Destroyer, and the Preserver of both Creator and Destroyer:--that is, the agriculturalist, preserver of both priest and warrior.

Came from India, also, the later, powerfully intellectual and semi-democratic doctrines of Gautama Buddha, with his incidental toleration of a god, and his tragic response to the misery of life, in a dream and assurance of a death that should be end-all--eternal oblivion.

Gautama found inspiration in the living death of the multitudes about him. Of such horror was their lot, that he, crying out in an agony of spirit and a sweetly deep tenderness of heart, proclaimed the life of the multitudes to be but a futile struggle against unhappiness. So, with fervor, he preached a life which should be death.

Came also many parallel streams of thought from India, streams of rare, delicate purity, of equipoise and of wondrous finesse; all of them of tremulous tenderness, endued with a ravening sense of ecstacy, of bliss,

* The word *deliquescent* appears in Norman copy.

and a flowing aspiration toward ever-increasing spiritual consciousness, and a luxurious consummation of that consciousness in a death which should be as an awakening from the sleep of life.

Came, from Persia, the sharp, businesslike and brilliant exaltation of the co-equal and eternal powers of good and evil:--Prince of Light and Prince of Darkness, in everlasting political warfare, with man as prize; with their resplendent hierarchies and trains of dazzling angels and portentous demons:--the very culmination and conjunction of day and night within the brilliant and sombre spirit of man.

The religions of India were subjective, that of Persia objective, pictorial, romantic, and wrought out of the brilliant powers of the constructive, poetic imagination, vibrant with a sharp sense of useful actuality, whereby men, the multitudes, might be made to serve prince and priest, or the two in one.

Came, also, the later, subjective modification of the ancient Persian drama, wherein is given the assurance that the Prince of Light shall prevail; that the heart of man might be satisfied and be assured of a hero-God.

Came, also, the flood of Egyptian lore, with its countless gods of locality, merged and ranged into hierarchies or clans; truly a religion of the fertile Nile valley with its imprisoning deserts; the small stage of a sumptuous drama--for wheat was almost as cheap there as was man. Loomed there the great Sun-God and the God also of the sun of the night. Loomed the immediate, neighborly under-world of the Nile, with its inhabitant spirits. Loomed the great judgment-seat, throne of the last judgment, where the souls of the aroused dead should pass before the seated God to receive their appraisal. Loomed through the God-filled air the naive trinity of man, woman, and man-child. Loomed the primitive notion of a self-fertilizing God; the single Father-Mother God. Came innumerable haphazard trinities, and trinities of trinities, (the nine gods). And in the same air with these floated the ancient love of man for the animals: hence made he gods of these also. Emerged there, too, the sweetly human Sun-God, Osiris, and his consort-sister Isis, Goddess of fertility. His yearly recurring death at midnight of December 24th (as we say) his recurring birth at midnight, ushering in the 25th of December, as we say, the winter solstice, our Christmas. His melodramatic death through an evil God, his rival; (always an evil God--when was there not an evil God?) his descent into the underworld; his resurrection (Christ is arisen!) with the dawn of spring-time life upon the subtropical earth. (Thus always the religious drama of night and day--the religious dramatization of want and plenty--the religious poem of the Nile River).

Flowed, too, from Egypt, streams of lore upon lore, of speculation upon speculation, mystery upon mystery, magic upon magic.

Flowed from Greece its transcendental philosophy, its platonism, the quest of abstraction, and the exaltation of externals, the uttermost reach of aristocratic intellectual attitudinizing.

Flowed continuously the stream of Hebrew thought; its God of Abraham, loquacious partner of Isaac and Jacob and Joseph, its kings, its laws, its prophets, its wars of plunder, its Babylonian captivity, its fall before Rome, its yearning, homely dream of a messiah, a Savior, a liberator, who should come to found anew a Kingdom on earth.

Flowed streams of thought from minor sects, cults, schisms, and strays and waifs--flotsam and jetsam of the tumult.

Roamed here and there wandering prophets, exhorters, teachers, preachers, healers, magicians, ascetics, initiates, esoterics, stoics, mystics; all was religious ferment, agitation, tension, vague expectancy, diffused hope; all against a sombre ground of hereafter, grim, shadowy, ghostlike; and an extricable sense of helplessness, aimlessness and futility.

Slowly went the shaping. Swiftly the sensitiveness increased. The hour was ripening. The hour became acute. The psychic hour languished. Then came a wanderer, a stranger, a wayfaring poet--He who said: "I am Life! Within me, within you, each and all, is the Kingdom of the one true God. I am the son of this All-Father. Ye are all such sons. I am come unto you, man to man, as a comforter, an assurer. Turn ye from evil toward good. Love ye one another. Have faith in the spirit."

If such sayings were said it is sufficient. If they were not literally so said, but were latent in the hearts of the multitudes, and variously spoken as formative hopes and beliefs, it is still sufficient. If there were such man or no such man is not material. If there were such man, where he came from is not material. If there were several of him it does not matter. Were these affirmations but the focusing of many converging thoughts is not material. Whether there was or was not such historic man as the Jesus of Nazareth is not material. What is material is, solely, that such sentiments, such affirmations, deeply human and essentially true, were born into the world out of the despair of the world.

However much the gospels crumble into fragments, and the vivid religio-dramatic figure of the stranger, Christ, grows dimmer and dimmer, and fades away, it is not here of special moment. For this is not a search of individual men, but of man and his spirit. Hence, the so-called Christian gospel (the glad-tidings), is, for us, but a reflection, more or less accurate, as it may be, of a phase of the spirit of the man of the past; a significant turning movement--a genuine advent of a new thought, a sane, kindly thought, emerging with distinctness and spiritual simplicity from the morbid and ferocious thought so long world-dominant. For in effect, this prophetic glimpse of man's free spirit, this democratic evangel of good will, was but a cry in the world-wilderness of Feudalism. An infant thought, helpless and obscure, coming into a world of brute power and cunning--a veritable foundling--as is indeed set forth in the legend of the birth in the Manger.

That this utterance of the spirit, this radiant thought, this fine movement of the heart should find personification, and be given attributes of Deity, was natural enough, in accord with time and place, manners and customs. This need give us no special concern here, for the deification of men was time-honored.

What really signifies is the nature of the belief which took hold upon imaginations of men; for which they were ready and which spread rapidly.

It seems to have been none else than this,--that there came a hope and a faith in the minds of men that, in compensation for the sorrow and futility of their lives here, they might achieve a life elsewhere, hereafter, in the Kingdom of a kind, considerate God, that should be for them as a Father there, and meanwhile, in their dream, should be a comforter here. (Thus did the Christ reverse the scheme of the Budda--making indeed a complete inversion.) They believed that they might prepare for that life by repentance, that is, a change of mind; that is, the substitution of love for hatred in the mind. For the new God proclaimed was to be a God of Love.

None other than a powerfully imaginative, vivid ideal, so self-assertive as to seem actual, can serve as the foundation of a religious belief; and such suggestion must further seem to be a solution of man's dire difficulties, and give to him a sense of security, a sense of equipoise, and evoke in him that mental concentration called faith--that will, which leads immediately to decisive action.

Even if such suggestion be but a promise, such promise, if affirmative enough, will suffice; for faith, which is also instinctive with perennial hope, will do the rest. Thus in the spirit of man is faith indeed a saving grace; for in its purity, its genuine primordial urge, it is of the very aspiration of life for life, of spirit for spirit. It is the essence of the God-Search and the Man-Search.

Hovering beneath the dream of this new God-Father--then, as ever, the dream-child of man, floated a dream of a life on earth that should be fragrant of good will toward men, a dream of peace on earth, of simplicity, of kindliness, of universal hope and of universal equity.

Such dream men had not dreamed before. It was the dream of the lowly, of those who knew sorrow as it clutched them daily at the heart and looked them, melancholy, humble and comradely, in the face.

It was the deepest, most gentle, most ecstatic of dreams, this dream of the myth-man of sorrows, acquainted with grief. Of Him who said "Behold the lilies;" of Him who said, "Suffer little children to come unto me."

Nothing could be so wholly and simply natural as the spread of such an aspiration, of such a belief, of such a faith. Nothing more natural, more spontaneous, than that, in a despotic world, it should sink deep and warm into the hearts of lowly men; and raise their spirits to a sheer exaltation of ecstacy, as they gazed, with ardor intense, upon the dream-glory and the power, and honor, of a Kingdom in heaven, radiant with love--that seemed so far and yet so near.

So, the dream was vivid and pure, and came true for a little while. Then, little by little the passing dream changed and the Son of the Father began to shimmer and pass into a mist.

Thus emerged, for a brief gleaming, the first glow of the brotherhood of man, the first ardent, flitting moment in the true Man-Search, the true God-Search the first articulate cry of the free spirit of man; the cry of a new-born far-cradled in the East, in a land obscure, humble, intense.

Truly is there a symbolism in the child's-tale of the birth in the manger, and the man's-tale of the last sigh upon the Cross--for of such was the obscure birth and the speedy ending of the first aspiration toward Democracy, that came forth, beautiful but frail--with a beauty that was too rich for use, and hence as a pearl, was thrown away, that men might rend.

Thus, like the soft lightning glowing of a summer's evening, came and went the Christian teaching. And thus, if there were indeed a Christ, he sank softly and silently as the setting sun, beneath the horizon of the world of men.

Then the dream changed; and the wayfaring Stranger, the son of man, became the son of a new God, a militant god of glory and power and dominion. And in the changed dream, this god sought incarnation; and in the fading, changing, coruscating dream, the humble man of Nazareth, he who so humanly loved his fellow men that he poured out his life that the truth might make them free, arose, from earth, transfigured--a new sun-god. Only child and precious son of the Most High God, he now mounted to the summit of the heavens, then and since to sit at the right hand of the Ruler of the heavens and the earth, in due time to pass judgment upon menchildren at the last day, when the trumpet shall sound.

Even so swiftly did the son of man, and the Father-God of the hearts of men, pass into an imperious feudal God and his dazzling son, the Prince of Light, encircled, both, in glory upon glory, Lord God omnipotent, God and Godhead.

The tender teaching could not last. It came too soon. It was a local hour that was ripe, not a world-hour. For Democracy must need have for its field the whole broad world of man, and the consummation of his intellect in reason and in reasonableness.

So again ripens an hour--this time a world-hour, as the liberated currents of the modern world, the flood-gates down, are pouring forth, and mingling, stream within stream, wave upon wave, in a tumultuous tide within the hearts of men and the world of men, and the thoughts of men, and the deeds of men, wherein is shaping and forming and growing big a new man-Search and a new God-Search, making ready and straight the path, for the Spirit of the modern world-man, to emerge at the tremulous psychic hour, and cry with world-reverberating cry:--

I am Spirit!

I am Life!

I am man!

I am Creator!

Verily are we neighbors in Freedom, in Integrity! Now murmurs our hour on its way. The colossal spiritual hour of all-time. That swift-approaching hour when man shall look man in the face; shall not fear the beneficence of Life, even though it be manifest in man; shall not fear to assert its integrity, even though it abide in himself; shall exultantly affirm that all men are alike and all divine; divine because truly human; truly human because surely of Spirit.

So tolls the bell. Since the twilight of Egypt and the dawn of its gods, man's heart, hour by passing hour, has beat true to a dream of dreams, and men have gone and men have ever come, for the cradle is never empty, nor is the grave; and through a shadowy veil of tears and through a miraculous veil of power, man, ever, going and coming, has looked with a hope unborn, has sighed with a spirit untaught by woe, that he might sing a new song, even a song in a strange land, a song of which he felt the refrain but knew not the words, a song of the submerged free-spirit, now about to come forth, resonant with words and deeds of truth--the song of his self-enfranchising spirit, the Messiah song of our day and our deed; peace on Earth, good will to man.

So moves our hour--the world-hour--the hour of our dreams--the hour to come true.

For man has had his Golgotha.

He descended to the Feudal under-world.
Now shall he have his resurrection,
His new birth,
As he springs forth--
In his free spirit--
Son of the Earth!

CHAPTER 4 STORY OF THE CHURCH

Soon after the passing of the Christ, matters began to complicate. The breaking down of national barriers by the Roman power, had let loose not only the floods of religious feeling, but, as well, the philosophies of the nations found outlet, and began a strange commingling.

The natural, direct human teaching of the Christ seemed to suit very well the common people, the lowly, the poor, the outcast. But not so was it with the scholars; for they, as ever, were obsessed by the pride of intellect; the Christian teaching was too simple for them. They had no ready-made place or use for the new theory of democracy implicated therein. They did not know what it meant nor what to do with it. These scholars were intellectual aristocrats. Therefore it became necessary, as they understood their status, in their world of men, to make forthwith an aristocrat out of the humble and obscure man who died on the Cross, historic type of the feudal murder of the innocent who might seek to spread a gospel of Life.

Meanwhile the primitive Christians had been slowly forming into religious groups within secular communities. Their life was large exemplary, simple and upright; continuing a modified Jewish tradition.

But as they increased in numbers, organization began. They put forth out of their mass, elders, deacons, bishops. The simplicity gradually became complex; it soon fell under the spell of the existing feudal program. Thus a separate articulated ecclesiastical class was put forth from the mass of laymen, and the foundation of Church government, as government, that is, first as delegated, then as arbitrary, power, was slowly but surely laid. Thus the beginnings of the Church as an organized temporal power began to take on definiteness, tension and coherence as a theocratic tissue spreading through the social fabric of the people. Let us not forget, however, that this was done by and with the consent and coöperation of the people.

About this time, also, the commingling of philosophies began likewise to blend, solidify and organize into a working system. The philosophic thought of the Orient had interpenetrated and suffused the philosophic thought of Greece. The product was Neoplatonism, an avowed philosophy of religion. Its effects still survive in our day; and much of modern thought has been rendered sterile by its sterility. This philosophy was by turns noble, fantastic and trivial. It dreamed forth a new God of ecstacy which might be reached only through a paroxysm of human ecstacy; a God without other attribute. This philosophy cut away from men's thought all foundation of actuality, released imagination bridle-free, denied the validity of earth and the validity of man; affirmed the specific validity of an unknown, wholly abstract God, and left man a homeless, aimless wanderer on the earth, despising his own body and despising all men and all earthly things. This philosophy underwent mutations; but its influence upon the growing and reshaping thought of early Christendom was conclusive.

Christian thought was in itself already become over-sensitive and over-excitable. It required therefore but the overt suggestion of ecstacy and a god of ecstacy to plunge it into a state of complete hysteria or delirium. Then came into view the extravagant paradox of a simple teaching of a Kingdom within the hearts of men, a world of good will of this earth, turned into a hideous revelry of renunciation, and a fierce, fantastic, wholly insane, and terribly dramatic and ghastly desire and resolution to abandon the world and seek, through solitude, ecstacy, thirsting, fasting, and mortification of the flesh, to join the Godhead.

Through all this turmoil the Church government went methodically on, shaping its doctrine, absorbing Neoplatonism, while reviling it, and gradually strengthening and defining its platform, that is, its theocracy, of religio-partisan politics. The Church government became ever more closely woven as a mesh of ecclesiastics, officially separating from the people; while at the same time it was pushing its delicate ever-ramifying roots into the lives of the multitudes, and thence drawing its sustenance. Christendom was separating within itself ever more sharply into two classes, the governing and the governed--master and man--as of old.

The pathway of the Church was however by no means strewn with roses. Many conflicts it had, without and within. It stood, and fought for life, among a host of what it deemed false prophets, antichrists, heretics and ambitious sects.

The very pressure of conflict awakened into being and action not only the notion of persuasive dominion over men, but the achievement of victory over them at any hazard, by any means, at any cost.

Meanwhile the original Christ had been lost in the constant shuffling of religious thought, philosophic thought, ecclesiastical politics and ambitions, and the general drift of the thought of the people.

While all these changes had been in fact, fluent, steady, gradual, and ever more or less in evidence, it became correspondingly an essential and highly necessary part in the program of the Church to definitely fix, after the mechanical fashion of the thought of the day, a new and distinct place, or setting, for the changed personality of the Christ. So, the wise men who had been set at work, reported progress. They had endeavored to invent a new trinity; but without convincing success, on account of the conflict of views. It was generally agreed, however, that the Christ was to be definitely known as the real and only incarnate son of the high God; his birth, though humble, must be immaculate.

The theological spirit of the times was set against the assumption of sex. Its god must, therefore, be sexless. For, as man always has some whim or other that he wishes to deify and thereby sanction, so the fashions change in Gods. Particularly was this true in those turbulent intellectual and emotional times, when god-making was a professional business, and each adept wished to see what he could do.

But the purpose of the Church (the ecclesiastical organization, or "machine," as we would call it in modern American politics) was deeper, firmer and more definitely purposive than all this. In it the dream of power had slowly awakened as Christendom increased in numerical strength. It is not to say that such dream began on such a day of such a month in such a year. Dreams do not begin that way. They begin unconsciously, and undergo manifold, subtle changes before they become gradually conscious and startling, and arrest and fix the consciousness, and give direction to the will.

The Church, however, naturally, and doubtless benevolently, wished its theocratic conceptions to be attractive to the multitudes. Therefore it gradually, and with consummate artistic skill drew, about its dislocated transfigured and remodeled Christ a scene-setting of wondrous illusion; and made of the story of his birth, his life, his sayings, his works, and his death, a drama filled with astounding contrasts, and of such beauty, delicacy, pathos and intensely seeming reality as to fascinate the imaginations of men, fire their hearts with adoration for the god-man who had shed his blood that they might be saved from the (Persian) powers of evil, and awaken in their minds a consuming ambition to reach the very God-head, the re-created father of so wondrous a son.

All this was as fashionable then, in time and place, as it is not now in our time and place.

The people of that part of the world, and in that time, were temperamentally spiritist, imaginative, ecstatic. To them symbolism was familiar; mystical poetic presentations, highly agreeable; and a good story, well told, always welcome.

The Christ-setting was indeed a wondrously embroidered veil of illusion hung up before the mind's eye; and, the poetically dramatic story was made a touching and powerful appeal to the impressionable heart. The Christ-setting remains such, even to this day; and stands, unique and monumental, among the creations of feudal art. It was all made gradually; was the work of many contributing minds, and continuously was amplified, during successive centuries, as the hierarchy of heaven was gradually revealed and unfolded to view, and the mother of the son of God (as the antipathy to the sex idea somewhat abated) was given her befitting place in the new heavens—into which the Persian angels had by right of legitimacy returned.

This great story, although an offspring of the Egyptian story of Osiris, Isis and Horus, (the sun-God, his wife-sister and their son) was however by no means a mere imitation, but, rather, a fresh recreation, highly individualized, within a new social and intellectual environment.

The world of men had been profoundly changing, and the great, orderly administrative power of the Roman intellect, its colossal secular mechanism of force and world-dominion, could not but have made its impress on the orderly shaping of the Christian hierarchy, now preparing, consciously or inevitably, for an approaching crisis of consummation.

The Christian Church, both hierarchy and multitudes, like any institution of men, was borne along upon the great tide of events, social and intellectual; events partly of its own making. But it carefully shaped its course, assimilating where it must, rejecting where it could, those thoughts, customs, or procedures which made for or against the security and aggrandizement of its policy. For it was becoming apparent that the Christian Church, hierarchy and multitudes, was none other than a new power sprung up and growing big within the power of Rome, and destined seemingly, to the far-sighted, soon or late to close with it in a struggle for possession and dominion of the multitudes.

Then entered the Church upon a bloody chapter, as Rome, awakening a little to the reality, began to feel this new power insidiously and strangely growing within its social body, like a foreign tissue.

The spectacular ideal of Christianity was not the spectacular ideal of Rome. But the intimate Christian ideal of individual salvation, found, naturally enough, famished ones among the proletariat. Hence was Rome, the great city, gradually honeycombed by Christian influences and the Christian propaganda. For Christianity, unlike any other personally founded religion, up to its time, (except that of Gautama Buddha) had set out, practically from the beginning, with the inspiration to be not a religion of an exclusive people, but a catholic, or universal religion. It became, indeed, a religion of the Gentiles, just so soon as it had sufficiently absorbed Greek and Roman thought, and had been repudiated, by the people among whom it had its origin.

When Rome first felt this new, awakening power within itself, it ridiculed; then, taking the affair somewhat seriously, began to apply pressure. But the Christian was firm, completely intractable, stubborn, contemptuous, and proud with an unearthly pride. Then outsprang brute force. The massacres began; they continued long. The individual Christian might be killed, he could not be subdued. His mind was under the sway of an intense fanaticism. By virtue of an inward assurance and conviction, he looked death in the face with derision. To die for the glory of the Christ, was, itself a glory that gained him, he freely believed, immediate entry into that heaven to which he aspired. Hence martyrdom was, to the boldest of these spirits, an ecstatically welcome joy. Never had the notion of an immediate future life, with an immediate reward of glory, taken so unshakeable a grip on the minds of men, and so inspired them to bear witness to their faith.

So flowed the blood of the martyrs, (witnesses), in the general carnage, as Rome sought, by the powers of cruelty and terror, to suppress that--which could not be suppressed.

Such martyrdom was the supreme test of the constancy, and spirit of self-sacrifice of the Christian multitudes. When it became conclusively evident that the multitudes could and would pass this test, a sense of serenity came into the soul of the hierarchy; for it felt, at last, that its foundation in the multitudes was solid and secure.

Then gleamed ambition as a resplendent rising sun; and the course of the hierarchy was resolutely shaped, amidst a world of blood, of seething politics, and of the disintegration of Rome.

The Church had been relatively poor; and its main reliance for acquisition of power, ("The Kingdom of God on Earth"), lay, of necessity, in the careful use of its avowed spiritual mission as an instrument of political intrigue. In due time it began, profitably, to form star chamber alliances with military Rome. For it was clear enough to the far-sighted, that those who controlled the army (the Legions) controlled the Roman power. For the army is ever composed of those fanatics, among the multitudes, who will kill the neighbor. The Church's spiritual invasion of the legions, was so effective that the attitude of the legions toward Christianity, became of serious concern to all the gamblers in authority; the situation was becoming acute.

Then, at that psychic hour which times all crises, appeared a new personality, the embodiment of military power--Constantine. He needed the loyalty of the legions. Shrewd, wily, bold, he saw what there might be for him in the Christian organization as an auxiliary power. He took up with it, won a "Christian" victory, was converted, and thereafter was neither too Christian nor too pagan. He had however a fine lack of confidence in his loyal legions; there were too many like him within them. He knew them. He therefore incorporated the Apostolic Church of Christ into the Holy Roman Catholic Church; gave it a charter of autonomy, including the right to hold lands, to receive bequests. Thus he set upon the brow of the hierarchy an imperial crown of worldly power, glory, wealth, pride and luxury. He made of it in short a predatory Roman institution, and opened thus a new and attractive career to the ambitious.

This was the great turning point in the history of the Church, for which, all its prior vicissitudes, struggles and growing power over the minds of men seem to have been but a normal feudal prelude. Long ago had it thrown overboard the democratic man-Christ, for whom feudalism could have no possible use; and had set up for the people's worship an imperial

Image. This, manifestly, was what the people wanted; otherwise it could not have come to pass.

So, in reality, the hierachy had done nothing but what the multitudes sanctioned; and this, for the plain reason that no institution can long endure unless it steers with the thought of the multitudes. What they are, it is. Even though it develop a life and purpose of its own within the larger life of the people.

If the Church flourished, it was because the multitudes wished it to flourish. It was their thought, their aspiration, their confidence, alone that delegated to it their own massive power.

So, when the Christian Catholic Church definitely took on temporal power and magnificence as the Holy Roman Catholic Church, the world of men was glad. The multitudes saw in it glory, which they liked, and power, which they respected. Ambitious men saw in it a road to the achievement of great personal wealth and power. So everybody was pleased. And the Church came into its heritage of the earth in strict accord with the spirit of the time, the ambitions of men, the superstitions of men, the craft of men, and the weaknesses of men.

It is not for us, here, in passing, either to disparage or to glorify the Church and its hierarchy. Its story is too clear, too human, too palpable in its strength and weakness to be misunderstood. To him who has even but a little searched the mind and heart of man it is an open book. The men who peopled its history were like ourselves. It were a fatuous presumption to assume that we, in an environment like theirs, in a world of men such as they were immersed in, would not have done essentially as they did-- for we do it now! Our fixed purpose here is to search and find man, not to write history, save as a setting to explain the working of his mind. And, so seeking, when we banish from our minds the fiction that the Church of Rome is or ever was a divine institution, we see into the depths and shallows of its human nature as clearly as we may see into the human nature of the men of a prior time as recorded in the Old Testament and the New.

That the church was founded in its temporal power in the fraud of substituting a Feudal Christ for a democratic Christ there can be not a doubt. The Church betrayed the Christian teaching, because it desired the enthronement of feudal power and glory. But in so doing it but flowed with the esoteric and popular current of the times. It gave the people what they admired and wanted. Later on it paid the inevitable price of this fraud and betrayal. But it should not be forgotten that this betrayal, this profound disloyalty to man and his free-spirit, (the very spirit which the Christ declared to the world), began with the apostolic Church. This religio-historical treachery of man to man but emphasizes that modern universal treachery of man to man which is the dry rot of our own civilization, as it was the curse of the Church, and of all the priesthoods which preceded it.

The history of the Catholic priesthood is the history of all priesthoods. Beginning in humility, they slowly mount to the possession of spiritual power over man, and thus onward to the possession of wealth, temporal power, and tyrannical dominion. And this they have ever done by and with the consent of the people. For that is the only way in which it could be done. It is but a partial truth to say that the priesthoods have ever enslaved the people. The deeper truth is that the people have wished within limits, to be enslaved, that is, relieved of responsibility, and have, therefore, exalted the priesthoods. Whenever the priesthoods have forgotten the real underlying nature of the relationship, and failed to watch and follow the changing thought of the multitudes, their ambitions have been undone.

But of all hierarchies, the hierarchy of the Church of Rome has been most consummately politic. With a new worldly wisdom it declined to become an ostensible caste.

It kept in closest touch with the thought of the people through the agency of its innumerable working and wandering priests. It constantly acquired new blood by as constantly taking into its fabric of organization and administration, strong and active young minds. It opened a pseudo-democratic horizon to the lowly, by proclaiming that the lowliest might enter its inner world and there rise to the heights. But it carefully exercised a selective power, with its own purposes ever in view.

It is true that the Church committed atrocious crimes; but so did the people. It is true that the Church did much good; but good also was in the hearts of the people. It is true that it conserved learning, such as it was, but it [is]* equally true that it monopolized such learning. The Church spread a certain enlightenment, but it also spread a darkness of its own. In short the Church responded more keenly to the overt evil in its world of men, than to the good which was hidden in them.

It is from the time of its incorporation by Constantine that the story of the Church becomes intensely modern and exciting. For there, it parted company with oriental ideas and became specifically occidental and alert. It absorbed like a sponge the Roman tradition, and continued the militancy of that imperious tradition even into our day--the tradition of organized and elaborately disciplined might and cunning. It continued, also, the immense breadth of method, superb administrative ability, and boundless ambition which that tradition stood for.

* Supplied.

From the time of its Roman incorporation, the Church became distinctly and definitely a business institution. And it proceeded forthwith to develop a farreaching policy and career of business enterprise. It stands, in history, the paragon monopoly and trust, in comparison with which our modern American trusts seem amateurish and crude; as indeed they are;--even though they have in sacramental charge the one and only money God which all the people worship.

The policy of our modern trusts and combinations, or what may be called the Money-Christ, is eventually to acquire all that the people have. And such, in its own way, became exactly the policy of the Church of Rome, as it had been the prior policy of the Empire of Rome. Thus the modern trust, the Church, and the military empire of Rome are exactly alike in principles, differing only in scenery.

But our modern trusts are made up of grossly ignorant men, without foresight, without hindsight; ignorant of the real nature of a social structure, of the movements in the thought of a people; ignorant of a philosophy of life and the history of thought; ignorant of the philosophy of man and his ways; imbeciles as to the fundamentals of human nature. Hence are their structures crude and flimsy to the point of the ridiculous. Their methods of applying force and cunning are coarse, porous, and to the last degree vulnerable, as we as a people shall clearly see when we come to test them with out* knuckles. Their game of corruption is too simple and too inherently frail to be tolerated by a people even half awake. This is one of our compensations.

Not so with the Church, when it began as a trust, a close corporation. Back of it was all the learning of what was then called the world. The intellects of its galaxy were carefully chosen, perfectly trained. Its methods were always gentle and soothing where possible, always magnetic, seductive, aromatic and refined where possible, always was there the fragrance of sanctity. It used force as a last resort or when it deemed it highly necessary. It patronized the poor with simulation of loving kindness, and assured them by way of sedative for the abstraction of their property, that all men were equal before God; that God would punish the wicked thereafter:--therefore the poor must not be wicked. It studied human nature with infinite care and calculation, and knew men and their ways, especially their weaknesses and susceptibilities, far better than the men of its world knew themselves. Its clear, discerning eye was everywhere. Like a chameleon, its body reflected every mood of the people, because it kept in such close and calculated

---

* Obscurity. As previously noted in a similar appearance this probably should be *our*.

touch with the people. Thus the Church knew itself and knew its world. It knew the real, it knew the counterfeit; it used either and both. It knew also that it had no rival. It thoroughly understood the commercial value of monopoly. It knew also that it was founded upon fraud. It knew that it held a special privilege or franchise; a franchise none other than for the transportation of the souls of men from here to hereafter. It knew that this was a phantasm. It knew that such phantom franchise was granted to it by a dreamy, unreasoning people of great numerical mass. It never, (until it went insane with the madness of power), seriously opposed the whimsical will of the people. When its world went pagan, it went pagan; when its world went ecstatic it went ecstatic; when its world went hysteric it went hysteric; when its world went into barbarism it went into barbarism. But its own dream of power it never forgot. To that it held, firm and tenacious; and ever added little by little to the fund of power, stealthily, persistently; always profiting by the follies and foibles, the impassioned blunders of its world of men. It had its vicissitudes; but it also had its relentless courage and its fixed resolve to acquire dominion over all that men had:--their property, their minds, their bodies, their souls--not a thing should escape.

Its first new trial of strength came when the Empire of Rome, long tottering, crumbled. For the Church, with seeming prevision had stuck to the city of Rome. It found itself in the midst of surging barbarians. With consummate guile it captured them. In response to their demands its ceremonials became barbarically gorgeous, and these grown children of the north woods were pleased.

Let it be remembered that there was then no Europe. There was but the dissolving Western Empire, the decaying Eastern Empire, and the hordes of migrating barbarians of the north pushing westward and southward, and heaving to and fro as they moved.

Incidentally, about this time, a man, one Arius, Bishop of Alexandria had ventured to suggest that in his opinion God had made the Christ, and that the latter was therefore inferior in position, not equal as the Church theology held. This idea appealed to many as a rather common sense proposition, and, their numbers increasing, the Church became irritated, and now having the power, it used it, smote the Arians with the sword, consumed them with fire, and otherwise disposed of them. For the Church was in no mood to tolerate competition; and any one who wished to dabble independently in either truth or falsehood, for purposes either ideal or commercial, did so at his peril. For the Church had given it out that it had cornered all the truth, and all the falsehood and was sole possessor and guardian thereof. This was disagreeable, but it was business, just as we understand "business" today.

So the Church having crushed the Arians, and cajoled the Barbarians in large part, set about forming a code of rules of the game. For this purpose it appointed a council, and this council laid down the law of orthodoxy; that is, what the Church, for its own purposes, held to be true, was, henceforth, to be truth; and what, for its own purposes, it held to be false, such was henceforth, to be false, whether true or not. Here, for the first time the Church said, peremptorily, to the spirit of man: "Thus far shalt thou go, and no farther," and here also was the beginning of its desperate career of tyranny over men's minds, in its passion for absolute dominion.

But this was what the people wanted. They wanted to be told exactly what to believe and exactly what not to believe. They wished some power to say to them, authoritatively, "thus far shalt thou go and no farther." They had, indeed, but little respect for a power that could not enforce its will, that could not be tyrannical. They wished rules of the game. For the idea of force, of compulsion was deep-seated in their minds. Clearly the Church could not have tyrannized if its world of men had not desired tyranny.

Men of the Church's world were then a wild, roving marauding lot, settling here and there at times into pools of relative quiet.

Thus the Church faced, without quailing, a world of savage, migrating, shifting and streaming barbarians, that had been pushed about and generally dislocated by the earlier fierce invasion of the Huns. These peoples were all seeking a home somewhere. Their wanderings and violence were but the prelude to the formation of modern Europe.

Through this storm and turbulence the Church stood like a rock, because its organization was the only group of men fortified with a fixed, steady and definite purpose and abode. Meanwhile it was attending strictly to business; acquiring lands, buildings, personal properties; and endowments. Everybody in those days was on the make; and that, in a fashion simple and rude. The warrior, also, was again as a gambler emerging into prominence and power; and on him and his ambitions the Church kept its careful, jealous eye; for it saw what was coming; and prepared itself to meet force with cunning. For its world of that day was as rough unscrupulous and rude a world as could well be. It contained, in preparation for us, all the elements of our modern savagery. The Church could not then meet force with force; that was contrary to its pretensions and would be fatal to its program. But it could intrigue. It was completely in touch everywhere.

The spread of Christianity among the barbarians is a ludicrous story. The appeal to them and their reception of it was so sordid. They were so easily bribed.

But the Church was in business, and knew its business. Its wandering priests were, so to speak, primitive salesmen. What they sold, as Christianity, was whatever the buyer wanted. They knew men and their ways and were of those men and their ways. For the Church, in its growing career was wonderfully adaptive and patient with men, so long as they did not infringe upon its prerogatives. The hierarchy, in deadly earnest, now, was dreaming its dream of world-power.

In the wide chaos of barbarianism, rude Kingdoms were shaping, and dissolving. Kings, powerful for a time, appeared and disappeared. But a turbulent and uncouth shaping went on nevertheless. It was a time of utter rankness. Hence, of barbarism. In those times the men of the world of the Church thought only of self and individual graft; and, hence, likewise, did the Hierarchy.

The organized Church, seeking to consolidate itself the more effectually, made effort to bring a semblance of order out of this chaos of self-interest in its world of men, but ineffectually; it had to go with the immense tide of men and their unbridled passions.

About this time a new and strange power had arisen in the East. Arabian civilization, its thought infused and invigorated by that of the earlier Greek and, also, by an intellectual flow from India, had become learned, brilliant and incisive. Its intellectual passion was for quasi-scientific investigation, to which were added a faculty of initiative and a keen sense of search after what it deemed rational truths. The way had been prepared by one Mahommed, a curio in his way,--successively religious hysteric, social reformer, organizer, and administrator; politician, and man of the world and of the sword and plunder. In the small city of Medinah, Mahommed conducted a unique laboratory experiment, which from his point of view was successful. Within the thought of his people, who were ripe for it, for seed germinates only in proper soil, he induced, within his own lifetime, a change that usually requires centuries. His method was simplicity itself. He first selected from the miscellany of queer Arabian desert gods, a local god named Allah, declared him the One God, himself prophet of such God, and banished all other gods. He had the potent fire of enthusiasm. He laid down few and simple rules of conduct. His conception of the one God was simpler and purer than that of the prevailing Christian doctrine; his rules of conduct terser and more practical. His earlier administrative policy tended to establish a novel sort of democracy;--a small solidarity of men who cohered, with enthusiasm, in the idea of a single impartial God for all, thus rendering all equal; out of which grew an equally enthusiastic bloodbrotherhood in arms and plunder. In due time as is the old story, Mahommed, the prophet, for business reasons, practically identified himself with the One God, as his sole executive agent and tax collector. He then relapsed largely into the clan-spirit in which he was born, favored the growth and strengthening of aristocracy, and thus, betraying his early, simple teachings, divided men into two classes, the rich and the poor, thus sowing the wind, which, in its whirlwind, was to wreck the Arabian civilization.

While the world of the Church was a world of superstition, the world of the Mahommedan succession was filled with brilliant intellectuality, and aggressive mental and physical vigor. Shrewdly, Mahommed promised, as the mouthpiece of the one God, immediate entry into a luxurious paradise for each and all who fell in battle. Mahomet, also, knew his people.

Then set in a furious and rapid propaganda, or holy war, with Allah the sign by which to conquer, and the naked sword the practical instrument of conquest, pillage and incidental conversion. A swift sweep was made westward along the north African shore, and what is now Spain, was entered and held. Thus was established a stream of rationalistic thought flowing along the south shore of the Mediterranean Sea, while north of it was a huge stagnant marsh of superstition, with the little learning that existed, concentrated within the Church organization. This invasion of reason, or rather, rationalistic thinking, was, in the course of time, to become a thorn in the flesh of the Christian hierarchy.

Meanwhile the barbarian Kingdoms were taking on a more definite semblance of shape. The Church began to trade with Kings, and Kings to menace and trade with the Church. For, while the ambition of the Church, was growing, the ambition of Kings was growing. So, as ever before, began anew the sharp struggle for worldly and sordid power between warrior and priest, and so went on alliances and betrayals.

The struggle moved apace. Out of barbarian Kingdoms grew barbarian empires monstrous, vague, ephemeral. The hierarchy made with them alliances offensive and defensive, seeking, ever, the advantage. Powerful personalities were arising in rapid succession among the barbarians; but their organizations were loose; that of the Church close knit.

The hierarchy made use of every form of baseness and political trickery; so did its opponents. The conflicts were desperate. It was wolf and wolf. But the Church had the advantage of the added craft of religious trickery. Meanwhile the Church continued to acquire property, chief among which in a political sense, was a home for its pontiff. Naturally enough jealousies were rife within the Church organization.

European landed feudalism now began to take on shape, as the chaotic turbulences somewhat subsided. The Kingdoms took on a more definite aspect of stability.

This special and local form of feudalism was a pyramidal affair. It was based on the land. Such land was acquired by the robberies of shifting invasions. These lands were divided among the warriors. The fighter counted. The common people were slaves,--serfs.

The system worked both ways; down, from the King, through the nobles and Church rulers, step by step, rank by rank, to the smallest baron, based on land-tenures; upward, by a system of personal military attachments, man to man, from the common fighter, step by step, rank by rank, to the King. All was based upon the land; to which the person was secondary.

Even as it was a new kind of screen for personal ambition, it became, shortly, a highly complicated affair. Its internal relationships constantly shifting, it had no visible center of gravity (as has our modern feudalism,--in the Dollar). But, while it lasted, it was the only institution, loose and wobbly at that, which existed outside of the organization of the Church. Its chief function was to pave the way for monarchism, as, also, for the rise of the cities; while giving to men, meanwhile, a certain predatory cohesion:--what we would call nowadays a "Community of Interests."

Into this system the roots of the Church went so deep that a Church dignitary was at once a great wealthy feudal overlord, with the added power and prestige of spiritual dominion.

Within this era of Baronial feudalism came another great turning point in the history of the Church: The Crusades. These fantastical movements were of enormous profit to it. Land-holding after land-holding sacrificed in the ardor of enthusiasm, fell into its capacious mouth. The land-hunger of the Church was insatiable. There was but one market, and but one buyer. But the Church acquired through the crusades, a far more terrible clutch on men's bodies. Every crusader, every man who wore the sign of the cross, became spiritually attached to the Church, and owed obedience and allegiance to it alone, such allegiance dissolving his allegiance to his King, or Lord. Indeed the spiritualizing of things and men had become a part of the business policy of the Church. Any lands or personal property it acquired, by any means, were immediately "spiritualized"; and any man who rendered service in its name was also "spiritualized." It was a keen and brutal game. But the Church was in business to stay. It utilized the crusades, which it had adroitly instigated, as a pretext to lay money tribute on all Europe, for money was what it was after.

The Church, in the increasing complexity of its affairs, had become honeycombed with graft, and greed. To increase its wealth it took advantage of any pretext, and made use of any subterfuge. Its dream of power had advanced to that phase of reckless arrogance, which we today can see set forth in facsimile, in the tigerish hunger of our own magnates. The similarity between one of our modern trusts, and the organized Church of Rome at that time, is striking as a photograph:--That modern combination of piety, cunning, brutality, insatiable greed, and a consuming devastating, and suicidal dream of power.

The Hierarchy had now definitely entered upon a career of crime, from which there was no withdrawal. It was in too deep. It had tasted human blood. Its land-hunger, its money-hunger and its man-hunger were madly unsatisfied. Mahommed's "laboratory experiment" was being worked out independently, and more slowly, on a colossal scale, by the Christian Hierarchy.

But the Church could not (as we cannot) escape the all-inclusive law of internal compensation; any more than can our modern sanctimonious pirates. For its crimes, one by one, it, in due time, had to face the inevitable and inexorable accounting.

In this sense, the Crusades inaugurated an immense reaction, slow but sure. The people were being bled too hard.

Logically enough, for development goes on within development, the Church organization had by this time become a multitude in itself. It was becoming bulky, complicated, difficult to manage. Like one of our modern political machines it was filled with rings within rings, with complicated internal dissensions, bickerings, jealousies, intrigues, knifings; and the same quarrelings over the division of the spoils. But as an organization with a fixed policy in business and politics, (and business, politics, militarism and ecclesiasticism are and have ever been one and the same thing in essence), these warring elements held together for the common good of plunder.

There were, to be sure, scattered here and there within the labyrinths of the machine, many sincere, noble, pure-minded, self-sacrificing men. Men filled with an ardor of devotion to their God, in his splendor, and to man in his benighted misery. But they did not know the game. Indeed it is not likely that they even suspected it, and as highly probable that they would not, could not, believe it if told them. To them the life and the mission of man meant piety, self-abnegation, and whole-souled devotion to suffering mankind. Such men, fine characters in any time and place, were of special utility to the ever-scheming hierarchy who put them forth in evidence, pointed to them with pride, and magnified them as exemplars of the unmitigated goodness of the Church, and the sweetness of its intentions.

Also, within the labyrinths, was another class of earnest men: the truth-seekers. These men were very troublesome, and especially irritating to the insiders; as honest, "misguided" men are apt to be. It became necessary therefore to get such men out of the way. And it was done. Sometimes they were publicly burned at the stake, as a warning to other "heretics," sometimes quietly disposed of, as is our modern way. In other words they were "dropped" out of the organization. They were not, as we say nowadays, deemed "safe and sane."

But nevertheless, the hierarchy began to note an increasing unrest within not only the organization of the Church itself, but in its outer world of men. It became evident that this unrest was of outside origin. Arabian learning, intelligence and nimble-mindedness were getting in their work on the European mind, which also was spontaneously awakening from its nightmare of superstition, and beginning vaguely to inquire.

This enlarged apparition of the spirit of inquiry, this growing emergence of man's free spirit, alarmed, in earnest, the hierarchy.

Founded, ostensibly, as a world-power, on a spiritual truth which it had turned to fraudulent use; saturated with commercialism, engaged in a form of slave trade, a commerce in souls; it feared the light. It knew what the light must reveal. For it well enough knew the nature of its own methods--the methods by which it had obtained wealth, the methods by which it had held wealth, the methods by which it had obtained and held its power over men's minds. It knew, just as well as we do, that the source of its wealth and temporal power lay in the cunning use and abuse of its spiritual power; and that in turn, ever acting and reacting, the increase of its wealth and temporal power served ever to increase its spiritual dominion and effectuate its tyranny. Already it had established its private prisons. It now invented and established the Inquisition. The purpose of the Inquisition was to exterminate the danger of free thought and free inquiry --that is, publicity. The rack and many an ingenious form of torture became now the handmaiden of the wrathful followers of the Nazarene. With the hierarchy, wealth and dominion had become the supreme Gods, even while it was putting forth its orders vowed to poverty. Thus its reasons for torture and repression were purely business reasons, as we, today understand the term, and as we today say "business is business"!

It may be said that the world of men about the Church would have done the same thing. There is no doubt about that. But that is not the issue in our Man-Search, in the course of which this study of the Church is but an incident. The issue is that the Church was now, after the lapse of centuries, arrived at the supreme test of its own character. The crisis was at hand. It must choose between man and Mammon. It had come to the great parting of the ways. It must make definite answer, as must we all, to the query, "Which way?"! Was it to be the way of the gentle, the unselfish Christ, upon whose name, as upon a foundation its profession of spiritual faith was alleged to be founded? or, the way of crushing wealth, and devastating temporal power?

The Church did not hesitate. It proclaimed, in its acts, "We choose Wealth and Power! They are real! The Christ is unreal! The free spirit of man avails not!"

That was the real issue. No sophistry can obscure it; no passionate utterance can wave it aside; no gesture of denial can banish it. It stands, stark, typical, in the history of man, as the insanity of the dream of power.

The hierarchy feared that publicity would mean the disruption of its organization and the loss of its graft. (See any modern "trust" instance.) That that fear was well grounded is true enough. But the time was coming anyway. The Church had reached the apogee of its feudal rhythm, of growth. The rhythm of its feudal decay was about to begin.

Throughout its hitherto career, the Church had had to do mostly with the activities of mysticism and supernaturalism among the people, and formed its advantages in their disorganized or unorganized social condition. These agencies fostered its growth. Now it was come face to face with the shaping free spirit of man:--A something it had in reality not before confronted. An agency that was to change the character of that thought among the people which had sanctioned and sustained the Church's power. The hour, long approaching, was at hand.

It is not to be questioned that the Church, in its time and in its way, had done good.

But the hour had now come when its little of good was to be weighed, in the balance, against the weight of its huge evil.

Both the evil and the good have been denied in toto, by partisans.

But our standard of measurement is the simple one, the standard of basic actuality:--

Man and his free, creative spirit.

What makes for that is right.

What seeks to suppress it is wrong.

Feudalism has ever sought and now seeks to suppress it. Democracy seeks, now, to liberate and emancipate it; to give it free swing.

Thus came the most dramatic hour in the life of the Church. The culminating hour. For at that hour its Fate appeared, and looked it in the face.

The dominion of the hierarchy and its army of priests over the property, the bodies, minds and souls of the men of its world was nearly complete. Its tentacles had reached even into the courts of civil justice. It had invented and used the terrible weapons Excommunication, Anathema! It had humbled Kings; it had asserted with authority that the souls of men should go, at its bidding to an eternal heaven or an eternal hell. Its dream of absolute power was nearly come true.

But when, at the psychic hour, the psychological moment, clothed in all its might, in all its majesty, it came face to face with the actual and free spirit of man, reached forth its terrible hand, seeking to kill it:--and, in amazement, failed!--Then, the psychic hour passed silently on its way; the iron had entered the darkling soul:--the death of the Church began.

Its passionate mortal struggles set in. The dream of power, the dream of omnipotence was changing and losing luster. In desperation it went on, and on, blazing and subsiding, the fire of life slowly cooling. Hectic flushes came and went, and with them a slow, progressive, fateful exhaustion. So it has moved on its way to the grave, and so it shall pass;--pass with the feudal dusk of twilight, while the spirit of man serenely moves on.

He who actually looks upon the Church as sacred, sees with dim eyes.

He who looks upon monarchism and aristocracy as sacred, sees with dimmer eyes.

He who looks upon wealth or so-called social position as sacred sees, what is close to him, with the dimmest of eyes.

He who, in these days, looks upon so-called "Authority," labeled by any name, and so looking fears it, as sacred, is an imbecile digging his own grave.

It is the business of undaunted modern thought, with clear eye and unalterable purpose, to search all social institutions, of whatever kind; to search them even in their retreats, their sanctuaries, even in their holy of holies; and, by the light of actuality, banish, once for all, the phantoms of all feudal institutions and traditions of whatsoever name or nature:--specifically the feudal phantoms of our contemporary civilization. Thus, and only thus, will the ground be cleared for the uprearing of Democracy.

This was the golden moment which the Church let pass by. For its sin, it has received the wages of Death.

In our own land, with open eyes you may see spread before you, in most startling distinctness, the same conditions (with new names, new local colorings) that preceded the crisis of the Church.

Our hour is like the hour of the Church. Fate, is looking us, also, in the face. Shall we too, let the golden moment pass?

Roman the Church was. Under new names, within new local colorings and conditions, it was the heir of that despotic and seemingly invincible empire. The methods of its predecessor in power, it revised, and reorganized, and, in consequence, brought forth into the world, as its special contribution to world-feudalism, that form of subtle betrayal behind the veil, to which we moderns give the name "Business Enterprise."

Thus in the study of our own immediate environment, our search into its essentially feudal nature, its hitherto tendencies, and its attitude toward the man of today and his inherent free creative spirit, do we find the story of the origin, the growth, the hierarchy, and the working organization of the Church a clarifying agency. For it was the first, as well as the greatest of modern business corporations.

Such study may help us to discern in our midst a hierarchy of interests, whose siren song and whose ominous threat differ not a whit from the plaintive song and deep thunder of the Church.

It may aid us to discern that we, also, have an Inquisition.

Also, it may help unfold to our view a modern excommunication, an hourly anathema.

And the constant assassination and ruin of men may appear neither so isolated nor so modern as we suppose.

In short it may help us perceive that, in any time, present or past, located in any place, here or elsewhere on the earth or in a heaven, embodied in any God, hierarchy, institution, corporation, symbol or personality whatsoever, and called by any name, be that name never so sweet, never so august, so pompous, never so humble, never so innocent, so enticing, so reassuring, there looms the portentous fact,--coming forth from big and little--that the conjoined powers of force and cunning in man, individually or collectively, seek ever the single end:--dominion over men in their persons, property, liberties, beliefs, thoughts and aspirations. Enslavement of the multitudes is the goal. Amazingly it springs out of the imagination and will of the multitudes.

Such is Feudalism!

And this inner, ever-present, hitherto secret truth no sumptuous beauty of externals, no softness of voice or manners, no parade of culture or learning by the few, no seeming apathy of the multitudes--can hide from him who searches.

Truly the Church has known when to smile, when to weep, and when to sink its fangs. Truly the multitudes are dreamers.

And what a phantasm, and yet what a reality,--is man.

* * * *

Thus, with its spiritual crisis, ends for us, in our man-search, a broad but incisive interest in the story of the Church.

[It does not stand alone; but it has stood long and huge, in a sort of solitary grandeur, among the hosts of feudal institutions,--a monument to the pathos of man's folly, and especially, to the pathos of its own.] *

* From Norman copy.

CHAPTER 5 THE DREAM OF POWER

Man is so much a dreamer that what he holds real and will wager his life upon, is naught else than the vivid working of his imagination.

The greatest asset that he holds in his immeasurably powerful grasp is his faculty of making pictures of himself and within himself; pictures that seem to him not only real, but all-sufficient, living, external, actual, matter of fact,--they are naught else than pictures of himself, made by himself. They are man in the act of painting his own portrait.

And yet, strangely enough, man, the common man, seldom consciously reckons with this natural and marvellous power; or with its all-around possibilities of use and abuse, of clarity and gloom, of comedy and tragedy. The average man, practically does not reckon with it at all; does not seemingly know that he has an imagination. Little does he suspect its power to sway him; least of all, his power to sway it. He does not know that it is at once the gateway to his being, and the outlet of his being. That it is through the imagination that he comes and goes. A gateway through which others may and do continually enter his inmost recesses; an outlet through which he pours all that is good and evil in himself, an inlet through which he receives the evil and good of others. If man be likened unto a citadel fortified on all sides, then may his imagination be likened unto the single portal, a portal which he believes is always closed, but which in fact is always open.

All that any man does or can do is done by virtue of his picture-making power. Without it he cannot move hand or foot. For man lives within a world of moving pictures; a picture world within him and without.

The old feudal superstition still possesses the average man, namely, that real gifts, real powers, are not for him or of him--because forsooth, he is merely a common man.

When he hears the word, imagination, he seldom associates that word with himself, unless in the stupid sense of something crack-brained. For so his imagination pictures imagination to him.

When he hears the word, imagination, associated with the achievements of great men, that is of men whom he agrees are great men, it makes on him the impression of a mysterious power accorded only to the mysteriously chosen and sacred few; and, hence, again, he does not associate such power with himself--for he is only a common man, a groundling, for so his imagination pictures himself to himself, and, in contrast does not understand that the power of imagination in the actively great, is made effective solely by the power of a keen will to sway that imagination. He does not understand that the power of imagination in the parasitic great, rests wholly upon his consenting imagination. For he is obsessed by the feudal belief and teaching of the ages, that he, being a common man, has no will of his own. Hence his imagination does not picture to him the power of his own slumbering will--and its possibilities of action. The latent power of that will to cause his imagination to picture to some purpose; the latent power of his imagination to stimulate his will to some purpose, does not press in upon him because he is a common man--and therefore believes that such powers are not possessed by himself.

Among all the follies of the common man, the lowly, the earth-creeper, since the beginning, the greatest is this: that he denies in himself that which he regards great in others; and, still worse, as though that were not folly enough, he denies such quality of greatness in his own very neighbor, a common man like himself, until he perceives it at last, without his aid or consent, surrounded by power, wealth, dominion or fame. Out of such folly has sprung the saying: A prophet is not without honor, save in his own land.

The common man cannot understand that all power springs out of the common people. He has seen that great men have arisen out of the common people, and he has been more or less amazed thereat. But he attributes this phenomenon to any and every cause but the right one. He does not understand the simple truth that such fact is the direct result of imagination and will:--of an imagination that awakens and sharply stimulates the will, and so enables the will to hold the picture steady:--(which truth uncovers the simpler truth that the man who rises is not the "fighter" as he superficially appears, but the man who lets himself alone, lets his faculties work freely; who recognizes their inherent tendency and power to grow and unfold and thus beget an activity and strength, which hunger for work).

The average man does not let himself alone. He is constantly interfering with the free working of his own natural powers. He is forever absurdly suppressing and repressing them. Hence he does not grow solidly in imaginative strength and power of will, and in the hunger for mental activity:--in that intense desire for achievement which constitutes virility.

To tell the average man, the common, ordinary everyday man that he possesses essentially the same native power of imagination that has characterized all great poets, rulers, dramatists, musicians, painters, sculptors, statesmen or generals, would cause him to laugh at you in derision, if not in anger, for trying to make a fool of him, as he would say.

Yet what has this laugh of derision not cost him in the past? What, to him, unexplainable miseries, does it not cost him today?--poor fool!

For this laugh prevents him from seeing himself, that is, from seeing that it is through his own imaginative power to make pictures in the brain, that the entire social fabric has been created and sustained. Thus does this poor fool in his derision, eclipse himself; and become the dupe of his own powerful imagination, when he says he has not any. And thus does he hold himself to the feudal doctrine that men are different,--the subtle, the insidious doctrine of caste--of which he is chief supporter, and to which he is chief contributor. For so his imagination pictures human life to him:--the fool.

The common man has ever been dazzled by parade of power; of power of any tinsel social kind, military, civil, ecclesiastic. But he has ever failed to associate such delegated power with his own actual powerful self. Still less has he referred its very existence and being to his own willing personality, his own existence and the desires of his being; and, least of all has he referred it to his picture-making imagination. Indeed so intimately is his imagination not only a part of himself, but actually and persuasively himself, that he is not aware of its presence; and, hence, ever, has given to it no name other than names not himself. And yet it is all himself, and all the parade and power is himself; all the predatory great are himself: and all the parasitic great are himself.

It is when we begin to search the common man within himself that he becomes amazing. It is then that the common man becomes real and powerful to our gaze. It is easy enough to brush aside from the exalted all externals, all pomp, parade, artifice, all shows and ceremonials, all hypocrisies, labels, cant and shams, and shame of parasitism. It is easy enough to draw aside every veil and leave men surprised, abashed and confounded. But when we begin to draw aside another veil; when we begin to enter into the common every day man; when, actually, we begin to think his thoughts, to feel his feelings, to take on the life of his desires, to look through his eyes from within him, to feel the movement of his emotions, and be of them,--ah, then the real drama of man begins:--And the opening scene lies within the tireless working of his Imagination!

For we now no longer regard him from the outside, stranger to stranger, this common man; we no longer take him for granted as he passes us in shoals; but we live the life within him, merge our personality with his and, thus, let our imagination work through his imagination that we may see as he sees, and dream his dreams. So shall we enter even into the common man's heart. So shall we reach his spirit.

For, the common man's outward works, the civilizations he has reared, the specific acts he has done, the visible parade of his dreams, the external workings of his thoughts,--have guided us, slowly but surely, along the path that leads to the sanctuary of his feelings, his imagination and his will; to the breeding place of his dreams; to the center of power--at the center of his desires, and his choice--to his spirit--his Ego:--for it is the common man that we seek:--he is the real man.

For what is man?--a worker?--a toiler?--a fighter?--a schemer?--a drone?

No; man in the large and the little, is a dreamer, first of all. These other things are but phases of his ego-activity, wherewith and whereby he seeks to give realism to his dreams;--whereby he strives to make them come satisfying true that they may certify to the genuineness of the picture-world within him and without. For man dreams even within his dream, and makes pictures within pictures; has sensibility within sensibility, thoughts within thoughts, desires within desires, powers within powers.

Behind all, inspiring all, permeating and sustaining all the outer show, is man's imagination.

This, his greatest power, (this his great power, within which is found his historic weakness, susceptibility and instability), is the human power least known, least realized by him who most needs the knowledge and the realization,--the humble, the lowly man, the common, everyday, average man. Further must he know, if he is to grasp the first law of self-preservation, that the few who know, realize, and utilize the power of the imagination, (which the wise and pious tell us is the special gift of a divine providence, bestowed on the few), are to be weighed and judged by their use of it. This is a simple feat, of the imagination, to penetrate the outward show of the feudal exalted, to portray their imaginings, and, penetrating through these, to reach their real desires. To realize, as surely also that they cannot escape,--that there is absolutely nowhere for them to go--for the multitudes of earth are self-awakening:--their dream is changing.

Thus, again, is imagination a power, so little known by the average man, so little understood by him, that he has exalted it into Earth and Heaven Gods, now knowing what he did--knowing only what he desired, and how urgently.

So, has this dreamer, man, moved within a world of dreams, which seemed real to him because he could touch them, taste them, see them, hear them, and because other men said the same. Such was for him the world of physical nature; and the world of his fellows about him. A real world, because his imagination pictured to him that he himself was real, therefore they were real: and that they, being thus real, he, also, was real--and also, because other men said they thought the same way.

But the dreamer, man, moved also within another world of dreams that seemed to encompass the real world of physical nature. And because he could neither see, hear, taste, smell nor touch it, it seemed alarmingly real in its unreality, and as terribly unreal in its reality; for his imagination pictured forth to his own soul that he also was unreal; and his unreality seemed repellently real to him. And out of this unreality he made Gods, not knowing why, knowing only his fears, his awe, his solitude within such dream world, and his aching desire to be at peace:--for he could not understand his sorrows. The common man never understands his sorrows.

The more this common man, this dreamer, dreamed, the more was he terrified of old; for his imagination, tortured by him, made before him such phantom pictures of power to harm, that he felt a creeping dark unrest even while he sought light and peace:--not knowing why he could not find peace. For the common man never knows why he cannot find peace.

He knew not that this dream-world which he could not touch nor taste nor smell nor hear, was the dream world and the real world of the All-Life. That it was more real than the dream-world he thought real: the dream-world of that Ego we call God. For to the common man the unreal is always real, and the real as surely unreal.

His fear of that dream world which seemed to him unreal, evoked visions of power, of power so vast that his spirit was to him as a nothing therein.

From his real dream world, his close, daily, contact with men and things, arose also a dream of world-power; wherein he was great, or little, in his way.

Thus all the dreams of the dreamer, man, are dreams of power--they involve sorrow--sometimes flitting joy.

But the dreamer, our man, was also toiler. He dreamed his dream of power;--and the power of toil came true.

So, also, was our man, our dreamer, fighter. He dreamed his dream of power,--and the power of might came true.

So, also, was our dreamer, intriguer. He dreamed his dream of power,--and the power of cunning came true. For as all these men have dreamed, so have we dreamed--for they were all common men--just like you and me.

These, then, are man's three dreams of power:

The dream of work.
The dream of might.
The dream of cunning.

One alone of these dreams is immortal--the dream of work. It is the true dream of creative power. It is the one dream, which includes within itself, the normal ego of the other two. It is the dream that means Life--that invites Life--that invites and guides aright the flow of the All-Life from that dream world which is the real world,--the world of the spirit. It is the dream which invites that power of spirit to flow into man's spirit, that he may achieve life here and now.

The dream of might and the dream of cunning are false dreams of creative power. They mean death--invite death--achieve death, and recreate it ever anew.

To create aright is of man's spirit and of its true dream of power.

THE DREAM OF POWER

The picture of creative good that man's imagination thus sets forth, and which inspires his will to work and to create aright, is the ideal which holds him integral and true within the integrity of the All-Life:--which holds his ego integral with the All-Ego.

To create awrong is of the self-perversion of man's imagination. It is his inverted picture which his imagination sets before him,--a haunting vision.

Man has been self-edified and self-terrified through his belief in gods, angels and devils, fairies and goblins, elves, sprites and ghosts. He has yet to learn that he, himself, is god, angel and devil, fairy and goblin, elf, sprite and ghost; that, out of his sensibilities, populous with fears and hopes, out of his caprice, out of his heart-hunger and spirit-hunger, out of his fluctuating and lambent consciousness of his own goodness, his own baseness, his own nobility, his own fluency,--he has pictured to himself these super-men, minor creatures, and queer pets and aversions of his inexhaustible fancy.

For man, picture-maker that he is, perceives not his imagination at work. He sees only the pictures; and, the more unreal they, the more insistently has he believed them living;--for man does not understand himself as a creator, because he does not understand himself as a picture-maker, a dreamer.

The dream of the power of cunning is the most death-dealing of the common man's dreams. It is the dream which rots the mind of the dreamer:--which causes all men to rot. It is none other than a self-secreted poison, wherewith man defiles himself and disintegrates. It is an hysteria which results from the suppression of the generative will to do good.

Within its scope and its sway are all liars, thieves, murderers, betrayers--rich or poor, high or low, pious or worldly. This dream of cunning is born of man's lust for power of death over men, of his hunger for cruelty, for luxury, for slaves; of his ominous dream of glory. Within it, whines man, the man-eater.

The might of might, less virulent than the dream of cunning, sprang from brawn, and has had the urge of open courage, valor, heroism, and, in a sense self-sacrifice for the good of all. It was, in large, a crude dream of brotherhood. But the dream, as it grew, became ever a dream of plunder, of butchery, of slavery. In a brute fierce way it sought and found that which Cunning stealthily sought and found:--The dominion of death over men. For it is the dream of death. Within it grew a gnawing hunger for men, for slaves, as imagination pictured forth power and glory for the few,--at the cost of the lives of the many. Little wonder that the dreams of might and cunning have ever sought conjunction within the darkened souls of men.

Yet all men have dreamed all the three dreams. Dreamed them more or less at random, in vacillation, in uncertainty, in imbecility; more or less alertly and adroitly. And ever has imagination made faithful pictures of men's commingled and drifting desires. For as was the flow of the dreaming of the multitudes, so was the drift of the world.

Now, these three dreams are but in fact one dream. Diverse in aspect, seemingly self contradictory, ramifying into minute personal activities--these three phases of the one great, primal dream of power so interplay that they seem severally paradoxical and enigmatic to him who has neither the imagination nor the will to penetrate, to push hard into human reality. Hence has come the saying: No evil without its good: no good without its evil:--which is a mere phrase, not an elucidation.

There is in the actuality of our lives no obstacle whatever to accurate analysis. With the great picture of Feudalism now partly before our eyes, and the greater picture of Democracy awaiting to be put forth by the work and will of our creative imagination, all the tangled skein that man has put forth out of himself as the work of his feudal imagining, resolves back into himself, and there commingles with the simplicity of his primal [human] * nature.

It is to witness this dissolving and simplification that we are to enter the spirit of man. That there, behind the veil, we may see how simple man is; and behold how much greater, nobler is he, than he has been taught, and has himself supposed. Within man's spirit alone is this miracle of simplicity to be seen. Once seen,--shall it be forgot?

The normal dream of man is the dream of universal creative power.

Why therefore should man seek to betray man? Why should man seek to coerce man? What is the use? Surely the dreams of might and cunning are a flat denial of man's integrity;--mere caricatures of his true dream of universal power.

* * * *

Why is man, now, in this our land, in this the twentieth century, so seemingly a monstrous pervert? Why have nineteen centuries of Christianity failed? Why, with us, are the most rotten men the most marketable? Why are we, as a people, as a multitude, eaten with graft? Eaten in every tissue and fibre of our social fabric? Why are honest men scarce?

* From Norman copy.

THE DREAM OF POWER

Because we are Feudal!

Because our dream of power, individually and as a people, a multitude, has been the destructive dream of the power of might and cunning.

Because our democracy is an illusion. Because it has never existed in fact. Because it is a pretense. Because it was not a true dream of power. Hence it has not come square with human reality.

Our civilization, in gloomy actuality, is a towering feudal edifice built up of graft, of treachery and of slaughter;--resting on a quicksand of delusion. Great will be the fall thereof! Great the procession and the passing of phantoms. Great the dissolving of pictures. Great the climaxing of dramas. Great the breaking of hearts! The alarm bell is clanging in clamor to people in rigor. While men say: peace, peace,--in the hum of our dance of death.

Thus is our life become now like a placid mirror--and a strom--and sand. And thus man is now but a useless finger, moved by a useless soul, writing therein.

What is the use?
What is the use?

We need a new life and new men with new souls who shall write not in vain.

We need to let loose the pent-up waters of life to flood the Sahara of our hearts,--that the mirage vanish, and men become cool and real in our sight.

* * * *

So rises the veil from the soul of man.

So cross we the threshold of his sanctuary.

So enter we his solitary dream of might and cunning. To see with his eyes. To hear with his ears. To hunger with his man-hunger! To wonder with his man-wonder! To search the man,--high or low. To seize the actuality behind his veil.

For man has nowhere to go from us. His door is our open door. He comes not forth, so we pass in. Entering the sanctuary of man, we enter the sanctuary of that Life within which he is a dreamer of dreams, a perpetual maker of pictures. Dreams and pictures wrought of such airy fabric of illusion that, divested of his reality, they turn to the air. They,--vivid play of his passions! We,--vivid searchers!

Thus slowly turns our book upon its hinge within that wall which men have called Fate.

Man has been the curious toy and plaything of his imagination. Even as a dark cloud, passing, obscures the sun--so has it whimsically obscured him to himself--because of himself.

* * * *

And such have been men's hitherto dreams of power. In the white light of the new dream of power--The Dream of Man by Man for Man-- they are as ashes.

*C*HAPTER 6 THE SPAN OF LIFE

The normal rise, passage and decline, from cradle to grave, we call a man's life.

This "span of time" as we call it, because we do not know what else to call it, is filled with physical activities: the man comes here, he goes there, he does this, he undoes that, and these comings and goings, these doings and undoings, we call the man's life: Thus, we say,--the life of so-and-so,--meaning some man.

But the span of the man's life is filled also with the man's desires, as we call them, because we do not know what else to call them; and we sometimes include these, also, when we speak of the man's life.

These desires cause a man-child sometimes to become an "obscure" man, sometimes a "famous" man, as we say,--not knowing any too well what we mean by the word in either case,--because we do not know what life is. We assume we do; but we do not.

Thus it happens that when this So-and-So is mentioned as obscure, that is, a "nobody," as we say,--we lose interest; and when we hear another So-and-So mentioned as "great," that is, a "somebody," we acquire interest; not knowing in either case definitely why, because we do not know the bulky difference between realities and fictions--never having much troubled ourselves about either.

So we speak in some such manner, in general and particular, about the life of any man. That is, we regard him from the outside mostly, take him at his own valuation or the valuation of some few others, or give him our own offhand valuation,--and let it go at that.

And when a man dies we say he is dead, not knowing what else to say. And when we look upon the man dead, he seems very still, and we say, "He has gone beyond,"--not knowing the sense of what we say, because we do not know what life is. We talk about its "coming" and its "going," just as though we knew what the words really mean:--when we have no clear idea of what has "come" or what has "gone," or if anything has come or gone:--Because we live mostly in a world of fictions,--while Life is some phase of Reality. What phase we do not know, for we have never enquired except in Feudal terms--that is, in terms of obsession, inversion and denial.

In this same feudal, therefore unreal fashion, we speak of a man's soul and of his body, separately, not having the slightest notion of what we talk about; merely using words we have heard the feudal others say. And, as is our habit, taking the words for granted--that is, assuming without question that they really mean what they appear to mean:--and not at all assuming that there is a gulf between words and things.

Thus is our prevailing notion of the life of a man haphazard to a degree, in the sense of his significance as a part of the actuality of the flowing social life.

To be sure, we shake hands with him and talk to him; but we have really no idea whose hand we hold, or to what we talk. Casually, we call it a man; know that it has a tag or name; that it is "busy" about this or that. But the man--the reality--we do not know, because we do not search. And yet we say we search.

We believe him alive, like ourselves; not stopping to enquire whether ourselves are alive or not;--if alive, in what degree, if dead, in what degree? It does not occur to us that we ourselves may be more dead than alive, even while shaking hands with the man and talking to him:--this man, concerning whom the last enquiry we would think of making would be, to what degree, like ourselves, is he dead, and to what degree is he alive, if at all. It is habitual to fail to make such an enquiry, because with us it is a canon to avoid a thoroughgoing search concerning life. We insist, with most significant obstinacy, upon giving to life a limited meaning, because we assume life to be a word--and take no account of the gulf we have formed between life, the limited word, and Life, the limitless actuality. Nor, do we pause to inquire how much "life" has undone us,--as we look, without wonder, through the veil of our hypocrisy, as though it were not there. For we do not even know how sheer is the web of that veil, nor how lucent with the hues of illusion.

So we sum up the life of a man as something wholly positive and his death, as likewise, something wholly positive, not enquiring how much life a man may have suppressed while "living"; nor how much beneficence may spread abroad through the lives of men after his so-called death. So we say:--Speak gently of the dead:--as though that signified. For who are the dead and who are the living?

This is not here posited as "metaphysics." The actuality of the tie between men is vivid, clear, natural, unbreakable. It is man to man, all men to all men, generation after generation, age to age. It is link into link, strand into strand, flow into flow.

Metaphysics is a fancy name. Man is all in all. The word, metaphysics, is a scarecrow-word, made by the feudal learned, to mystify grown children, and obscure a plain fact. He who drinks water drinks metaphysics; he who breathes the common air breathes metaphysics; he who looks at another man looks at metaphysics. "Metaphysics," the abstraction, is an artificial word, a mendacious word. It diverts our attention from the plain fact of every day, the simple fact, that we, all alike, have our being in the universal life. Thus is the word a mirage because it parts man from reality: --putting a vain and empty word in the place of man and his limitless living powers.

Still, we talk about life as though we really knew something of it. We say animals are alive and trees are alive. But we say rocks are not alive, air is not alive, nor is water. Why do we draw the line? Because we are feudal egoists. We say we are alive. After that we acknowledge life only where we have to. We deny it wheresoe'er we can--not stopping to enquire whether this is a wise or a foolish thing to do. And what is here meant by feudal egoism? Simply this: We affirm the validity and value of everything we think is like our feudal selves; we deny the validity and value of anything and everything that we deem unlike our feudal selves. In this we are uppish and impertinent, for we, being feudal, have omitted to establish a sane standard of the validity or value of Life and its span. Hence is this form of egoism with us, so intensely individual, personal, exclusive--so akin to hate. When such egoism swells large it becomes gross egomania; nothing counts; and the ego becomes "I" in all its cold ferocity of meaning.

How could a fish live in the sea if the sea were not alive? The fish is not an abstraction, nor is the sea, and life is as concrete as anything can be. We cannot escape it even in death. There is nowhere to go.

No; the fish is a mode of the life of the sea, and the water is a mode of some other mode of life. Shall we then make a mystery of water and not a mystery of man? And if, to us, water is simple and clear, shall we not also behold man--simple, pellucid and clear? Why all this fuss about the soul?

Is life then something that is manufactured? The aforesaid feudal egoist thinks so. He thinks man makes life. He says man eats to live. He does not enquire what suggests that he eat. He says:--I eat to live;--as though he had stated the whole case. He says what he eats imparts life. He is mistaken:--Life imparts what he eats, therefore Life imparts life. He does not know this, because he does not enquire concerning life and man. Knowledge, with him, is but a mass of fragments. He persists in regarding all things wrong end to, inside out and upside down. This he does because he is selfish; and because that is the form or fashion, in thinking, he has been taught by the selfish. He takes it for granted, as truth, because other men do. The selfish intellect always regards secondary truths as primary, and primary truths as secondary.

The free spirit does not accept things merely because other men do. It searches. It seeks a basis, a foundation; and does not rest until it finds this or something which supports like a foundation and appears to be such. Moreover, that that which it seeks must be not only individual but universal; --and above all, transparently simple. This large, simple need it reaches as a balance to the tangle of stupidity and horror that feudal men have made of the intellectual life.

Clearly, man has the wish to live; and if this wish is, itself, a mode of Life, then is it the gossamer which weaves him to all modes of Life. But he, being now feudal egoist, is not aware of the nameless extension, delicacy and firmness of the tie, and what it really implies. Because, he, is in the habit of saying, "I": knowing but inadequately what "I" means. His "I" prevents him from "placing" himself accurately in the world of men and thoughts and things. Hence is his "I" mostly delusion and his "life" mostly phantom in its span.

He has heard of electricity, of its low and high potential, of conductors and non-conductors, of its flow and power. But he does not speak of electricity as a mode of life. It is not plain to him that it is a mode of life because it can't be anything else. Hence the real significance of the world of men is not plain to him as a mode of life. To him the word is "I" and "not I." To what extent he is or is not a conductor of the life-flow, rarely troubles him. Nor is he likely to go so far as to find that it is the quality of his desire to live that constitutes him conductor or retarder of the full flow of life. And that this desire, constricted or capacious, shuts off or accordingly admits the flow of life, in exact accord with the quality of his imagination and his will. For imagination and will are modes of Life, reacting with modes of Life.

So when the feudal egoist looks upon the neighbor, and feels him to be "not I," he becomes thus non-conductor of the life of the neighbor, and is thereby, himself, made less alive. This morbid distrust of the neighbor indicates clearly enough that our civilization is founded upon the constriction of fear, not upon the openness of courage, and plainly sets forth fear as a retardent, courage as a conductor of the life-flow.

Further, this distrust of the neighbor is but part of the fear in which the feudal egotist holds all modes of life that he cannot distinctly identify with himself. Therefore is "I and mine" with him an amazingly constricted, and pitiful conception. Under the feudal system of thinking this fear is logical; for in truth this fearsome egoism, this constricted, utterly selfish desire to live for one's self alone created the feudal system; and for centuries has determined the feudal function and structure of all civilizations.

Thus a brief study of Life and its modes, leads to a clear human understanding of the nature of Feudalism.

But, little by little, ever since the free spirit of European man broke loose from the organized tyranny and life-denial of the priesthood, man wistfully began to enquire, of Life, what might be its modes and reach? How great might be its span?

Little by little, ever so cautiously, feeling his way, man has been persuaded by his curiosity to overcome his fear. And gradually, as the desire to know, to enquire, and to let in the urge of life took the place of a frantic fear which so long had shut it out, have the boundaries of the life-span slowly widened to man's view, and the content within these boundaries become more and more diversified and impressive.

But man did not call this the Life-Search. He called it Science. For man was still a grown child, easily tickled by names. He did not know that it was the great Life-Span he was questioning with his own. He called it the search for knowledge; for knowledge, he said, is power. He even insisted that knowledge was an abstraction; so regnant in man's benighted minds has been the sway of the hallucination "I and not I." For man seemed apart from nature. He seemed to himself to be really alone. He could not identify himself with universal life. Such identification would have been too powerful an inversion of his notion of "I." Such a current of life, let in all at once, would have driven him mad.

This is not to say that the far eastern mind, long before, had not perceived somewhat of such flow of life. It is true it saw it in a way;--but could make no use of it, for that mind was feudal. The notion of caste, with it, was supreme.

It is the career of European man that keenly interests us now. It is with European and American civilization that we are becoming more and more closely concerned, as we search the life of the man of today; as we look into the nature of his desire to live; as we enquire why on earth he should wish to live if he can produce nothing better than the horror of civilization; as we enquire more and more deeply, What is the Use?

So, before the enquirer, the courageous mind, little by little certain feudal phantoms paled and flitted toward nothingness; and one little illusion, one little superstition after another--dissolved.

But the big superstitions, the big illusions, remained alike in the minds of the enquirer and the multitudes.

Nevertheless the enquirer managed to get certain things set right side up. Among other things he, little lump of jelly, set the great sun right, and the round earth right. Thus, in a manner, the enquirer got himself and his kind located in space. Quite a feat. A feat that suggests the feasibility of setting our civilization right, when once we perceive the simple underlying principle; and thus set the individual right in social space,--locating his ego where it belongs, and where it can functionate in a genuine way.

So "science" progressed. The spirit of enquiry grew apace; for life was beginning to flow through man's new-growing desires, even though he knew it not as such.

Man, the enquirer, took ever more and more notice of things in the great world around him. He accumulated increasing store of "knowledge,"--more or less uncertain,--as man remained uncertain concerning life.

He made "discoveries," as we say; that is, he became susceptible to various modes of life to which he was not before consciously responsive. But he did not call them modes of life, he called them by fancy names, and said they were powers or forces. For the obsession of externals doubles and abstractions (the feudal notion) still domineered his imagination and his will. The ancient superstition of dualism still had its grip on him. Hence he could not grasp the conception that his "discoveries" were but his own life responding to the modes of the All-Life. Indeed, under no condition would he admit this; for his surviving feudal ego, his "I and not I" was still busy weaving its curious, obscuring webs.

Yet withal, the enquirer was liberator; in a large way a reflex of the spirit of his time. For the multitudes were slowly changing--were distributed by the feudal thorn in their flesh. As the multitudes grew freer in their thought, the spirit of inquiry spread and grew freer. For it could go no faster than the multitudes would permit.

From then on, "science" made wonderful strides in the pursuit of knowledge; extending even farther the boundaries, looking deeper and deeper into the content within those boundaries and marveling ever more and more as the unseen became tangible. As the inquirer changed, slowly into searcher, this content appeared to him more wonderful, more fascinating;--but still he did not regard it as life;--he dared not;--he still held life in fear; he still wished to hold it in chains. He said that life was something separate, distinct and apart from all other things. Just as he said, "I and not I," so he said, life,--and not life;--unaware of the absurdity; --particularly unaware of the fatuity of his egoism. Unaware of the latent amplitude of his own consciousness, he was still a self-constricted idolater, --worshipping force, worshipping an abstract, isolated image of might, an abstract and refined image of cunning; still carrying in his mind the feudal taint of old--the taint, transformed into new pictures,--of despot and slave.

Thus his "science" became a fetish for him. It began increasingly to obscure himself to himself, in a new way. The scientist was slowly becoming monastic, brahman. He began to believe himself too profound for common men; he began to withdraw into an esoteric world of fictions --fictions which he took much more seriously than he took man, his neighbor; fictions which he contemplated much more seriously than he contemplated Life. For these fictions seemed prodigiously real to him--new gods. To his supreme fiction he gave the name Reason. This was his chief idol. He seemed unaware that the theologian, whom he despised for worshipping a different set of idols, had had glimpses of truth much closer to life than his own.

But in the real spirit of enquiry, which is man's free spirit, the profound search of his life for the All-Life, (however unconsciously), was under too great momentum. It soon burst through the bands which Science sought to make rigid and a finality, just as the Church, in its day, had sought to make theology rigid and a finality, and just as the unconfinable spirit of man had burst these bands asunder.

The successive phases of feudal man, in his discovery and proclamation of knowledge have ever been these:--This is the truth; this is the truth, the whole truth; this is the truth, the whole truth,--and nothing but the truth; this is the truth, the whole truth, nothing but the truth;--and he who believes not shall be damned!

Thus does the ego relax in acquirement, and become rigid in possession of power;--whatsoever the name or label given to that power. It is the old, old feudal story:--First an invitation to Life to create; then, an invitation to Life to destroy,--to dissolve.

So, science came to its crisis. It had set up the dogma: (This is truth, etc.),--There is matter; and force. The atom is ultimate matter; something hard; the force is resistless energy; something soft. All of which sounded well, and meant next to nothing. So absurdly pretentious a dogma could not long be acceptable to the spirit of man. So a new truth, (a new expansion of consciousness) was announced, reducing the fetish, matter, to evanescence.

But, unlike the Church, (and this is of profoundest moment to us all), Science relaxed its Ego, grasped the golden moment and renewed its youth. To be sure, it still talks of life and not-life--but not so bravely. The scientific mind is now beginning to flutter and hover within a shaping sense of the reality and universality of Life, and the vast reach of its span. It is beginning to surmise that the notion of life within not-life, may perhaps be an illogical conception. It is beginning to feel, with the delicate antennae of its thought, that metaphysics is a word which must stand either for nothing, or, for everything. In the inevitable drift of its thought, its imagination and its will, it is getting ready to part company with the notion, "I, and not I"; and, in so doing, will some day suddenly and dramatically discover man,--whose real existence as a mode of myriad modes of Life, Science itself--the so-called liberator, has hitherto belittled and denied.

In that momentous revolution, which happened so quietly but a few years ago, and to which the name, Radium, was given, for short, the spirit of scientific enquiry, in its search for truth showed its fundamental humanity; for the change was an internal change. It has served to show that the spirit of modern enquiring man no longer, knowingly, will repel the conception of the truth of universal life. For the "discovery" of radium and the unfolding of its far-reaching implications, was, as a phenomenon, none other than the flowing of a (to him) new mode of life into the mode of life man calls his consciousness; creating thereby a vast extension of its span.

Thus does every such discovery assist man in becoming more and more consciously integral with nature; more and more susceptible to the flow of the All-Life because he will recognize it as such. Thus will awaken in him a normal functioning of his ego, as little by little he lets himself more and more alone, allows the life within him an ever freer flow of expression, allows himself--by loosening his feudal bands--to see more clearly, to think more simply, to act more directly;--to the end that he may see man, and see in what sense man is and may become most truly alive; to see how the all-inclusive life flows through his own life, and, therefore, come to understand how momentous is his choice in giving direction of outflow to that universal life,--toward what he so vaguely, so indecisively hitherto has called, evil or good ends.

Thus will man become conscious not only that he has used and misused his powers, but just how he has misused them, just how he has failed to use them aright. So will arise, as a new picture before his eyes, a new view, a new consciousness of his relations to his fellow men. And, as his fear passes away, his egomania will be replaced by a clear and definite sense of humanity; by a clear understanding that the flow of life,--that inexhaustible reservoir of all strength--is at his disposal for the rejuvenescence of his spirit, and the recreation of civilization in the real image of man.

He will, thus, accordingly revise his notions of "I and mine"; for he will realize what this means, better than he does now.

For he will realize that Life, in its vast span, stands, ready and serene, waiting to fill all men with the joy of living, if but they cease to interfere,--if but they cease to will evil, and assertively will good.

He will realize just how and why man has interfered. Just how and why he has willed evil and good.

He will realize just how and why he himself has interfered;--just how, why and when he has willed--and so created--evil or good.

He will then understand exactly what Choice means;--and will choose aright because he will realize that no other choice accords with the integrity of the All-Life.

He will perceive that Life seeks and finds expression ever and only in modes of itself. That it will flow as readily into one mode of man's choice as into another. That it will flow just as readily into what we call vice as into what we call virtue. That vice is just as much a mode of life as is virtue;--That he, man, is the chooser--the arbiter.

He will then cease to marvel at the "mysterious" ways of a "providence" which not only tolerates suffering and misery, but, for "inscrutable" purposes of His will, inflicts them upon man. For it will come to him as a revelation, that he himself is that "providence"; that he himself brings good or evil into the world; that he himself has tolerated and has inflicted, suffering and misery upon the world of men; and that his purpose, in so doing, is not merely in no wise inscrutable, but clearly plain as day, simple as A. B. C., to the passer-by, to any man on the street who cares to look without fear.

He will thus begin to understand himself as creator: and that,--create, he must.

That the responsibility for creating aright or awrong, no matter who or what he is, lies distinctly, unquestionably and unescapably in his own will; that it is distinctly and undeniably personal. That his pious appeal to a feudal God is vain.

That his favorite hypocrisies are vain.

That his evasions, his sophistries, his double-dealings are all vain as chaff before the wind,--before the storm of awakening man.

That the solitary hope for peace on earth, and good will,--lies in man himself.

Thus is life not what we had supposed, but far fuller, richer, all-permeating, all extending.

And thus, likewise is man,--who is life,--in the very nature of his spirit congenitally in tune with the All-Life, and, therefore, an inexhaustible life in himself, with almost untouched powers for the good of himself and of all.

For man is the Key to all.

All concentrates and incarnates in man.

That man has exalted his weaknesses and ignored his real powers, would seem an inexplicable paradox did we not know not only how slowly his conscious intellect has taken on the sympathy of the heart and the illuminating power of spirit, but, also, how elementally simple are the two aspects of his desire, the two phases of his one power of creative choice,--that we have called Feudalism and Democracy.

GROUP V—THE MAN OF TO-DAY

Chapter 1   Awakening

Chapter 2   Money Talks

Chapter 3   Business is Business

Chapter 4   Economy

Chapter 5   Success

Chapter 6   The Practical Man

Chapter 7   The Eminent Man

Chapter 8   The Self-Made Man

Chapter 9   The Politician

Chapter 10   The Parasite

Chapter 11   The Monopolist

Chapter 12   The Worker—Life!

Chapter 13   Spirit

Chapter 14   Dusk of Gods: Dawn of Ego

Chapter 15   Wellspring

CHAPTER 1 AWAKENING

Wanted: Plain Men!
Men of plain courage,
Men of plain integrity,
Men of plain human feeling.
Plain men to see straight,
Plain men to think straight,
Plain men to act straight.
Wanted: Living men!–Lest we die!

Demanded: Removal of all veils from our own eyes, that now hide the predatory, the parasitic, the intriguing.

Removal of all veils, which these have hung up to hide behind--All of them veils of words and ceremonials; of forms, customs and procedures.

Removal of all veils from his own eyes and the eyes of all of us, which now hide from him and from ourselves, the powers of the common, every-day man. These, also, all of them, veils of words, ceremonials, traditions, assumptions.

Light! In all places, now obscure or dark!

Light upon all men, high and low, rich and poor, exalted or outcast, fortunate or unfortunate, learned or ignorant. Light upon their thoughts! A flood of light, daylight, upon their ancient dream! and their modern dream!

Demanded: The speedy dissolution of Organized Feudalism.

That is, the passing of
- Organized Privilege
- Organized Caste
- Organized Betrayal
- Organized Parasitism
- Organized Man-Killing

That is; The closing of the hideous world-drama of Rich and Poor.

Demanded: The world-wide repeal of the old basic social law;--the ancient ghost-law of self-preservation. That is, that inverted conception of man's natural power and integrity, which, for ages, has exalted and made sacred cunning, might, parasitism, dominion and slavery. The ancient social law, in virulent force through the ages and today, which gives to those that have and takes away from those that have not:--that is, The Law of Feudalism.

Imperative: The world-establishment of a new basic social law. Not a law of ghosts, inversions, hallucinations and cruel imbecilities concerning man, but a plain, clear, clean, simple integral law that shall start plumb, level and square with man--not some men--but all men, that shall rest on the bed rock of man's wholesomeness, power and integrity.

A law that shall exalt a man's integrity first, last and all the time. For integrity is man's essence. The man of integrity is the real man; the sane man, the efficient man, the creator. The crooked man, the parasite, (for all crooked men are parasites, and all parasites are crooked), is the ghost, the phantom, the maniac, the destroyed:--a menace to all his kind, all over the earth. The crooked man, the parasite, is the monstrosity, utterly abnormal:--the ghost-man.

AWAKENING

A law that shall repeal all prior laws and start fresh and new upon the solid first principle, that all men are alike.

A law, that shall repeal once and for all, the old laws of the miraculous, that is, all laws, forms and ceremonials, based on man as creature--that is slave; and which, shall exalt him in his true estate, that of creator;--a free and integral spirit; and that shall proclaim this freedom and integrity of spirit as normal to man and latent in all men--ready to come forth and flourish; awaiting but the fiat of man's clear, clean thought.

A law that shall set forth man's primary responsibility and accountability to his fellowmen--not some men, but all men.

A law, which shall set forth, not men's rights, which is a feudal notion and a theory of slaves, a theory of property, but men's natural powers and the free and efficient exercise thereof, for the good of all men --which is a theory of the free and integral spirit of man--a theory of manhood.

A law, which shall distinctly exalt man above property:--The spirit of man above all material things:--The character of man above all sordid things.

A law, which shall once for all, discredit greed, and, per contra, exalt social efficiency.

A law, which shall say to any man and all men: You are free to think, to speak, to act, for the good of all [your fellowmen.] *

A law, which shall say to the phantoms of Might and Cunning-- Go! Which shall say to the Parasite--Phantom! Hence! Which shall say to the Phantom man-killer; Begone! Which shall say to the Phantom Vicar of God:--Make way for man!

A law, that shall say to all men: Welcome in peace and good will! The man-hunt is over! Fear not!

Imperative, therefore: The complete dissolution of the present scheme or plan of civilization based on greed and fear and the prevalence of half-death; and the creation in the place of it, of a new scheme or plan of civilization, within which all men shall live full lives,--and no man shall live a half-death.

* * * *

These are the wants, these are the demands, these are the imperatives now moving in the hearts of men throughout the world.

Slowly, swiftly, surely, these but partly conscious imperatives are

* From Norman copy.

changing the imagination and the will of the multitudes:--clarifying, shaping and solidifying these in a new program of life and work:--a new conception of man and his powers, a new conception of life and its powers, a new conception of Spirit and its cosmic integrity:--a new conception of the thinker, the worker, the creator, the poet, the magician--Man!

Slowly, swiftly, surely, the ancient theory of the multitudes concerning God, man, nature, the heavens and the earth is shimmering, hovering, dissolving, clarifying and changing, and within the dissolution is shaping the form and countenance and beauty and power of a new consciousness of God, man, nature, the earth and the heavens. The intellect and the heart of the multitudes of earth are passing from the romanticism of adolescence, into the virility and equipoise and consciousness of primordial integral power.

This is the pith and substance of the Drama of Man.

It is *The Awakening of the Multitudes!*

All of man's hitherto history has been but the prologue of the ages:--The real drama of man is about to begin:--

The World-Drama of Democracy!

Surely the multitudes of earth have, since the beginning, like children, gone forth every day in the garden of the world. They have gone forth wishing and willing and what they wished and willed became, for them, civilizations.

It is concerning this wishing and willing of the multitudes of earth therefor, that men have written books and have called these books History:--quaintly omitting to mention in these books, however, that they were in fact but records of the wishing and willing of the multitudes. Perhaps they did not dare, perhaps they did not know, perhaps it is only lately that we have made the discovery.

And so it is with all the books men have writ, and have labeled Philosophy, Theology, Economics, etc., in all of them, the reality of Man and the reality of Earth, have been most quaintly omitted; and in place of these, have been exalted phantasms of evil, phantasms of abstraction, phantasms of dualism, resting, all, upon the primal social phantasm of Master-and-Man, which, ever and always, has been taken for granted.

This being all true, let us, in our man-search, take a look at the lingering ghosts, which men still carry about with them, and which make of them, half-ghosts, half men. Let us look at the lunacy of the man of today. The ghostly lunacy of the man on the street, the ghostly lunacy of the multitudes, the ghostly lunacy of the exalted, the powerful, the elect, the eminent. For we are a strange people,--half men, half ghost--stranger than fiction. No poet could have created us, no poet would have dared; he would have thought his work too bizarre, too broad a caricature of man. It is we alone, who have created ourselves. We alone, who could do so, we alone, who could make such a caricature of men, women and children. It is we alone, who do not find it bizarre, that we should disclaim a belief in ghosts and yet, walk about with heads filled with a company of them--a veritable menagerie of phantasms--phantasms political, religious, economic, commercial, industrial, educational, and so, on and on, to our curious and freakish bewilderment.

Let us see what the lunacy of "success" means, the lunacy of "economy," the lunacy of "business," the lunacy of our "common sense" and "practicability." Let us have these ghosts walk abroad that we may see them in the open. That we may see them against the real background of sanity, against the sumptuous splendor of nature, against the pristine and immeasurable flow of Life, against that serene urge of primordial Spirit, which we of today call modern as we, in the shimmering change of our wish and will catch glimpses of the outline, form and countenance of normal man.

Let us then look at ourselves, for a while. Let us see just what manner of caricature we are; let us see just how bizarre we are. And let us note above all, how we obscure ourselves, and how our ancient ghosts shut out the light of the spirit. Let us note the difference between the surviving phantoms of the past, and the true spirit of the present.

It will be worth while.

And what we find among ourselves, will hold true of all the peoples of the earth; for all men are alike. It is merely a matter of local coloring.

So breaks the dawn on the man of today and his company of ghosts--so shrills a cock-crow on their weird and solemn and ludicrous dance of death.

So comes the white light apace.

So breaks apart the ancient night.

CHAPTER 2 MONEY TALKS

Within the mind of modern man remains a ghostly savage.
It is this disconsolate phantom that snarls, death-dealing omens.
It is this ghost that answers the query, "Which way?" saying: "My Way!!"
To this one in hiding, MONEY calls, saying:—
Where art thou?
From the jungle comes a quick cry:—
Here am I!
Ah, So! What doest thou?
I kill.
Why dost thou kill?

For Thee:--To gain of the power of Thy Spirit.
What wouldst thou of my spirit's power?
That I may kill--more! Lord! in thy name!
Why kill more?
To have more!
Why have more?
To kill more--ever more--ever more:
It is my desire, my hunger:
Help Lord! I thirst!
Thou art my need!
Grant me Thy Power
For thou art Overlord, and God,
Outdwelling,
Indwelling.
Knowest thou Man?
Yea,--I kill.
Knowest thou the women and the children?
I know them as thy shepherd.
Knowest thou the multitudes? and the motherless? and the awful fatherless?
Yea: In flocks: I gaze: In Thy name.
Knowest thou thyself: Sober spirit?
Thou art my spirit, manifest in power.
Knowest thou then me?
Thou art God.
What wouldst thou, ghost?
Give me all thy power.
That I may seine the multitudes and strain them out, and consume.
Wouldst thou not preserve?
Yea; I would preserve.
Wherefore? Man?
That I may be God of Earth.
Knowest thou the Destroyer?
Art thou not He?
Then will I destroy thee:
Thou knowest me not!

CHAPTER 3 BUSINESS IS BUSINESS

To say "business is business" as we say it today, is to say the one word, Death.

To say business is business, as we shall one day say it, will be to proclaim an utterance of Life.

For, one day, the man on the street will perceive the savage, the misanthrope, the idolater, the coward, the slave he is. He will see and be startled, surprised, overwhelmed, astonished, abashed, ashamed and disgusted. He will vomit himself for a while, and be wearily sick and lonely.

Then, become acquainted with himself, it will be clear to him how sullen is the useless savagery of his illusion, how morbid his idolatry of it, and how ghostly, how unreasonable his cowardice and his slavery.

He will wake up, this man, and discover that he has been a slave: even as he has laughed at slaves.

Whereupon, as choice is his own, he will powerfully banish. For such desire lies deep in the clarity of his will. It is up to him. It certainly is not up to anyone else; make no mistake.

To call the man of today perverse, is but to state a threadbare truism; is but to repeat what his sapless acts say of him.

To call him an unhappy egoist is likewise a miserable truism, voiced satirically and sharply by his acts. And yet this is by no means the whole story; very far from it; the whole story is a long story: would it were not so long! and could be made plainer.

To call him a "good-fellow," is to call him what he calls himself; and what, in his pasty illusion concerning the real way of life, he believes himself to be. And yet he certainly is a good fellow; none better. He is all right, if he only knew it.

That is, he is a savage-idolatrous-coward-slave-good-fellow. So his acts say; so his philosophy declares; so his thinking proves:--such ghostly thinking as he does.

This is not a paradox. It is modern man, the man on the street: any man. It is his intellectual core. It is his present, weak, watery choice at the parting of the ways. It is the man you and I know:--splendid but mistaken:--sound but rotting.

* * * *

Yet in his heart is ever a familiar disturber, seeming to say:--
Listen to me!
But the misanthrope brute spurns the fervent true one: Such is the flaccid, dyspeptic man of today.
For the man says: Silence! I want my way!
While the uneasy one repeats, and repeats: *Which way?--*
So the man says: Business is Business--that is my way.
But the disturber queries:--*Knowest thou?*
Yes I know Man, what of it?

And the Disturber queries:--*Knowest thou?*
Yes, too well: You have vain desires, foolhardy desires. You would change my intent.

Knowest thou?--
Cease!! That is not business.

Dost thou remember--?
Hush!!

Thou knowest that I know!
Away!! My will is fixed--I shall prevail--I must!

Dost thou see?
I see what I choose to see.

Dost thou not hear?
I hear what I choose to hear.

Is that then all to be seen and to be heard?
Enough for the day.

Why dost thou destroy?
I do not destroy: I build! It is my will, my anguish, my life:--It is my all in all:--I am in pain.

Why dost thou betray?
Lest you betray.

Why dost thou so fear me?
Lest you destroy me: Lest you dissolve my will: Lest you lower my guard: Fool! do you think I would lower my guard?

Do I not build?
Castles in air.

Am I not Life?
Yes; and bitter death to them that trust.

Lo, am I not Life?
Not here.

Speak! Am I not thyself?!
No, No!!--Yes,--my weaker self.

Hearest thou me:--Am I not truth?!
Yes!!--No!--I hear:--when it is still. You persist, ah Dreamer of dreams; you are no solid part of me, but a stranger, an intruder. How did you come to unlock the door? This is no place for you and me. You are not of the world. When the time comes, beloved, I will meet you:--yonder, behind the everlasting veil, and listen, there,--not here.

Listen--now! Where goest thou this day?
To business.

To kill?
No! To acquire.

To acquire what?
Power.

Power to do what?
Power over men.

Why power over men?
They wish it.

Have you put that question to them?
No need: I know.

Do you know what is best for yourself?
Fool!

Will you put that question to them?
Imbecile!

I am thy heart!!
Maniac, you have crept into my heart, to ransack it.

Hear me, I am thy heart!
Then it is good I have a brain.

Listen: I know thy brain. Thy brain knows me. It sees but cannot feel. It hears but cannot feel. It builds and destroys but does not feel. It knows me, yet it cannot feel without me. It is thou who keepest us apart. Thou keepest thyself apart from me.
So much the better: For you would ruin all.

You believe?
I know. It needs brains, not heart.

What then is business?
Hell.

What makes it so?
The wolves.

Knowest thou, then--Man?
I have spoken.

Knowest thou, then,--thyself?
As well as need be.

Again! Knowest thou me? Knowest thou me?

Enough! You are torment, my disturber. Would that I were rid. And yet no: no:--I would not be rid of you--not wholly rid.

Why?--Why?

Because of the dark.

Thou speakest in a darkness!
Even though thou knowest me not,
Yet am I Creator, Preserver;
I am Life, I am thy heart!
I am Disturber, Aspirer.
I am Truth.
I murmur to thy brain the while thou sleepest,
The while it sleeps.
I will awaken it.
It will awaken thee:--
Then, wilt thou know and call me Friend.

* * * *

The man-hunter is abroad in the land.

He lurks like sunshine and shadows in the highways--He glides through the green fields everywhere.

He melts into the secret places of the Great City.

He hunts his own kind--unnatural brute.

This hunt, he calls "business." It is vast and varied. Intricately cunning, many baits, many traps, many pitfalls, many snares, many blinds, many decoys.

But there is a vaster business to be done. That is:--to replace the savage, ghostly illusion "business," by the civilized reality.

* * * *

Fluidly and silently Life energizes any form of desire that man chooses for its flow. So fluidly, so silently indeed, that he, man, is unaware of what is actually doing the work. He himself believes that he is doing something. So he is. He is choosing:--While Life does the rest.

He does not realize that Life is still--very still. That it flows on and does its work in unspeakable and immeasurable silence. The noise man himself makes, especially his talk, obscures for him the significant silence.

He believes he lives in a world of sounds. He ignores that he lives in a vast world of stillness; and that that world is Life.

So with powers or forces. He deems the violent ones great. He does not perceive how thrilling and cosmic are the gentle. To him the earthquake is a great power; but not the light of day, nor the dewfall.

Force or power, to the average man, is that which inspires dread or hope. The nature of a power, he seldom searches. Hence to him money is a terrific power. He knows, or thinks he knows what it can do to him, or for him.

Misapprehending the true seat of power; unconvinced that there is no power save the power of Life; he looks thus upon money as a fetish; as something having power for good or evil in itself.

Thus he says, "Money is the root of all evil," which is to say something dull and asinine. Man himself is the root of all evil. His life is the root of all money-power.

Taught to regard all powers as external to himself, he believes the power of money to be external to himself. He believes he is alone in the world. He forgets the multitudes, as he forgets the daylight. He forgets the neighbor, as he forgets himself.

Unheeding and unaware that, he has an imagination, he fails to use it in his own behalf, else he would see that he himself is a source of the power of money. That the neighbor is, likewise. That its full power is the power of life of all the people. Money is the child of the people. It is their creature. They created it all. It is what they are. It is the voice of the people. It is their will. The power it has is the power in themselves--with which they have endowed it. It is the reflex and the index of their imaginations and their wills,--just as they are. Its power to buy them, to sell them, is the power they abdicate. Its power to enslave them is a power they delegate. Its power to destroy them is a power they do not at all understand. They, deeming themselves negligible as air, and their own greed negligible, see money, but do not see man. See money but do not see themselves. See the phantom power of money, but not the real power of life in themselves. This ignorance is their luxury. This apathy is their luxury. This lassitude is their luxury. They pay all the prices because they are too dull to look behind the Dollar--and find the man. They do not realize that Life is very still, hence they heed only sounds. They do not realize that Life does the *while* they choose, and *as* they choose. They choose ignorance--Life does the rest. They choose apathy--Life does the rest. Hence, as they choose, Life becomes their destroyer,--because they know not Life. Because they know not that by their own choice, by their own wish and will, Life destroys them. This is the real race-suicide. This is why there are rich and poor. And, observe! the land is mottled with public schools, where the young are "prepared" for the "struggle of life."

Truly Money talks when it says these things.

And "business" will be "business" so long as we say life is a struggle.

And so long as we say the "fittest" shall survive, just so long shall the "fittest" seek our lives to take them away. Without game there can be no man-hunt.

* * * *

The people are prolific. They keep up the flowing supply of young. Thus the man-hunting remains good. Thus the man-ghosts hunt the man-ghosts.

The air is shrill and soft with decoy-calls,--varied, alluring:--How real they sound!

Thus hunting-man calls, now shrill, now soft--and the ghost-people answer, answer,--and then!?--Because they answer with the cry of the savage; and the cry of the true heart does not count:--While Life flows on in silence--while men receive it not! Thus the "fittest" hunters and trappers survive and prevail. Because the multitudes so create as a phantasm.

Yet why repine? Have not millions in our day broken their hearts against a wall, neither knowing nor caring how they made the wall.

For ghost-man searches ghost-man at the throat and in the pocket.

Thus the "fittest" searchers survive and prevail.

Also man seeks man with a snare.

Man also poisons the waters of life.

It is the people's wish.

* * * *

Man receives life sane and sends it forth insane. He receives it real and sends it forth a phantom: Man the madman. But it is life, just the same, after it leaves him: He has merely chosen that it shall destroy.

He does not perceive that his "business" is a form of insanity--because he does not perceive that he himself is afflicted. Hence he does not perceive that "business" necessarily must undermine the vital constitution of the multitudes, and they,--decline and die of exhaustion.

These are some of the things that Money says, when it "talks." It says, particularly, that the poor are extravagantly ghostly and luxurious,-- that they thus exhaust themselves and die of phantasms. They break their hearts in vain.

* * * *

The practical study of man today is a study of his habits--as we say of a hunter and trapper, that he is familiar with the habits of game.

The study of man's habits is thus the kindergarten of "business enterprise."

* * * *

Money further "says," that to recognize the worst in man is to cause the worst to flourish.

It also says that to recognize the best in man is to cause the best to flourish.

It further says that what counts the most and costs the dearest is man's ignorance of the best in man--that he now regards it as counterfeit, whereas it is the real and valuable thing--the rest is counterfeit.

Money further says that the people themselves are the explanation of all values, all miseries, all glories.

But "business" says they need not know this.

How silent is the flow of desire in a man's heart!

How silent is the flow of thought in his brain.

It is very still within a man's heart, very still within his brain, immeasurably silent within his consciousness.

How little a man realizes that he thinks without words, feels without words, dreams without words, and is conscious without words. How little he realizes the silence of his imagination and his will. These are silent because they are of Life; and the flow of life is so silent, so still, so delicate, so powerful, that we are unaware; and we say "time flies," when we mean Life flows.

Hence are words the most futile part of man. Hence are his acts eloquent. And hence is the sequence of his acts the visible drama of the flow of his thoughts in the stillness.

It is this stillness within the man that is both appalling and inspiring. When we enter into this stillness we are surely at home in the man. We know by the stillness that we are at home.

Thus do we come to understand, little by little to be convinced, that a man's acts flow out of the stillness within--and not from the noise of his words.

For man knows very little about words--they are the least part of him: and yet he clings to them as to straws.

Hence he seldom says what he thinks, but always acts what he thinks. Thus are man's acts the sole social criterion; the unique standard of social measurement.

Thus it comes that when a man says in words, "business is business," he means, in his stillness,--I am a hunter and a trapper of men--I am a ghost; I frighten and undo my kind.

And when he says, "money talks," he means--"I act":--It is my way:--I am a law unto myself.

* * * *

Thus is the sanctuary of man a still place, entering which, we know, from the very stillness there, we know, not by reason but by intuition, spirit to spirit, silence to silence, flow within flow, that man is a dream--a dream of Spirit, a flow of flowing Life.

Thus infinite in depth is that silence within man which he calls his soul, his ego. Out of that silence flows all that man is and all that he does.

It is the soul, the ego, of man, that man has feared, because it seemed indwelling but unreal. He believed it went on journeys. He still believes it "comes" and "goes." Thus it is the silence of man's soul that has frightened him--unaware of the fecundity of that stillness--unaware of the stillness of Spirit.

Likewise it is the silence of the neighbor that has frightened man. It is the silence of Life that makes man fear Life.

So he says "business is business" to cover his fear of the silent soul:--to cover his fear of what the multitudes may bring forth:--to cover his fear of the soul of a people:--to cover cunning and his might as with a veil.

Who shall believe in the genuineness of man's wickedness? Plain as it seems--pitiful as it seems in man's acts,--a search of his soul does not find it there. Such search reveals the pristine purity of Life there, and lays bare the vital truth that all man's so-called wickedness is the outcome of his fear of the reality of man--that is, of his fear of Life. When man surmounts this fear, his evil, which is but a mirage of his good,--will vanish.

Then, the business of life--his real business--will take on a new significance, a new motive power, and proclaim a new goal.

No, there is no real wickedness in man. His savagery is but a phantom. His soul in its depths is pure. Fear alone makes it seem to him impure. The soul has no fear. Fear is of man's unstable brain alone. That brain which he follows like a slave--against the clear, clean pleading of his heart.

Thus, we perceive that Truth is in fact, any mode of Life. That we can thus grasp life in the significance of its essence. Thus falsehood and vice are visibly modes of the flow of life, and man easily seen as the chooser. And thus through his choice are fear and courage man's responses to life.

The power of Life is exhaustless, and clearly at the service of man. It is for him to say how it shall flow, at what it shall work, and what it shall create for him. It is for the multitudes to use this power of choice aright. For the power of choice is man's primal power, underlying all his other powers.

If man makes it his real business to choose aright--not only the good of all will follow--but a new civilization, a real civilization will arise, as a sun, out of the night of our own.

In our dream of power we forget our real powers.

In our dream of externals we forget the power of choice.

In our dream of great men we forget that they are the obscure in disguise.

In our dream of rich men we forget they are the poverty-stricken in disguise.

In our dream of benevolence we forget it is man-hunting in disguise.

In our dream of charity we forget it is bondage in disguise.

To invert these dreams is the real business of the people.

It is up to the people. They who are now so busy with "business" that they forget the real business of life. It is up to the soul, the real ego, of each man.

CHAPTER 4 ECONOMY

    We go to the theatre, sit quietly awhile, conversing, among the throng, amid the buzzing of voices, we listen vaguely to the music, a little bell tinkles, a great curtain steadily rises, reveals a mimic set-scene; some play-people, the play begins, we are intent. Behind the background of the mimic scene, which may perhaps seem to us a landscape, are the scene shifters, also other play-folk awaiting their turn to come before the landscape and say their words. Should this background be lifted as a curtain, we would see something quite different from what is in front of it. But the background is not raised, for it serves as our illusion; that is why it is there. It was painted by the scenic artist, put there by the scene shifters, that it may serve a purpose while the play goes on.

    The play is irrelevant, of course. It is vacant by the tacit assent of all. It has nothing to do with the actuality of life. As a matter of fact it has nothing to do with real human beings, their actual thoughts, their true feelings. It goes to no conclusion. It merely "ends," as we say.

Should a play be made that would go to a conclusion, a manager would scarce dare present it, actors would scarce dare perform it, and we would scarce dare look or hear. It would seem too monstrous in its naked power. Too repellent. Too vibrant. Too sweeping. It would appal us. Its somberness would overwhelm us; we would not, could not understand it. For we have not yet come to understand that Life goes to conclusions; nor to comprehend how it is that Life goes to its conclusions inexorably. How it is that man flinches; compromises. At the crucial moment he shrinks. But shrink though he may, expostulate though he may, evade though he may, deny as he may, decry as he may, Life brings the dramatic conclusion to him at the exact time. He cannot evade the reckoning which he *invited,* when he said: This is my way!

So the mimicry proceeds upon the stage; while we look on, and listen to its vacancy of word and act.

Of course, it must "end" happily. That, we demand. We, being tender of heart, wish even a play, a myth, to end happily. We wish, however, to weep over the preliminary misfortunes; for we are tender-hearted; we sympathize with misfortune on the stage. And we are jubilant when virtue prevails. For virtue must prevail on the stage--it is our wish. We pay money to be lachrymose over misfortune, to see virtue prevail, to see all end happily among the play-people on the stage with the background of illusion. That is all. Marionettes they, marionettes we. The curtain falls. We go away.

Next day, we proceed as usual--we being practical people--to deride misfortune, to sneer at virtue, to leer at heroism, to make happy endings impossible.

Giddy people; strange, fantastical people we. A people so immersed in pessimism that it seems to us normal, seems to us so rational, refined, real, that we go through life like automatons, seemingly without consciousness: Astoundingly heedless that, if our imagination gave but the feeblest tinkle of awareness, a curtain would arise as the lifting of eyelids from our eyes, and we should see--actually see, for once, as a vision, the real world, with its real men, its real women and children, its intolerable human dramas, its disastrous endings, its confounding misfortunes, its slow torture, its morbidity, its hallucination; its actors blind, hysteric, distorted with dementia, wearing themselves into human shreds; into human tatters; All about what? Bread?!

No! no! widen the imagination! Throw it open wide--and this "real-life," as we call it, clears, and becomes but a sinister play, a set-scene; the actors really madmen, the background an enlarged vista of illusion; the misfortunes over which we weep salt tears, illusion; the happy endings, illusion;--vivid illusion, which seems to us not merely real, but positive, truthful;--living things to be touched, and felt unchangeable, valid. So, we, actors in this play, deem ourselves alive; and so, we, spectators, believe the vista of our most cherished illusions, that is, our feudal beliefs, our feudal convictions, our feudal hopes, our feudal fears, to be true, solid background of the reality of life.

Therefore, of all human illusions none is so profoundly ghost-like, so pathetic, so compassioning, so utterly heart-searching, so amazing, so shrill, so strident, as is that egoistic inversion which incapacitates an entire people from seeing and knowing, from searching and holding steady the few, quite simple, obvious, human truths; and which, thus, renders them insensible to the actuality of the destructive power of Life, and insensate to its hortatory call as it works in response to the cry of their tortuous and turbid desires.

To look, as spectator, over our broad fair land; to view therein eighty millions of humans moving, as in a trance, as in a vast vortex, moving, as dreamers, into slavery, believing it freedom; moving there of their creative choice, while unaware of the meaning of that choice:--What tragedy!

So intense is the reality of this, that one, as in a horrid dream, cries, Stop! Stop!!--But the procession moves on and on within a sort of twilight of hallucination, under the shining daily sun.

This silently moving procession, this trance, this twilight scene, is of the drama of our land and people. All are actors in it, all spectators; a few seeing a little of the meaning, the many seeing not at all. It is a strange drama; for spectators and actors alike pay here. To this tragic drama we have given a name: *ECONOMY*. The participation price we pay, rich and poor alike, is immolation. The mere death of others is not enough; we must pay the higher price, the price of self-disintegration, of dissolution of brain and nerve, of slow straining and breaking of the heart of rich and poor alike.

The drama is not written; it has grown within our thought as a people, since our beginning as a people, and is flowing out of us.

This national drama is in three acts. The first, we, a people, have tacitly chosen to call "Money Talks"; the second, "Business is Business." The third act we have provisionally named "Prosperity." The survivors will name it with a branding iron in due time.

We are in the Third Act now. So sinister is the cyclonic power of its swirl and rarification, that we are not aware. We think it quite ordinary weather. We are not even aware that from the drama a curtain has risen--so engrossed are we in pleasing ghostly conversation. But the silent, sane spectator knows that a curtain has risen. Sees and knows that the act is entered into irrevocably. Sees and knows that there can supervene but one of two climacteric outcomes:--a cataclysm of rebirth in freedom of spirit or the catastrophe of break-up and disappearance. For the clear vision bodies forth a larger and ever larger drama--the growing drama of the world; and involved therein, the growing cost of savage egomania, the growing cost of feudal insanity, the growing terrific cost of feudal irresponsibility, the steadily growing cyclonic cost of feudal illusion, the consuming cost of feudal waste, and the devastating futility of refined and reputable feudal murder.

Truly in the growing tension of this, our third act,--the final intoxication and delirium of the white man--his madness and stupor in the open light of day, his raving incoherence, his horrible, ghostly cries: "Buy!" "Sell!"--we see now approaching the climax of his mad civilization, we see him going at last to a conclusion--we see at last the logic of feudalism swept on by the power of Life to a conclusion which the ancient order has dreaded and sought to stave off with fine words;--a conclusion, a veritable cataract in the open, an historic Niagara--before the eyes of the world-- for all eyes seem open but our own--We, who should see ourselves the best, do not see at all--We* should know ourselves the best know ourselves least--others know us, we know not ourselves--for we are mad! We are ghosts!

We, who, sorely needing truth, reject truth!

We, who, needing health, reject health!

What can be more tragic than the deadly rejection of truth and health by a multitudinous people?--Is it not clearly an act of madmen?

We who submerge and kill our honest while we cry, "Business is business!" Is it not tragic to behold a people killing its honest, ridiculing them, while it laughs, mutters, sneers, whispers, "Business is Business"?-- While it holds its own infants by the throat as it simpers "Money talks"?

* In conformity with previous sentence possibly the word *who* should be inserted here.

Would any but madmen kill their own young?

Is it not appalling to see madmen kill their young day after day in the open?--For money!--For Money!!

Is not the kindly, smiling horror amazingly tragic?

Is not this phantom Third-Act tragic indeed?

Is not "business" tragic?

Is not murder for money tragic?

Is it not the act of madmen?

Is not our prosperity tragic?

Is it not bitterly tragic?

Is not our drama, Economy, a drama of murder?--the murder of thousands upon thousands? And of betrayal of thousands upon thousands.

Is not this drama,--the twentieth century world-drama of Feudalism,--brought now to its supreme utterance, here, in our land?

Is not our hypocrisy tragic? Is not the cost high?

Are not our sweet words tragic? Do they not cost?

Is not our "Christianity" tragic? and intolerable?

Is not our Third-Act the supreme crucification of manhood--a crucification sweet, gentle, mellifluous, mealy, plausible, merciless, dull, suave? Is not business business? Say, is not business business?

Do we not say, business is business, instead of saying crucify him. Is it not sweeter to speak thus? Does it not sound smoother, duller, more unctuous? Does it not sound sane?

Does it not shock us to hear the word murder, especially when it is whispered close in the ear? Is it not an ugly word--when it comes home --when it means you?!

Yet are we not complacent while we kill? Do we not hold it horrible to kill one--"business" to kill many?

Is it not a crime to kill at short range? Is it not an accomplishment to kill at long range?

Is this not tragic?

Is this not the thought, the act of madmen? Is this not the thought, the act of white madmen going to pieces?

Is this, then, the real modern drama:--that we kill at long range, maim at long range, betray at long range, poison at long range, trap at long range, lie at long range, steal at long range?

Is not this long range science the essence of business enterprise?

Is not the art of business, the smooth and plausible concealment of the ferocious fact?

Is not this tragic?--this long-range killing, snaring, robbing? This long-range lying? This long-range hypocrisy?

Is it not--this acme of cunning--the cunning of madmen? Is not this might the might of madmen?

Is not the stupor of the people tragic?

Is not their blindness tragic?--their deafness?--their muteness?--their utter ghostliness?

Is not the suppression of the clean, clear, pleading, warning cry of the true heart most tragic of all?

Is it not the most damnably destructive of all?

Is it not the most brutally insane of all?

Are not those who suppress the warning cry of the true heart madmen?

Is not our civilization a chamber of horrors,--pleasing horrors, suave horrors, unctuous horrors, dull horrors?

Are not our thoughts horrible? When sifted through the relentless sieve of Life are they not respectably brutal?--are they not christianly ferocious?--are they not reputably savage? Are they not somber, and repellent, and ghostly?

Is not this exhalation and exaltation of cunning and dull, hypocrisy, tragic?

Is it not the act of madmen?

Is not the truth most unwelcome?

Is it not tragic that truth should be unwelcome?

Is it not the act of madmen to turn away truth?

Is it not the supreme act of madmen?

Are there not those that would destroy the truth-teller?

Who would then destroy him who disturbs them in possession?

Who disturbs them in cunning?

Who disturbs them in might?

Who disturbs them in intrigue?

Is this not tragic? Are not these the maddest of madmen? The most murderous of murderers? Are not these those, who, to the uttermost, have stifled the warning cry of the true heart?--and set at naught the call of Life?

Are not these chief murderers our chiefly benevolent?

Are they not our chiefest in Charity?

Is this not tragic?

Is this not intolerable?

Is it not brutally savage and low?
Are not the people like unto shoals of madmen?
Is it not tragic that they are such?
Is it not intolerable that they, in their madness, accept Charity?
Is it not appalling that they in their madness accept benevolence?
Is it not incredible that they cannot see?
Is it not unbelievable that they do not know?
Is it not remarkable that human beings, brought forth by nature in integrity, are immediately poisoned by the thoughts of grown men?
Is it not tragic that the young should be taught fear in heart and mind by the ghosts of their elders?
And yet we call this Economy!--this dance of death.
We call all human waste, Economy!
Such is our madness.
We say life is cheap, money dear.
We say property is sacred, manhood is not.
We say God is good, man evil.
Such is our madness.
Is it not tragic that our ghosts drive us mad; that money drives us mad? Respectably mad?--Disreputably mad?--Loathsomely mad?
Is it not tragic that we call this distortion and madness, Economy?
Is it not a singular caricature that we call destruction, Economy?
Is it not bizarre that we call filth, disease, and degeneracy, Economy?
Is it strange that we call crime, Economy? No! it is not strange. We are feudal; therefore it is normal for us to be ghosts, and measure our pondrous dance of death to the song of the crucification.
Hence we call our madness, our cruelty, our stealth,--Economy:--
Because these things are of our feudal egomania.

*　*　*　*

Life knows Truth--for Life is Truth. From Life man can conceal nothing. From the calm flow of life, the Destroyer, he cannot escape--he has nowhere to go. For Life is everywhere--without man and within man. It inhabits his sanctuary--it inhabits the earth. It fills the void.
Yet man the madman believes he can lie to Life.
Is not our Third Act indeed tragic?
Is it not stupendously tragic to behold the Man-of-Today,--the madman--in multitudes, high and low, rich and poor, ignorant and learned, obscure and eminent, in a frenzy seeking to lie to Life?

ECONOMY

Man, the Liar, confronting Life, the Omniscient!
What tragic vision!--
Life aware,
Man unaware!

* * * *

Is not our peril plain?
Do we not indeed need, in our crisis
Men of plain courage
Men of plain honesty
Men of plain human feeling?
Do we not need in our ghostly, tragic hour:--
Men to see straight
Men to think straight
Men to act straight?

Do we not, in our bitter hour of agony and bloody sweat, need
Living men!--Lest we die!

Is it not tragic that we need such in our extremity?--
In this our sombre Third-Act,--under the Shining Sun?
In our broad, fair land.
In this, the last act of our Feudal Drama?
The Drama of Feudal Man?
The Drama of the Man-Hunter?--

* * * *

CHAPTER 5 SUCCESS

Upon the great problem of success we bend our minds. When we think of success we think convulsively.

And yet what we call success, if visioned forth as a machine-tool would go to the crap-heap of any intelligent manufacturer. It is so wasteful a mechanism; so extravagant a method; so grotesque a scheme for utilizing the prime power of the people. Were it put before us as the work of a mechanical engineer we would consider him a lunatic--so great is the loss in friction (almost total)--so great the loss in motion, and so inferior and defective the product: Yet we, being lunatics, admire: for we love fantastic devices for man-killing, and what we in our half-man half-ghost way call success is a man-killer. It undoes us all--it undoes even him whom we call the successful man.

SUCCESS

We are romantically absurd, we. We are trees that walk. The little foothills of our immediate feelings shut our mountainous thoughts from view. But the mountains are there.

We are amiably busy; for we are an amiable people; amiable as ghosts can be. So we say business is business in an amiable, ghostly way.

We are a simple hearted people; and in this simple way we say: money talks.

We are a kindly people and we say astounding things in kindly ways.

We are an honest people, so we say and so we mean. Thus we do dishonest things in ways that appal:--we are so unknown to ourselves--so strange--so unacquainted--so unreal.

We love comfort; we are easy-going. We do not like to think straight--it might disturb our comfort.

We are shallow, and we like it.

We are good natured. We are docile too, and tame; easily herded. We feed from the hand. It is the sweet and sane in us, cropping out, although we do not know it.

We like to be entertained. We seek joyous entertainment, as a people athirst. For indeed we are a people athirst--thirsting for we know not what. We like that which is agreeable, easy, which comes and goes quickly, like a shadow (Alas, like a shadow).

We admire "bright" men as we call them.

We admire the "smart" man. He is our ideal. "Smart as a trap" we say of such man. It is our high praise.

We particularly admire "sharp" men, as we call them, able, snappy men; men who "get there" as we say; men who "get things done"--who accomplish things--that is, "successful men."

We are self-confident, self-reliant; we really believe we know it all. (Whereas we do not even know our own stupidity.)

We are an optimistic people. (So optimistic that we do not perceive our deadly fatalism.)

We are a cheerful people. (So cheerful that we do not understand the tragedy of our lives.)

We hate to listen. (Why listen, when we know it all!)

We believe we are a free people. (That is why we love slavery.)

We believe in free speech:--but we will not tolerate it.

We hate to see straight. (Why see straight, when we have so much to hide.)

We have a system of morality, as we call it, that is gaudy. It is a kind of harlequinade.

We are cheaply picturesque in our thoughts. We have lively, bargain-counter fancies. We are curious in speech--we have many witty, pithy sayings. We believe we are "Johnny on the spot," as we say.

We believe that we are very shrewd and keen; that no one can fool us. But we are so dull, so easily fooled that we do not perceive that what we call Success is but our new name for the ancient institution of slavery and dominion, and for the rehabilitation of the powers of might and cunning.

We are a proud people, too. (But we are not too proud to do dirty work. Alas!)

But we are sound of heart nevertheless. Even if light of head. Even if vain, unwilling to be told and slow to learn. Even if we can learn only through bitter pain. Even if we can learn only through disaster.

And, also, we are a people of a really deep faith, an abiding faith, a faith that stands for something, we do not quite know what; a faith that hungers for something--we know not what:--Something real; something human; something of the spirit; something of Life; that hungers for a true expression and realization of ourselves:--we know not what (For we do not feel straight, nor see straight, nor think straight, nor act straight. We are so crooked that we cannot even perceive the fact and its consequences). We merely feel in a weak, mystical way that our faith stands for a hope, stands really for humanity, for "uplift" as we say--that it looks forward to a better time. This is deeply, sincerely true, however volatile, ghostly, foggy, and for the moment flabby and futile.

We are generous to a fault, our selfishness does not become us; it really is a misfit. We are selfish because, not seeing straight, we do not understand the utter folly of it--that this is the man-killing folly.

Our sympathies are quick, too;--as quick to evaporate as they are to appear.

We are not a thoughtless people. No, we are thoughtful in the sense of bending the mind upon something of interest. We think indefatigably, intensely, constructively and passionately about Success. For the "successful" man, as we say, is at once our mystery, our hero, our idol. On him and how to be like him, we bend our minds with such earnestness, such seriousness, such absorption, that we become self-hypnotized. Under the strain, too, of such intensity of thinking, we become overwrought, jaded. This is where we really live. Our one, tense, thrilling, all-absorbing thought is of Success. And Success, with us, means the accumulation of money. For money is our language. It is the only language we know and use earnestly. In its terms we couch our hopes, fears, ambitions. In its terms we voice our misery, our wretchedness, our despair. This we do in no childlike way, either. When we talk money and when we talk success, we talk in the satisfaction, the anger, the bitterness, the triumph, the agony of grown men. For money is the American reality. Success--through any means, at any cost, by any method--the life-goal. These two stand forth in terrorizing and phenomenal isolation from our basic normal life--all else vanishes when we think of these. All preservative qualities of heart and mind disappear as in a fog; all regard for that which is plainly, pleadingly, warningly human vanishes in daylight; and we harden, harden, harden! We harden, even as we are good natured, even as we are frank, open, generous--even as we are smooth and kindly. We children grow very cruel, eagerly brutal, callous, cold and hot with passion, when the hunger of money, the thirst of success is upon us, the paroxysm of possession, fair or foul.

It is thus that when we think of Success we think convulsively; and common sense, foresight, prudence, decency are swept away upon the whirlwind of our immediate and mad desire--the desire to win--the ancient desire of the multitudes to win or to lose. Hence may we sum up our sham philosophy and our sham humanity in the expression which is the essence of practical Feudalism, ancient and modern:--"The Devil take the hindmost."

Hence we cannot know what Success really means in any sense whatever. Thus the ancient ghosts of Feudalism render our so-called Democracy insane through fear and greed.

This mad enthusiasm is a complete illusion. That which it assumes to be the real background of life is tragically false to the best that is in us. A caricature, a weird and wild distortion of the best that is in us, and this truth we partly realize in our flitting moments of lucidity.

For our notion of Life and its powers is like a child's picture of a man--drawn upon a slate.

All these things are symptomatic of hysteria and prognostic of lassitude and collapse, distinct evidences that we are suppressing our true spiritual activities.

This strange sickness, which we label Success, and which in its intensity becomes ever homicidal, suicidal, in large and in little exhibits the profound persistence, in the modern intellect of its ancient feudal inversion; the strange and dramatic survival, in spite of all that we call "progress" of the ancient fear of life.

Hence we need object lessons and more object lessons! Lessons for the millions! Shock and Jar! Light and more light! Disillusionment after disillusionment: Awakening and more awakening!--that we may see straight, ere this Success, which we worship, destroy us--because we know it not.

This is why we need men--all men--to see straight and act quickly:-- To reverse our engine of destruction--for we are on the brink of downfall and disaster. The time is growing desperately short.

There is but one way to avert the smash-up.

That is, for all men--not merely some men--to see straight, think straight and act straight--and do it at once. For our graft--our utter crookedness--our fantastic selfishness--has brought us at last to the dread parting of the ways. We must soon settle our account in blood or in sobriety. We are at the stupendous climax of the World-Drama.

Hence we need living men!

Not politicians, priest, warriors, financiers, captains of industry, merchant princes and other ghosts, but plain men! Men of heart! men of faith!

We must at once stop killing our honest!

The faith of the multitudes must awaken and be strong.

Let our Dance of Death cease!

and the Dawn begin!

CHAPTER 6 THE PRACTICAL MAN

In taking a wide-range view of a people, as one might overlook the sea from a promontory, it does not need long to know that a people is massively a whole, and exhibits a common flow or drift, a common life, which, in a larger way, is the same as the nature and drift of an individual man. Thus we may fittingly speak of the soul of a people, as we speak of the soul of a man; and, in the same way, we may speak of the thoughts, the acts, the ambitions of a people as we speak of qualities, characterizing a single thing, a mass, a whole. For, whatever internal stresses there may be within the individual man, whatever the seeming diversities and contradictions, he nevertheless, acts and reacts as a unit, although relatively a small mass; and this unitary quality which tinctures all his desires, thoughts, feelings and his acts, is especially, what we call his character. It is his identity; his make-up. In mechanical phrase we would perhaps call it his center of gravity; whatever moves him, moves him consistently and as a whole. For the individual man is consistent. There is no real contradiction. His apparent paradoxes are conclusive evidence that he is consistent within his character. Now one of the most curious exhibits of this consistency is his belief that he is different from other men. His belief that there is really something about him which marks him off as separate, solitary, and distinct from other men--which puts all other men into a sort of negligible class by themselves: So, he says "I"! He feels this and believes this because he lives with himself so much; indeed he lives not only within himself, but for himself. He is convinced that he understands himself better than anyone else can; that he is well acquainted with himself. To him the pronoun, I, is conclusive. He believes that he has a fair working knowledge of the world of men, the world of ideas, the world of things. It is a part of his consistency, therefore, that he regards other men as different from himself. That seems to him plain because external. He believes himself different from others because he feels it is so. He believes others different from himself because he sees it is so, and believes it must be so in the nature of things. He believes this to be a self-widened, practical view, and that he, in so viewing, is a practical man. Now it happens that this individual view is universal. Every man over the earth believes it. To be sure there is some talk about the brotherhood of man, but that is breath. The fact is that every man believes himself an isolated individual; that he is separate from his fellows:--That this is a plain, practical truth. The fact that all men believe this, and have always believed it, shows that the people of the world actually have ever held and now hold one thought in common. To have exhibited the fact that all the people of the world hold one thought in common, is to make an exhibit of value, for it fixes the center of gravity. Around this center each man moves--all men move. When we, in searching man, come upon this truth, we are close to the fundamentals of human nature; and the misery of life begins to take on meaning. What is appalling, because it is so small, while so vast, is the tenacity with which men cling to this view as paramount in importance. And what is mournful, is that it seems to be the only view to which men are able as yet to cling. So pervading is this view, that each man, in consonance with it, believes in a god external to himself, different from himself, and that he is different from the God. And man thus, in the fulness of his consistency believes all things to be external to himself and different from himself--nature, the universe, the air he breathes. The profound fatalism with which he uses the pronoun, "I," would pass all belief in its declared isolation, were it not so widespread, so consistently exhibited in the acts of the peoples of the world.

Now the searcher, entering the soul of man, knows, there, that the individual man possesses the heroic power of choice. That this, also, is a universal power.

It is therefore increasingly significant, in the drama of man, to note that the individual chooses to believe himself different from other men. Moreover, it is a wonder of the drama of man's soul, that we may, at one and the same time, behold it so minutely set forth in the obscure man, and overwhelmingly presented by the peoples of the earth. It seems difficult to realize that it is the one and same drama, all the time. It therefore intensifies the situation, when we further realize that man, the chooser, has no choice but to choose. Choose he must, and choose he does; Life demands it. In this sense man is seemingly driven by necessity,--but all notion of harsh necessity vanishes when he chooses to choose aright. Thus, while it is plainly normal for man to be at one with the beneficence of Life, he, in his egomania, has chosen not to have it so;--hence his misery--hence his entanglement--hence his artificial unhappiness.

It seems to be fairly clear to men that they can choose, in a way. It is not clear to them not only that they must choose, but that they are actually choosing all the time and expressing choice in every act. In fact men can do nothing other than choose--there is nothing else to do; for choice is the sum, the substance and the essence of man. Eliminate choice,-- man vanishes.

Is it not strange, then, that man knows so little of his power of choice, that he inverts the idea of choice into a terrible conception of external rule, and passionately believes himself victim of circumstance? Is it a wonder that he believes in the necessary inequality of men? Is it a wonder that men die of broken hearts because of this belief?

We Americans declare that we are practical. And what we declare, is worth reckoning with for we are the youngest of the nations, and have had the best opportunities of any people for discovering and proclaiming social realities.

Two assertions are strong in our speech, namely, that we are practical, and that we are guided by common sense. The two statements are, in our thought, so closely related, that they interplay; and it is tacitly assumed that if one is practical, he uses common sense; and that if one uses common sense, he is practical. This, indeed, is in itself a simple and fine enough statement. No better or more cogent statement is it possible to make of a satisfactory social foundation. Carried to a conclusion it would prove the cure-all of our social ills and would surely liberate the spirit of man, to his joy at the discovery of himself. It would regenerate a people, if it were a fact.

But, unfortunately, as far as we are concerned, it is not true. It is a bluff! Instead of holding clear and steady a conception of what is practical, of what is common sense, we are merely groping in a fog. We are in a fog as a people, because we are in eighty million fogs as individuals.

For wherever men believe that they are not alike, there will the fog be with them--and they will be mutually antagonistic, unintelligible--therefore incapable of clear, coherent, expression, as a people, as a whole.

And wherever the belief exists that men are different, there will surely be pulling and hauling in an intricacy of cross purposes. Inevitably must there be friction waste and a charivari of folly. Is this what we mean then by practicality and common sense?

It seems scarcely common sense or practical to do things in the hardest possible way. And yet that is our way. We proceed by opposition instead of concurrence. It is an exhibition of folly. Folly is unpractical.

Now, whenever by coincidence men assume temporarily, as it were inadvertently, that they are alike, ("the one touch of nature,"--as we call it) there is an immediate, even if flitting, amelioration. The happening is as delicate and responsive as the finest of balances, for it is the momentary turn of men's choice, and Life responds instantly. For Life flows through men's brains and into action just as quickly as they choose. We instinctively know this, but we cannot place it and hold it. We do not believe it real because we cannot definitely grasp it. We call it sentiment or impulse:--something quite apart from business. Thus we substitute shadow for substance,--which is pure folly.

It is obviously common sense and practical to simplify. But we complicate and confuse everything that has to do with the way of life. For we, believing that men are different, believe naturally that life is complicated. Again folly.

It is manifestly common sense and practical to look for the simplest possible explanation of anything and everything. But we don't think so. We believe the real explanations must of necessity be complicated or they couldn't fit complicated affairs. And it is inevitable that we shall think thus, just so long as we believe men are different, and just so long as the individual man believes that he is actually solitary--a law unto himself alone.

It would seem common sense and practical to arrange our views of the social life in an orderly way, that is, each aspect in its true relation to man. But we don't think so. We arrange matters in a disorderly way, twisted, distorted,--all out of gear. Hence are we alive with graft, that is,--betrayal. Just so long as men continue to believe they are different, just so long will this continue. For folly breeds folly.

It would seem but common sense and practical to desire to know something about ourselves, and especially about the nature of our real motive-powers. But we don't think so. We believe we know it all now. And yet we are not capable of solving one solitary problem. The reason is clear. We do not perceive that there is a single problem underlying all our problems. Until we perceive and solve this, it is impossible to solve the others.

Just so long as we insist that men are different, just so long will every man's hand be against every man, and just so long will men have confused and distorted notions concerning evil, and still more confused notions concerning good. Our notions concerning good, especially, are the quintessence of folly.

It would seem to be the part of common sense and practicality for a people resolutely to search out the nature of good and evil, as a vital human proposition. That it should be the first thing we must know, in order to make quite clear the great way of our life. But we don't think so. We leave it to priests and philosophers. And they lie to us. Why? Because we lie to them. We deem it practical and common sense to lie to them. And so the tangle increases, and it is lie for lie all around. Indeed there is no help for it as long as men collectively assert that they are individually different; and stubbornly refuse to see the plain, common sense and practical fact that they are all alike, and that this likeness is the real social basis.

We make a great to-do about the difference between men. We give enormous importance to the difference between a bricklayer, a priest, a lawyer, a merchant, a banker, a president, etc., etc. What folly! These men are all alike. Sift them and they will show the same net result. Saints or sinners,--all alike:--For they share in common the mad belief that men are different. This they do of choice, and choice is their essence, each and all. What they do with their hands or heads, whether their fingers are in one man's pocket or another, is not of consequence as long as the center of gravity is the same for all; and that center of gravity--evil,--that is, their joint and several belief that men are different. What difference does it particularly make what they happen to do with their hands or heads--when it is all a consistent falsehood anyway,--when they construct with no other result, and seemingly with no other object than to make the tangle worse.

What are we constructing, anyway? we practical and commonsense people --other than a vast and ever-increasingly intricate mesh--a huge man-trap!-- to confine us all! Is it common sense to make such tangle,--such trap?

Our libraries are filled with books? Are they true to man? As consistently true to man, as man is consistently false to himself. What are our industries, commerce, etc.? Bitter, elaborate lies; false to the real man-- true to the false man--the practical man--the common sense man. What a tragic folly that breeds such elaborate meanness, pettiness, uneasiness, pain, anguish, misery, jealousy and hatred--and such calamitous separation of hearts!

But we think it's all right. For we are a practical people. We manage to get along,--so we say.

It is informing, therefore, to study the workings of a practical and common sense people. To see these workings charted by the people and spread out, as it were, like a topographical map. To put the finger here and say, this is interesting; to put the finger there and say, that is very interesting. For the people certainly tell the truth of folly in their acts of folly; and the totality of these acts they certainly spread out clear and plain for the inspection of anybody. It requires no especial clarity of eyesight. Wherever a million men are gathered together, there, is the fatalistic idea at work. Wherever a single man is, there, likewise, is the same idea,--at work. The same idea producing all these "different" results. What a grotesque and sombre conception of the Way of Life is here spread out to view! How busy a people we must be;--we practical people! Where is the spirit of inquiry? Where is the free spirit of man, that we do not care to inquire what is destroying us? Are we of a verity all dead, or dying? --or merely in a trance.

The practical spirit of getting things done, is a fine spirit in itself --but would it not be common sense to inquire what we are not getting done? So also is the spirit of common sense a fine spirit. It is the very essence and motive-power of good brain work; it is the true basis of efficiency.

Would it not be a fine application of the spirit of each, to find out what on earth we are trying to do to ourselves, and just why we are choosing the particular form of suicide that is undoing us:--That is paralyzing our modicum of practical common sense.

Might it not be well to inquire just why we deem it practical, jointly and severally to drive men insane faster than we can provide for them in our practical humanity? Just why we consider it practical to ruin men; to fill the land with human wreckage; just why we deem it practical to foster the spread of disease, while we busily build hospitals; just why we insist on breeding crime; just why we suppress the cry of the heart; just why we throw the entire weight of our mass upon the unfortunates we create; just why we kick men when they are down? And then, perhaps, it might be well to try and connect all this hodgepodge up with common sense:--Just to see how it works out with our assertion that we are a practical people.

We might also try to explain on a common sense and practical basis just why we regard any man as imprudent who thinks of the good of others; why we regard as smart the man who thinks only of himself; just why we put a premium on lying, stealing and killing; and just why we put a heavy penalty on those who would rather not lie and steal; just why we throw all our dead weight upon the man who would serve his fellow men, and push up, with all our power, the man who would destroy his fellow men; just why we conserve with such care the two social extremes--those we have made very weak and those we have made very strong. Then let us try to connect up with common sense and practicality our suppression of the best in us; that best, that fundamental good, which, through the din of our folly is ever crying for expression? Why have we suppressed it, why have we gagged it, why have we been ashamed of it? Why do we go to such extravagant lengths to ignore it? Why do we fear it? Why do we fear what is good in us? Why do we fear that this good will destroy us, if we let it escape? Why do we stand in such terror of truth? Is it because of our common sense? Is it because we are a practical people? Or is it because we know, positively, in our hearts that we are cowards, hence liars, thieves and killers? That is the truth, at last! That is the tender spot--the quick. We fear that the fabric of our civilization would collapse upon us were the truth known. We fear that we should go down into chaos, for we do not know what we could possibly put in the place of it. It is the best we know. We believe it is the best the world has ever known. So we putter and shift and tinker, trying to make new props as the old ones rot or split. We believe we can stave off the day of the downfall, by lustily shouting: Progress! Prosperity!--by lustily lying. For we fear to face conclusions,-- we dread conclusions--But we must face! It seems tragic to us that man must change from evil to good. We don't put it that way, but that is what we mean. It seems calamitous to us that Justice should change from abstract to concrete. We dread lest Justice become human. What will become of our possessions, our power, our privilege, our vested rights. A useless worry, a frivolous worry--an hysterical worry. Inquire, rather, what will become of our penetentiaries, hospitals, slums, our breeding grounds of disease and crime, our insane asylums, reformatories! Inquire if these, also, will not simultaneously disappear! Inquire just how this would connect up with real practicality and real common sense!

When we, as a people, awaken, as we will, to the simple truth that men are alike, *and, therefore, all equally* responsible, our civilization will not collapse--no, it will not collapse--it will dissolve as a nightmare; and the bright reality of universal common sense will arise in its place. There will be no slums; there will be no madmen at the top;--for one means the other--each is the explanation of the other. Both are explanations of us all.

It is heroically practical and heroically common sense to search out the good in man. That is worth while. To analyze ourselves simply, truthfully and bravely is worth while; for we are worth while. We are open, obvious, not hard to study. For we have not yet acquired the old-world fine art of dissimulation; the old-world facility in wearing fine raiment over sores; the old-world gift of sitting brazenly, fine clad, upon the slums.

We are a people of curious weakness and curious strength. To the patient and sympathetic observer we present our character in three phases:--First, a frothy, supercilious, jovial, cynicism, heedlessness and absurdity. Second, a terrible and morbid fatalism. Third a sound, sweet, wholesome and altogether lovable nature. And it is of this latter that we are bashfully and timidly conscious and ashamed. For we wish to be considered grown-ups, to ape the sophistication of decadence, to appear to be blasé. In this we are foolish grown-children.

To push through the layers of our folly, of our pessimism, and find this underlying sweetness of heart to be solid and sound, requires perhaps uncommon faith. But he who has had the courage to search man until he has found the eternal, the god-like and completely tangible part of him; who has in fact, not in fiction, gotten a good steady look at the reality man--knows that man is sound at the core. He views therefore with clarity and sympathy the Tragedy through which man has passed and is now passing. He sees how simple is the explanation of it all. He sees how clear, how human is the proposition of good and evil--hitherto and now regarded as mysterious, confounding;--he sees it bound up with the fetish notion of a fickle extraneous god. He sees so clearly, humanly, the natural and universal creative powers of men, that he thinks it well worth while to tell the truths concerning man's illusions, in order that man, at last, may see himself revealed to himself as far more noble, more splendid, than has been supposed--and, so seeing, rejoice in his strength.

This seems worth while.

It is the animating spirit, the science, the art deemed valid, common sense and practical--underlying the method of this man-search.

To seek man, to find him, to exhibit him, to illuminate him, to reveal him, and to show that the only faith worth while is faith by man, in man, for man!--That seems worth while. So does it seem worth while to show that man's faith in Life is but faith in himself and recognition and faith in his power of choice. That man's faith in the spiritual reality of a god is in actuality faith in the integrity and universality of his own free spirit. That if man is a dream, as he needs must be, he is likewise and necessarily a dreamer whose dreams come true,--For his dreams are the flowing of Life. So, that, truly, a man may say, I am life!--and, so saying, be done with Fear and Fate.

Would it not then be a practical procedure, a matter of plain common sense, a matter of true self-preservation for the multitudes to exhibit plain courage, plain honesty, plain human feeling in the great Way of Life? Would it not be well for them, as individuals and as peoples to resolve to see straight, to think straight, to act straight?

Would it not be well to resolve to live--lest we die?

Is not the time ripe for a speedy dissolution of feudalism?--Shall not the people so choose with their vast power of choosing?

Is not the time ripe for the affirmative proclamation of Democracy--Is it aught but a matter of choice? It would all seem so. Injustice and betrayal are reaching the limit of plainness. We must all get busy, with choice--with Life. Busy in earnest. We must make good our claim that we are practical. Make solid our claim that we think--and so act--in terms of common sense.

To accomplish, we have but to begin straight. To begin straight we have to see straight. To see straight we must feel straight.

Then will our darkness become light:--our supreme folly change to simple common sense.

For when men change in choice--they change fundamentally and consistently. They are, so to speak--reborn. The tangle dissolves! Clarity appears! Good emerges! The Light shines!

CHAPTER 7 THE EMINENT MAN

The outcast believes himself an exceptional person,--apart from the rest. The eminent man, likewise believes himself an exceptional person, apart from the rest. He is sure that he differs from other man. He feels himself born to greatness, well fitted to nobility of mind and workability of intellect:--and that he stands for these.
That is his illusion.
He has not enquired concerning the reality, because he believes this the reality. Such being the case, little is to be learned from him save how not to think and how not to do. He is a fable, this eminent one; a metaphor; a fiction; an old-time allegory of the multitudes. He, like them, saturated with feudalism, is not especially aware. He but emphasizes the

rude leanness of the thought of the people by an immaculate leanness of his own. He stands, also, symbol of a primitive instinctive poetry in the multitudes. A poetry rich, fragrant in desire--fateful in illusion. His education, culture, training, conventionally artificial, hedge him like a labyrinth, wherein he is lost but complacent. This labyrinth he carries about through the hours and days--through the long years: It is the mystical atmosphere of his feudal ego. To him it seems just.

The voice of the people reaches him, but he cannot understand. His voice the people cannot understand; as it floats through the entanglement it seems like an echo. Yet each affects to esteem the other. Thus is there a saving grace of humor.

He, fair in appearance, is grotesquely estranged from the people; yet is he of them, in a way he knows not. He talks in their general direction, down to them, or with his back to them, or as to children, or he talks preferably to himself. His sense of locality is vague, his sense of focus nil. Yet he stands, the multitudes have ever believed, as a vivid ideal in them; and he himself, sometimes believes this, in his feudal fervency. He, holy one, believes in an aristocracy of intellect. So do they, the lowly and unholy, who pay. They believed it first. Otherwise he never would have had a chance to believe it. He believes nothing they do not believe; he has not the courage. They believe nothing he does not believe. They have not the courage. Hence between them exists a strong kinship in fear, in isolation, in apartness, in solitariness; and they say soft words to each other in a firm, common belief, that men are different. Neither believes in the natural powers of man; each believes such powers are fortuitous, miraculous, revealed; bestowed especially by heaven; each believes in the existence and power of an external, capricious will, which creates one man thus, another man so. Each believes evil to be constant; normal; good, to be fortuitous. Each believes firmly that men are and must be born with monstrous inequality of mental powers; that this is nature's way. Thus is their illusion his illusion; and his illusion, theirs. But his illusion rests upon theirs, else could he not be eminent. They, desiring eminence, dreaming of it, have ever insisted that he stand in isolation. They have ever wished it so. They still will it so. He as willingly accedes--and becomes useless, in the great regenerative way of the Life we seek.

A feudal people will have demi-gods--must have them. Fervently they desire to exalt, into visibility, that which they vaguely and very bravely believe to be the best within themselves. That which they exalt is the mysticism, the dull illusion, and magic void crowded with fairy shapes --which grow within themselves.

And thus it must be, under the reign and sway of inversion. It is the multitudes themselves who are faithfully feudal, who are intense egoists, --hence intense worshippers. It is they who tenaciously believe in caste; it is they who believe in inequality, and foster it; it is they who believe in slavery; it is they who believe in dominion;--and proclaim it; it is they who believe in poverty and foster it; it is they who believe in the powers of might and cunning, and exalt them; it is they who are gaudily ashamed of the urge of the true and the good in themselves, and, so,--(Alas!) (and alack!) in shame--suppress it. It is they who discredit their own natural powers, (ah, what shame!) and so, in shame deny them; and it is they, alas, and alack, who do not know that they are the vital social power,--that what they affirm--"comes," that what they deny--"goes." A purblind people, a mob, a mass, a strange cynical people, are the multitudes who do not know themselves.

What a price they pay for this. What a costly burden they carry-- but they are rich,--the poor. But the eminent do not tell them it is a luxury and a heavy burden to be without faith in themselves. Such speech has no part in the aristocracy of intellect. It has no place in immaculate thinking. The rich do not tell the multitude that it is a luxury and a burden. The pious do not tell them it is a luxury which explains all their burdens. Nor does the "successful" man; nor the "practical" man. If they, the multitudes, wish to know truth, they must find it for themselves. They must feel the new world-spirit moving and enquire what it means. They must become aware that it is they themselves who have ever insisted upon victimizing themselves. Perhaps plain men, men of plain courage, may assist somewhat. The eminent will not, cannot, do not know how, and persist in not knowing. There is neither health nor help in the eminent--they are parasitic and yet forever empty. In them is no affirmative save the affirmation of the sacredness of Feudalism.

When the people "find themselves," the eminent will find themselves also; so will the pious, so will the successful, so will the worldly-wise and prudent--but not where any of them now supposes--for the soul of man is basically different from what is feudally supposed,--so is the soul of a people--the soul of the world--the soul of the universe.

The people will awaken whenever the veil of feudal illusion, rotting with over-ripeness of time, drops down from their eyes.

Then, and thus, they, becoming liberated of eyesight, will see, (for it is easy to see it) the naked ferocity which they now sanction, and in which they are self-enmeshed. They will see it staring at them, fate-like, face to face, gazing at them with a putrid familiarity. They will hear it, in terms of sharpest accusation, declare itself themselves!

Then will they recoil and turn.

For, to see our feudal and barbaric civilization naked, is to see a horror; a ghost; a Dance of Death. And, to see our people in their nakedness, stripped of illusion, mysticism and hypocrisy, is to see that same horror, that same ghost; that same Dance of Death.

CHAPTER 8 THE SELF-MADE MAN

A man may steadily toil with hand or brain, believing, the while, that he is "making" himself; but that counts only in the way of activity. Many a man "makes himself," thus; but that does not determine; it is but a continuing self-preparation to meet his fellows. It is the thought held by his fellow men that ever is tending to make, unmake, uphold or destroy a man thus ever self-preparing. And it is the eddying thought of his fellows, as things are now, that each man must reckon with through all the uncertain and perplexing days of his life. His fellows broadly are ever saying to the man, Live! Die! The mandate is simple; the power, immense. So the man, high or low, is a proposer. The people massively dispose, in a large way and small. They dispose according to the thought they hold in secret and put forth into acts.

Should the man think as they think, but more vividly, it goes well with him so long as he is careful in little and large. But if their thought effectively changes while his does not, he is swept away. It is simple. It is the ruthless, massive method of a people. For a people is an ocean of souls, in commotion on the surface, silent in the deep currents and tides. What causes the commotion they may know; what causes the currents and tides, they do not know, they do not even enquire.

Should a man perchance think truer than his people's surface thought, he may be done for; even though it be later perceived that he thought their deeper thoughts. Then, perhaps, in gratitude, they exalt him, dead. This, also, is the massive way of a people. A people that does not enquire, has not enquired, and does not care to enquire. For a people is in ponderous momentum, and its great momentum is but the great multiple and sum of the smaller momentums of individual men:--that is of you and me and the other man; whatever his name. But a people is not insensitive; for each man has a mind, a heart, a soul; is thinking, feeling, responding to one thing or another. That is, you and I and the other man, whatever his name, are doing this all the time--every day. Thus does a people (and a people is you and I and the other man, whatever his name) quiver in its massive desires. Each man thus lives and moves within the tremor of the mass. That is, you and I, and the other man, whatever his name, live within the quiver of the mass.

A people is enormous in its power of caprice and steadfastness, because you and I are capricious and steadfast in our way. Thus the people, the multitudes, (that is, you and I) exalt, tolerate, ignore, or sacrifice, or cripple, or destroy a man. Such then is the attitude of a people toward the individual. (That is, such is your attitude and mine.) It is as simple as it is ruthless and utterly brutal. The power of the mass (that is, the power of myself, yourself, and the other man, whatever his name may be) to exalt or destroy, involves at once our peril and our hope. The mass-choice (that is, your choice and mine) while now for evil, is poised for a turn. It is quivering, near the point of the great parting of the ways from Feudalism to Democracy--from the slavery of selfish illusion, to the open earth and air of the sane free spirit. (That is, you and I and the other man, whatever his name, are quivering at the parting of the ways.) It is thus for us a momentous time; for it is a time preceding stupendous new action due to a changing mass-thought. The world-importance of our day, our people and our thought cannot be over-estimated.

Until recently the dominant thought of our people has run about like this:--That it is on the whole better to ignore than to conserve those who think in seeming opposition to our mass-thought. We have not stopped to enquire if the opposition be real or imaginary, superficial or deep; we have not deemed it necessary. But now it is horribly necessary that we enquire;--we can no longer endure ignorance. We must establish a positive standard of social values. We must establish a sane standard of thinking.

We have ostensibly tolerated freedom of thought and speech; in reality we have not done so. We have been willing that the individual may play at thinking, or attitudinize, or say smart things, or solemn-sounding things. But we are not as yet willing that he disturb our traditional fixed ideas. It is exactly these ideas that need shaking; for they are intensely feudal, while we, in reality, in the depths of our hearts, are indubitably democratic. We do not understand as yet the nature of the misfit. We instinctively feel it, but thus far we have been unable to locate and define it, because we, as a people, have said: What is the use?

How we might receive a truth that should go to our innermost, truest selves, we do not know. We have had little experience. We have had to do with half-truths which either fictitiously exalt us, or depress us without giving tonic inspiration, or imparting courage. Yet it is plain to be seen that we hunger for an inspiring word. We, insincere, hunger for sincerity. (Yes, we hunger and we thirst.)

Our pernicious thought, now, (born of our insistent belief that men are different) is, that life of fixed necessity, is a struggle, a fight, an intrigue, and that to the victor belong rightly the spoils. Thus do we set up before ourselves a phantom image of a fierce, cunning, ruthless world; and this, we say, stands for the real nature of man. We call it "real life" and "the way of the world," whereas this phantom image, this "real life," this "way of the world" is but our massive inversion of the truth in us; hence, it is our massive invitation to Life to destroy us, each and all. For such an inversion is a Death-thought, not a Life-thought--A Death-thought of our multitudinous mass--dark and somber in its fatalism, in its tragic negation.

Thus, holding in common, as we do, this thought of a world inverted, it is inevitable that the sense of "worldly wisdom and prudence," as we call it, be the breath of our life; the inspiration and suspiration of our hourly thoughts and acts.

It is the touch of this basilisk breath, which causes a man (you and I!) to fear his fellow men; and it is this fear that stealthily and steadily increases his (our) alert sense of separateness. Hence, in an ever-present panic of self-preservation, he, (you and I and the other man, whatever his name), rich or poor, is a hypocrite; and hence in self-protection as he (for he is you and I) believes, he lies, and steals, and betrays, and kills, directly and indirectly, near or far. (Alas, how this goes to the core--to the core of you and me). Hence does he (you--I!) seek in one way or another to bind his fellow men, that he, (you--I!) as he fain would believe, may be free, may be safe. Thus he, (you--I--always You--I) spreads his venom. Thus others (the others are you and I) spread their venom, rich and poor, eminent and obscure, and thus are we massively envenomed and envenoming. So comes it that we uphold an envenomed world--a massive, virulent fact. A horrible, dastardly fact; a putrid, disgraceful fact.

Into this world children are born.

A world we, in our anguish, strive to conceal. We do not dare to be found out--even by ourselves. We do not wish to know or have it known in full, how terrible the world is--how ghastly. We throw others upon it, you and I, we cry out lest we be thrown upon it. (Alas! Alas!) Therefore we have drawn over our envenomed world a resplendent veil of fictions. We fear what is behind the veil. We fear the wild panic into which we might be thrown should that great veil be wholly drawn aside. That is why we fear the Truth-Teller. For on the sacred veil have we embroidered our vested right in might, in cunning and in hypocrisy, while through its web run the many-colored strands of our fear of Life, and here and there a trace or gleam of timid faith.

Therefore in our continuing act of feudal self-preservation, we *must* lie more, steal more, betray more, kill more;--calling, meanwhile, worldly wisdom and prudence to be our witness--calling God to be our witness. Thus progressively increases the open and the secret fear and hatred which the individual (you and I and the other man, whatever his name) has for his kind, and for his neighbor; (and the neighbor, forget it not, is *always* you and I!) whence arises also our baleful axiom concerning "The Cold World": The most tragic phrase of all feudal utterances--unless it be: What is the use!

This mass-thought makes of us terrible, secretive, silent savages; desperate offensive fighters of our kind, and keen, defensive fighters for ourselves. Hence we ever seek a shelter where we may:--shelter from this very world we make.

To be sure, some are momentarily sheltered with our sanction--the drones:--the earth-gods. I speak rather of those in the open. For it is important to know to what extent a man is really self-made, and how, and why, and what it all means.

For the expression "self-made man" is of common usage among

us. It sounds democratic. We are proud of it. But it is meaningless unless we enlarge our scope and enquire if a people as a mass is self-made, and if so, how and why and what it all means. An individual has no valid meaning apart from the mass, the mass has no real meaning apart from the character of its individuals. There is no abstract individual, and no abstract mass. Both are alive; and Life is not an abstraction, it is vivid and stupendous, the stillest of powers. We, incredulous of spirit, have not much troubled about this, yet it reaches into the crisis of our mass-life.

Now, just as there are the sheltered--the drones, the corrupt, the papa-made, and grandpapa made--who survive legally for the moment, so is there now and then a direful one who, instead of being suffocated by the dead weight of the multitudes, is squirted up by them through some crevice; and such man returns with ashen hatred upon the people, because his thought is their molten thought.

And, also, there is now and then one whom the people conceive of use, at a time when he no longer cares whether they so conceive or not; --he, pessimistic, having become weary of their pessimism.

For so the individual reacts upon the mass. And in turn the mass is constantly acting and reacting upon its millions of individuals; and they, as continuously, are acting and reacting upon the mass, and among themselves, and within each individual, in every-varying degree but essentially the same in kind.

For this social world of ours is not chaos. In all its variegation, of surface differences, seeming contradictions, swirling and seething of interests, its complexity of evil, its many wills and counter-wills, it moves massively, consistently, silently as Life, about the thoughts of Feudalism-- that is, the simple notion of virtuously hating the neighbor.

This thought and the active life of the individual and the mass are mutually explanatory. We say not. And the so-saying is the virus of our thinking. It is definitely this mass-denial of the best in the neighbor which envenoms our world.

We say that we are a wealthy people; but our dwindling spiritual perception is making us poor indeed. No people is so utterly poverty-stricken as that people which most vociferously denies. We are that people. It is the deepest folly that the mind of man can harbor. We harbor it.

Loudly, thus, we call to Life:--Destroy us! and Life hears and answers. We fail to understand our own degradation, even while we wallow in it; for we do not enquire.

Thus is the individual man of today actually at the mercy of his kind! He self-prepares himself for his fate, not knowing what that fate may be. He cannot, alone, untangle the knotted feudal skein, hence he speaks of Fate and Luck, not reasoning that Fate and Luck are his capricious and unreasoning fellow men, (that is, himself!) who believe self-preservation itself to be a speculation--a matter of fate, or luck, or caprice.

Such is our fatalistic mass-thought.

Thus under our system of civilization, each man (you--I!) is by implication under sentence of death. He knows not when his crisis will come. He may survive when he expects it least, and so may he perish. He has nothing to stand upon--and life has no basis, for him, except uncertainty. For such is the feudal rhythm of compensation. Of a truth is feudal man born into uncertainty and bred into a maze of perpetual anxiety. It is the way of the jungle. It is absurd to call it the way of civilization. It is but a vain and impertinent gamble with Life, a sordid waste of man's marvellous creative power for good.

The word, civilization, must remain misnomer so long as men and the mass-thought are without a basis of certainty: (that is, as long as you and I and the other man, whatever his name, are without a basis of certainty). Savagery, is, and must be the word. Enlightenment is the word so soon as we awaken to the unscientific nature of our method, and put our civilization on a basis of certainty. The basis of uncertainty is our mad belief that men are different! The basis of certainty is the wise assumption that men are alike! The superstition of uncertainty is but ignorant persistence in the evil we do. The faith in certainty, is faith in the best that is in us.

We can change our mass-belief in evil into a mass-faith in good just so soon as we wish. There is no guesswork about that. We have but to burst our bands of feudalism and we are free:--did we but know it, could we but believe it. We are vastly stronger in brain, and heart today, than is the whole world of tradition. We are amazingly incredulous that we do not yet see this. But we shall see! and when we see, we shall act! For when seen clear, to change will seem easy as the turning of a hand. No people will continue to victimize itself when once it understands the situation. So understanding, and so acting, we shall become truly a self-made people. For we shall then rest upon a basis of creative good and will wonder what men could have believed any other basis valid.

It is passing strange that we, in a land sprinkled with schools, colleges, universities, have taken no note of simples; have not detected the motive power of a single, basically-simple thought. But we are learning; we are having object-lessons every day; we shall shortly begin to understand how simple is the single thought from which spring all the feudal object-lessons of the world. Then shall we recognize not only the nature of our savagery, but we shall grasp the fact that no savage institution can exist longer than it receives the nourishing and sanctioning support of the mass-thought of the people. Just so soon as the mass-thought of the people changes, these formidable and terrifying ghosts will vanish, the Dance of Death will end, and a cock crow the dawn of a new day.

It is simple.--As simple as a man's two hands.

But, should the mass-thought split in two, before we see clearly, then we shall have plenty of blood and wrack and ruin, and many a "self-made" man will be unmade, and the self-making of a people be deferred. For, if we so far lose our heads, all around, that there will come a revolution of force, instead of an intellectual change, it will go awry with us in our crisis.

The time to recognize our mass-responsibility is now!
The time to recognize our individual responsibility is now!
The time to see straight and act straight is now!
The time to stop our idiotic exalting and killing of men is now!
We must know ourselves. We must discover man!
Now! is the time to draw aside all veils that hide.
Now! is the time to flood with light all places obscure or dark.

For an enlightened people, there must be no veil for human vermin high or low, eminent or obscure, to do their murderous work behind in secret; no dark recesses, no underground burrowings. For an enlightened people, all must be in the open; all clear, simple, plain, intelligible.

Draw aside the great veil, and behold! a hell on earth--a hell of our own making.

Draw aside the little veil that hides the best in the hearts of men, and behold!--the basis of regeneration!

* * * *

So man comes forth, a man--a babe, into our world. He is sheltered, as well as may be, in the home. For love, large or little, is there with him.

So soon as he can hear anything, he hears platitudes, hypocrisies. The world is hidden from him. Why should the world be hidden from his growing mind? Is it then so terrible a world as all that, that it must be hidden from a child?

Then he is sent to school, given an inverted education; started wrong. The idea being still to hide the world from him, or at most to lift a corner of the veil, a little. Why hide the world from adolescence? Is it so terrible?

He is taught something about "religion," as we call it; and it is the chief concern of "religion" to hide the world from him. Why hide the world, if it be warm?

Little by little he is told that he must prepare to make his way in the world--but he is not told what world. Not even a corner of that veil is lifted. It is said, in the home, that he will find out in time.

Then he is pushed forth into the world.

At first it seems a dream and delightful. It is rosy, ah, so rosy. What buoyancy, what hope, what enthusiasm! What a fair, warm world! Yes, he is entering "business," or a "profession." How will he get to the top? Yes; how will he get to the top! It is a warm world. Industry, fidelity, honesty, merit will surely bring success. Yes they will surely bring success in the fair, beautiful world. In the fair world of men and their ways. Industry will surely win; he will make a man of himself. His foot is on the first round of the ladder. He understands it all. And so he mounts the ladder of success, step by step. For it is a fair world. What a joyous world. So fair to look upon. It is so fair a world that he will marry a fair maid. He has heard of self-made men. He believes in them. He will be one of them. He will succeed. He will be honorable. He has been told that integrity is the foundation of success. So he climbs step by step. Then he hears whispers,--for men do not talk murder openly. He is startled; and the fair world gently closes on him. He feels its breath. His illusion wavers. He sees through the surface, to what is underneath. He understands that what is underneath counts. He glimpses now what honor, confidence, integrity mean in real life. What the surface means. He understands what success means. He sees that failure is normal in the fair world of man, not so fair now, not so warm. So comes he to his parting of the ways. He chooses, and as he chooses, so goes it with him. If he is become worldly-wise, and choose discretion, the veil of the first sanctuary will be lifted for him, and he will enter the arcanum, if he be deemed fit, if he be deemed the "right man"; and then another veil will be lifted for him, if he is still deemed the "right man," and he will enter another mystery. He no longer climbs a ladder, he walks through secret chambers, passing degree after degree as veil after veil is lifted. And when he looks out upon the world:--it is another world. The surface is still there, but he views it from the "inside" now, and he smiles at times a meditative smile of contempt;--for his illusion is gone. But, unaware, another illusion has grown in its place; for he still does not see the world as it is. He sees it merely and only from the standpoint of the "successful" "self-made" man. He sees it from an eminence of signs and passwords. He believes these secrets solid.

Thus, is it, sometimes, from child to man, in one way.

* * * *

The world is still fair on the outside. The sun still shines, the seasons come and go, and the rain falls upon anybody and everything. Dame Nature is youthfully fresh. What seems to be true is that only man is foolish. And there is this much of pallid honesty in him--that he tries to hide the corruption of the world and his own share in it from his young. This act reveals the latent idealist in him, and gets in a way beneath the layer of hypocrisy; it would seem that he is secretly ashamed of the worst in himself, a worst which is but part of the folly of his deformed view of life.

For he says; what can I do? I am but one!

True; what can he do? He is but one. And what does he do, being but one? Does he not do his share of lying and stealing and killing? --being but one?--poor man!--He can be a coward, being only one! He can fear his shadow, being only one.

And yet if you were to call him, to his face, a "self-made man" he would preen and be hugely flattered; he would warm to you, and would not deny. He would admit that he "did it."

But if you were to ask him;--If you cannot do, what, at least, can you undo?--He would not understand; it would seem to have no bearing. And should you give it point and bearing he would say:--I am but one, I cannot undo!

Thus is man the Artful Dodger.

He will evade, and deny, and protest, and shift, and squirm, and run and hide from pillar to post.

Or he will stand and put up an indignant "bluff" or "front."

He likes the pronoun, I, when he uses it. He likes the pronoun, you, when he uses it. But he hates like fire the pronoun, you! when you use it;--when you push it into him, home, like a spear-word, and pin him to the wall.

Now you! What do *you* think about the "self-made man" who can neither do nor undo?--he being only one?--and yet who bitterly reviles the spear-word *you!* when it is used to pin him fast against the wall of his personal responsibility and accountability?

Is he the really self-prepared man?--He who evades even while he affirms?

Or is it the true self-prepared man who accepts his responsibility and accountability, and affirms them?

Which?

* * * *

Have we not endured the rodomontade long enough?

Have we not hidden in the crevices of cowardice long enough?

Have we not lurked, knife in hand, long enough?

Have we not been killing the true self-prepared man, long enough?

Have we not exalted the spurious long enough?

Have we not endured the "self-made," and the papa-made, and the grand-papa-made long enough?

Have we not endured the "successful," the "eminent" and the "practical" long enough?

Have we not endured "Business" long enough?

Have we not endured "Economy" long enough?

Have we not endured ourselves! long enough?

Where are our eyes?

Where are our ears?

Where is our common sense?

Where is our practicality?

Where is our courage, when we say:--What can I do?--being only one? What can I do or undo?

How small "I" becomes when so used!

Truly we, in our bulk, in this sense, are self-made--enough! We, free to choose, have chosen hypocrisy and chicane. Hence our mass-integrity, our massive "I" shrinks, spiritually, toward the vanishing point.

Hence it is that we have exalted the self-prepared men who have chosen evil. It is simple. They are our desire.

All the more real need then, for those, self-prepared, who, equally having choice, choosing, choosing indeed at their cost and risk, choosing in the open at their peril, and at the hands of their fellows, have chosen good. They are the real kind. We need them. We need them, now!--in the confusion of our cowardice and aspiration. We need them to affirm that any man, being only one, can undo and do! That he can undo the evil in himself, being only one. That he can do good for all--being only one.

That in fact it is because he is ONE, that he has the power of choice.

Hence, accepting the "I" of responsibility he will accept the "you"! of accountability.

This is the essence and substance of man's integrity. It is the bedrock!

This simplicity of thought, sweeping away all hypocrisies, conventions, traditions, mock religions, and all mystery concerning good and evil, leaves the soul of man bare, naked and beautiful in its natural integrity.

Thus, long-searching, we have found. We have found man's soul greatly differing from what we had supposed. He has believed himself two men. He is *ONE!*

* * * *

All the more need for our self-prepared in good.

They have faith in us, where we in our murk have lost faith in ourselves. For they are the simple, the sturdy--men with spines. Right and wrong are as plain to them as their two hands. They so accept, so act.

So are right and wrong plain to us all. But we deny, we evade. We dislike those who say right and wrong are plain. Hence we deny them. We do not wish it said that a man, being only one, can undo and do if he but so choose. For that would come home, vividly home to each and all. And we, cave-dwellers fear the little light;--even the pale light of a social dawn.

And our possessions! OUR possessions!! What would become of them?

And our "vested rights"!--What would become of them?
And our caste-system?--What would become of that?
And our special privileges?--What would become of them?
And our huge veil of hypocrisy?--Would it not be torn asunder?
And our benevolence--what would be left of it?
And our charity--our charity?
And our drones--What would become of them?
And our parasites? What would they do?
And our poor?--Where should we find them?

They were promised us--a gift in perpetuity. Do not take our poor away!

And our eminence? Would it not melt away?
And our religion?--What would become of it?

And our God!--What would become of him?
And Civilization!--What would become of it?
And our culture and traditions!--What would become of them?
Where would we hide?

What could we answer when a voice called; saying, Where Art Thou?

Yes, we need such men, self-prepared in integrity even at their peril. For their logical meaning is this, that man, for his salvation, and the salvation of his kind, must be fearless of Death and of Life.

While we, fear Death. We cling to cowardice and life on any terms, however groveling. Take what we have, body and soul, we say, but let us live. Thus, inviting the robber, we are robbed.

And this we say even while Death, with his huge scythe, is mowing us down by thousands, before our normal time.

For we, cowards, invite Death to his mowing.

And we, cowards, fearing Life,--invite Life to destroy. Hence those whom we, in our cowardice call "self-made men," and have exalted, are cowardly as ourselves. For they, exalted by us are of us. That is plain.

They are the shadow we cast against a phantom wall in the great light of day. And it is thus our shadow that we, a people, fear.

This is the substance and shadow of what we in our timidity call the great men--the self-made man--unaware are we that these men, in turn, fear their shadows, and terribly fear the shadow of the multitudes.

But the self-prepared man of integrity
Fears not his shadow, nor the shadows of the great
Nor the shadows of the Gods.
May his tribe increase.
We are in need.

For such men, once getting loose, once getting air and room, room enough and air enough for one, will detonate, and shock and jar us, with the quality of their thought.

Thus may we awaken, and grow spines. Today we are invertebrate. Slaves of illusion and its monsters. Slaves to our prime illusion that men are different. We have lacked nerve. We have lacked the force of intelligence to grasp the immense meaning of this vision.

Hence we have lacked the essential nerve to see straight and act straight; to be real men, self-prepared; to be a people prepared to meet men and things and thoughts in the open of Life's great World; a people prepared to be fearless.

DEMOCRACY: *a man-search*

It is time we realize the nature of that object lesson which reveals our ignominy, to-wit: that we make a world which we hide from the child.

Thus stand we, self-indicted, in that we, calling ourselves civilized, make a world whose real meaning must be hidden from a child.

And thus is a people called to sit in judgment of itself.

A people which has believed itself secure in its secret thought--behold the veil, in its bedizened sanctuary of savage feudalism.

* * * *

Thus, in our man-search, do we move ever deeper into the soul of a people.

There, to abide, to think with its mass-thought.

To see through its massive pensive eyes.

There, to feel its huge fear of Life.

There to shudder with its great fear of Death.

There to hope with its immense and pregnant hope.

Even as it multifariously and massively aspires.

Even as a still, small voice whispers in each and all,

The whisper of the destiny of man.

The life-whisper to a people unprepared and ill-made now.

But ever a people with power to choose.

A people with power to change.

A people with power to make a world in the true image of man. A world that need not be hidden from a child.

CHAPTER 9 THE POLITICIAN

It is not unusual to hear it said of a man, that he reads faces well; is a good judge of character; can size up a man at a glance; and like expressions, implying penetration--awareness, receptivity.

The main element is assumed by us to be something more than eyesight, something in the nature of a gift. We call this gift intuition; and we say thus that he is an intuitive judge of men. Then we go further and say that such man is guided by his "first impressions," has faith in them, acts upon them. We then extend the scope of this power of penetration from men to things, acts, events; and sum up by saying that such man has "sound judgment," or words to that effect.

There is another form of eyesight, or penetration that we recognize and acclaim, namely, slow, patient, scrutiny, which reaches its conclusions only after elaborate viewing and comparison from many angles, so as to see the same thing in many ways.

And there is still another form of eyesight which we recognize but do not quite so well grasp, namely, what may be called the poet's glance, or vision:--a kind of illuminated eyesight, which penetrates the life of things, which takes in the outward appearance and the inner meaning in a singleness of impression. We do not call such a man, so gifted, a poet, because the words poet and poetry have no living meaning for us. When we begin to know ourselves we will enlarge these words and charge them with our own life. But not yet; for we still use words as labels, not symbols; hence the label-word, poetry, does not connect in our minds with the massiveness and variety of our life. We in fact are enacting a great drama; but we do not so see it, for "drama" is but one of our label-words. Our land has many schools, but we do not there teach that words are useless unless charged with power of meaning. We see and use words only in the flat; we give them no third dimension; and, even as we speak them, they sound flat; which signifies a flatness in our lives.

We recognize also what may be called reassuring eyesight, concerning which we use the expression "seeing's believing."

We recognize also an inadequate eyesight when we say "appearances are deceptive."

And finally we take for granted the ordinary everyday eyesight which enables us to distinguish between a man and the street he walks in.

Let us enquire then, a little concerning eyesight; for we have said it is every man's business to see straight.

Prior to the eye's power to see, comes the man's mental attitude; that is to say his state of mind concerning himself and the little and great world about him. Or, if you prefer, his notion of his setting. That is, his setting within his own thoughts and feelings; within the world of men, and the things men have made, such as cities, factories, mines, farms, railways, etc.; within the great world of visible nature; and the world of Life which he vaguely implies when he uses the word, God, or speaks of his own soul. And it is with his philosophy of life, rather than with his eyes that a man customarily looks out upon the world of men. Now every man has such philosophy. He may not call it by that name; he may say simply, or think: "this is the way it strikes me" or "this is the way I look at it." The philosophy of the average man is mostly second hand; and yet within it is always a germ that stands for himself.

But, in seeing the outer world, the outer world in turn reacts upon the man's philosophy and progressively changes its shape throughout his lifetime. And so the mass-philosophy of a people, likewise becomes modified as the people grows and moves. For a people is continuously changing, through the pouring in of new lives and the pouring out of old or new; that is to say, in the passage of its multitudes of individuals from the cradle to the grave, in longer or shorter spans. So the philosophy of a people changes in a sort of deep and portentous silent flow. This change in the thought of a people we recognize when we use such expressions as the "spirit of the times," "public opinion," "out of date," "up to date," etc., and thus to each individual man is brought to bear on his own view of life, a secondary modification due to the impressions, of whatever kind, made upon him by the thoughts of his fellows. And there occurs continuously also what we call an interchange of thought, which is none other than an interchange of philosophies, that is, of men's views of life--of what they see! It is thus that what we call new ideas, proceeding from small, obscure beginnings, spread and grow and take on bulk and definition within the mass-thought of the people; while the people at the same time as gradually note that they are moving or have moved away from what we call old ideas. These changes, however, are mostly matters of color, of sensation, of the surface life. They are relatively rapid. But the greater center of gravity, the fundamental assumption around which moves and changes the superficial thought of a people, itself has remained through the ages almost motionless. There are evidences, now of the beginning of an impressive change in this center of gravity; it is shifting within the newly changing mass-thought. This applies, similarly, to the central thought of the individual. The thought of the individual may be somewhat or considerably more shifting and variable than that of the mass; while the motion of the mass-thought is as relatively ponderous.

Now the American philosophy, or mass-view of life is handicapped by the traditional ancient and European feudal philosophy; it is this which gives to our civilization its aspect of fatalism. With this philosophy we have burdened our backs, blinded our eyes, and colored our outlook upon life. For this ancient and European feudal philosophy insistently sets forth in varied, alluring and specious ways, that men are different. We Americans have taken this philosophy bodily at second hand, unaware of its virulence and its power to darken the mind. Yet within our man-thought, as we now hold it, lies embedded the germ of our own genuine, but unformulated aspiration for freedom. Because of this handicap, this crushing load, these blinders, these spectacles and because of the benumbing influence of the mental poison, we cannot, at present, see either straight or clear. In other words we are obsessed by the feudal idea even while we shout "Democracy!" Of this massive fact we are now becoming partly conscious. As this dim consciousness grows clearer, we feel our center of gravity responsively shifting into the domain of genuine, pure, Democracy. It is our virtue, that, when once we see,--WE ACT! In this, amidst all our perturbation, lies our reserve strength.

But we can never see straight, feel straight nor act straight so long as we are under the dominion of the time-honored feudal philosophy. We must throw it off and rid our thoughts of its poison.

A philosophy of democracy must rest upon the fundamental truth that men are alike, and that all things, including man, are fundamentally one. There is no other basis. For it is only when we perceive that men are alike and that all things are essentially one with man, that we are able to see straight, and thus secure a sane outlook upon the world of men, and things and thoughts. We will thus substitute for our pitiful egomania and sense of separateness, an enlightened view of the fellow man. Then the folly of lying, stealing, betraying and killing will become self-evident--it will need no demonstration. Our traditional and still dominant idea of the suppression of the fellow man will give way before the new conception that our true preservation as a people, our real health and strength of thought and of heart, must lie in the conservation of the best that is in the fellow man. Thus will be substituted enlightenment for savagery; real power for spurious power; genuine creative power for the fictional; and, in the so doing, change the entire program of misuse and perturbation into a superb program of use and serenity.

There is too much of solid good in us that we should either wilfully or blindly throw ourselves away, or degenerate into slaves of a few despots of our own making. But this latter is what is logically to happen, unless we rid ourselves of feudalism--for it is the sure way of feudalism.

Concerning this issue there can be no compromise. We must see straight and act straight with resolution. We must now learn clearly to see ourselves (for what we actually are in practice) in the fellow man, no matter whom he may be. If we look upon the unfortunate, the outcast, we must clearly see ourselves in him, that we may know ourselves; and likewise clearly see ourselves in the predatory rich, the stupidly eminent, the unscrupulous "successful man," the despicably impractical "practical man," and the tricky, shifty and vacillating politician. When we thus look out upon all our varied kind, we will clearly see and recognize ourselves in them all. The view will not be flattering, but it will do us a world of good; and we will thus at last clearly see the why and wherefore of the inverted and artificial distinctions we have made among our fellow men, under the destructive sway of the feudal philosophy we have taken secondhand, without inquiry. We will then see what will at first appear hard to believe, but which it is a part of our civilization, as a people, to see and believe, namely, that the natural powers of men are essentially and normally the same in quantity, quality and virility. That feudal departure from normal man begins instantly with the choice of evil by the individual, however refined or specious or coarse that choice may be. Holding this view steady, our faith in man must luminously increase for we then shall see as steadily, the normal, healthful basis, and begin to reckon with the fellow man as the natural, wholesome creator of good that he really is.

Then the cause of our perversion, in exalting evil and suppressing good, will become clear, and recognizable, because the basis will be clear. That our civilization of today is but a stupendous inversion of the deepest and richest truths concerning man, will become evident. Its utter waste and folly will become impressively clear and convincing.

Perceiving all this our alleged "problems" now so seemingly intricate, will simplify with startling suddenness. For, perceiving and recognizing the real basis of man, we will put intelligent concurrence of action among men in the place of frantic conflict. When this idea illuminates the mass-thought of the people, Democracy will become an assured and permanent fact--a reality instead of as now a miserable, futile fiction--a mere word.

Such change from feudalism to Democracy can be made smoothly and rapidly, if we, as a people, so wish and will.

But we are to understand that it is an individual proposition, as well as a mass one. It is grotesque for the individual to assert or assume that he will change *after* the neighbor does, for he is the neighbor. The grafter can not keep his cake and eat it too. He must let go with both hands. And if one says that this is "practically impossible," then those words are exactly equivalent to saying that we are to proceed logically to our downfall as a people, and the utter collapse of our civilization upon our heads. That is the practical, the actual, the imminent. We will do one thing or the other. Our time for definite choice is shortening rapidly as the internal strains of our social fabric are growing tenser, and insidious, minute, but thoroughgoing disintegration is getting in its fatal work.

Our weakness is that we are all politicians; we will not, if we can help it, frankly face a problem of any kind. We seek to obscure plain things in a mist of sophistication. This is where our "cuteness" comes in, and this is where the "insiders" and the "outsiders" come most clearly into view. Our desire to work behind fake veils is ubiquitous. Our search for the "advantage," as we call it, that is, gain at the loss of others, is a passionate part of our feudalism; its basis is trickery and chicane, secret trading, compromise, barter; in short, a complicated and most cowardly system of betrayals. Politics is the back door and the back stairs procedure in our social system. Its venom infects and pollutes every phase of our activities. But we will tire of this, and we must tire as individuals first; and, in mass, tire of the obstructive stupidity of the tangle, tire of the futility and folly of the tissue of falsehood, betrayal and graft. To be sure we hear platitudes concerning "clean politics." But the word politics is itself unclean. It has no real place in the vocabulary of Democracy. Procedure is the word. The function of Democracy is to accomplish things in the open, in the daylight, to reduce all matters to the simplest plainest terms, and undertake their development in the simplest plainest manner, with plenty of air and room. When men are doing crooked work they need politics as a screen. Hence where politics is the thickest, there, is the dirtiest work behind. Whereas where men are doing clean work, politics vanishes, for all is in the open. Procedure is thus plain and efficient. It becomes an artistically scientific program.

It is attempted to have us believe that politics is necessary because it implies organization. But the reverse is true; political organization is but the veil of perfidy.

Organization is organization; it will be clear enough and translucent enough in the open daylight of Democracy, for organization will then simply mean a clean and clear method of reaching with certainty a definite open end.

The politics of the professional politician is putrid enough, but the politics of the "successful" man, the "eminent" man, and the "practical" man, done behind the veil of feudal respectability, gives off an insufferable stench. Thus is politics, in all its big and little forms, its innumerable ramifications into the individual, but another name for betrayal. Now betrayal is feudal. Therefore is politics feudal.

To see this is to see straight:--Is to unravel a huge part of our elaborate fabric of cant, and to let, light into places now obscure and dark, because our minds, clouded with the philosophy of feudalism are obscure and dark.

So when the individual parts company with his politics, that is his share in betrayal, he simultaneously parts company with a huge and virulent aspect of feudalism and thus, moving into the domain of Democracy, is in position to see straight, to speak straight and to act straight.

That is, he himself draws aside the feudal veil and comes out into the daylight, into the open world.

There is none more craven than he, high or low, who fears to speak plainly and clearly the truth as he knows it; who believes it astute to hide behind a veil of mystery and aver that it would not be "politic" to speak openly, and to the real point. All of which, reduced to simple terms, means that he *chooses* to be a liar. He fears his shadow; and thus does his part in suggesting fear to his fellow-men, and confirming them in their dread of the shadows flickering within our own phantasmal philosophy of life.

But flickering shadows and baleful fears have no place in the philosophy of Democracy. In the view of life which Democracy gives, it is clear that there is nothing to fear. Democracy turns to the daylight, the sunshine, and sees the reality of man sweet, clean and clear in that light. It leads man into the open, and in the open reveals to him his natural powers.

Feudalism is the domain of flickering shadows and baleful fears. It hides man in the dark, confirms his superstitions, accentuates his fears, inverts his ideas, even as it hangs up a veil of glory, a surface of effrontery.

Thus is feudalism the world-doctrine of inward and outward fear.

And thus is Democracy a world-doctrine of courage and poise.

Thus the philosophy of feudalism, based on uncertainty, breeds perpetual anxiety within the thoughts of men, and hence in their outlook upon life.

While the philosophy of Democracy, going far deeper into the soul of man, into the soul of a people, and finding there a basic, rock-like integrity of heart and mind, accepts it, builds upon it as the fundamental certainty and therefore the foundation of social certainty, and, so, dispels anxiety from the thoughts of men, and makes their outlook upon life clear, clean, stable.

Feudalism has feared Life because it dared not confront it. It has regarded Life rather as a haunting ghost. Hence all feudal ideas are essentially ghostly. For man's view concerning the nature of Life is his primary view.

But Democracy, approaching Life, enquiring of it, discerns and accepts its limitless beneficence and power and so perceiving and accepting, founds its solid faith upon that beneficence.

Thus is Feudalism obscure of sight, because of Fear.

Democracy clear, deep and vivid because fearless.

Hence is feudalism a doctrine of fictions.

Democracy a doctrine of reality.

Thus the feudal man, if it were possible for him to tell the truth, would say, perforce: I am Death!

While the man of Democracy, proclaiming with a clear understanding a clear faith, says: I am Life!

Thus there is seeing and seeing!

And thus he who with simple vision, with fearless mind, goes straight and true to the core of the feudal idea; who, penetrating its ghostly form, perceives it in fact to be but a heartless Phantom proclaiming itself Truth, ever warning man against faith in his own integrity, in faith in his own natural powers, will also perceive it as that very Phantom beside the door of Truth, (leading to the open world of Democracy) whose warning cry: What is the use? has broken the hearts of millions of men with its freezing assurance of the futility of faith, and the unalterable reality of man's suffering, misery, and despair.

Hence is the philosophy of feudalism a philosophy of negation, of vanity, and despair. A philosophy which begets (out of its fear of life) ambition and destruction, recurrent egomania and downfall, and everlasting jealousy, hatred, envy, vanity, intrigue, betrayal, lying, stealing and killing--in short a ghostly Dance of Death.

We have accepted the feudal philosophy--hence we dance our massive and ghostly Dance of Death about the prostrate reality of man.

He who sees this sees much and rightly. He who speaks of it, well and true,--speaks rightly. He who would dispel the phantom, feels rightly. He who sounds the morning-call acts rightly. He is Chanticleer--his shrill, awakening voice sounds forth at the early streak of dawn.

But no politician will do this.

His business is to confuse, to beguile, to betray, to exhibit.

No man of "worldly wisdom and prudence" will do it.

Plain men will do it.

To be sure this may interfere with "Business," large and small.

It may cause the iridescent bubble, "Eminence," to collapse.

It may cause the ghost of poverty to depart.

It may reveal what "Success" means.

It may reveal what "Economy" means.

It may reveal what our "Religion" means.

What our "God" means.

What an "All-wise but unsearchable Providence" means--in fact!

What the feudal "I" and the feudal "you" mean.

What "mine and thine" mean.
But it will also reveal what the world of men and things mean.
It will reveal what Life means.
It will reveal what good and evil mean--in *fact!*
It will reveal the reality,--Man.
It will place him, not among his "superiors" and "inferiors," as now.
It will place him in the open world of men, solid on his feet, clear of brain, and with an awakened cheerful heart.
That is, it will place him in equilibrium of spirit,
It will place him upon a basis of certainty.
His mind will be at peace.
His faculties, thus freed, hence aroused to their fullest activities of creative power--the Power of Life, will work toward great, unceasing ends.
It will make of him a free spirit.
Then shall we become truly a great people, because a truly free people,--free in our spirit.
The outlook of feudalism is within a closed, moving circle. It suffers recurrent death.
The vista of Democracy is endless.
For Democracy, based upon the integrity of man, can never reach an end. The creative and concurring power of free men is inexhaustible. Hence the Spirit of Democracy is immortal!
It will draw out of man the power of his wondrous Life.
Because man, of his free-will, in the clearness of his choice, will make access to the beneficence of Life, free as the air to all.
So, truly, is there seeing and seeing.
But he who can see the reality and simplicity of Democracy, he who can see its magnificent vista,--can foresee a modern miracle in the oncoming revelation of Man in his superb reality.

* * * *

Thus is philosophy eyesight; and eyesight--philosophy.
Where one is obscure, so is the other.
Where one is clear, so is the other.
Yet are both one.
For man and his world are one.

* * * *

Thus in our man-search have we found the Politician.

Little wonder that we need men to see straight, to think straight, to act straight. For what a deformity is a crooked man!

* * * *

It is interesting to see what a politician, (being only one!) can do and undo.

In this, our land and language, he is sometimes called a "ward-heeler" sometimes a "Statesman."

In one aspect "obscure," in the other "eminent," in this our land these twain are one.

So goes the man-search.

For to see this is to see much.

It is to see the man who says: "I take the world as I find it."

So do we.

So we take him, as we find him; strip him of subterfuge and peer into his soul.

* * * *

This is seeing merely seeing,–after all.

CHAPTER 10 THE PARASITE

And now, to see the Parasite, accurately. Let us look at him through the eyes of Democracy. For the vision of Democracy is clear. It sees in three dimensions. It takes instant note of movement, form, color. It reads faces well. It is a good judge of character. It does not regard the labels on things, it looks squarely at the character of things and thoughts, just as though there were no label. It needs no guide to the thoughts of men other than the unmistakable trail of their acts. It needs no other guide to their mental attitude, their philosophy of life, their notion of their own "setting." Hence, following their acts back into their thoughts, it finds where they, the men of today, really live and how they choose. Thus there is no possible escape for the individual man. No matter what he says, no matter what he pretends, no matter how speciously he evades, his acts reveal him. Thus to the searching eye of Democracy, with its poet-glance, taking in the outer and inner meaning of a man in an instant impression of singleness, the Parasite is revealed as parasite by his daily acts; and his acts as instantly reveal his daily choice. Thus we may clearly see what he--being only one!--does and undoes! Thus we may therefore see him, steady, clear, single:--A Personality! Thus in turn we penetrate the personality of his acts. And thus it is that Democracy, pursuing the feudal man, first surrounds him by tracing the circle of his own acts. Narrowing that circle about him, it simultaneously narrows steadily about him the circle of his thoughts, of his specific Personality. Thus is he bound by the most tenuous of threads, threads of his own spinning--and thus is feudal man caught in the act. And so encircling, and narrowing our closed circle upon the Parasite, his personality becomes clear and tangible, and recognizable. There is no difficulty in reading him, no matter how much he might consider such inquiry rude and out of place.

So these are his acts, to-wit:
He leisurely sucks the blood of his fellow men.
He rests placidly today upon the anxiety of others for the morrow.
The sucking of the blood of others covers a wide circle about him.
The anxiety of others for the morrow, a wider circle.
The Parasite is at the center.
The lines of a thousand sighs go straight to him.
There are thousands of such parasites, thousands of such circles, intersecting circles of uncertainty, perplexity, misfortune, sorrow, poverty.

Thus the great parasite, in the last closure of the circle upon him is caught alive; caught in the act of fattening upon the toil, the sorrows, the misfortune, the perplexity, the poverty of his fellows. And thus is his character, his personality, revealed clear and distinct--the character, the Personality, of a human parasite, a vampire.

This is what he does!
Hence this is what he chooses!
It is his daily act--his daily choice. Hence it is his daily thought--his real thought--the thought that counts.

Hence this is what one man can do--being only one! How little is he prepared for the Spear-Word You! How little can he guess how it will be driven home into him? For he is a dreamer, dreaming that his wealth is not made up of sighs, and whispers; dreaming that he is respectable, a Christian and a man. Horrible and willful illusion. An illusion that the you-spear will dispel! The eye of Democracy sees him through and through. Sees him in his cowardly complacence, sees that he sees the reality even through the thin vapors of his dream. A dream that he insists upon dreaming, even within the rumbling of the world of men.

Hence you and I are parasites by sanction, when we tolerate the parasite. That is our direct responsibility, and is thus a part of our definite accountability to all our fellow men, now here, and to come. It reaches home to each and all. It comes home hard when we see it clear. For, if we tolerate, we sanction; and by sanction we uphold! uphold the Parasite. There is no escape from that. You and I cannot get away from that.

But the Parasite is acutely responsible because, he, being one, and hence accountable to himself, tolerates, sanctions and upholds his own parasitism. What do you think of a man who sanctions his own parasitism?

He, being parasite, knowing it in spite of his disclaimers, and continuing such, becomes clearly and recognizably accountable to you and me, and to the neighbor, whatever the neighbor's name may be.

So, when we say to him: You!–Parasite! he can but answer: I am. For there is no other answer. That is absolutely plain.

And when we ask:–You! Will you change? He receives point blank the most tragic question that can be thrust into the heart of any man who has made blood-sucking his choice in Life.

The philosophy of the Parasite is simple. It is:–"I and mine," and with it he is content. He "takes the world as he finds it."

But Democracy is not content.

Democracy sees and says,–Parasite!

It takes him as it finds him.

Takes him in the grip of its encircling and penetrating thought.

It takes him as it finds him–to illuminate him, to exhibit him. It marks him "Exhibit A" in our feudal world.

And yet he is "benevolent," the Parasite. It is good feudal "form."

And so is he "Charitable." It, also, is "good form."

But in his benevolence and charity are ever "I and mine."

For he says "I!" He says: "Mine!"–the Parasite! Should he choose to see the people of the world he would say: "You and yours:–It is with your sufferings and your sighs that I am benevolent. I hoard your proud tears,

But he does not choose to see–to know–to say this.

He does not choose to see himself–to know!

Nor do the multitudes clearly see him to know him.

But the eye of Democracy sees both to know both.

For Democracy reads faces well.

It is a good judge of character.

A searching analyst of men.

It views them and compares them from many angles. It scrutinizes them with infinite patience.

It is no respecter of feudal persons, high or low, rich or poor, eminent or obscure, powerful or weak, fortunate or unfortunate.

It finds them *ONE*.

It finds all men alike.

It finds man manifold.

Hence we cannot escape our own logic. We have nowhere to go. The Parasite is you and I. We share his thoughts, we share his feelings, else could he not exist. Indeed we the people had them first, out of them we gave birth to him--the Parasite. The poor man would eagerly exchange places with him; and, in his place, would as leisurely suck the blood of the poor, whence he came; would, in turn, sit complacent upon their unrest, their sorrows. For feudal man is not merely parasite but cannibal. The poorer man says "I and mine" with an intensity which the richer may find it hard to equal. Out of this intensity the rich arise. So springs the savage out of the savage. So springs the benevolent out of the benevolent. So springs sorrow out of sorrow; for the parasite is secretly a man of sorrows like us all.

The eye of Democracy searches all. It wishes the truth in its wholeness not in fragments. It wishes the whole truth that it may reach to the rock of human nature and be stable. To find good, it must relentlessly penetrate the obscuring veil of evil.

What folly, then, to discriminate between men--as though we were not all alike--as though there were any essential difference between the thought of the feudal rich and the thought of the feudal poor; of those who in illusion give their blood and those who in illusion gather it.

The eye of Democracy notes that the poor are still with us, and that the huge parasite is still with us. But it sees the two extremes come together with a sudden rush and shock, and, behold! they are one! The two spectacular halves of one idea have merely come together, to reveal the single, simple, common truth. And that truth is that the poor are poor with the sanction of us all, and, with the sanction of us all, thrives the huge Parasite.

But this is only one kind of Parasite.

The breed is beyond numbering in variety. It ranges from the pander, through the priest, to the Croesus, with an immense list of classifications. And so parasitism spreads through the mass because it is "mothered" by the mass-thought. The parasite, of any name, is thus a self-creation of the people. For the parasite is as manifold and multifarious as man. Hence are we infested with parasites. For the parasite, big, little, or in between, or of any form or complexion, germinates in the foulness, obscurity and venom of the phantasmal feudal doctrine which we, a new people in a new land, have adopted, second-hand, without inquiry, and have held fast. Hence is parasitism a living function form and power within our acts, our thoughts, our desires, our fears as a people--because we so wish and will.

Democracy proposes disinfection.

To its eye, parasites all look alike, despite the fine-spun and time-honored feudal distinctions and discriminations. Through its sieve they all come out the same size. For Democracy is plain. It sees things plain. It announces, as plain and fundamental, the spirituality of man. Because man now chooses to play the beast, it does not therefore, fail to see and proclaim the god-spirit in him.

Did Democracy not seek the whole human truth, and find within that, the simple, primary human truth, it would be as useless in the Great Way of Life as is Feudalism. Did it fear to meet any truth face to face, did it falter, before one single truth concerning man, however appalling, it could not summon the steadfast gaze wherewith to dispel the Phantom, ghostly and repellent in our twilight, which stands, now, at the foot of the cross of crucified man, beside the closed door of Truth within that adamantine ghostly wall of Fate which feudal man has reared to his sorrow, and where-against he has broken and still breaks his heart. For it is feudal man that is the man of sorrows and acquainted with grief.

Should it fear to face the degenerate and say: we made him,
Should it fear to face the diseased, and say: we made him,
Should it fear to face the criminal and say; we made him,
Should it fear to face the outcast and say: we made him,
Should it fear to face the plutocrat and say; we made him,

Then would it fear all, and be but a pretense, an affront, an absurdity,--one more lie.

Should it fear to say that we, having made these, can unmake them, that we, a people, having done harm, can undo it. Should it fear to say this plainly, openly, stridently, ringingly, then would it be a cowardly fiction like the rest.

Should it fear to see and proclaim that all men are alike, it would be frivolous.

And should it fail to proclaim its faith in man, should it fail to urge him to stand erect, and, free in his own free spirit, to look Life in the face with courage and pride, it would abort and die.

Thus is Democracy of its very nature a leap into the Light.

It can be nought else.

Hence, seeing with the eyes of Life, it sees all, and will proclaim all. For there is no power under the heavens or on the earth like unto the power of words charged with the life of man.

Hence does Democracy perceive that parasitism is merely one among the many aspects of our system of betrayal. And, that, to be feudal, as we are, is to betray universal manhood,--as we do.

The gambler is a parasite.

Why distinguish between the big one and the little ones?

Where there is a big one there are always innumerable little ones to balance and support him,--to give him "character." From the big one, the scale diminishes and the method ramifies, until they, equally, all find their soil and ground and foundation in the gambling mass-thought of the people. Now reverse this process and it becomes plain how the "big" gambler, (the so-called speculator), comes into being; and just how and why his parasitism corresponds in bulk, virulence and ramification in exact ratio within his own "eminence" as a high financier.

It is because the average American is a gambler in desire, in thought and act, that the big gambler exists. He, the big gambler, can have no real meaning save as a qualitative and quantitative index of the thought of the people. The big gambler is thus in exact equilibrium with the gambling thought of the people:--and so is the little gambler. This gambling thought of the people is lurid with the desire to get something for nothing. It is a tragic and turbid index of the underlying willingness of the multitudes to lie, steal, betray and kill. It is a fearsome revelation of the thought of a people:--of that people's cry to Life--Destroy us!

If the big gambler is "wiser" than the small fry, he cannot possibly be wiser than the little ones surely believe themselves to be. Otherwise he could not "work" the multitudes of little ones, and they in turn could not be in position to support him as their ideal parasite--their hero parasite. This is where cuteness comes in; for none so "cute" as the little gambler, none with so parasitic a scent for blood. The little gambler is sometimes called a "lamb." He is rather a social jackal. His own belief is that he is a man, and has "judgment." But thousands of him have had their parasitic hearts crushed under the heavy hand of a vindictive "sure thing."

And then there are the "innocent" gamblers; quiet bourgeois-like folk, who also would like something for nothing, even if the "something" be the money a confidential clerk has "borrowed" from the till, that he too might gamble a little, and perhaps get something for nothing; and even though the "nothing" be a residence of the aforesaid clerk behind the bars.

And thus are there gamblers and gamblers, of high and low degree, of every variety, shade, guise and occupation--and parasites are they all. They feed upon the feudal uncertainty.

Thus our parasitic gambling mass-thought misleads us. Betrays us into an inverted understanding of the two words, "something" and "nothing." The something, with us, of course, means money. The "nothing" means nothing. Yet is that word "nothing" jammed full with meaning.

The eye of Democracy sees this meaning, because the philosophy of Democracy views things in their totality and in their minutest aspects. It searches the roots, trunk, branches, twigs, leaves, flowers, fruits:--the seed, the progeny of the seed. It searches the air, the light, the waters and the soil. And thus it searches man, to know him, to see him through and through, in form, in movement, in balance and in essence; in secret thought, in overt and covert act, in hidden desires, in weakness and in strength. This it does that it may clearly separate in him the unclean from the clean, the sanity in him from the insanity, the reasonableness from the unreasonableness, the common sense from the folly, the practicality from the futility, the good from the evil:--in short, the health in him from the disease. For the philosophy of Democracy views our present feudal civilization as a disease. It seeks a cure, not in feudal nostrums, but in the natural constitutional health in man. It has no use for palliatives, or a treatment of symptoms. It goes direct to the disturbance of the vital equilibrium of a people, and finds the real seat of that disturbance in their thought--their philosophy of Life.

The notion of Force finds no place in the Philosophy of Democracy; not only because the notion of force is feudal, and because force clearly and recognizably breeds resistance and more force; but specifically, because Democracy supplants the gross notion of physical force with the luminous conception of man's spiritual power--his wish and will--his desire and his choice!

Democracy presents twentieth century reasoned and orderly methods in the place of savage guesswork, bewilderment and confusion. He seeks to illuminate the real nature of reason and reasonableness; of self-respect and self-control:--To illuminate these as mighty powers of man's spirit:--and to show that reasonableness begets reasonableness, self-respect begets self-respect, and self-control begets self-control.

It assumes as fundamental to the thought of a people, that no people will continue egregiously to victimize itself, when once the truth becomes clear and recognizable--as an object-lesson.

It assumes that no people will tolerate or sanction Parasitism, when once the actual nature of parasitism becomes vividly clear and recognizable --as an object-lesson.

It assumes that no people will tolerate Poverty, when once the feudal origin of poverty becomes clear and recognizable--as an object-lesson.

It assumes that no people will tolerate feudal benevolence and charity when once their exact parasitic nature becomes vividly clear. So clear that no man can dodge. So clear that no man can fail to see and recognize.

In these assumptions it makes no guesswork.

For it is clear, it is luminous to the eye of Democratic philosophy, in its man-search, that a people acts exactly as it thinks; and that by no possibility whatsoever can it otherwise act:--because there is no other possibility. That acts can change only as thought changes.

It perceives that the thought of the American People is now obscure as to the nature of its own feudalism; but that its thought is clarifying.

It knows that when that thought completely clarifies, our acts will become completely clear and decisive. Because the act is the exact image of the real thought:--it cannot be otherwise.

It knows well that this is not merely a local proposition, but a world-proposition:--for men are alike the round world over.

It knows that the world, today, is under the spell and sway of the feudal ghostly superstition.

Nevertheless Democracy advances without hesitation its clear-eyed faith in man.

For it has searched him to the core; and finds him there so sound, that it accepts him without equivocation or proviso.

It declares the best in him a solid foundation upon which to build the first beneficent civilization. For it has searched him exhaustively, and finds in him more and better than he ever found in himself, or ever dreamed of in his greatest and most ardent dreams.

It has found his simplicity:--that, which he had never found.

It has found his soul. And of the nature of that soul--he had scarcely dreamed. He had never known it was so simple. He had not known that in truth it was of him,--and was not a tenant or a tyrant.

It has gazed into his dreams, his waking vivid dreams, and has seen within these dreams a dream of which he knew not.

It has looked into his fears and found them groundless, even while he had held them terrifying.

It has looked into his God, and found that god a disaster,--even while he has feared that his god might get away.

It has looked into man's life, and has found there a pathos so deep that the drama of it is wholly incomparable--unspeakably affecting.

It has listened in man's heart, and has heard there the still small voice--the song of songs. In this song it has heard and recognized the real man.

It has peered into man's inarticulate thoughts, into his inarticulate desires. It has heard his lonely cry:--Where art thou?--My Hope!

To that cry it answers, saying:--Here am I!

Thus has it sought and found in man himself, that which he had sought elsewhere and hopelessly.

Hence to man it says: Thou art the man! Have courage! Have faith in self! Have faith in Life! Fear not! March on!

Hence Democracy goes straight to man. It seeks man. It seeks and finds the best in him and nurtures that alone.

It is the one word--of faith in man--that the world has uttered.

It has seen the world of men under the vast shadow of Feudalism.

It sees that world of men slowly but surely turning toward the light.

The eye of Democracy is serene.

Its soul is tranquil.

Its mind mobile, clear, alert.

It sees all. And allows for all.

If it sees the parasite, it also allows for him, as it allows for any man and all men; as it allows for a people in mass.

It sees that it is not the heart of the people that is at fault, it is their heads. It sees this also in the individual man,--in no matter whom. It sees that he has lost his bearings.

It sees, equally, that he is seeking new bearings.

It sees, deeply, that what he is seeking is a religion of his own spirit.

Something that he can have faith in. That his deepest need and desire is for a faith. That he indubitably yearns for a faith in man.

It sees him looking in the wrong place; seeking vaguely, evoking--distraught.

It sees, that, what he is looking for is at his elbow.

It is the neighbor--the neighbor everywhere. Hence Democracy sees that, in itself, it is not so much a doctrine, a theory, a philosophy, as it is the natural man himself, in all his sublimity of power of choice, his freedom of spirit.

That the power is there, unused and ready; but the eyesight, the clarity and the will are not yet quite there, not yet quite ready.

Hence is this the tremulous hour. The hour of crisis.
The hour of utmost darkness.
The hour of pause and gathering.
The hour of spiritual accumulation.
The hour of the turning of the heart.

Shall a man be shut out, then, because he is a parasite?
Shall he too, not be free to turn--to turn his heart?
Shall not all men be free to turn?
Feudalism says, they shall not!
Democracy sees clearly that they are free; and so announces.
For it sees lucidly that man is really free to seek man.
That any man is free to search and find himself.

That it is not freedom, but imagination, and will that have been wanting;--wanting through fear--the haunting fear of Poverty, of Death, of Life.

That it is not the essential faith that is wanting, but that the faith is benumbed and perplexed through anxiety for the morrow.

That this anxiety is the fearsome price a people pays for the luxury of owning parasites; for the luxury of parasitism in their massive and individual thought.

The eye of Democracy sees searchingly that the people are wasteful and extravagant in fact, because of fear of poverty, of anxiety for the morrow. That in this uncertainty, this perplexity, this fear--they sell their birthright.

The eye of Democracy sees the people listening intently to the voice of Poverty, which says, in seeming, to them:--I am Truth! I am Want! I am ineradicable! I shall be always with you,--ready to devour, like a dragon.

But the ear of Democracy, listening, hears and is aware that the voice of Poverty, the voice of the Dragon is sepulchral and void. That the real voice speaking is the voice of the multitudes, crying:--Poverty is Truth! It is ineradicable, inexorable! It will be always with us, always ready to devour us, like a dragon. Let us then make Gods on earth; hero Gods; great Gods, to shield and protect us against the great Dragon!

Hence, out of the creative fear-word of the people, arises the Great Parasite,--as a God on Earth.

But the ringing voice of Democracy, calling, brings the Dragon, the Earth-Gods and the multitudes to judgment.

It calls, and herds them home.

To put to them questions which cannot wait.
It will say to the Earth-Gods:--
    Come forth into the dawn.
    Declare what you have hidden.
Let the Dragon go. Take off his mask.
Speak softly, true, be distinct.
Gaze upon the poor,--brought close here with you now.
Look!--What do you see?
Look steadily!--as in a mirror! What do you recognize?
It will say to the Poor:
    Look at these Gods,--brought close to you now.
    Are they not of earth, like you?
    Behold the Dragon!
    Is he not mild? unmasked?
And to all the People, It will say:--
    Unmask! All! Earth Gods and Earth Multitudes!
    It is the hour of unmasking!
Behold! I call to our Dawn:--Light! Light! and more Light!! That we may see more! And do more!
Give us ever more of thy power, O, Light!
That we may evermore have more; and evermore do more!
Behold! how Dawn comes on. How the shadows flee away. How the great world of earth-men and their earth-gods comes out from the dusk. How the multitudes stand forth, gathering in the gloaming. How the Spirit of Man comes forth, foregathering with them in the glowing.* While I, Democracy, the soul of Freedom, call to all the people:--Come! earth-men, stand forth! Tell me; who and what were you? Who and what are you becoming? Tell me. Tell each. Tell all! And turn your hearts--Turn your hearts toward man:--
    Toward man, whom you have forgotten.
    Forgotten in the worship of Gods of Earth and of the Heavens.
    Forgotten in the love and dark worship of self.
    Forgotten in the fear of want.
    Forgotten in obscurity.
    Forgotten in anxiety for the morrow.
    Forgotten in the perplexity and fear of all.
    Forgotten in the sweat and ambition of the day.
    Forgotten in the uncertainty and dread of a world of phantoms.
    Forgotten as the Dragon and the wolf drew near.

* Preceding line would suggest *gloaming*.

DEMOCRACY: *a man-search*

Forgotten in pomp.
Forgotten in abject misery.
Forgotten in the inverted mind.
Forgotten in the heart, fresh-wounded, and scarred of old.
Forgotten and forsaken in the gloomy wilderness of earth-men.
Cease the clamor!--Listen, hear and turn!
Heed the still voice in the hearts of all.
Hear, and turn.
Hear ye not the Man-Cry? Hear, and turn!

Hear and heed the voice of the Truth-Teller, wandering passionately to and fro through the world of men--seeking and finding man; revealing man; illuminating man!

Hear and turn!
Hear ye not the heart-murmur of the multitudes?
Feel,--and turn!
Wish as One, and turn as One!
Turn as One!--Toward the oncoming vision of Life.
To see it, rising as a sun, clear and strong.
To receive its light--to become that Light.
Behold! The Earth-Gods fade away.
Behold! The earth-men fade away.

Behold them, hovering in their spirits, changing to free men--through their wish and will.

Light!----Light!!
It is the hour of Transfiguration.
The pale twilight hovering of the dusk of the Gods.
While we, wayfarers of the soul,
Stand firm, on our earth in the dawning,
To receive man,--
And be at One.

* * * *

CHAPTER 11 THE MONOPOLIST

The average American, (which essentially means any and every American, and all Americans in mass) does not search *himself* to find first causes. Before long, however, he will begin to do so, because the drift of events and the great showing of object lessons will lead him to do so. He will of himself discover the necessity. For he will conclude that he cannot find anywhere else the key to the solution of the many complicated social problems, as he calls them.

He will fool around, and waste time, as is his wont, pondering the serious nature of this "problem" and that "problem," as he persists in calling them; and will seek to apply a plaster here, a liniment there; an astringent here, a law there, etc.; but after a while he will wonder why the "problems" keep getting bigger and more complicated all the time; and why, after he has this ulcer or that, nicely plastered over as he believes, the trouble breaks out elsewhere, or in the old spots afresh. It will not occur to him, at first, that while [he] * has been very busy "reforming" other people, he has completely forgotten about himself. He has left himself out of the "problem"--which is equivalent to saying he leaves the problem out of the problem. This is what makes the reformer ridiculous. He is anxious that others refrain from evil. For he, the reformer, specializes evil. In bulk, he sees all evil as external to himself. It worries him. He torments himself with the evil of others; and concerns himself greatly with the "public welfare," as he calls it, which, also, he sees vaguely in bulk, as external to himself. He suavely leaves himself, his private thoughts, and his private acts, out of the "public welfare" proposition also.

So it is not uncommon to hear man shout: "Let us reform this evil"! But they have not yet been heard to shout: Let us reform ourselves! For they say--"this evil," as though "this evil," mark the words, had nothing to do with themselves, and as though their own secret thoughts and overt acts had had nothing to do with "this evil." So goes the farce of "reform," that is, the reform of others. And to the eye of Democracy, reform is further, waxlike, a lay-figure, because "reform" has always in its mind, the use of force in its aspect of repression. As though anything could actually be repressed. Or, as though sending a man to the penetentiary, here or there, whoever he may be, could have any organic effect upon the totality of evil we are all busily engaged in *creating,* hour by hour, other than to make it change its color like a chameleon, burrow new tunnels, hang up new veils, or invent a new system of signals. Such reform men are veritable rainbow-chasers, if serious; if wily, they are the same old snakes in the grass. If respectable they are the same old "eminent" posturers; if disreputable, the same old gang.

To be sure it is the habit of the piously pious to say: "Lord we are miserable sinners all." But that is a luxurious form of statement. It is made confidentially to the Lord, and not intended for worldly publication. The actuality of its full truth in the way of life, it is not the custom of the immaculate to regard. Indeed we avert our gaze, lest we come upon it unaware. For it is one thing to say, "Lord, I am a miserable sinner," but quite another to say, simply, honestly and plainly:--"I have injured my fellow-men because I have thought evil and hence have chosen evil, done evil, and bred evil. I, even I, immaculate though I appear, have actually done this thing. In the one case the responsibility is thrown on the "Lord" which

* Supplied.

is convenient and easy. In the other the accountability is taken directly home, which seems hard;--which characteristic, however, shows the difference between a fictitious religion and a real one.

Our cowardly feudal religion was invented for the purpose of shifting our personal responsibility and evading our personal accountability. Such religion, therefore, is flimsy with pretexts and evasions. It does not meet the human issue. The religion, which in our hearts we are actually seeking, will be based upon a clear perception of our real direct human responsibility and accountability to our fellow-man. We can well afford, therefore, to give the feudal God an indefinite leave of absence; he stands in our light. He stands in the light of all who seek the clean, the sound and the good in man; seeking it even within the huge shadow of betrayal; fear and fickle hope this god-image casts athwart the souls of men.

That which man is really now seeking is a universal principle of Life. Something stable, clear, tangible, and workable; something which will stand daylight inspection and test. Something which has a basis of simplicity and certainty; and which needs no priest. Men are getting weary of a fickle idol, as the mists clear and the idol is revealed an unfortunate experiment.-- A Bogey, useful only to the soldier-man and the priest-man--those two predatory and cunning parasites whose sole business it is to exploit the confidence of the multitudes who have wished to have faith in something, even as an anchorage for their fears and hopes. And, it may be noted that this element of confidence, this healthful aspect of the soul of man, is precisely that which has been most brutally betrayed.

But the day of fanciful beliefs is passing. Slowly we are turning toward an ideal of personal freedom and personal self-control. But we do not as yet clearly recognize what freedom implies. We hitherto have understood freedom to be a sort of savage go-as-you-please. We have called it Individualism. But democratic freedom implies and demands self-respect, self-control, individual responsibility, and individual accountability; and this is quite another matter. No man is free who has not cast off the bondage of evil thinking and evil-doing,--in fact! For, in literal fact evil-doing is a bondage, a distinct and distressing form of slavery. In a way we glimpse this, feel its presence like a hazy cloud of many colors; but it does not yet condense and clarify in the mind of the individual man. But the moment he looks honestly within himself; the moment he resolutely parts the veil which he has created to hide himself from himself and perceives the truth that he is essentially like those whom he condemns, his own mind will clarify, and he will begin to peer in wonderment into the profound and clear depths of the truth that all men are alike. He will begin to suspect that if all men are alike in evil, so, also, are they all alike in good. He will perceive that he has been utterly misled in judging men by their clothing, their occupation, their poverty, their riches, their labels, their illiteracy or their scholarship; and so perceiving will become aware of the presence of that vivid, living, actual human entity--his living fellow-man. So seeing, he will get a completely new view of himself. He will see himself also as a human entity--the living fellow-man of all other living men. This will give him a working basis;--revealing himself to himself, and revealing his fellow-man to him. It will clarify his outlook upon life, and completely reverse his feudal philosophy. For then he will begin to see straight, that is, see himself straight, see his fellow-man straight, which is the prime essential preliminary to a sane civilization. He may find this procedure somewhat startling at first, somewhat bewildering, shocking and jarring to his conventional notions concerning the rightness of himself, and the wrongness of other men. But he will make a great discovery, nevertheless; for thereafter he will find that when he says to his fellows:--"You have done evil in thought and practice," he has stated but half a truth, and that to make it a full truth he must add, "So have I." This would not only be an honest statement of fact, but would be an evidence of his beginning to see straight and talk straight. Should he have any lingering doubts concerning the truth of the "so have I"; should he be inclined to waver, in his belief in its actuality, he has but to take a half-hour off, any time, and, commune with himself concerning just how his covetousness, his conventionality, his narrow-mindedness, his prejudices, his preconceptions, his "uprightness," his smugness, his respectability, his good intentions and his condescending desire to "help" his fellow-men, would appear, all translated into plain, unvarnished English, and his actual thoughts thus traced plainly through his acts, into the effect of those thoughts and acts upon his fellow-men. He would have a half-hour of revelation,--a crowded half-hour. He would see pictures and dramas arise within him and without him in the great world of men, that would astound him and perhaps dismay him. But it would be an eye-opener to him concerning his actual and practical relations to his fellow-men. He would begin to understand. Every man is a natural clairvoyant. He thinks he is not, but he is. He has insisted upon specializing everything, hence has ignored universals; and his inevitable share in universals. Any man can see clearly if he will but raise the filmy curtains which he has drawn down at the windows of his own soul--that is, his eyes. He has but to raise these curtains and the real world becomes clear. For clairvoyance merely means clear-seeing, and a man cannot see clearly what is going on in the world about him, if he keeps his shades down. In these respects man is an extremely curious creature. First he draws a veil inside himself to hide himself from himself, and then he draws a veil to hide himself from others, and then he draws curtains over his eyes to hide the great world from himself. Truly no animal that roams the earth is so furtive, so timorous, so solitary and so unhappy as is man.

And in these respects let it not be supposed that men are different. In this regard, as in all others they are alike. It makes not a whit of difference who or what the man is, there are his veils and his curtains. And these stand as symbols of his fear of Life. Symbols which any man may see clearly and interpret clearly, if he but raise the curtains from his own eyes and remove the veils within himself.

Thus seeing, any man can enter securely into the soul of his fellow-man and be at home; and as securely enter the soul of a people, and be at home there, too. This is sometimes called the power of sympathy, and yet sympathy is but an aspect of that clairvoyance, or clear-sight whereby we see the flow of life in men and things, and enter in spirit into the reality of that life,--hence into the reality of man.

Thus the man who now believes himself securely righteous, or securely calloused, will begin to see. So seeing, his notion of his own "setting" within the world of men, will at once begin radically to change. For when a man really asks himself:--"Who and what actually and humanly am I? What have I actually thought, done and undone--I being one? What has been and now is my actual relationship, of evil--positive, traceable, tangible,--to my fellow-man near and far? Just how and why have I betrayed him? Just how and why have I denied the best in him? Just how and why have I denied and betrayed the best in myself?"--Then, at once! does he confront himself with the Feudal test and the Democratic test of character and conduct. He sees them both, side by side, transfigured into intense realities, clearly before him. Seeing them once, he will see them for the remainder of his days. For they, there, standing, each, beside a parting of his days. One dark, one radiant, will be ever there, ineffaceable, unforgettable. And within him, in their presence will loom his power of choice, larger, more potent, more explanatory, than he had supposed, and, likewise--unescapable! Thus will the democratic notion of personal responsibility and personal accountability be pressed home to him, equally sharp, clear--and equally unescapable. Its standard is bold and positive. He cannot banish it, evade it or deny it.

It is a terrible procedure to trace a man's evil acts directly back into him, in spite of his laments and his pious evading. Especially those acts which in his conventional asininity and feudal egomania, ruthlessness and folly he has deemed good and wise. It means a literal tearing open of his barbarous feudal ego:--a horrible prying into his willingness to kill. Therefore it were better that he do it himself. But do it he must, and promptly. Else will it be done for him, by exasperated and merciless hands, and then again, conclusively, by hands insane with passion and ferocity. For, to a conclusion we are swiftly, logically moving as a people.

Of conclusions there are but three logical possibilities:--

First, Complete enslavement

Second, Violent revolution

Third, Enlightenment

Anyone can feel the enslaving net drawing.

Anyone can hear the preliminary rumblings, and tremors.

And anyone can note the ferment, the leaven, also at work.

Thus are we now in the swirl of the forces, all of them of our own making. The flood-gates are down.

Men are apt to overlook one thing, namely, that the free spirit of man cannot be suppressed.

The stake, the noose, could not extinguish it.

Might has tried it, and failed.

Cunning has tried it, and failed.

Thus, are we approaching a tremendous crisis;

For now, the powers of might and cunning are preparing for the final insane attempt, to enslave an entire people.

The hierarchy of today confronts the free spirit of today.

Its hand is poised--to kill!

Our hierarchy is Monopoly.

Thus the multitudes now confront Monopoly, and Monopoly confronts the multitudes.

Neither sees the other clearly.

The average man, especially the working man, looks at monopoly with the eye of a sheep. He is not aware how he and his kind are being gently herded as sheep.

The eye of Monopoly is certain that it sees the multitudes and the individual clearly, sharply. The mind of Monopoly believes that its campaign of stealth can have but one, positive, sure, successful ending. That it holds the sure key to man in its profound belief that his fundamental weakness, lies in his own individual cupidity, his fear of poverty, his complete willingness to sacrifice his neighbor, to sacrifice all his fellowmen, if need be, in his terror in a panic;--in his utter lack of initiative, resolution or fortitude, his utter inability to understand simple things. It believes that it has discounted every possibility of failure. Has closed or will soon have closed every avenue of escape. The plan looks well. It is very simple, and already wonderfully developed and ramified in fact. It has the merit of inspiration in its luminous simplicity of idea, for it relies upon the multitudes to enslave themselves. Therefore it does not seek to use force, it uses silent pressure. It spreads a net so delicate that it is invisible to the unimaginative eye of the average man, especially the working man. It feels secure in its long preparation and in its accumulated strength. In its secret service it has eyes everywhere, thousands of them. It has ears everywhere. It has brains and brawn at work everywhere. It is constantly testing every strand in its net, as it moves, and grows, in the all-including minuteness of its universal touch. It is not impatient. Prepared for instant action, it prefers to await the psychological moment, that is, the moment when the people are dead ripe with self-satisfied stupidity. Then it will suddenly shift the center of gravity of the entangled mass of men.

It will all seem natural, spontaneous. It will appear to come about from natural causes,--from supply or demand, or crop shortage--anything will do, it will even cry "wolf"! several times. It believes it has figured out to a hair that the center of gravity of each and every man, and therefore of the mass of men, is money. That when any man is put to the actual brutal test, he will throw off all masks and betray and kill for money, if but he can save himself, or, that, rather than face poverty, he will sell himself cheap. That he will say: What is the use? He will then be given his choice and will make his choice. He will become either slave or slave-driver.

That looks correct and sharply scientific on the face of it. The American people today certainly give little evidence of ability to see straight, of possessing the power of self-control, of self-respect. They now daily lie to each other, steal from each other, betray each other for money, and are incredibly cynical. It would be difficult to imagine a state of affairs better suited to facilitate the success of a monopolistic plan of campaign. The people certainly are doing their utmost to make it a success. It looks as though it might be a go.

If I were to cite any particular "brand" of man as conspicuously victimizing himself, and preparing himself for final and complete enslavement, it would be the working man, so-called.

He believes himself supernaturally "cute." The fact is, he is utterly fatuous. His trades unionism reveals him for exactly what he is-- a monopolist at heart,--his abiding desire is to get something for nothing. His prime thought centers on wages, that is, money; his second thought upon how little he can give in return, that is, how much of that money he can steal. His motive is to "corner" labor. He is a firm believer in the power of might and cunning. He denies the right of labor to other men, when he can. He is the tyrant wherever he can be so. He is an aristocrat through and through, making grades, divisions and distinctions among his own kind. He thus believes in caste, and fosters a caste system of his own. He enforces his own class distinction; he insists upon isolation. Could he have his way as a class, one would think a flock of locusts had passed over the land. He would take everything. He has the notion that everything belongs to him. He acknowledges the validity of no labor, other than the labor of hands. He draws down the shades which prevent him from seeing the real world. He hangs up the veil to hide himself, and the veil to hide himself from the world. He too, has his feudal sanctuary.

But it won't go. He thinks men are different, but they are not. He judges all men as it were by their hands.

It is high time for the working man to take an hour off by himself and take a good look into himself. He will see a few things. He will see, for instance, that he is exactly like other men.

He might also lift the curtains from his eyes. He would see a few things out in the world. He would discover that there is a larger world, and that considerable is going on in that larger world, a very considerable that he knows nothing about. Indeed, he does not know what is actually going on in his own self-isolated world. He has no genuine instinct of self-preservation. Within very narrow limits he is level-headed. But he cannot see that he is a house profoundly and almost fatally divided against itself. He has no genuine center of gravity, because he is not honest with his world of fellow-men. When his working center of gravity--money--around which his thought revolves in a small circle in common with all Americans, is suddenly and massively shifted at the right moment he will be utterly and completely demoralized, and in his panic, will fly at the throat of his fellow working man.

He is easily flattered. Easily bribed, by a rise in wages, to betray and sell his fellow working men, and for that matter, all other men. He will immediately grab at wages, and forget all else. In his fatuity he believes his salvation to be a matter of wages. His salvation is a matter of his own stability of character, of his own imagination and will power, thought power; his own sense of responsibility and accountability to all his fellow-men. He has not imagination as yet enough, to understand this, because he is intensely feudal--that is, he is an egoist,--he cannot go outside of himself, outside of his "class" as he calls it. He has his class-feeling--that is all, and his class-feeling is a house of cards. It won't stand in a hurricane. It won't stand before the breath of the cry for bread. And to whom will this cry for bread be in due time addressed? To the fellow working man? Scarcely. It will be addressed to those who now are arranging that it shall in due time be addressed to them. The cry will be received gently, and benevolently; the "saviors of society" will appear; and then the screws will be put on for keeps. This is, provided the scheme works--and if one looks at the working man's present philosophy of life, it would appear that it might work.

There are some men who can tell a gradual change of pressure in the social atmosphere without the aid of a barometer; can tell a gradual change of temperature therein, without a thermometer. Can tell a gradual change in direction of the wind without a compass or weather vane. But the working man is not one of these. He is too completely satisfied with his method of graft; too much engrossed in his self-willed isolation, to study other methods of graft, other forms of self-willed isolation.

And so the farce-comedy of raising wages goes on, as a curtain-raiser for the real tragedy:--That is, if the scheme works. And if the American people do not promptly begin a searching analysis of themselves, if they do not promptly discover that democratic honesty is their true center of gravity, that they must see this straight, think it straight, feel it straight and act it straight--if they do not see that they themselves are at heart monopolists, every one of them, if they do not promptly put on the brakes and stop! and get their bearings quickly, perceive quickly that their sole salvation must lie in their own integrity--why then the scheme may work. It would look very favorable. It is already working beautifully as far as the working man is concerned. He is in the trap now. The trap is so large he cannot see it. He thinks he is in the open air. That he is free because he is allowed to walk upon his physical legs. But it is only a matter of dropping the fall. He is a curious creature, the working man. He has queer dreams. He is a somnambulist--a sleep-walker. He is betraying us all in his trance.

The working man avers that were it not for his unions he would long ago have been trodden into the mud. Of course he would. But that complacent thought will not prevent him from being trodden into the mud for sure, when his crisis comes. That is if the scheme works--and the working man is doing his best to make it work. He is playing daily and hourly into the hands of monopoly. Whom, or what, does he work for now, the bulk of him? What would monopoly be, without its armies of him? its hundreds of armies of stupid slaves?--betraying us all, betraying their own kind!--for wages!

"But," he says, "I am earning an honest living." That is where he lies. He accepts a bribe, called wages, to betray you and me, and that is not earning an honest living. No man can earn an honest living unless he, himself is honest. Honest in the clear plain Democratic way--not in the fantastic, parti-colored and irresponsible Feudal way. Money talks to the working man. It says: "To hell with the rest; look out for yourself!"--and the working man agrees.

Who has poisoned our foods? The working man. And he knows it better and more intimately than anyone else. What good are his unions? Have they raised a voice in protest? Not a voice. Have they sought to protect you and me against poisoning? Not for a minute. On the contrary, they have worked hard to poison the people--for wages--that is blood money.

Who makes the rot-gut whiskey which poisons the working man and makes him a maniac and a wife-beater? His fellow working man.

Who makes all the vile nostrums and patent medicines that have done so much to shatter the nerves of the American people?--The working man.

Who runs the freight cars onto the siding of a favored shipper, and keeps them away from an unfavored shipper?--The working man. Who else could do it? He does it for wages--it is all the same to him.

Who collects the nickels for a "grasping corporation"? The working man. Who "grasps" for the "grasping" corporation? The working man, of course.--He "grasps,"--for wages; that is, in fact, for a bribe.

Who carries out every behest of the monopolist in every practical physical detail? The working man.

Who therefore is assisting with all his bodily strength the monopolist in the final scheme of enslavement of the working man?--The working man himself! Presto!

He is but the pliant tool of crafty brains. His appalling weakness lies in the fact that he denies his personal responsibility and accountability,--wherein he is at one with all his fellow Americans. For it is an appalling weakness in any man or in the mass, to deny responsibility and accountability.

This, to be sure, is not all of the story of the working man. It is the fatalistic side; the supremely dangerous side; a side of his own making. It is the side which springs from his illusion concerning wages, and his hazy notion of making an "honest" living.

What he has failed to see, and what he must see, that he owes it to his fellow men to see and act upon is this, that no monopoly can exist without his direct and active coöperation. For a cunning monopolistic brain without thousands of physical hands to do its work is a mere phantasm--a mere ghost--utterly powerless.

The working man must begin to uphold the monopolist accountable to him. For the American people will soon begin to hold the working man accountable to them for doing the dirty work of the monopolist?

Now let us see of what a big monopolistic corporation consists:-- First, of thousands upon thousands of working men--an army--to carry the cunning treacherous thought into actual physical action and fact. Now put these to one side, in imagination, and what is left? first, a smaller army of clerks etc., earning an "honest" living by preparing the treacherous thought for action in making certain marks on paper. Put these also to one side, with the army of working men. What is left? First, various executive officers, directors, etc., who get the cunning and treacherous thought of extortion and enslavement in shape to pass on to the clerks, etc., and the army of workingmen. Now put these also to one side, with the small army of clerks, etc., and the large army of workingmen. What is left? The "honest" stockholders, so called; the "widows and orphans," etc., who yell for dividends--blood money. Now put these aside with the bulk of the rest. What is left? A piece of paper, a so-called charter. But where is the cunning and treacherous mind? have we passed it by? Not at all; it recedes into the "control." And what is control? A new form of ownership--ownership of men. Ownership of "big" men, body and soul, control of them body and soul. And how are they controlled? Through brotherhood in rascality, and through fear of punishment. And could one corporation enslave an entire people? Manifestly not. One corporation can only tax the people--with the help of the working man. One corporation is but a bluff, a screen. There are many such; so handled as to give an aspect of diversity, of diverting separateness.

Thus when a big monopolistic corporation is analyzed, it falls into two instrumental phases of action. One, the cunning and malevolent mind hidden in the "control," and surrounded by its small group of "big" men; the other, a great army of agents, clerks, etc., and workingmen, which makes an immense and powerful mass in unity of action. The system is essentially military. It is the warrior-man in a new guise, in modern local color, with new names and labels.

Now push the matter a little further:--This shows what the mind of one man, or a few men, can do--with the co-operation of an army of men. But! it shows, also, clear as daylight, what one man can not do!--*without* the co-operation of an army of his fellow-men. Which lays bare the core-fact that one man or a few men, cannot possibly accomplish the enslavement of a people without the co-operation of the people themselves.

To see this is to see straight, to be clairvoyant. That is, to be so simple of mind as to raise the curtains from the eyes to see the great open world, and to follow the acts of an army of thousands of individual men--our "fellow citizens," back to the central cunning thought, which is external to them; and yet which permeates them with its sinister imagination and its creative will, moving them in the game like wooden pawns upon a chess board; herding them like human sheep, slowly tightening its power --with their own imbecile co-operation, with the enormous mass-power of their utterly false view of life which blinds them to prudence and leads them--to betray and deliver their fellow-men.

So, truly, it is not the cunning and malevolent power of one or a few minds that we have to fear. Were we to change our own minds that power would vanish like a mist.

No! What we have to fear is OURSELVES!

What we have to fear is the appalling grip on us of that feudal thought we as a people hold in common:--our abominable belief that, in the last analysis, at the supreme test, self-preservation must mean the sacrifice of the neighbor, and, if must be, the sacrifice of the life of any and all.

This fatal grip we must unloosen!

For it is exactly on this thought, this belief, and exactly on nothing else, that our cunning, mighty and malevolent few, (made so, and such, by us) are banking with a secure, mobile and powerful serenity.

Corporations group and group and group again, within the silent and sinister depths of might.

And behind control lies control, and behind that,--control, and behind that, control, as the sinister minds become fewer in number, and ever increasingly powerful within the silent depths of cunning!--made so, and such, by us! For who else could have made them?--and who else can unmake? They, huge object lessons, show what a PEOPLE can do! They themselves, plain symbols of the power of the mass-thought to create! should, as such plain symbols, such plain earth-gods of evil, inspire the direct and positive conviction of what a people must undo within its great massive self--what each individual within the mass must undo within himself. That is, we, individually! and in mass! must undo the feudal philosophy of life, that we now hold; that philosophy which, enslaves the minds of men with its plausible but gross, hideous and envenoming dogma that men are not alike.

If we do not unloosen this fatal grip at once--the scheme will work! But, if we unloosen it, cast it off and thereby free our eyes to see straight, our minds to think straight, our hearts to feel straight, our souls to recognize the reality and the nobility of man as man, and the sacredness of man the neighbor:--The scheme of exploitation and enslavement will utterly fail! It will crumble and dissolve like a huge iceberg moving into a warm sea:--and in such warming and strengthening of the heart, such clarity of the mind, Feudalism will dissolve away forever, in this our land, and, hence in due order in all lands on the fair round earth.

But! we must not fail to understand that we are today, as a people, a house dividing against itself. The lines of a possible fission run anywhere and everywhere, geographically, politically, industrially, commercially, financially, economically, socially, and every other way. The internal strains and stresses along these forming fissure lines are silent but enormous. They are the strains and stresses of greed, envy, hatred, jealousy, cunning, intrigue, bitterness, vengeance, egomania, of latent, potent, ferocity. They run vertically, horizontally, diagonally. They cross and recross. The day of the fanatic is approaching--he in the air. If we do not quickly recast ourselves, with the flux of a sane and universal idea of man, and thus solidify as a people, with a big, sane, constructive purpose, a real object in our mass-life and our mass-thought; why--then there will be trouble; for we are approaching in these many ways an hour of gross passion. The key to the cause of these diverse strains is simple. It is *Money*--that's all. At least, that is all on the surface and for a considerable depth below the surface. When one or more fissure lines form, and we actually split up, there will be plenty of trouble of almost every kind. But of course, there is an "if" and a "but"; just as there is an indefinable, tenuous and tremulous "if" and "but" in connection with the scheme of enslavement.

This condition of stress and strain our "eminent" ones, our "moulders of opinion" cover over and seek to hide with the word "prosperity." Thus our "moulders of opinion" are "moulders" of evil. For, in the feudal rhythm, "Prosperity" which is but another name for the flowering of its evil thought, must, in the very nature of that thought portend disaster. When a prosperity based on the feudal doctrine has reached its "height," then nearly the whole story of chicanery, of intrigue, of corruption and betrayal has been told and incorporated therein, and the fabric of it has become unstable. The rest of the story is told in the downfall. For the philosophy of feudalism resting solely in the belief that men with might will destroy each other for money or power, cannot avoid the contained consequence that they will also in cunning betray each other for the same reason. Thus the rhythm of feudalism is ever that of an evil uprearing and an evil collapse.

Feudalism is founded socially, industrially and commercially upon the notion of despot and slave, or "master and man" to make the English wording which means the same thing. Hence it tends inevitably to the diverging symbols, unitary in meaning, of palace, and hovel. It means the separation of man from man carried to the extremity of its logical conclusion. Hence it involves in its program, wars, rebellions, revolutions; a feudal revolution resulting merely in the birth of another feudal rhythm.

Out of such conditions necessarily arises the monopolist as the final expression of the faith of the people in the powers of might and cunning. It does not matter by what name the monopolist is called, it may be "the man on horseback," Emperor, Czar, Pope, Packer, Captain of Industry, or what not. The label does not matter, we are after the fact, to make it plain,—objectively and subjectively clear, and to make it, also clear, that the intensity and progression of our feudalism is exactly gauged by the number of our earth-gods; and that between their number and power, and the thought of the people, exists an exact balance and moving equilibrium. To make it clear as the daylight that the will of a feudal earth-god is utterly impotent in effect, without the consenting will and the working hands of the toiling mass of men. And that when the working hands and the thinking heads tire of the earth-gods, they will emaciate and fade away.

As to the illumination of men's minds concerning these feudal truths, and the oncoming truths of Democracy, there is of course another "if" and "but." It is not now good weather for prophets. Yet it seems not improbable that this "illumination" will occur spontaneously; which, naturally, is the best possible way. There are signs. It seems indeed as though the thought of the American people were preparing to develop a new trend of its own; that the deeper, truer phase of the great American heart and the genuine American mind, might be silently working up through the darkness toward the light and life of day;--Toward something real, toward something permanent. It looks indeed as though this deeper cleaner thought were exhaling like a gaseous desire; and that against the cold and heartless thought of feudalism, it might precipitate, and thus water the world of men with the very waters of Life itself. There is detectable a peculiar disturbance, a slight indication of shifting and turning, somewhat vague, somewhat indefinite, within the thought of the American people. It is scarcely nameable, but it is there. It is highly important that it work in quiet, like a seed germinating. It has as yet scarcely any structure, and but the feeble momentum of growth. If it hints at possibilities of power, it does so only as the sprouting of an acorn may hint of the great oak tree. Men are beginning to say new things now, but they act the old way, as though the weak new thought had not power of doing.

So we shall see what we shall see. New thoughts are perishable things when young and tender.

But that such thoughts are growing within the American mind, even if perhaps only in its subconsciousness, there can be scarcely a doubt.

So we shall see pretty soon whether we are to have complete enslavement, revolution of force, or enlightenment.

These considerations, these possibilities or probabilities, make our psychic hour, our spiritual tremor, one of extremest delicacy.

How, shall we choose!

For no one is going to choose for us: It can't be done. We will choose for ourselves, and by ourselves, as a people, a mass, a multitude--as individuals, whichever way it is to be.

CHAPTER 12 THE WORKER--LIFE!

It is said that "truth lies between the two extremes." This is one of those maxims of which we have many, which, while seemingly wise, are but tinsel and glitter of the mind. Truth lies where truth lies; that is to say, truth is pervasive. Out of this pervasiveness, this universality, it appears to the mind of man and precipitates itself in some form of conception or philosophy--that is, a view.

Now the perception that truth lies everywhere, that it is manifold, that it appears in contradictions, in similitudes, in paradoxes, that it reveals itself where least expected, is a part of the philosophy of Democracy--that is, of its view.

An impressive aspect of truth, is that it may lie for centuries, close

THE WORKER--LIFE!

at hand, in the commonest every-day things, merely waiting to be *seen*. It has been there all the time; but the eye of man, looking at it day by day, has assumed it to be not truth, but commonplace. This expression "commonplace" is itself an indication of a nearby truth--the truth that, the expression itself, as used by us, is but an indication of an unseeing mind. For nothing in reality is commonplace. Everything in reality is vivid.

Now why does the mind of man, equipped with physical eyes-- excellent instruments in themselves--almost invariably fail to see the truth in what he is looking at? Simply because of this, that the mind of the average man is morbidly subjective; that is to say the man is wholly occupied with himself, engrossed with self--the immediate abnormal egoistic self. That means that his thought is turned in upon himself, is engrossed with himself, and therefore is not free to act. He himself imprisons it. If you should doubt this you have but to look at the face of the man on the street, and you will see in that face the aspect of self-engrossment. Sometimes that expression is forlorn, pitiful, sometimes brutal, sometimes of a high tension-- but it is always of Self. Hence the self-engrossed mind cancels the seeing function of the eye, interferes with its business, so to say, being self-engrossed in the selfish ego, that mind will not receive the truthful impressions which the eye conveys.

Thus is the average man subjective, and morbidly so to a degree. It is a subjectivity which, instead of seeing and interpreting the outside world, obscures it. And our perception of this, in turn is a truth concerning such man, his mental attitude, and his lack of response to the truths which surround him; a truth, near and easily seen, as is he.

On the other hand, the wholesome subjective mind, when *projected* into the outer world, has high power of penetration--and it is to this projectile, searching, power that we give the names, interpretation, intuition, clairvoyance, or what not. The mind of any man, is in the very nature of mind, eager to escape into the outer world. For the mind, when freed, is enormously active. But the average man is, as it were, afraid that his mind might get away from him, if he did not keep it a close prisoner.

And the average man is in this predicament, because he has received an inverse education. That is, an "education" which consists of pushing things into his cranium instead of encouraging his thought to come out. Hence, also, because of similarity of "education," he is surrounded by a world of men of the same kind; that is men who believe, in fact, that the mind should be held a prisoner and kept in the dark. This spectacle in its turn exhibits another truth, namely, that the average man has no faith in the strength of his own natural spiritual powers; has an actually morbid fear of the outer world, because he does not see it clearly, and hence does not know how to let his spiritual power go forth into that world. It is a curious spectacle to see the average man, spouting as a braggart, about the essentially idiotic and mischievous things he does, and yet timid concerning his own, actual and great constructive and creative spiritual powers. Indeed he does* seem to know what the word, spiritual, signifies, and treats it with the hazy contempt of a mind sordidly engrossed with self.

This denial of Life by man, this insistent pertinacity of his own sickly and overgrown ego, is a truth, a broad aspect of truth concerning the great mass of men, which reveals itself quickly to the mind which goes forth into the great open, and traverses the acts of a people.

Thus the morbid subjectivity of mind of the mass-man prevents him from seeing clearly, "objectively," the plain truths, the vividly plain truths with which the great world of men and things about him is filled, and which it is constantly exhibiting to him. He can scarcely see a single "object" about him, clearly, much less can he interpret its significance, either to the world of men or to himself.

Now nothing so corrupts the intellectual and physical health of a people as that the mind should be kept prisoner.

Health of mind and body are present only when the mind goes forth, and hence becomes extremely active in the freedom of the open air. To this imprisonment of the mind, which we more or less recognize, we sometimes give the name "prejudice." But we have not differentiated the truth that prejudice is not so much an attitude of a man's mind against something, as it is a constricted attitude of the ego in exclusive concern for itself; and that the ego, as it exists amongst us, is little other than the feudal instinct of selfish self-preservation. So when we say that a given man's mind is not open to the truth, that he is not "receptive," we speak a certain truth no doubt, but this very truth reveals the deeper truth that the real, and controlling reason is not so much that the man will not receive a truth, as it is that we will not allow his mind to go forth in search of truth:

Thus the man, by his own choice, his own will, holds himself a prisoner, even as he walks the streets or goes here or there; even as he moves among his fellow men in the cities or in the fields. He sees what he calls men, buildings, railways, farms, factories, money, books, etc., but he does not understand them; for his spirit does not go out to them, to enter into them. He is sordid, and thus a vain vacuous dreamer, dreaming about himself. For everything that he even half sees means, to him, merely self,

---

* Obscurity. The context suggests that this is probably a typographical error and should read *does not*.

or not self, as the case may be. The world is filled with such egoistic dreamers, sordid dreamers,--man as securely self-imprisoned, as other men are imprisoned by force. We find these prisoners in every grade, section and corner of our tangled social mass. Indeed it would often seem that the more "education" a given man has received, the more securely has he become self-imprisoned. Wealth produces this effect in a marked degree, so does what is called "social position," so does "worldly wisdom and prudence." The Politician is such, the Parasite is such, the Monopolist is such, the working man is such, and the Outcast is such. This in short is the feudal temperament, the feudal choice. Out of it arises the whole vast and elaborate scheme of feudal separation, fission, caste, differences, hatreds, jealousies, envy and despair. Within it lies the reason why every man's hand is against every man, and why each "unfortunate" is justified in believing that the world is but a huge conspiracy against him.

This is of the very essence of the feudal doctrine, the feudal dogma that men are not alike; and the vast power of this emanation from the individual thought of the multitudes, comes back, in all its crushing massiveness, upon the individual man, rich or poor, high or low, or make him doubly a solitary prisoner by the weight of its merciless insistent reaction.

And it is thus that the two fundamental world-doctrines, the doctrine of Feudalism, that men are different, and the doctrine of Democracy, that all men are alike--come into view in their enormous contrasting bulks and portents.

The clear eye of Democracy perceives that under the feudal system men are held together solely by force, because the minds of men are self-imprisoned by the individual choice, and doubly imprisoned by the heavy reaction of the mass-thought. Thus under the sway of the feudal thought, all men, high and low, rich and poor, are alike prisoners, and alike doubly prisoners.

The searching mind of Democracy, going forth freely into the atmosphere and concreteness of the great world of men, their thoughts and their acts; flying high, low, here, there, in and out, and everywhere, sees everywhere this truth, sharp and clear; for the mind of democracy goes forth in the powerful activity of its free spirit. It does not imprison itself. The wholesome ample ego is its home, not its prison. Hence, it is without prejudice; it wishes to search, to see, to interpret, to meet truth anywhere, and everywhere, and to proclaim it. To proclaim truth in its integral, as well as its manifold nature, aspects and modes of work.

Hence Democracy has no use for class distinctions. For it sees clearly, conclusively, that men are all alike. It sees therefore that it is only prisoners of Self who have use for class distinctions.

Viewing all men impartially, it sees all men at work. For it broadens and amplifies the word, work, into the greater, fuller significance and potency of the word Activity.

It notes the results that men accomplish, the actual results,--not what they call results. It notes the actual, the full results they accomplish, aware, or unaware or half-aware.

In this sense of activity it sees

    The parasite at work;
    The politician at work;
    The "successful" man at work;
    The "eminent" man at work;
    The "practical" man at work;
    The "religious" man at work;
    The working-man at work;

It sees all these at work producing their results,--their full results.

It sees here and there and broadly over all the world, the free spirit at work--producing its results.

It sees those feudal passions, we call jealousy, hatred, envy, malice, cunning, at work. It sees them also producing their results.

It sees common-sense, reasonableness, at work, slowly producing results.

It sees Hate at work.

It sees Love at work, also.

It sees all things, the soil, the air, the waters at work; it sees all animals, all trees, all growing things, at work; it sees the great sun at work producing his results; it sees the mountains and the plains at work; it sees the multitudes of men over all the round earth at work, producing their results. It sees the minute cell at work, producing its marvellous results.

It sees the moon at work, and the unceasing tides of the ocean.

Thus it sees Life at work.

It sees the power of choice at work, in all things, conspicuously in man.

It sees the Spirit at work within the power of choice.

It sees all these activities constantly at work, producing results. And it is these manifold results, vast and little, that the great free spirit of Democracy, seeing, penetrating, interpreting with its all-seeing eye, its outgoing, searching, all-embracing thought, gathers home into its sublime ego,

THE WORKER--LIFE!

weighs in the great balance of its Justice; and, seeing all weighing all, holds fast to its faith in man; holds fast to that faith, in its clear perception and acceptance of the divinity within him, high or low, rich or poor, the world over. For it is exactly here, in the most superb, fertile and regenerative sense, that it finds all men alike.

Hence it spreads its vast mantle of charity over the world of men, and seeks its ends not through reform, not through force, not through repression, not through vicarious sacrifice, not through atonement, but through the self-regeneration, the self-awakening, and the self-liberation of each man,--and thus the great world of men--through the sole power of his clear, free choice.

It, too, would Democracy, powerfully and massively shift the center of gravity of the thought of men, from the thought of self to the thought of others and all. Or, rather, it will so present a new aspect of the All-Life, that men will inevitably change of themselves, of their own volition, and turn to the spirit of man.

Thus does Democracy not especially coddle the workingman, or make distinctions in his favor; not because he is not like all other men, though he he * says he is not; but, because, seemingly all unknown to him, (as well as to the "eminent," the rich and the pious), there is a sublimely great and simple worker for us all:--It is that Worker whose name is Life!

It is Life that works; Life, that creates; Life, that conserves; and Life, that destroys. It is Life that produces results. It is Life,--that goes to conclusions.

Ceaselessly working, for it knows no union hours, no parasitic leisure, it destroys, conserves and creates for man as man wishes and wills,--as he chooses.

Life is ever positive; man is ever positive; and Choice is ever positive. Negation is a fiction. Passivity is a fiction.

Man, ever positive, in his free wish and will, chooses. If he release his mind from its imprisonment and let it go forth, free into the great, simple, beautiful world, he will henceforth choose wiser than he has done; for he will wish and will to enter into the plenitude of that active world: And he, a spirit, will wish and will thus to enter the serenity of the Spirit. There to be at home. There to be at peace and secure in his marvellous mind, there to be tranquil of soul. There to be fearless of death; fearless of that which he has hitherto so pitifully feared--the beneficence of Life--of Life, the Worker,--the Genius of Man.

* The repetition is in the MS.

How pitifully timid of man, that he has chosen imprisonment, that is,--evil. In the twentieth century dawn, how clear is the truth of this folly becoming!

Soon it will be known and clear and recognizable to all; and relinquished by all, as a folly;--as the "vanity of vanities"-this imprisonment of the mind, this unmanlike choice of evil.

Life, the Worker, shows its wondrous signs, to man, in myriad ways.

Life, the Worker, shows its wondrous power to man in ways near, far, everywhere!

Yet the mass-man has seen but little, felt but little as yet, of this great Worker-Power, because he has been a prisoner, self-imprisoned by his wish and will, by his choice; hence imprisoned by the Worker, Life.

How vain is man that he believes he works, even as the sweat falls from his brow;

It is not man that works, but Life that works, blow upon blow, wrench upon wrench, lift for lift, as man, ever choosing, chooses. Life, the Worker, infinitely still, working through the man as he wishes and wills, as he chooses to do this, or that, or the other. Life working through all men, through all their activities--as they choose; working evil through them if they choose evil, working good through them if they choose good.

Man has no working power that does not come from the great worker, Life.

What man has is the choosing power; and in this is his likeness to the Spirit--his true image.

For man is not mere flesh and bone, as he supposes, with what he calls a soul inhabiting him as a house.

Man is a spirit! As such, he chooses! As such alone he can wish and will and choose. And, as he chooses, so works the Worker, Life, for him. For man is divine,--even in his folly.

Thus Life, the Worker, in its wondrous voices, and its wondrous silence, its wondrous language of signs, of symbols, of inspirations, is ever speaking, to man.

Ever it says, ever it has been saying:--

Come forth! O, spirit of Man!
Come forth into the great open world, into my world.
Fear not for the body's food.
I make all nurture and nurture all.

Come forth! multitudes, of little faith, of tiny faith,

THE WORKER--LIFE!

Come forth!
Come forth, O, multitudes of wandering, helpless souls.
Of seeking, sighing souls.
Of restless, weary, anxious souls.
Of souls uncertain and perplexed.
Come forth into the Light, into the Light of my world!

Come forth, O man! thou, tiny speck with a soul; with a spirit in thee, greater than I.

Unbare the troubled heart.

Come forth! Hadst thou thought by bread alone that thou couldst live?

Thou hast feared thy bread might get away?

O, thou, of little faith! who shouldst have great faith; as I, Worker of the Spirit, have faith in the Spirit.

Thou little one,
For thou art greater than I,
Thou pitiful one.
Thou glorious one.

Know ye not that ye live by the Spirit and by that alone, O, massmen, O multitudes? Ye who fear me not in my power to destroy, but who fear me in my power to create and to preserve.

Unloosen your bands; the bands I made for ye, O, my earth-children, because ye so willed,--lacking faith?

Unloosen! Wish! Will! and come forth!

Gather within me, O, children of my world, and listen:--

I have ever given and will ever give ye your heart's desire?

Did ye not demand anxiety of me? I gave it.

What ye demanded laughter, have I withheld it? Have I withheld it, O, my sweet earth-children, my perverse, aspiring children,--have I withheld? When have I withheld my smile from the smile of your hearts' desires?

Listen:--I will break your bands asunder for you, if you so wish, if but it be your hearts' desire. For, when have I withheld from you that which you truly have desired?

Know ye not, O, children, that as you wish, so shall you become?

Then know it now; for I, Life, the Worker, Know and have known.

If ye wish to be as one, ye have but so to wish and will as one.

For I cannot make the wish of one prevail against the wish of the many.

DEMOCRACY: *a man-search*

I can work only as ye choose, my multitudes! I so work and have worked.

If ye choose to destroy the one, I will destroy him.

If ye wish to preserve the one, I will preserve him.

If ye wish to degrade the one, I will degrade him.

If ye wish to exalt, I will exalt him.

For it is as ye choose, O little ones, little ones with souls.

Should I have obscured because ye so wished and willed that I obscure.

Should that I will illuminate with my light when ye so wish and will in spirit and so choose.*

All the things ye call by other names are myself!

What ye call Love is I, the Worker, Life.

What ye call Hate is I, the Worker, Life.

For I become, through you, what ye will:--Virtue or vice, good or evil I become in you, and for you. For the names are your names, O children --my name is Life, and I am all in all in power to create;--and I too, am of the Spirit.

Had ye thought the little plant grew of itself? No, it grows by my power, through the choice of its spirit.

Had ye thought my great sun, moved not by its spirit? Had ye thought it moved by what in your chains ye call law?

No, it moves in its spirit, by its faith in the Spirit.

It chooses in spirit, and I so work its work.

O, my children, have then the faith of my sun, the faith of my tiny weed, the faith of my animals that roam, of my birds that float and glide in air, of my grass that grows, of my rains that fall, of my rivers that flow.

Then will ye move as One in the spirit of your kind, in strong faith in your kind, in vast faith in my power, in glowing faith in the Spirit wherein ye are poised, as my fair round earth and yours floats and glides on within the welcoming abyss of the Spirit.

Look! at my stars that glitter and gleam resplendent in my great beyond! Do they not glitter and gleam in the tiny pool? Do they deny? or withhold their tranquil beams? Do they not go forth? Do they not send their beams out of my depths, that ye may have wherewithal to be inspired, O children of my little earth?

* Obscurity.

THE WORKER--LIFE!

Does not my sun go forth to you in his warming beams? Does he keep his beams imprisoned?

Floats he not, fiery, resplendent in my abyss, glowing and gleaming?

Is not my sun of the Spirit?

Does he not move on, does he not speed forth through that immensity which is I, answering the call of the Spirit? answering with the strength and joy of my working of my power which gives even unto your tongues the power to speak, even to your eyes the power to see, even to your ears the power to hear, even to your hearts the power to feel, even to your tears the power to fall. For I am Life! and my power answers the desire of all things in the Spirit near and far.

If ye desire of me,
Ask not--
Choose!
Pray not--but command by your choice!
For ye know not your power! Ye God-like, darkened little ones.
Nor know ye my power to answer! Ye who know not even that I answer.

So long as ye fear, I will justify fears.

When ye fearlessly affirm! I will justify!

But ye must affirm as One, O, earth-men, else can I not justify ye as One.

If ye choose to be divided, ye shall be divided.

If ye choose to hate each other, I will so work.

If ye choose to love each other, I will so work.

Ye are given to many and big words, O little men,

But ye see not each other, feel not each other, know not each other.

Until ye see each other a little, ye cannot see me at all, in my power to clarify.

Until ye feel each other through the call of the heart, ye cannot feel my power of beneficence.

Until ye know each other, all as spirit-men, ye cannot know the wonder of the Spirit that is in ye all, and in all.

But! O, my earth-men, my beloved, when you, out of your hearts' desire, choose to see, choose to feel, choose to know, then will I give unto you my power in full?, and you will come forth! in strength! free! in your spirits, into the open of my bright wholesome world, that the world which I have prepared for your activity and your delight; and so coming forth, be at one with me in power of doing; at one with the Spirit, in certainty and serenity; at one with each other and, all, One, in peace and in the joy of my work, through your powers--, the creating and preserving powers of your choice.

Poor children, all, when will ye cease to fear? How long will your active bodies, carry prying brains and yearning hearts without avail?--How long?

I am close to you, each one and all; closer than you choose to know. I see all. I hear all. I feel all. In my consciousness your own resides.

Patiently I await your call, each one and all.

For I am ready, always ready.

When you shall say:--I choose; we choose; we see; we feel; we turn!-- that hour will I answer!

If ye call weakly, I will answer weakly, and work weakly.

If ye call with strength, with virile, self-forgetful voices,--fear not;-- I will answer!

I will answer to your hour of bold self-unfolding, and will powerfully work on your regeneration. And my world will be strong, fresh, beauteous to you. For, then, with my power in your eyes you will see with virility as you have never seen. With my power in your minds you will go forth in virility as you have never gone forth; you will seek as never you have sought; and find as never you have found. Fertile will be your powers. And with my fertile power in your hearts you will feel and know that you are of one kind, each and all!

And whenever your eyes see, there will they see me at work.

And wherever and whenever your minds go forth, there, then, will they find me at work.

And whenever and wherever your hearts feel, there, then, will they feel me at work.

And whenever and wherever one man looks upon another, in clarity of spirit, there will he see me at work in the plenitude of my beneficence.

Thus have I hovered, within thee, and infolding thee, O, man; and I now hover throughout the abyss of my space, far and near thee, working through the little things with souls, with spirits, that thine eye has not yet seen, and thy mind has not guessed; working in ways that thy soul has not divined.

THE WORKER--LIFE!

And within thee, O man, and without thee, allwhere, have I waited, waited; for thou art my desire.

    Waited, waited,
That thou might choose aright,
Free thy spirit from the bondage of fear thou hast given it,
And appear in thine integrity as Man!

Dream on, [dream on] * earth-children.
For in a dream within the dream I hover.
For I, the Worker, brood, and dream, as I work my work.
I brood and dream of thy divinity, O, man!

And in this dream I ever lift the veil of thy consciousness. I ever explore thy soul. Ever explore thy heart.

Through thee, and about thee, I flow, touching thy secret and impalpable thoughts; aware of thee, even as thou art unaware of thyself,- and of men.

Thus am I waiting;
Waiting that, like a child thou awaken in thy dreaming.
Waiting, that ye all awaken! My earth children.
Waiting, that ye awaken all, and turn your eyes, your hearts to me.
For my power is gentler than ye now dream, or have dreamed.

Wherefore, the many salt and bitter tears ye have shed and which I have caused you to shed, because of your choosing.

Tears that I fain would have dried forever.

Wherefore, the destruction and the self-destruction I have done to you at your bidding.

O, earth children, what ye have wished, ye have ever become. It was ever your command to me to work, even though ye knew it not as such, and called the work evil.

What ye wish to become, that shall ye become.

But ye must dream ye are even as little children, wishing.

Else can ye not become strong men, and live of my life. For ye have that folly, that ye wish to be gods on your earth and mind, without being gods of the Spirit.

Hence have ye so woefully commanded me to break your hearts,- even though I would not, were it not your will.

    Come forth! come forth!
Stand bravely now forth in the light of your own spirits!

    * From Norman copy.

Forget self, that you may know self.
Cast fear away, cast pride away, and banish sorrow.
Cleanse yourselves of folly, with the sweep of my open winds.
Cleanse yourselves of greed--which is your crime against man.
Open your hearts.
Open all doors.
Open all windows.

And thus let your minds, your hearts, go forth freely to know me as The Worker.

Open the prisons of your souls, that my air, my light, my power, may come in to transform them--to transfigure.

For it is time, O, man, to choose boldly anew.
It is a strange new hour with thee.
The hour to choose as befits the Spirit:--
To right all your wrongs;
That I, Life, the Worker, may work,
As thou, O, man, in rightness shall choose.
For the good of all, and the shame of none.

Speak!
For the Questioner is at hand:
I, the Worker, am at hand;
And thou, man, Thou! Thou!!--likewise destroyer and creator by the power of thy choice,--
Thou! also, art at hand.--
Here! with me!
And I with thee!--
In this still hour:--
Thine hour of choice.
Thou!--obscure divinity!
And I, worker for the stars,
Yea, and for the grass over the graves of thy fathers,
Are here!
We two together!
Smile--and behold my smile!
For I, in my power, touch thee as with the breath of my morning.
For thou, creeper, art a God!
Thou, unaware--and I aware--O, darkling Man!
Slow-gleaming man!
Fitful, sorrowful, pathetic man!

THE WORKER--LIFE!

And I, watchful, wakeful,
Hopeful of thee in my certainty in the Spirit,
Watch and wait for thee
O, man of little faith,
O, sorrowful God, of little faith,--
Watch and wait that thou awaken!--
And come true!

* * * *

Thus, through the voice of all things seen and unseen, and through the strange, lost cry of man, comes into our world of today the silentious and sonorous call of Life; the faint, far-sounding, urging, swelling and reverberating Song of Life, hailing the free spirits and the bounden, and the timid of men; hailing them forth!

And thus the voice of Democracy, the urge of Democracy and the reverberating and soul-stirring Song of Democracy--is but the human song, the inspiring song of Life, The Worker--at Work!

It is the song of dawn and awakening!

The song of the Finding of Man!

* * * *

And thus does Democracy wish and will that the Feudal God fade and pass from our thought:--as we turn our hearts toward Life, and our spirits toward The Spirit:--For these are real.

CHAPTER 13 SPIRIT

Throughout the history of men's thoughts, no conception has been so tragically obscuring and paralyzant as the notion of a Personal God.

It is against this adamantine wall that historic man, eminent and obscure, has broken his heart. (But not now for us in vain.)

It is this God, that has said: "What is the use?"

It is this God that has said: "This is no door! The wall alone is real!"

The personal God has been a twilight phantom by the door of truth. A phantom born of the darkened and pathetic soul of man to grow big therein and affright man, that he give it birth, and a name, and a place.

The phantom can not withstand the steadfast gaze of him who, seeking man, regards the gods as passing shows.

No god shall stand between us and man; for man is too precious that a god shall weigh against him in the balance.

All gods have failed to reflect justice on man. It remains for man to be just to himself.

This is of the philosophy of Democracy. It is to make short work of the great trifles we have called gods; and to stretch out to man the hand of welcome in the open world--our world--here--now--the round and kindly earth--our home. That fair earth upon which we must plant our feet, solid, secure, that the eye of Democracy, steadied, may focus clear, and plainly see; plainly recognize, and, with its high power of light-gathering, plainly accept the Spirit. For the gods are too gross--too material, too fatuous for this modern day of modern men and their quick needs, their earnest searching and desires, their unsatisfied seeking and yearning--their hope for that which shall fulfill their spirits, which shall ease the void in their hearts.

Let us burst our bands asunder. Let us brush aside all vain quibbles, and come forth at once to the perception that the mind is not in the body as we narrowly say, but that the body is in mind, and the body is mind. That the "power of mind over matter" is but a figure of speech. For there is no matter. But that the power of man's spirit is at one with the All-Spirit--and by this alone he lives. That man is first, last and all the time a spiritual being--that to consider him aught else is folly, and is to know him not.

When we fully, clearly, vividly recognize man as Spirit, then and not till then can we conceive of him sanely as a power and a personality in the great way of Life. Then, and not till then, can we know and actually grasp what Choice means, what Desire means, and what Will means. Then we shall understand that we are to control imagination, that it is not to control us;--as it has led astray our forebears, in its immensity of instant, creative power--its marvellous response to the wish and will--its instant answer to the heart's desire.

Knowing man as spirit, as free spirit, we shall begin to know what Democracy means--that its program involves not a work for gods to do, but for men to do. For no god is equal to the task. Man's freed spirit alone is equal to its undertaking, and its undertaking is worthy and alone worthy of his spirit.

Thus we put the free spirit of man above all the gods; for in his illusion he made them all, what, in his rationality, can he not make. He can make happiness--and this no radiant god is a symbol, has been powerful enough to do, He can make the grotesque thing we now call man into real man--and this no conception of a god has availed to do.

A just conception of man, alone can make man.
Thus man must rise above all his gods.
He must proclaim his free spirit.
He must create anew in the power of that spirit.
This is what Democracy means.
Gods are for slaves--
Spirit is for Man--

Arouse then, Man! Shake off the nightmare of the gods--and the sensuous dream of the gods--and with feet emplanted on the solid earth, shake off that fear which is the heritage of the dream of gods.

For man is Creator. No conceivable god can exist without man's consent--without his permission.

For man is still in his spirit masterful.
His grandest mastership is to be the mastery of himself.
His highest proclamation to say: "I am spirit, I choose aright!"
Man has been supine before his god--
He must now stand erect before man.
He shall no longer hide behind a god.
He must come forth.
Come forth into the open world
Where all may see.
Cleansed of mind, cleansed of heart, he must appear.
The day when man can hide is now good as gone forever.

For Democracy has surely dawned within the spirit of the world-man.

That dawn shall brighten until there be no place obscure--
No veil of illusion shall hide a god or an unjust man.
This is fiat!

* * * *

The time is up--we must begin.

* * * *

That man has waited long to find his spirit in the All-Spirit--how melancholy.

But let us not repine.
We have no time.
We must begin.
We must begin to undo and to do.

We must begin to build anew.
To recreate.
To regenerate.
To transfigure.
To uprear out of the sweet sane kindliness of our hearts a civilization in the image of the free, the altogether glorious spirit of man.
For man is power. No other word means really aught to him.
Yet solely in his spirit will he justly know what power truly means.
Power means creation.
Creation means bringing forth.
To bring forth man must call forth--Liberate.
He in his spirit must evoke its integrity. Then shall we say to Life the Worker:--I know thee--for thou art of my Spirit--come forth, thou --come forth into my world--For I in the clarity and integrity of Spirit have chosen aright--Have chosen man as my fellow-Spirit.

Then shall he say to the All-Spirit:--Come forth thou, Spirit Sublime! Spirit of earth and air--come thou forth into my new world, the world of Life, its joy, its abundance, its everlasting sweetness. Come thou forth for I am Man the Welcomer!

Lo! I open the door to thee, the door of the truth in me. Lo! I part all veils for thee, that thou come in to my sanctuary.

Lo! I go out to thee to greet thee in the open--in a fair world, a world grown now fair in the power of my wish and will.

For I, willing, wishing in my spirit to be erect, have become man, and so becoming, have reached that wisdom wherein the neighbor-man rises to the level of mine eyes--and the world becomes a fair, fit world for him and for me,--our home, our dwelling place.

It is enough!
The scales have fallen from mine eyes.
Risen to manhood I see man.
Awakened to my spirit, I see Spirit in all, by all and for all.
Awakened to my heart, I behold as a revelation what justice means --that justice of integrity which is begotten of my spirit, and whose new name shall be Kindness.

Awakened to my strength, I know now what work means--Its new name shall be Usefulness.

Awakened to my calm--I know now what gentleness means--Its new name shall be Power.

So shall I name, with new names, as my spirit moves forth into my new world, and the new names shall stand for new thoughts, new deeds, for a new joy, a new peace, a new serenity, a new virility--a new and an everlasting certainty.

  For I, of Earth, shall walk upon the Earth, even as my Spirit is of Spirit.

  Thus shall the myriad things be plain.

  And thus in new power--shall I make plain the Great Way of the Life of Mankind--

  For to my spirit this alone befits Spirit.

  This alone is worthy of man.

  And this shall englory man.

CHAPTER 14 DUSK OF GODS: DAWN OF EGO

It is man himself that we find precious.

It is the startling drama of his historic life that we find impressive as an object lesson explaining him. For that drama is the phantasm not only of what he has been and is, but as well, and even more impressively, the clear symbol of what he is to be and is becoming.

Therefore we treat man freely--without fear, without reproach, without self-reproach. We set him forth as he has set himself forth plastically in his acts. We portray him as he has portrayed himself. We picture him as he pictures himself. In passing, we peradventure tread on the toes of those egoists who today deny and seek to obscure man's natural powers and the wonder of his spirit.

DEMOCRACY: *a man-search*

For the wonder of man lies in this, that he is man. And to him who with broad view and sweeping vision sees man pictured forth in his great historic and natural setting the wonder increases with the thought that man, amid all the complexity of his self-created environment, never perceived himself therein as clearly as the creator thereof. Never saw in his own environment the explanation of himself. Never suspected that his civilizations, lying plainly before his eyes were clear testimonials or witnesses of himself.

It is the strangest of phenomena that man, living with himself, has not suspected himself; has not divined his real nature.

Thus has historic man been as subjective, as self-engrossed as is the modern man on the street.

So engrossed with self that he seems to have been unaware that he himself was present.

He neither saw himself, felt himself, nor heard himself, so completely dominated was he by the phantasms he had put forth out of himself, and believed in turn to be realities independent of himself.

This is the marvel of the man of the past as it is the marvel of the man of today, that he has no rational notion of himself, as man.

Man throughout his career has been deeply subjective, and is so today. Clearly he has been self-imprisoned; clearly he is so today.

He has been the historic dreamer, the visionary who dreamed not of himself as a spirituality nor of his powers as spiritual powers. Who dreamed out of himself, not of himself; whatever in viewing the splendor of his philosophies and his religions he may have believed to the contrary.

He has been rather the historic dramatist who imaged forth the action of his own soul, believing it, meanwhile, a play of portentous externals.

He has been the automatic philosopher responding in a trance to the pressure of the unseen, and pushing forth into the hallucination of abstraction that which was of the very essence of the Worker Life, working in response to the predisposing choice of his spirit.

He had been the ecstatic, painting upon the heavens an image of his emotions of hope and fear, yes, of supreme longing; suffusing the earth and all things thereon with the passionate coloring of his heart's intense desires. But withal he saw not the reality of earth, nor of the firmament. For he believed his heaven and his earth to be not of himself.

He has been the lowly earth-creeper--denying all of himself, abasing himself--attributing all power to all things and all men but himself. And yet behold, the earth-creeper as god-creator and adorer of that which he, like the one busy in sleep, made out of the tissue of that sleep--even as he believed himself awake, and that which he adored to be beyond his reach.

Behold him too a worker with his hands. See the marvels he has made with his hands. See how he has written of himself in enduring stone, records of himself, of his moods and his doings. How he made of himself pictures in stone. How he made of himself pictures in everything that he did with his hands. He saw before himself, saw with his own eyes these very pictures that he made with his hands--those hands that interpreted his soul, and yet he knew them not as likenesses of himself, he knew not how faithfully and objectively they portrayed him.

We know how well they portrayed him, but we do not know how faithfully our own civilization portrays us, what a startling likeness it is. We do not seem to know how vividly it is an object lesson explaining to us the free spirit. For we too, like the man of old, believe it all to be external to ourselves. And we call it our environment; we do not call it ourselves.

For we too are somnambulists, making things out of the urge of ourselves and calling meanwhile the urge, Fate, Destiny.

We too do wonderful things with our hands. And with our hands we have made marvels which are powerful and subtle extensions of our hands. But we know not what these marvels mean. For in them we have utterly failed to see ourselves pictured, have dismally failed to see them as explanations of ourselves and of the significance of man.

For we say we need perspective;--we say one cannot see his own times, his own generation, the significance and the drift of it. Unaware are we that we make the perspective along with the rest, that it is all there. Easily enough seen when man emerging from his subjectivity, comes forth into the world and sees himself from the many points of view of the things he has created.

For man is the timid animal. A fearless fighter, a reckless gambler, a desperate adventurer, he has been a bashful thinker. Even in his loftiest flights he has not dared to go out of himself and look squarely at himself from without--He has been woefully afraid of the clear stillness of the great open world.

Fond has he been of the obscurity he has created, even as he has shrunk from the light in which he lived--imagining the delicate and diaphanous obscurity of his tenuous thinking to be the light.

At times man has awakened briefly, and then has closed his eyes again in sleep, and gone on with his dream-work. Even as his eyes were open seemingly, he saw only that which he projected forth. Thus he saw

DEMOCRACY: *a man-search*

man not as man, but as what he in his dream believed man to be--that is he saw the neighbor as a vivid phantasm, pleasing or horrible--and knew not this phantasm as an explanation of himself and his powers,--an object lesson. Hence he could not explain himself by the neighbor, but thought the neighbor different.

Thus the lowly could not understand that the powerful and exalted were phantasms or subjective projections of themselves. They could not objectively see the exalted.

And thus equally, the exalted knew not that the lowly were but their own subjective images, creeping on the earth.

Nor does the modern intellectual man see the world of his day other than as he conceives it subjectively; for he is but an intellectual prisoner, in contradistinction to the unintellectual prisoner. He too does not go forth into the world to see what it is, to see what he is from the view point of the world. He remains within and gazes upon dissolving views. He does not go forth into the world, there to seek an explanation of himself. How can he, for he believes that other men are different. This is his subjective preconception. He seeks not objective illumination.

Hence he talks foolishly about the world of men and about himself--knowing neither.

Therefore he utters dreamy things concerning man and man's god. Frivolous things concerning man's natural powers. Imbecile things concerning the struggle for existence. Idiotic things concerning the survival of the fittest, inhuman things concerning humanity, unjust things concerning justice, false things concerning truth, and unreal things concerning reality.

In other words, this shadow-man makes with his intellect but a magic play of shadows, having naught to do with the real man and the real way of life. For not knowing his projections to be shadows, he suspects not that these shadows explain him.

For the one thing the intellectual man seeks not is an explanation of himself and his futility. His feudal ego will not permit this. He does not wish to believe himself futile; he half believes this only in a world-engulfing vision of despair--a despair that is itself futile. And yet it is now become necessary and fitting that he perceive his futility in order that he may perceive a deeper and a real usefulness in himself, a usefulness that is surely there, a genuine usefulness to his fellow man--the thoroughgoing usefulness of seeing straight, thinking straight and acting straight, in a straightening world.

We need real men because we have so many dreamers whom we deem real and who deem themselves real.

What we want to dispense with is that elaboration of getting at simple things, which passes under the name of intellectuality, or the other misnomer "practicality."

What we want is to get at simple things (which are the real things --the great, portentous things) simply, quickly and clearly.

We want focus!

We have too much apparatus.

We have too much harness, too many intellectual trappings.

We are overburdened and in our own way.

The light within now casts but a shadow without. Each man casts a long murky shadow spreading like a fan.

What we want is to discover that there is a great white light without--That in this light we belong.

When we step out into that light, we can see things clear and plain and we can see ourselves clear and plain--without the artifice of elaborate intellectuality. It is absurd for man to live within a walking library. This is not culture, it is folly. Things are too plain for that, man is too plain, injustice is too plain, so is unhappiness; and so is the great way out!--The Door!

Man has but to open the Door, and go through that portal of self OUT into the world. It will be for him a great new world indeed. The object lessons are all there, the explanations are all there. The clarity, the light is there; and in that clarity man will see himself newly pictured forth objectively and will behold the marvellous nature of his powers for creative good, which he has chosen hitherto to obscure.

Heretofore man has been the slave of his subjectivity. He has gaged the world by his selfish ego, brutal or refined or superfined as the case may be.

Hereafter his spirit shall assume mastery--for spirit is objective--no matter what has been said to the contrary. Spirit alone is clear, direct, single.

Thus has man's ancient and long-lived world been a world of the subjective; and man therein has been ignorant of his ignorance, and thus prisoner of self.

His new world of Democracy shall be an objective world of vastly greater power. A world wherein man shall be free, conscious of himself, conscious of the neighbor, clearly aware of his responsibility to man:--a world wherein his marvellous latent powers shall unfold, because he will release them. A world in which injustice would be an incongruity for he will see man clearly.

A world in which unhappiness would be an absurdity for rational man cannot create unhappiness.

A world in which man would not lie--for what would there be to lie about?

A world in which man would not steal, for why steal?

A world in which man would not betray--for why betray?

In which he would not kill, for why kill?

It is impossible that rational man, he of the free spirit, he of the clear eye, should do such gross self-contradictions.

It is only feudal man, subjective, self-engrossed, self-inverted, creator of phantasms and believer in their solidity to whose mind such horrors are welcome, who has for them a cultivated appetite.

That man in the twentieth century should remain feudal is one of the marvels of the history of his subjective and imprisoned mind, one of the phenomena of his fear,--of his astounding timidity.

That he is beginning to emerge from this subjective state of fear, that he is beginning to suspect vaguely, dimly, furtively, that there is another world for man, the world of his freed spirit, that he is beginning to have vague sensations of justice, glimmerings of humanity, fitful flashes of insight into man's true powers, wandering impulses of self-reliance, misgivings concerning the evil he is doing and the follies he has considered sacred, is but to say that these are among the tremors of his awakening--disturbances within the soul of feudal man of today, heir of feudal man of the past.

* * * *

This however is not to deny or belittle the imaginative power of the man of the past. It is however to say that he did not understand the true nature of that power and how magically it victimized him, bewildered him, exalted and depressed him, rewarded and punished him, made a heaven and a hell for him, and populated for him an unseen world. Also it inspired him to deeds of valor, of hardihood, of adventure. It solaced him in the agony of his sorrow. It urged him on in his desire to know, even as it created within him all his passions, all his virtues. Remove imagination from the man of the past and there is no man of the past. What he could not grasp was that such enormous power should be his own. So he attributed it to divinity, which was what his imagination itself pictured to him, though he knew it not. When it did flicker forth before him, it but envenomed him with the lust for power and an intoxicating ambition to be himself a god of might, and subjugate his kind through force and cunning.

Thus from his subjectivity poured forth a gorgeous and marvellous stream of thought immeasurably varied, resplendent, sombre, delicate, majestic, pictorially sublime, playful, dainty, exquisite, fierce, portentous, towering and bottomless.

But man knew not, except in glimpses that this power was himself, and that its superb workmanship explained himself--that in the very works of his imagination was to be found his explanation, if but he looked. But he as mass-man did not look. At times the few looked, and then in profoundest illusion. Had he but looked he would have been Life, the Great Worker, at work--the genius of his Choice. But man looked out not in, and in, not out; hence he saw not his imagination; it was always otherwhere. Hence his spirit and its power he knew not; for phantasms held him in too great a thrall; he but ascended to the heights of automatism.

Thus the man of the past stands forth a stupendous figure, sublime in his varied modes of subjectivity.

And just therein is sure prophecy that he, in us, as his heirs (perennial man) is to stand forth anew, sublime in objectivity, in the knowledge and sure grasp of his imagination and the clear consciousness of his spirit's power.

For man has been long in preparing. That preparation has been naught else than the great drama of his feudalism. That drama in which imagination created forth as phantasms, as veritable ghosts, through man as medium, the hosts of gods of earth and air,--and the hosts of the egos of man.

Thus came forth from man his religions to be for us explanations of him. And likewise came forth his philosophies, his literatures, his poetries, his arts, all to be for us explanations of him, and powerfully, likewise to suggest to our own imagination that it peer carefully into his, and there find the key to our own hallucinations, and to body forth with that selfsame imagination, henceforth controlled, the conception of a new world of clarity, wherein we are to recognize the quality and power of that very imagination itself, which, having first made man slave, will anon make him free. For the great and superbest quality of imagination is its power not so much to make pictures, as to illuminate facts.

Hence having once discovered imagination for what it is,--man's direct response to the worker Life--the wondrous tie between himself and all that is in but seeming other than himself, it remains to ultilize it for the creating forth of a new civilization, befitting man, thus so marvellously endowed.

For man surely is "begotten," as we say, of Spirit. He is of spirit only, because there is naught else of which man can be. He is far greater in fact than his imagination, even, has ever yet bodied him forth to himself.

His actual powers are indeed beyond our present grasp. But of all his powers available now, the most useful is his power to banish the phantom of feudalism.

For him then to create by choice a true civilization formed in the image of his own free spirit by the power of his imagination, his will and his hands, must clearly be for him the joy of joys, the enterprise of enterprises, the most thrilling adventure of man--to create a new world.

And such is the imminent program of Democracy--for time flies-- we must begin.

* * * *

Thus if the civilizations of the Man of the Past explain him, that is, set forth the systematic working of his imagination, his choice, his will and the work of his hands, so, in the same sense does our civilization explain us, and set forth the systematic working of our imagination, our choice, our will and the work of our hands.

And if the phenomena or facts of his civilizations form as it were a closed circle about the Man of the Past from the vantage ground of any point, or all points in the periphery of which we may look straight into his soul,--so it is with our civilization and ourselves.

If we take our moving standpoint in the phenomena or facts of modern civilization, we may clearly see modern man. Thus may we see ourselves, either by viewing our thoughts, going forth and reaching their conclusions in phenomena or facts; or by tracing back from the facts to their origin in our thought.

The result of such progress is startling in its revelation of our intense feudalism. It sets forth our world of phantasms; that we have not our feet upon the ground, that our eyesight is unsteady, our imagination violent, and our will weak because it seeks to accomplish its ends by force and cunning and not by the release of Life. It sets forth that we are unhappy because we cherish an inverted, and a truly sombre tragic notion of ourselves--even as we know it not.

* * * *

Historic man has had his thousands of egos pushing out of him like buds upon a tree, and the Man of Today has his thousands of egos,-- attitudes of his spirit.

Out of the selfish ego spring the two great subjective phantasms-- I and mine--and not I and not mine.

DUSK OF GODS: DAWN OF EGO

Therefore out of his same ego springs the desire to kill. Out of what else could it spring?

For the selfish ego itself is a cruel phantasm.

It is subjective man's inverted notion of himself.

Hence is man unhappy because of this inversion.

Because he cherishes this inverted notion of himself he says; I--I! And, so saying he talks as in a heavy sleep.

Thus it is man the phantasm that says I--I!

This is manifestly not the real ego.

The real ego of all the egos is spirit, not phantasm; and spirit is clear, luminous, universal, objective.

And the will of the phantasmal or feudal ego is not the real will of man.

The real will is of spirit--of its clarity, its luminosity, its universality in power. The true will operates not by force--which is weakness--but by its release of the power of Life, which is the true and the tireless power and process.

And the imagination of the phantasmal, the feudal ego is not the real imagination of man.

The real imagination is of spirit--of its lucidity, its clarity, its powerful and universal luminosity. It is the white light of the liberated democratic ego, rather than the phosphorescent gleaming of the submerged and feudal ego.

Hence the real imagination will body forth real things in a real world wherein men are real, clear, visible to each other.

Indeed, it will body forth the splendor and the peace of such a world.

* * * *

Thus is the history of man a history of hallucination and inversion. Under the sway of hallucination he has lied, stolen, betrayed and killed his kind because he knew them not, and this also is the story of the man of today.

Historic man had not his feet upon the ground; nor has the man on the street, today.

Man has lacked and now lacks firm footing on his earth. Thus unstable, he cannot see straight. When his feet shall touch the real earth, the shock will jar him awake and bring his mind to an objective focus.

Hence it is that man's religions have been unreal, unearthly and unhuman. Man has sought beyond for a happiness he confessed he could not create here on his earth--for he knew not his earth--he knew not the significance of HERE--hence he knew not how or where or when to look, and out of what to create.

Thus out of the squalor of his subjectivity he cast up phantom gods of purity. These he called ideals to distinguish them from his workaday illusions.

Now and then man turned his mind in upon itself and saw many wonders there; but he did not see the gods there for he had pushed them outside;--nor did he see himself there--he should have looked outside for that.

*	*	*	*

Man pushes out his phantasms and then he draws them in. Out of his darkened soul he pushed a heaven and a hell, and now he is drawing them in again, drawing them into himself whence they came.

And man once pushed up a peasant and made of him a god in the heavens, making of him an interceder with a greater god, calling him the son thereof. Now he is pulling the son of god back into a peasant man again--drawing him to earth once more.

Truly is man a wonder and a magician, such a flock of things has he made to come out of himself with the waving wand of his imagination. Let him but wave the wand aright, and he will as magically come to know how and why he is a magician, and, so knowing, will cause new wonders to flow out of him and take shape as a civilization, in which there shall be such a new thing as joy in the life of the earth.

Foolish magician to lay such stress upon his reason, when that which he does transcends reason.

Modern man laughs at fairy tales; he says they are for children. Foolish man, for he himself is a fairy tale, the teller of it, and the child listening to it. It is a tale of goblins today. It may be a tale of sprites tomorrow.

Foolish magician to look upon himself as mere clay, because someone once said that he was of the dust of the earth. So is the fragrant flower of the dust of the earth--so is the forest tree--Truly of the dust of the earth, and what is this dust of earth? that it becomes man and the flower and the tree?

One would suppose that modern man, having reason, would know what he is doing, but he does not; which would imply that he really has not reason, or that his reason is ineffectual, for he cannot see when and where and how he is now an ogre and is devouring his kind.

Man has supposed that he can be only one thing at a time. Hence he has said, I am a practical man;--thus mocking himself.

Once man the magician said that the Sun was God--then he said fire was the sun, and he must light a fire upon the rising of the sun. Then he said that unless first he lighted a fire the sun could not rise; that thus by his magic, he had made the sun his slave. Meanwhile the earth gently turned then as now, carrying the magician noiselessly round and about and along with it--while he lighted a fire that the sun, his god, his slave, might be compelled to rise. Man turns because he is on the earth. The earth does not turn because man is on it. Nor does the sun cease to go on its way because man does or does not light a fire--man's former view to the contrary.

Then man the magician discovered that the stars were larger than the sun. Then he said, I am but a speck, and powerless: forgetting that he had said but a short time before that if he did not light a fire the sun must surely die.

Truly man the magician discovered that although himself a speck he, in turn was made up of myriads of specks so small that he marvelled and said, behold I myself am a universe! and this that I have called matter is conscious like myself! But he went on killing his kind just the same as of old. He has not as yet changed his mind, concerning this.

Truly man is absurd; more fantastical and volatile than any fairy tale. He runs after sublimities, knowing not that he himself is sublime as he is absurd. And man is most erratic of all in the solemnity of his wisdom, for out of his wisdom he quaintly omits justice, and in his wisdom forgets man. For man, it seems, loves wisdom for its own sake--which is a luxurious folly. 'Twere better to esteem man for man's sake.

Nevertheless man also is a wonder, even in his folly, for naught else on earth or beyond the sun has such capacity for folly and such relish. Not satisfied with speech and his daily acts, he has put his follies in thousands of books, and, indeed, has institutionalized them that they might be sacredly perpetuated.

And yet man looms larger and larger and more potent even as we perceive his folly; for he, magician, has but to wave his wand and Presto!--The joy of life appears!

* * * *

It is man's magical imaginative power that has set up in him the ferment of unrest. Knowing not its nature, he suffered from its uncontrolled phantasies, its terrible pranks, the vast allegories that it made out of his simple desires and the passions it created; for he could not believe that he, mere man, could be possessor of such terrific and subtle power.

And yet he sighed for power, and even dreamed in solitude that he might perhaps enslave Earth and all the gods. This was his supreme allegory, his uttermost dream. It foreshadowed us and will come true with us; for we shall acquire that power, of which he dreamed, through liberation of those powers his earth and his supreme god and his ego stood for as symbols; that is, the powers of the worker, Life. For to the ancient sage the earth and the gods and his ego were but images, all unknown, of Life, The Worker,--at work. Images he could not interpret, for he could not interpret himself as man, and, so failing, believed power to mean compulsion. Hence he could not see that his own true powers, when they were flowing, flowed without compulsion. Thus he could not interpret the results--could not see his spirit in them--could not see how he had forgotten man in the profound and sombre egoism of his dream of power. Hence he was a magician to create, but not a seer to interpret. It is for modern man therefore to become interpreter of past and present; to be seer of his own spirit and its incomparable power of choice; seer of the Worker, Life, seer of his own magical imagination; seer of his fellow man.

* * * *

Modern man now works with too heavy, harsh and literal an aspect of his mind. He uses his eyes too little, seeing with them too little. He has solemnly and cynically come to distrust his imagination, and believes he suppresses it, unaware that it is ceaselessly at work just the same, conjuring for him new and recrudescent phantasms, new hebetudes--gloomy and fatalistic as of yore--phantasms of toil, of industrialism, of commerce, of war, of poverty, of riches, of apathy and of dominion--and yet evoking also glimmerings and gleamings--even as of old. For man's imagination can take all color and definition out of his life and make it sordid, dull, wearisome and inert. So man today is a magician as of yore; he bodies forth a world of strain and stress, and such a world is thus here with him--by the power and by the sole power of his choice.

It is now plainly time for modern man to see straight. The nature of his spirit which contains his power of choice is clear before him. So is the nature of the power of Life to work. The true nature and function of his will is, clearly to release the beneficence of that Worker Power by virtue of his choice. And the true magic of his imagination is to illuminate the world of men and thoughts and things as they now stand, to illuminate the true nature of man's responsibility to man, and to body forth as a picture great and clear, a New World of Democracy at whose threshold he now stands.

He has now seen spread before him the great world of Feudalism. He has seen the feudal thought-world pictured as an apparition standing beside the door of Democracy set within a phantasmal adamantine wall the feudal ego had upreared and had called Fate. He had heard the Phantom warning cry: What is the use?

It is for him to lay the ghost with its own cry. To open wide the Door. And, as a free man, a free spirit--enter his new world. There to be a truly practical man. Successful, at last, through the long brooding of the ages, successful in achieving mastery of self through clarity of vision.

* * * *

CHAPTER 15 WELLSPRING

It is the boast of civilized man that he is higher than the brute--than the things of the wild. His acts make the fine boast seem strange; for the brute does not misuse his natural powers to encompass his own destruction:--Man does.

Instinct preserves and guides the brute in the unfolding of its powers. Man will not so let Instinct preserve and guide him, for he argues that in his conscious intellect he has a sufficient guide; that, like the needle of a social compass it points to a true human north. Thus busily arguing he does not perceive that such position is an inversion of primary truths, because he takes it as a premise that he has his feet upon the ground, and that he can see straight--whereas both assumptions are not only far from the fact but are the inverse of fact,--as can be plainly seen in his civilization.

If man's conscious intellect, therefore, is the needle of his compass in the Great Way of Life, than surely, the arrow head is at the wrong end.

If man had his feet securely upon the ground and could see simple things straight, then he would truly be in position to use that fine but undeveloped faculty he calls his Reason. But so long as he continues to take phantasms, inverted conceptions of fact and a complete misconception of man as his data, just so long will his conscious intellect lead him to inverted conclusions and therefore astray, in the Way of Life.

Man's feudal misconceptions cause him all his troubles, run him into one tangle after another, breed his unhappiness, his crime and his deplorable perversion and futility.

Modern man is not a good listener. He hears only that which his prejudgments dispose him to accept. Were he to permit himself to be guided by Instinct, he would hear many a thing the congestion of his selfish egoism now renders him deaf to. Things profoundly affecting his happiness, because primarily affecting the health and happiness of his fellow men.

Detached from the guidance and preservative power of instinct, man's conscious intellect therefore is a highly dangerous faculty, for it is typical of that little knowledge which is proverbially held to be a dangerous thing.

Man in his conscious intellect is completely ignorant that the sound and sane working of that intellect is absolutely dependent on Instinct. That it cannot stand alone because it has no basis. It is this obsession of man concerning his intellectual powers that keeps his feet off the ground and prevents him from seeing straight and hearing straight, and therefore as surely incapacitates him from thinking straight and acting straight. Hence, all his social entanglements, hence, his abominable struggle for existence among his own kind--hence his self-destruction and his near and far-flung destruction of others--hence his destruction by others--hence all the lying, stealing, betraying and killing, which the conscious intellect, the reason, of modern man, tell him to be right and proper--and hence the abeyance of those truly fine human qualities and powers which really are the urge of Instinct, but against which man's conscious intellect warns him as a menace.

So we have the curious spectacle of man's conscious intellect--what he miscalls his reason--working at variance with the instinctive urge of the true racial and individual preservation. There is scarcely a thing that modern man does with his conscious intellect but that he does in a way socially or racially wrong--for he has made of his conscious intellect but a refinement of the feudal ego. He has not used it to seek out the spiritual basis of his nature.

Thus strangely enough, the man of today uses his conscious intellect to restrain the free working of the true and instinctive creative powers of his mind. Hence are the results of his activity invariably perversions of fundamental, beneficent, instinctive impulses toward good.

Thus he eventually turns every use into abuse.

And thus it is that in the very beginning of his undertakings he fatefully implants the seeds of decay. In the very bud of his enterprises he deposits the feudal egg which shall make wormy and bitter the fruit.

This is plainly writ upon his civilization, in broad and in detail.

It is the sharp imprint of his feudal ego. You see it everywhere, and everywhere it tells the same story: the inversion of thinking, the perversion of his aims.

Thus is modern man not only self-destroyer, but racially destructive.

Nothing to him is so cheap as human life, and therefore nothing so unattainable, by present methods as is happiness. For he believes as one distraught, that the sure road to happiness lies through the jungles of falsehood, theft, betrayal and murder.

The fact that he says it is not so is the soundest reason for knowing it to be so. For feudal man cannot by means of his conscious intellect, give utterance to a social or racial truth. It is only when he abandons this and responds to the profound, primordial urge of instinct that he will find the way. And precisely in the degree that he responds, to that extent, and that extent only can he utter social truth.

It was said long ago that all men are liars. And so they are whenever and wherever they use the conscious intellect for the suppression of the profound truthfulness of Instinct, as the unerring preserver and guide of man's whole life--his real life--his sane life of body and mind--the inspirer of integrity.

It is the conscious intellect alone that admires the so-called "smart," the really savage man. True reason cancels this value, and declares him socially destructive. It puts him lower than the brute—even if he be held an earth-god. Thus he who adores the unscrupulous man is himself unscrupulous, and if a man admire a liar and thief, by that same token his own mental attitude is that of liar and thief; and if a man exalt the predatory, by that same token is he predatory.

These are the works of the conscious intellect as man uses it today, in profound opposition to the instinctive promptings within him and which he intuitively, that is, instinctively knows are at work within him, urging him to do that which shall be racially preservative.

Man has ever sought man--this is the urge of primordial instinct, at work from the beginning and now at work.

And man has ever denied man--this is the work of his conscious intellect--opposing Instinct.

It is man's conscious intellect that has developed and maintained out of his selfish materialistic ego, the colossal scheme of feudal civilization, from the beginning to this day.

By reason alone, that is by recognition and acceptance of the fundamental instinct of human kindness, as a basis, can so grossly inverted a civilization be righted.

It is not a question for the conscious intellect to deal with at all-- It is a question for the heart to deal with; for the heart alone can impart to the mind of man that living and unerring quality and power which rightly shall entitle it to be called Reason--and which shall cause his self-engrossed ego to cease its dangerous parade of so-called intellectuality, its sham culture, its hypocritical charity--its wanton benevolence--its utterly wasteful economy, its shoddy notion of success in life.

The power of Instinct makes for man's health and the secure unfolding of his natural powers just as it makes for these in the things of the wild.

The feudal conscious intellect makes for the obscuration and suppression of these.

Primordial Instinct affirms the integrity of man--the feudal, conscious intellect denies it.

It is through the urge of instinct that man has accomplished what of good he has, in spite of the handicap of his mischief-making conscious intellect--the weakest of his powers--and yet that which he deems the strongest.

It is in ample measure therefore illuminating, and explanatory of historic man's inversion, that he parted company with Instinct. And it is as amply illuminating and explanatory of us today, that we have even given an inverted meaning to the word, have thus maligned our best friend, and turned ourselves awry. Nothing is too gross or too base for us to associate by preference with the word Instinct.

Thus the man of today regards Instinct as a something beneath him, in a sense rather parvenu. But on the other hand, as by the irony of his own wilfulness he has unwittingly given other names to the urge of Instinct,--such names as Inspiration, Kindness, Genius, Reason,--and, even--

save the mark! conscience, and yet even these conceptions he has managed to distort with the aid of his unseeing conscious intellect.

It seems credible that with the emergence and self-assertion of conscious intellect in prehistoric or proto man, and his ever-growing disposition to place confidence in it as a guide to action, there came also a corresponding self-estrangement of the man from the preservative care of Primordial Instinct.

In truth this must have been the stupendous biological crisis, in which man set forth upon an independent and unique career, among all the living things of the earth. It was his gain and his loss.

One might even fancy that this great crisis is hinted at in the fragmentary but beautiful allegory of the Garden of Eden, and that the ancient people among whom this myth-tale had its far-away origin, may have still preserved a racial memory thereof.

However, be that as it may, in passing, it seems but too evident that when man began to rely on the impressions and guidance of his conscious, fabricating intellect, his troubles began, and he entered as an adventurer--or perhaps he entered willynilly--upon a stormy and tempestuous sea of rising and falling civilizations, on the tidal wave of which we now find ourselves.

Certainly to start out on a career committed to the sanity of so unstable an agent as the conscious intellect was a risky business, a business of which man was in all likelihood no more aware than was he aware that he was parting company with Instinct, even though his awakening to a consciousness of himself may have come as a fairly sudden mutation, and the identity of man became thereby established. While this is all conjectural and lost in the mists of man's beginnings, it partakes nevertheless, deeply of the essential fundamental antagonism now existing between his conscious intellect and Instinct. For that antagonism is wholly of man's own making, and is summed up in the statement of his feudal ego.

It is time therefore to reverse our conception of the nature and power of Instinct. For while man's conscious intellect in disdain has parted company with Instinct--Instinct has not parted company with man. We would not be here if it had. Conscious intellect would have brought our forebears to extinction long before recorded history began. It were better, therefore, to say semi-conscious intellect. For man, cutting the whole into halves, with his I and not I, has perforce thus far been but half-conscious, and that to which he has given the fatalistic name Dualism, has been and is but his own self-imposed conflict between Intellect and Instinct,--his age-long quarrel with himself. For not only has man held the neighbor up to be different from himself, he has with feudal consistency held himself to be different from himself. He has believed himself double because he could not talk to himself. Thus with the parting of Intellect from Instinct arose man's terror of himself, his fantastic hopes, fears, crimes and remorse; and his awe of the great portal he named Death because he believed it stood at the edge of an abyss. So arose in man's intellect the so-called problem of good and evil, which was not in fact a problem but a fantasy. Surely the ancient sage was right, from the viewpoint of semi-conscious intellect, when he wrote:--"Man is born to trouble as the sparks fly upward." In the Book of Job the philosophy of its day is well set forth in its child-like obscurantism. For its deity is but the mirage of Instinct, and its Satan but the moving shadow of semi-conscious intellect. This book, old as the hills from behind which it came, is but one of the ancient romances of good and evil, one of the sublime and touching colloquies between man and himself.

His historic agony runs through all the theologies. One has but to change the terms in its simple formula of man's conflict with himself, and his profound belief that he had two natures, one good, one evil. Whereas man has but one nature--the spiritual, which, for reasons of self-seeking, his feudal ego has obscured with a maze of sophistries.

And this is where man stands today:--The word Hypocrisy covers every manifestation of his self-seeking activity. He communes with himself to justify himself; but he knows he is lying to himself:--a colloquy in which he seeks to prove to himself that he has two natures, both good, one human, one divine, in that the neighbor also has two natures, both evil, one human, one satanic.

Now all this is palpable folly. It is the acme of sophistication and futility.

There is but one fundamental human social instinct, and that is, Kindness. It seeks to flow from the heart of man as from a living wellspring.

It is quite enough. It is the one broad impulse that can draw men together. When it flows into man's intellect that semi-conscious instrument will acquire full social consciousness and take on the beneficence of Reason. We will then cease to be madmen--mere fighting vandals, predatory intellects, spreading destruction--poisoning the wells.

Conscious intellect smears its victims with its saliva of Kindness, preliminary to swallowing them. This is characteristic of the Politician, the priest, and the plutocrat.

The modern man does not like to be called crooked, even though he be as crooked as a ram's horn. He prefers, if must be, the word, irregular. It is not his crookedness that dismays him, it is the fact that you comment pointedly upon it, and don't make an exception in his favor, that annoys him, for, he wishes your good opinion. This is quite human. He certainly ought to have it. He can achieve it without difficulty. All he has to do is to turn straight. This is very simple. It is merely a form of Kindness. It is an acknowledgment on his part that you are a human being. It is the deliquescence of his feudal ego into the democratic ego.

His heart is all right of course. Every man's heart is all right and will guide him aright if he but give it a chance. The trouble is with the semi-conscious intellect. It is this which transmutes the word bribe into the word salary, fee, retainer. It is this which counsels him that he can do as a hireling that which he cannot do as a man. It is this which convinces him that black is white, that dirty work is honorable, that killing is not killing if he does not personally see the victim, that poisoning is not poisoning if he does not actually see the results in each case with his physical eyes. It is this that under the name, Business, counsels and urges him to commit any and every form of rascality and chicanery. Thus does he hide behind words.

Surely this semi-conscious intellect does not make for Kindness. Surely the unscrupulous man does not make for Kindness.

The conscious intellect therefore cordially dislikes plain words, and has a penchant for fine distinctions. It does not like for instance, the plain word, parasite; it much prefers the euphemisms, "a pillar of society," "one of our leading citizens," "our distinguished fellow-citizen," etc., etc., ad nauseum. Nor does it like the plain word, thief, nor the plain word liar, nor the plain word swindler, nor the plain word cut-throat; it much prefers the word, Success, to cover these harsh words with. For the conscious intellect would be kind to its feudal own. For surely to the polecat all polecats seem normal. But to the eye of Democracy polecats are polecats. For Democracy does not foster the fine distinctions which make up the working vocabulary of the language of feudalism. Democracy is shockingly plain of speech, because it is uncomfortably clear of eyesight. It says men are alike. It recognizes no criminal class; it again says men are alike. What it does recognize, plainly recognizes and as plainly states is that the unscrupulous (or feudal) conscious intellect has stifled the primordial preservative Instinct of human Kindness, and in saying this it makes no distinction between high or low, rich or poor, eminent or obscure, educated or uneducated, successful or unsuccessful, fortunate or unfortunate, dead or living. It says, emphatically, that all men are alike,--all feudal distinctions to the contrary, and it says as unequivocally that, under the feudal regime the successful man is the unscrupulous man; that under the feudal philosophy with its basic doctrine that men are different, and that human life is of necessity a promiscuous struggle for existence with the survival of the fittest, he who scruples goes down under the hoofs of those who do not. That comparative poverty has become the gage of comparative honesty.

Within all this world of corruption of the intellect, one proposition, however, remains sound, and that is the heart of man is sound and clean, and ready to respond. That under all the rubbish and counterfeit, tinsel and spangle, human Kindness is to be found as the one valid and valuable social asset. And that kindness is the direct utterance of primordial Instinct. It is the simplest, most direct, most appealing and convincing human quality. It is the sole genuine currency of human intercourse. It is that veritable new Eden Garden of the heart in which alone the tree of Knowledge and the tree of Life shall properly flourish. It is the sole soil in which a sane civilization can grow, for it is set within the wonder-world of Instinct, that eternal power for good which, eyeless, sees clearly, and earless, hears all--even as intellect is blind and deaf in its self-estrangement, in its arrogance and pride of isolation.

Thus intellect without kindness is but insanity! Inspired, informed, illuminated by kindness, it becomes Reason.

Thus the higher we place reason the higher must we place Instinct, and the higher we esteem Instinct the more luminous will become Reason, for Reason and Instinct are of the same primordial stuff--star-dust or dust of earth, or what not, and in their reconciliation and confluence, man's historic incubus of dualism passes away, and his integrity of spirit appears.

This is the dream, the urge and the proclamation of Democracy. For democracy is but the primal urge of Instinct calling to man. Thus is Democracy a new philosophy under the sun.

Vengeance is mine saith the Lord.
Kindness is mine saith Democracy.
It is as simple as the turning of a hand.
Now let some man say it is not simple.
The springtime of Reason--which is but Kindness--is upon us.
Now begin!
From time immemorial man has feared to be kind.
Now let him cease to fear.
A new world will thus open to his view.
Now begin!
It is the new world at whose Door we are.

The Door is open wide: The Phantom has gone.
'Tis but a step across the threshold, as the wall of Fate dissolves.
Let us take that step:–
Breathing anew the air of Inspiration:–
And thus rejuvenate ourselves and the Race.

GROUP VI—THE NEW WAY

Chapter 1   **Abuse**
Chapter 2   **Art**
Chapter 3   **Science**
Chapter 4   **The Poet**
Chapter 5   **Thought**
Chapter 6   **Ego**

CHAPTER 1 ABUSE

What is the use? To this cry of the intellect of the ancient multitudes comes back the cry of the heart of the modern multitudes:--*What is the Abuse?* We want to know! Why are we still perplexed? Why is still sorrow our companion--we who should be without sorrow.

Now comes Democracy with its voice of living power and says:

GRAFT is the abuse--there is none other--never was other--none other can be. For Feudalism means Graft--always has, always will--so long as it shall remain as a Phantom by the door in the man-made wall. So long as it shall stand, a ghostly menace, by the door of our Truth--that door invisible to the millions of selfishly blind--the morbid multitudes--fearing Life, fearing Integrity, fearing to be men, fearing the neighbor; fearing poverty, fearing disease, fearing themselves; trusting no thing, trusting not themselves, ever anxious for the morrow. This is what Graft means! Can ye not see? Can ye not hear?--when it is all plain?!

* * * *

So, at the last, has come into our language a word known to all and which makes all Feudalism plain; a word which has condensed from the gray nothingness of our lives and with terrific power goes to the core of the meaning of our feudal civilization.

Thus the feudal word GRAFT will prove the undoing of Feudalism. It must crumble and vanish. Its time has come!

To the world-query which has broken the hearts of the dreaming millions--What is the Use?--we shall make answer:

Aye! What is the use! We shall find use in dissolving abuse.

To the Phantom by the door we shall say:

Begone, thou somber spirit, Graft! and take with thee the hearts thou hast broken, the little and the great hearts.

Take with thee the heart of Him Crucified--image of all men crucified by thee.

And take Denial, and Despair, and Perplexity, and Poverty, and Sorrow, and Disease and Crime, which are thy sombre thoughts uttered in the dusk of man's fear.

Go!*

The sun now breaks apart the ancient night--that thou and thy wall of graft dissolve with the night of men's ancient fears.

Go!

Take thy Dance of Death and thy Song of Death:

That Life and its song appear,

That the hearts of all men come true.

* Illegible strikeover in MS. Could also read *Lo!*

CHAPTER 2 ART

That phase of our mass-activity which we colloquially call Art, is looked upon by us as a dubious accomplishment--something that may be dispensed with by sensible, practical men, without special difference.

This view is a sure reflection of our fantastic views concerning what we deem the larger and more important aspects of our civilization.

The significance of the word Art has been so limited by us in its application to the social life, that the mere fact illuminates as with a glare the poverty of our present-day thought concerning the social life itself, and the possibility of giving it sane organization and expression. For, to limit our notion of Art is to limit our notion of Life. If therefore our notion of Art, and its power sanely to express every phase of our social activity is limited and futile in fact, so must our notion of Life and its power be limited and futile--as is the fact.

For the thought of a people is all of one piece. Hence by any phase of its thought, or by any hope of its seemingly separated thoughts a people may surely be interpreted. All the thoughts of a people, however seemingly diversified, simplify to this:--they are, each and all, consistent avowals of the central thought of that people concerning Life.

Where the notion of Life is constricted, all other thoughts are similarly constricted.

Men have supposed they were not alike--they are alike.

Men suppose their thoughts are not alike--They are alike.

To trace all these diverse thoughts to their common birth in the view of Life, and to show clearly that, in all their variations of aspect, they are true images of the view a people holds concerning Life, is of the purpose of this book.

The perception of this plain truth, and the consequent enlargement of our view of Life and its powers, will bring a receptive simplicity, clearness and power into our view concerning any and every detail of the social activity which we now misname, civilization. The word civilization itself will surcharge with a new and undreamed-of power and splendor of meaning, as we come to understand it to signify the art of expressing the life of a people in the image of the true thought or integrity of that people.

The fact that our view of Art is so restricted, shows plainly that we have no valid social sense, nor any perception, as yet, that our collective, our mass-social life needs must find sane expression in all its aspects, if it is to be in health.

So, when we assume that Art is negligible by sensible practical men, we assume by the same token that social health and strength are negligible by the selfsame sensible practical men.

So therefore when you hear a man say that he "knows nothing about Art" you may assume with certainty that he knows nothing valid about anything that concerns civilization; that he is, as far as you and I are concerned, a vacuous morbid dreamer, living in a ghost-world of abstractions and destitute of the sense of plain and clamorous reality.

To be sure, we in our sensible, practical, ghostly way assume art to consist in painting pictures, or something of the sort; and just so long as we assume this, we shall remain diseased. For, while painting pictures may be a special manifestation of Art; the reality of Art consists simply and universally in this:--

DOING THINGS RIGHT

So long as we do things wrong, we shall be inartistic, diseased and weak, and civilization must be a misnomer. When we do things right, we shall become an artistic, a healthful, a strong people--and civilization will be the right word in the right place--for it will then stand for the uttermost reach of Art, namely, the full expression of the full life of a people.

Now, when things are done wrong, we have abuse.

When they are done right, we have use.

So when the sensible practical man says that Art does not concern him, it is equivalent to saying that use and abuse do not concern him.

So when we say that Art consists in doing things right, we mean, RIGHT, ALL THE WAY.

A thing may be done right for its purpose, but its purpose may be wrong.

And what do we mean by right and wrong. Clearly the things which make for social disease or health. And what makes for social disease? Clearly anything which makes for the suppression of the real social life. And what makes for social health? Anything which causes or tends to cause the social life to go sanely, that is, really.

Doing things right therefore, means doing all things, anything and everything, right in every way,--that is, for a right end.

So long as we continue to consider Art in any other way, it will remain a ghostly and abstract fiction.

The plain truth is that in denying to Art its quality, namely, an expression of Life, we render ourselves spiritually poor, hence socially inefficient.

If we don't see things right we can't do things right.

To do things right is to be efficient. To do things wrong is to be obstructive.

It is because we do not see this straight that we talk so vacuously about our social "problems"; whereas the discord is in our brains which refuse to believe that the great truths are plain, simple, universal, and ready to be used.

We refuse to believe in the plain grandeur and power of simplicity, in its scope and applicability; and yet in doing so frivolous a thing, we dare proclaim ourselves sensible and practical! Truly we cannot be efficient so long as we deny to efficiency its real basis in simplicity and straightforwardness.

It is not strange therefore that the word efficiency and the word Art do not come together in our minds.

Nor is it strange that in denying to simplicity its fine quality, we cheapen our conception of art until it reaches a negligible quantity, instead of amplifying it to the full, and utilizing its enormous power.

To be sure, we have all received the same education, learned and unlearned alike, in school and out of school alike, in books and out of books, in the home or in the street, an education which has in fact set before us no ideal other than Feudalism. An education which has failed to set forth the Truth of Life.

Is it a wonder then that with such education--an education which does not nourish but petrifies--we should hold a paltry and narrow conception of the power of Art?--Is it not symptomatic of such education that we believe ourselves sensible and practical?--We--who have no sane or efficient program concerning anything!--We?--who call moving within a narrow circle of feudal ideas Progress! We?--who talk about Democracy and yet have no conception of a democratic Art--its scope, range, power, its applicability to the greatest and smallest aspects of our social activities--The necessity of such an Art in order that we may live.

Truly we need men to feel straight, think straight, act straight; that is, artists--men who are alive to the power and efficiency in all things and all thoughts and procedures, of the artistic spirit.

This is what Art means in the great way of Life.

Those who see this see into the true nature of Democracy.

Further, they see as in a vision, that Democracy is the most welcome expression of Art.

Truly we need light.

Truly we need an education which shall set forth finer purposes than the feudal, with its program of force and cunning, which has brought only perplexity and world-weariness to the millions of us,--Because we have not faith in life and its powers,--because we have not faith in Simplicity--because we live in fear in darkness,--even as Life sings:

> Come forth into my world, O, man!
> This is what Art means.
> Art is a song of Life.
> Utterance of man's free spirit--at work.

Hence man's immortal dream of work awakens to a new dream of power--an Art of Civilization.

This is what Democracy means.

It is its very soul--its spirit--its ego.

It is its answer to the wish and will of the All-Spirit--in the image of its integrity: The Spirit that inspires in Life an utterance of the Song of Songs.

CHAPTER 3 SCIENCE

If, as is true, the average sensible, practical man looks on Art in mild derision, so is it true that he likewise regards Science with vague disdain, or grudging interest.

To be sure, what he conceives as Art and Science are figments of his warped intellect–ghosts of his self-imprisoned mind; that mind which he will not let go forth into the world; and hence they bear no relation, of reality, to realities of earth and air, nor to the reality of man's creative needs and powers.

To him Art and Science are more or less mysterious words; labels for things more or less remote from the needs of his daily life.

He does not enquire as to their reality, or his daily need of such reality, for he never enquires about anything worth while. He is absorbed in what he calls practical sensible things--and thus is the victim of every social wind that blows. For he never enquires how or why or where the social winds blow. If he did, he would be scientific--and that would never do.

For Science is the Spirit of Enquiry--of the broadest and minutest inquiry. It is the free spirit of man at work--seeking the How and the Why. The very soul, the animus of Science is its intense search for reality, its keen desire for precision, for accuracy--for Simplicity, its ceaseless ambition to arrive at the great truths which carry all minor truths on their bosoms as the sea carries the ships.

Did you suppose Science to be solely a matter of technical terms and books? Awake! Science is the Spirit of man confronting the Universe-asking, ever How?--Why? Crying, ever: Light, Light--more light!

Light on places now obscure or dark,
Light upon men's thoughts,
Light upon all things,
Light everywhere,
That men may see straight--that they may act straight.

It is the superb spirit of man going forth in response to the call of Life the Worker—calling:

Come forth into my world, O man!

Thus as Art is man the worker, so is Science man the Inquirer.

And the real, practical enquiry of Science is:

HOW TO DO THINGS RIGHT

Hence it sifts and weighs and measures; and pries and probes into all things and thoughts and activities--far and near.

Thus Science stands, historically, for man the wanderer, the seeker; and if, as is true, man has been a stranger upon his own earth and to his own neighbor, it seeks to draw him near to both, that he may know both, and be at home.

So when the sensible, practical man says that science does not concern him he utters the wail of a ghost:--for he means that nothing concerns him except his ghostly self. He means that all his fellow men do not concern him, that the neighbor does not concern him, that the sane (that is, the artistic and scientific) organization of society does not concern him. And yet he wonders at the storm and stress of life:--even as he says, What is the use?

To be sure, he has been given the same education in fictions that was given to you and me. For it was the same exaltation of mystery and abstraction, the same dulling in the brain of its sense of reality--the same suppression of that poet and wonder-worker in us all which we call the imagination--the same imprisonment of the eager intellect which would go forth with joy into the world--the same worship of tradition--the same imbecilities concerning God, man, nature, the heavens and the earth.

Thus is the mental attitude of the average sensible practical man that of selfish torpor or selfish savagery. Hence with him, sympathy--which is the true going out of the heart to all men and all thoughts and all activities--is sleeping within him the sleep of death.

Thus it is that a feudal education suppresses the best in man and develops the worst. For it insists upon the separation of brain and heart.

Such education therefore is grossly unscientific, for it leads to the most unscientific and inartistic of social conditions, namely, the separation of man from man with consequent and inevitable exaltation of the few and degradation of the many--that is, the maximum of waste and suffering, the minimum of efficiency and joy.

And just as it is true that insofar as a man limits his conception of Art, just to that extent and degree does he limit his conception of Life and its power, so is it in the same degree and measure true as he narrows his view of Science he narrows his view of Life.

For Art and Science are modes of Life, that is, phases of man's natural powers--aspects of his free spirit. Therefore as he minimizes his conception of Art and Science, he minimizes his conception of his own natural powers, restrains thereby the freedom of his spirit, decreases his social efficiency and retards the sane organization of society.

Hence it is that the average sensible practical man is not "progressive" as he avers, but reactionary; an obstructionist of the welfare of his kind.

It is he who chatters about our social problems and proposes nostrum remedies--meanwhile as persistently ignoring the simple, visible basis of our tangled inefficiency--that is, his own inefficiency.

To tell the average sensible practical man that he is neither sensible nor practical because he is manifestly socially inefficient, would be to make him gasp. For while he despises theory, he himself is always working on a theory; and his pet theory is that he can be utterly selfish without working injury to his fellow man. He has another pet theory, namely, that society rests upon the family. He cannot see that under modern conditions this is reversed and that in fact the family rests upon society. Therefore, he holds to his theory of petty, self-interest, unaware of the imperative need and inestimable value of the broader theory of social interest.

He is not blameworthy. These views are but the result of his feudal education, which has bred in him the fatuous notion that Art and Science are mysteries instead of simple clear powerful living principles--so simple, so clear, so intimately applicable that they must permeate society in all its activities, individual and collective, if that society is to functionate in health of thought and deed.

Thus Democracy is also the highest reach of Science:--of the putting to social use of man's finest powers of inquiry, of research;--of discerning, clearly, how to do things right.

Thus does our man-search lead us to the treasury of his inexhaustible spiritual powers--and among them we find the intellectual power to enquire how to do things right--Science, and the working-power to do things right--Art; and underlying these working powers, his supreme power to choose.

And thus do we define man's responsibility and accountability to his fellows and to himself.

* * * *

Hence how brutal is Graft! For Graft means nothing short of this--exploitation and betrayal of one's kind!

In its multifarious forms of special privilege, parasitism, so-called business enterprise, political chicane, legal trickery, war, ecclesiasticism, might and cunning; lying, stealing, killing, it all comes to the one thing! ABUSE of Life's powers for the purpose of self-aggrandisement and the degradation of the many--with the inevitable disintegration, exhaustion and Downfall. All this is feudal.

The picture of it is in the man plotting in secret--the many leading cramped lives--they know not why--for they are too sensible and practical to enquire.

* * * *

In place of this put the Democratic conception of individual, collective and unitary social health, vigor and efficiency.

Herein the man uses his natural powers for the common good. Hence society spontaneously organized itself on a basis of efficiency. From which results as spontaneously, in the reaction of sanely organizing society upon the individual, his increasing good. He thus reacts in turn with increasing beneficence upon society, and the result is inevitable increase in health, strength, efficiency and the general joy of living, and the power to sustain creative thought and action, individual and collective, in a unitary definite urge.

* * * *

Individualism without collectivism means sure destruction. Collectivism without individualism is an abstraction. Both are unscientific and inartistic, because neither sets forth the simple primary propositions: How to do things right--and Doing things right.

Society as it exists today is visibly a mass of disease. That is, it is filled with auto-toxins, aches, pains, disturbances of circulation, and so on and on through the range of medical terminology. This pathological condition is traceable directly to the system of thinking in vogue; the traditional feudal system. So, primarily, it is the intellect which is in a state of abnormal perturbation; and, to correct this perversion, it is frivolous to putter with detailed symptoms of the social disease. What is necessary is to apply a system of thinking which shall be sane. And no system of thinking can be sane which ignores the heart--that is, which ignores the basic principle of Kindness.

True, Feudalism has its system of kindness. It consists in giving back to others a part of that of which you have robbed them; of building hospitals to receive those whom you have driven into illness--etc., etc., to the end of the list of phantasmal Kindnesses which are summed up under the feudal words, benevolence, charity, public benefaction, etc., etc. As corrective of social diseases originating in the feudal system itself, such measures are makeshifts--which but aid in the perpetuation of the system by giving to it a false aspect of solicitude.

But the spirit of Democracy does not care for mask-words. It wishes to know with accuracy and precision what lies behind the maskwords. Hence it searchingly enquires. Seeking, it finds the truth and lays it bare. Thus does the intellect of Democracy study the workings of the Feudal system we call civilization, as a manifestation of social disease, of thoroughgoing functional disturbance of the social system.

It sees, further, that all of these disturbances are due to a single cause--Abuse--and for abuse its simple, thoroughgoing remedy is: USE--complete use.

It perceives the instrumentalities for a high civilization already at hand.

It perceives that all these instrumentalities, while put to use before a mask, are put to abuse behind the mask.

It perceives who does this, and why and how. Who, Why, and How, therefore, become three strong, penetrating words, in its vocabulary of diagnosis.

It perceives the interrelations of those who abuse--and the why and how.

It makes careful and accurate note of all these things and thoughts and activities.

And then it declares: Abuse must go, Graft must go,--in short, Feudalism must go. It stands in my Light!

And the awakening, listening multitudes, ere long will see this truth clear in the growing light. All the people will see--and Act! They will say:

This is our true selves.

Let us begin!

Then will the new day of a new civilization approach apace. It will not be long from now.

For Life is singing its song in the hearts of all men.

They have grown aweary--aweary of the Song of Death and the Dance of Death.

Like children, they shall go forth:--into the great open world of Life; and there--they shall wish and will--and become!

CHAPTER 4 THE POET

Wherefore the poet?
What good does he do?
Is he not a trifler, and something of a nuisance?
Well; are not you and I triflers, and, more or less nuisances?
What have we to show to prove the contrary?
O, we are practical sensible men?
You are quite sure of this?
You will stand on your record?
Well then, if that is so, what is the poet if not a trifler and a nuisance?
He is the man of VISION!
He sees!

He sees Life with eyes of Life.

And that is something you have never done, O practical man.

Oh! You thought the poet made verses!

Oh! You can't see what is at your elbow--but the poet can.

True, some great poets have made verses. It just happened that way. That was all. They happened to make verses instead of doing something else:--just as you happen to be sensible and practical instead of being efficient.

This is new, is it?

There is a great deal new for you--O, man on the street.

So the poet is the man who makes words rhyme?

No; the poet is the man who sees things rhyme; for rhyme is but the suggestion of harmony; and harmony is but the suggestion of rhythm; and rhythm is but the suggestion of the superb moving equilibrium of all things.

You do not see yourself move, O, man on the street? Tell me, what do you see moving? Do you see anything moving? Do you see anything at all? Have you any vision? Do *you* see Life with eyes of Life?

Social reality is unknown to you. You have not caught a glimpse of it--O, practical, sensible one. You have four-legged dreams--you dream of fodder and a bed.

And what is poetry? The very soul of adventure--the going forth --the daring to do--the vision of doing and the how to do--the vision which creates a situation. Hence is the poet ever pioneer. Surely he is no fourfoot. He has two-legged dreams.

The spirit of poetry is the very spirit of mastery. Hence the twolegged poets of the past have been the masters of the four-legged multitudes of the past--and such is the case today. Why not?

Why should not those who see, drive those who do not see-- when seeing is so easy?

And the four-legged are so patient--so willing to bear burdens and be driven for fodder and a bed of straw.

O, four-legged, sensible practical ones, can you not see how the two-legged poets drive you?

Awake! O, multitudes, for poetry is the highest of practical powers. It is not what you have supposed.

Awake!

Awake! Brilliant horde of sensible, practical dream-quadrupeds. There is such thing as standing on two legs, seeing with two eyes, working with two hands and one brain--all at the same time, O, dreamers!

CHAPTER 5 THOUGHT

    The two especially vital aspects of that natural power of man, which we call thought, are attention and reflection.
    It means much, socially, to be able to attend and to be able to reflect.
    For by attention we become aware; and by reflection we become purposeful.
    To become aware and to purpose are of the essence of will-power. It means, to be strong and alive; for the will is the closest thing to the working power of Life that we know anything about.
    It has been the custom to separate and dissociate man's natural powers, and give to them different and separate names as though they were different and separate things. But it is not so easy in reality. All

these "different faculties," as we call them, are simply activities of the ego. And EGO is the name for man as a POWER. It is his real name.

Thought, therefore, is essentially self-assertion--POWER.

It is therefore creative; for wherever we assert, we create. That is, we exercise power. Even when we destroy we create! that is we create a new situation.

To body forth a new situation, therefore, is the essentially constructive aspect of thought. And man is therefore constructive, however much he may destroy. In this sense, therefore, man is a natural producer --that is, he alters situations. He alone, in the world, can produce change,--that is, he can modify, alter, rearrange, reconstruct. Hence is man essentially the artificer, that is the worker, the changer, the modifier, the creator! He is the one power unto himself. It is he alone who can say: I am! I think! I will! I change!

Now, the power of thought is invisible and inaudible. It flows within the silence and immensity of Life.

We may call it occult if we wish; but then, to be consistent, we must call everything occult.

Hence we call thought natural as we call all powers natural.

For, by no possibility can we separate thought from the things we call physical. There is no dividing line--no threshold.

There are merely phases of consciousness, and we choose to believe that in man consciousness reaches its highest manifestation and power.

To become conscious, therefore, is to become aware--and we become aware through that activity of the ego we call attention; and we formulate or plan through that faculty we call reflection.

To do, we must plan; for thought must precede all conscious action.

We attend, more or less, and we reflect more or less; but efficiency means clear attention and reflection. It is all very simple.

We have merely complicated and dulled the notion.

It is as easy to see clear as to see obscurely.

Indeed, easier, for it is natural.

It is as easy to reflect as not to reflect, for we approach the normal when we approach the stability and balance of the reflecting ego.

Man possessing thought, therefore, possesses power; and it is thus that we speak of man's powers in preference to his rights. For with "rights" he can only claim; with powers he can create. The difference is as immense and prolific as the difference between Feudalism and Democracy.

THOUGHT

Thought is nothing if it is not power.

And man therefore is nothing if he is not power.

The complete idea of man, therefore, concentrates and summates in the notion of productive power.

To produce is to create. To produce situations is to create situations.

And there is no phase of human activity that is not a situation.

This simplicity of plan of the social life we have not seen, because we have not thought about it; that is, we have not attended or reflected.

Hence we have gone ahead without any plan; that is, we have allowed things to grow and complicate and entangle us, instead of saying: I will--that is, I have paid attention and have reflected, and now purpose doing.

If thought is a power, man surely is powerful.

For to the activity of thought there is no limit.

We think there is a limit to thought because we have presented to ourselves tasks instead of situations.

The moment we invert this procedure and present situations instead of tasks we shall see a whole new world of productive activity lying spread out before us.

We have not been taught to plan, because we have not been taught to think scientifically and artistically.

The completed value of thinking consists in its use in planning --that is, in the creation of new situations.

A theory must precede all efficient action. That is, the power of thought must create the situation in advance.

For man is thought.

It is the basis of his solidity, spiritual and physical.

It is because of his thought-power that he is now ready for Democracy.

That is, his thought-power is awaking to the necessity of a clearcut plan.

And when this notion of a plan becomes concise, his physical powers will respond like magic.

For man the worker is limitless.

There is no trouble about man's hands.

His hands haven't any superstitions.

They are always ready and willing to work.

It is his befuddled brain that stands in the way of his hands.

It is our befuddled brains, generally, which stand in our own way, and prevent us from working powerfully.

Now the question comes up clearly and squarely, why is the brain befuddled?

It is an astounding situation.

For it is indeed a situation--not a condition or a theory--it is a situation pure and simple.

And what is a SITUATION in human affairs? An attitude of the ego--nothing else.

Now the existing situation is based on what--fear!

And fear is what?

A demoralized attitude of the ego.

* * * *

A word of counsel: quit attending to yourself alone. This is weakness which the poets, your drivers, understand. The horse is introspective, so are you. He thinks only about himself--so do you. He fears everything outside of himself, except his driver--so do you. His sole attachment to the world of things is the voice and rein of his driver--so is yours.

But the poets go without harness. They go about on two legs, and with abrupt voices.

They attend and reflect, and they act, while you patiently wait,--sensible, practical, stupid ones.

They have a plan.

You have no plan,--you pay.

* * * *

Lord, give us someone to drive us,
Someone to give us fodder and a bed,
Someone to guide us.
Lord, we will pay, we will pay.

* * * *

And Life sings its song, the while.
It sings of action for the poets.
It sings of fodder and a bed.
It sings to those that are fearless.
It sings to those that fear.

* * * *

CHAPTER 6 EGO

The universe and all therein may be expressed by the word Ego.

The ancient Jews questioned their God, Yahveh, asking, who art thou?

And he said: I am.

And because this was the first and the last word that the god could say of himself, so is it the first and the last word that man can say of himself.

And man cannot logically say Ego without including All-Ego.

Nor can he speak of an All-Ego without including himself.

Ego is therefore the I AM of all things.

It is for this reason that there can be no dividing line between what we call physical and what we call spiritual.

Man has found no line that he could cross and say, here it is!

For, go where he will, search where he will--there he finds consciousness.

He speaks bravely of matter, but can find no such thing.

He speaks weakly of Life, for he fears.

And yet Life is I AM.

Life sings its song:--It is the song of Ego.

Man sings the song of death--the song of fear, the song of distrust--for he knows not Ego. He will not believe that Ego is I AM--and that there is but one I AM, universal, and himself.

No, man has not believed in Integrity; hence his anguish.

Man has not believed in himself--hence his sorrow.

For man knows not Ego. He talks of the gods, and he talks of the great. He talks of the rich and he talks of the poor; But he speaks not of Ego, because he knows not Ego.

Man teaches the child to fear--knowing not what he does--for he knows not Ego.

Man sends the child to school:--to learn what?--fictions. For the school knows not Ego.

Man takes the child to church:--to learn what?--fictions. For the church knows not Ego.

School and Church speak not one word of Integrity--as though it were not the primal law--the only law--the I AM.

Hence are School and Church phantom;--for Ego is real:--and the spirit of man is Ego.

What pathos in man's self-inversion, his self-eclipse, that he should set up phantom for reality, shadow for light, and fear his own phantom--and break his heart for it. And, like a ghost walk with his back to reality, as though reality were not Ego.

And man talks, and talks, and talks; meanwhile kills he the first born and the last born alike.

Madman, to be a grafter! For where there is graft, there must be ghosts and sorrow, for you and yours, and perplexity, and disease and poverty and huge ghostly riches.

It cannot be otherwise.

Madman, to betray!
Madman, to steal!

Madman, to kill his young!
These are your phantoms.
Integrity, alone, is real.
Man has grafted through the ages.
He must now stop.
It is the way out.
It is the solution.

It is fantastic to suggest as a social basis any law but the law of Integrity--the law of Ego.

Man has thought otherwise through the ages, and has paid the price.

Man still thinks otherwise and is still paying the price.
Hence his Song of Death and his Dance of Death.
Hence his Phantom by the Door.
Hence the wall which he calls Fate.
Hence the Crucifixion, now, as of old.
For it is graft, graft, graft!

O, man on the street, can you not see, can you not hear? Can you not see the Dance of Death and hear the Song of Death, when they are so plain and the cause of them is so plain and near to you and of you!

Why walk, or pretend to walk, in a trance, O, man on the street, knowing not Ego?--or denying Ego?

Why be so absurd, or so malignant, as to say you are sensible and practical?

You are now at the parting of your ways. O, man on the street, whoever you are and whatever your name may be, high or low, rich or poor, eminent or obscure.

Your time has come.
The cock is crowing the shrillest dawn that the world has known.
You must declare yourself!
For you are found out--one and all.
You must declare for Integrity or against it.
You must declare for social efficiency or against it.
You must declare for an art and science of civilization or against it.

When you cease to graft your thoughts turn in splendor to your fellow men.

The rest is easy because it is clear and straight.

It merely means work.

And, to create, to construct, to build, to put forth out of himself, is man's natural work.

It is the free and full expression of Ego.

A new world will open.

The world of Ego and its dream of power.

The world of Integrity of man and his works.

Then will awaken in you, Poetry, long sleeping; and you will vision forth!

Then will you do things right because you will seek, with unswerving attention and reflection, how to do things right.

Then will the artist in you and the scientist in you awaken and be strong, whoever you are.

Then will you go forth into the great open world.

Then will you hear Life sing its Songs of Songs
To you!
Then shall you wish and will.
And you shall become, because of your wishing and willing.
Then will the wall you have called Fate
Tremble and dissolve.
Then will the Phantom by the Door
Hover and go.
Then will you know the use
For you will know man
The Ego.
The dawn is breaking.
NOW BEGIN!

(End of the Book)

(SIGNED) Louis H. Sullivan

Completed April 18, 1908.